尾田栄一郎

When you buy a CD single, sometimes around the third track there's a song without vocals labeled "instrumental."

Moms, when you've forgotten to buy the ingredients for miso soup, you should tell your families this: "Tonight's miso soup is an instrumental."

During a test, when you can't think of the answer, everyone should just write this next to the empty space: "This one is an instrumental."

When, in the manga, I've forgotten to draw various things and readers point this out to me, those places were, of course, "instrumentals."

    -Eiichiro Oda, 2005

Eiichiro Oda began his manga career at the age of 17, when his one-shot cowboy manga **Wanted!** won second place in the coveted Tezuka manga awards. Oda went on to work as an assistant to some of the biggest manga artists in the industry, including Nobuhiro Watsuki, before winning the Hop Step Award for new artists. His pirate adventure **One Piece**, which debuted in **Weekly Shonen Jump** in 1997, quickly became one of the most popular manga in Japan.

ONE PIECE VOL. 38
WATER SEVEN PART 7

SHONEN JUMP Manga Edition

STORY AND ART BY EIICHIRO ODA

English Adaptation/Megan Bates
Translation/Taylor Eagle, HC Language Solutions, Inc.
Touch-up Art & Lettering/HudsonYards
Design/Fawn Lau
Supervising Editor/Yuki Murashige
Editor/Megan Bates

VP, Production/Alvin Lu
VP, Sales & Product Marketing/Gonzalo Ferreyra
VP, Creative/Linda Espinosa
Publisher/Hyoe Narita

ONE PIECE © 1997 by Eiichiro Oda. All rights reserved.
First published in Japan in 1997 by SHUEISHA Inc., Tokyo.
English translation rights arranged by SHUEISHA Inc.

Printed in the U.S.A.

Published by VIZ Media, LLC
P.O. Box 77010
San Francisco, CA 94107

10 9 8 7 6 5 4 3 2 1
First printing, March 2010

www.viz.com

THE WORLD'S
MOST POPULAR MANGA

www.shonenjump.com

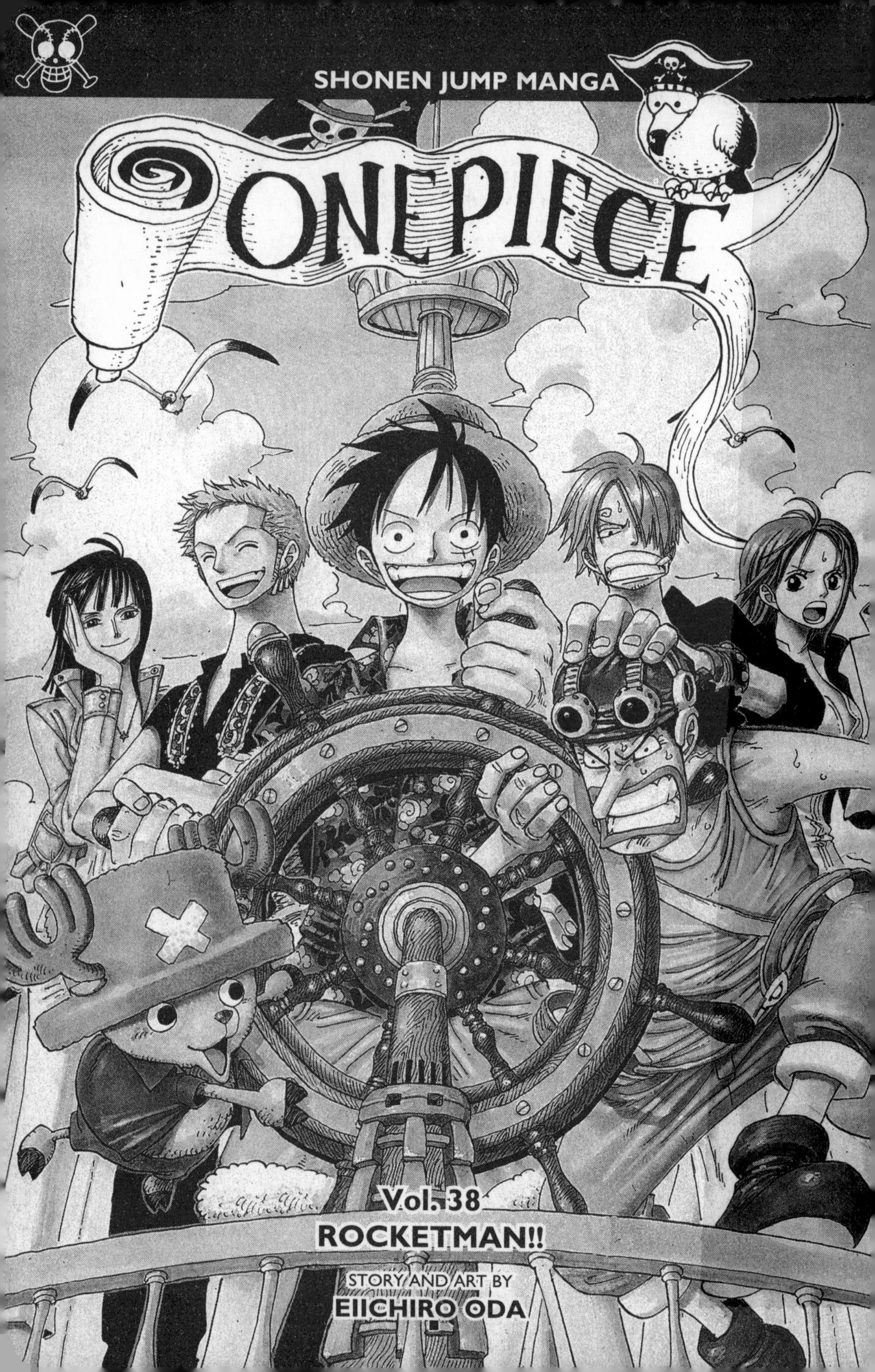
SHONEN JUMP MANGA
ONE PIECE
Vol. 38
ROCKETMAN!!
STORY AND ART BY
EIICHIRO ODA

The Franky Family

Professional ship dismantlers, they moonlight as bounty hunters.

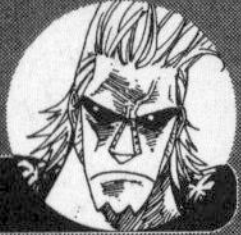

The master builder and an apprentice of Tom, the legendary shipwright.

Franky (Cutty Flam)

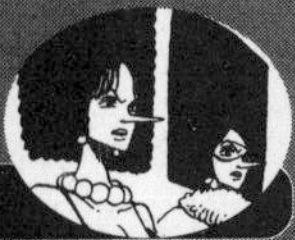

The Square Sisters

Kiwi & Mozu

Cipher Pol No. 9

A covert intelligence agency under the direct supervision of the World Government. They have been granted the license to kill un-cooperative citizens.

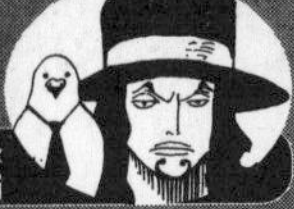

Rob Lucci & Hattori

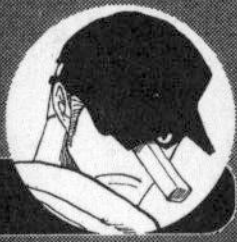

Kaku

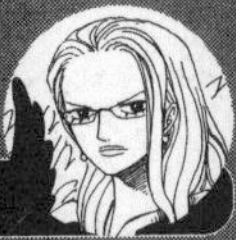

Kalifa

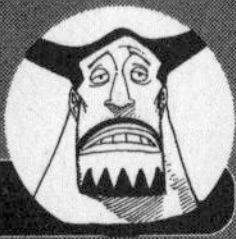

Blueno

The Straw Hats

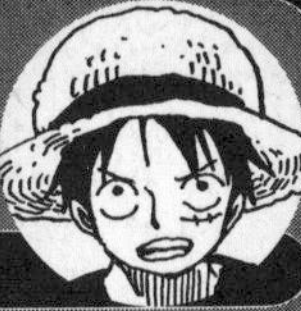

Boundlessly optimistic and able to stretch like rubber, he is determined to become King of the Pirates.

Monkey D. Luffy

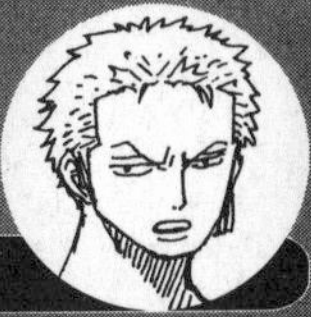

A former bounty hunter and master of the "three-sword" style. He aspires to be the world's greatest swordsman.

Roronoa Zolo

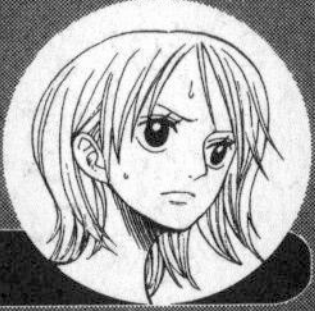

A thief who specializes in robbing pirates. Nami hates pirates, but Luffy convinced her to be his navigator.

Nami

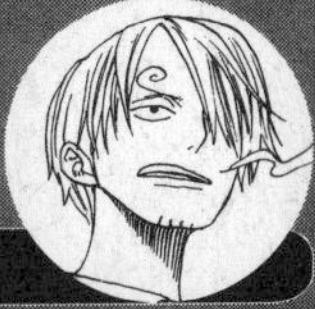

The bighearted cook (and ladies' man) whose dream is to find the legendary sea, the "All Blue."

Sanji

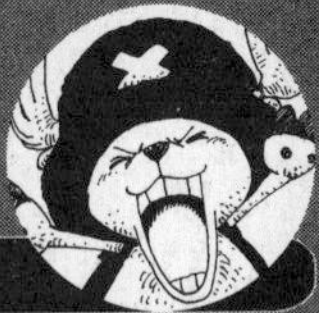

A blue-nosed man-reindeer and the ship's doctor.

Tony Tony Chopper

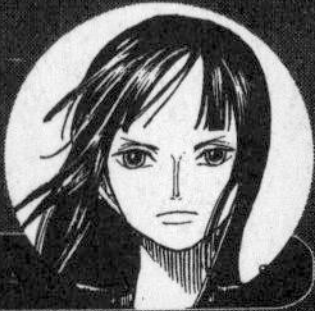

A mysterious woman in search of the Ponegliff on which true history is recorded.

Nico Robin

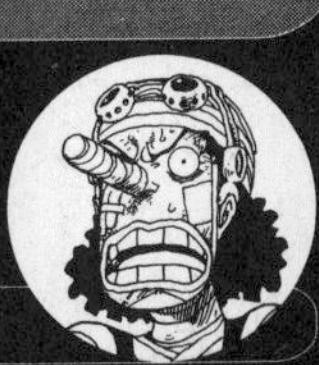

A village boy with a talent for telling tall tales. His father, Yasopp, is a member of Shanks's crew.

Usopp

THE STORY OF ONE PIECE

Volume 38

Monkey D. Luffy started out as just a kid with a dream—to become the greatest pirate in history! Stirred by the tales of pirate "Red-Haired" Shanks, Luffy vowed to become a pirate himself. That was before the enchanted Devil Fruit gave Luffy the power to stretch like rubber, at the cost of being unable to swim—a serious handicap for an aspiring sea dog. Undeterred, Luffy set out to sea and recruited some crewmates—master swordsman Zolo; treasure-hunting thief Nami; lying sharpshooter Usopp; the high-kicking chef Sanji; Chopper, the walkin' talkin' reindeer doctor; and the mysterious archaeologist Robin.

After many adventures, the Straw Hats' ship, the *Merry Go*, is less than seaworthy. In order to get her repaired, they head to Water Seven, home of the best shipwrights. When told that *Merry* is damaged beyond repair, Luffy makes the agonizing decision to get a new ship. Furious at Luffy's decision, Usopp leaves the crew. And when Robin is linked to an assassination attempt on Mayor Iceberg, her betrayal and then desertion leave them flabbergasted. When the Straw Hats are blamed for the crime, they set out to learn the truth. But what they find is more deception—the other assassins are agents of CP9, a covert agency working directly for the World Government! Their real motive is to secure the blueprints of the Pluton, the destructive ancient weapon, and they need Robin to decipher it! Robin's been taken prisoner and is headed for Enies Lobby, where she'll be tried for her crimes. The Straw Hats are in a madcap rush to save her...before it's too late!

Galley-La Company

A top shipbuilding company. They are purveyors to the World Government.

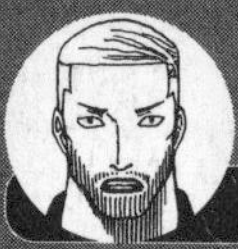

Mayor of Water Seven and president of Galley-La Company. Also one of Tom's apprentices.

Iceberg

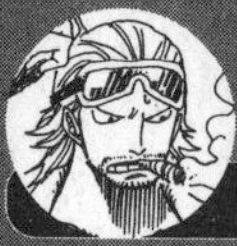

Rigging and Mast Foreman

Paulie

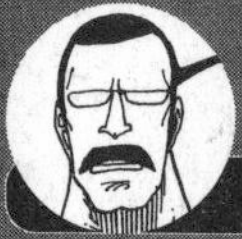

Pitch, Blacksmithing and Block-and-Tackle Foreman

Peepley Lulu

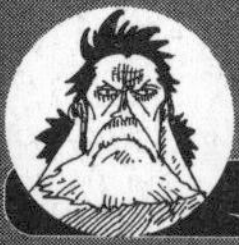

Cabinetry, Caulking and Flag-Making Foreman

Tilestone

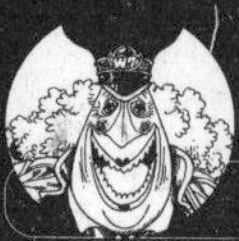

Formerly the beautiful secretary of Tom's Work
Now stationmaster of S
Station.

Kokoro

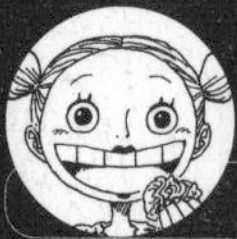

Kokoro's granddaughter

Chimney

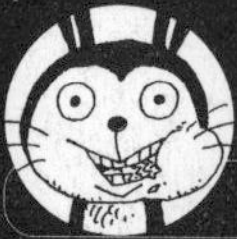

Cat (but actually a rabbit)

Gonbe

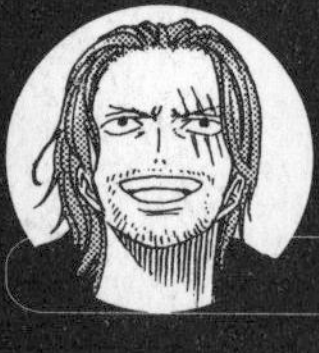

A pirate that Luffy idoliz
Shanks gave Luffy his trac
mark straw hat.

"Red-Haired" Shanks

Vol. 38
Rocketman!!

CONTENTS

Chapter 358: REACTIVATION

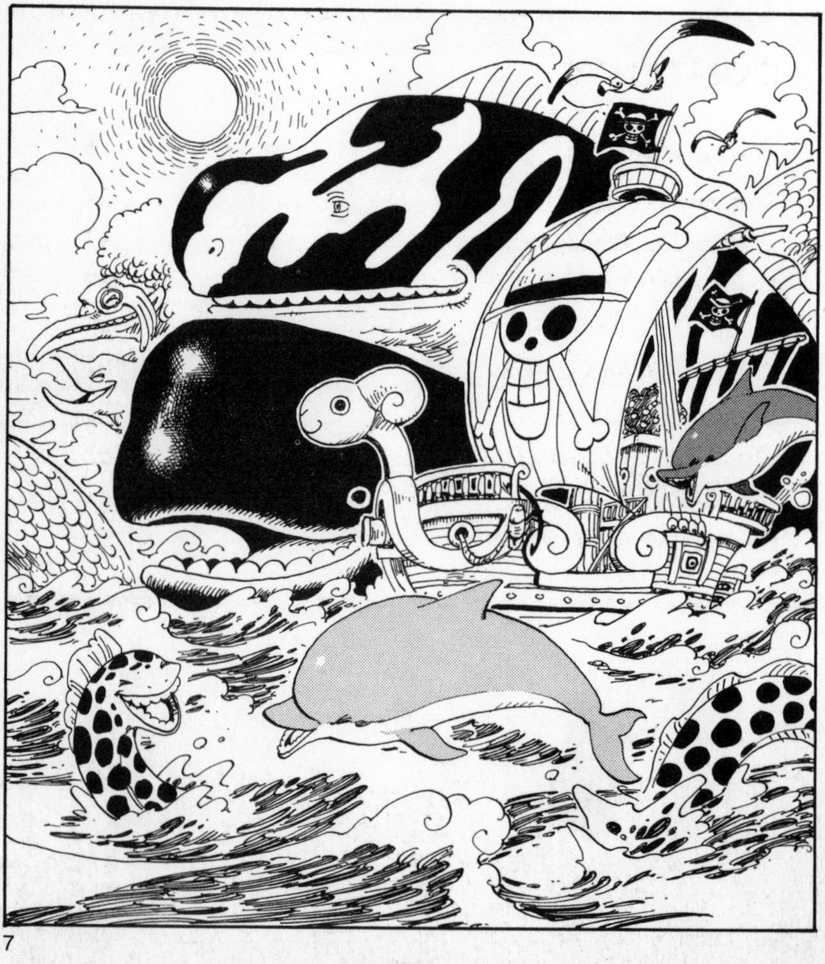

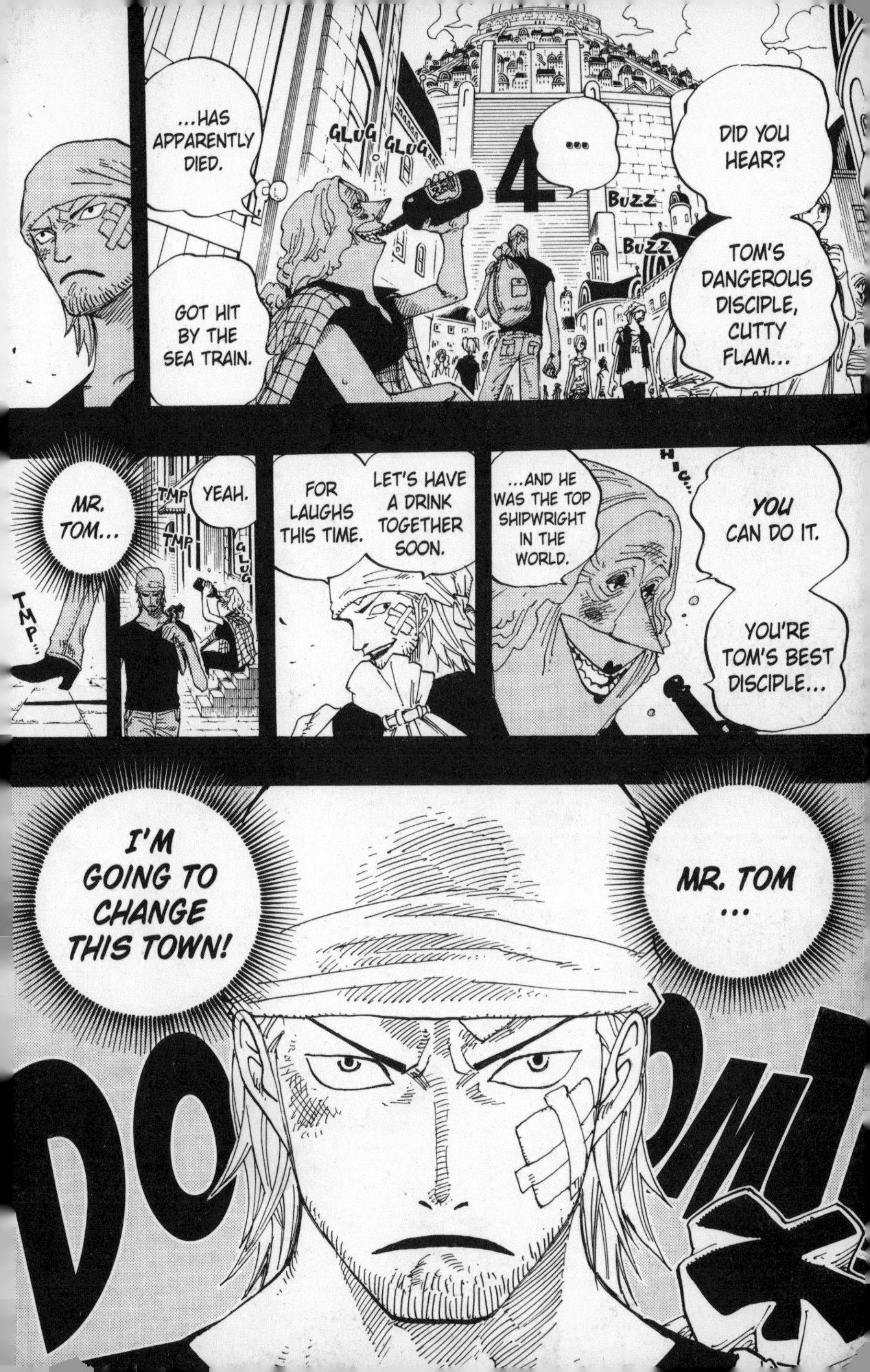
DID YOU HEAR?
TOM'S DANGEROUS DISCIPLE, CUTTY FLAM...
BUZZ
BUZZ
...
4
GLUG GLUG
...HAS APPARENTLY DIED.
GOT HIT BY THE SEA TRAIN.
YOU CAN DO IT.
YOU'RE TOM'S BEST DISCIPLE...
HIC...
...AND HE WAS THE TOP SHIPWRIGHT IN THE WORLD.
LET'S HAVE A DRINK TOGETHER SOON.
FOR LAUGHS THIS TIME.
YEAH.
TMP
TMP
GLUG
MR. TOM...
TMP...
MR. TOM ...
I'M GOING TO CHANGE THIS TOWN!
DOOM!

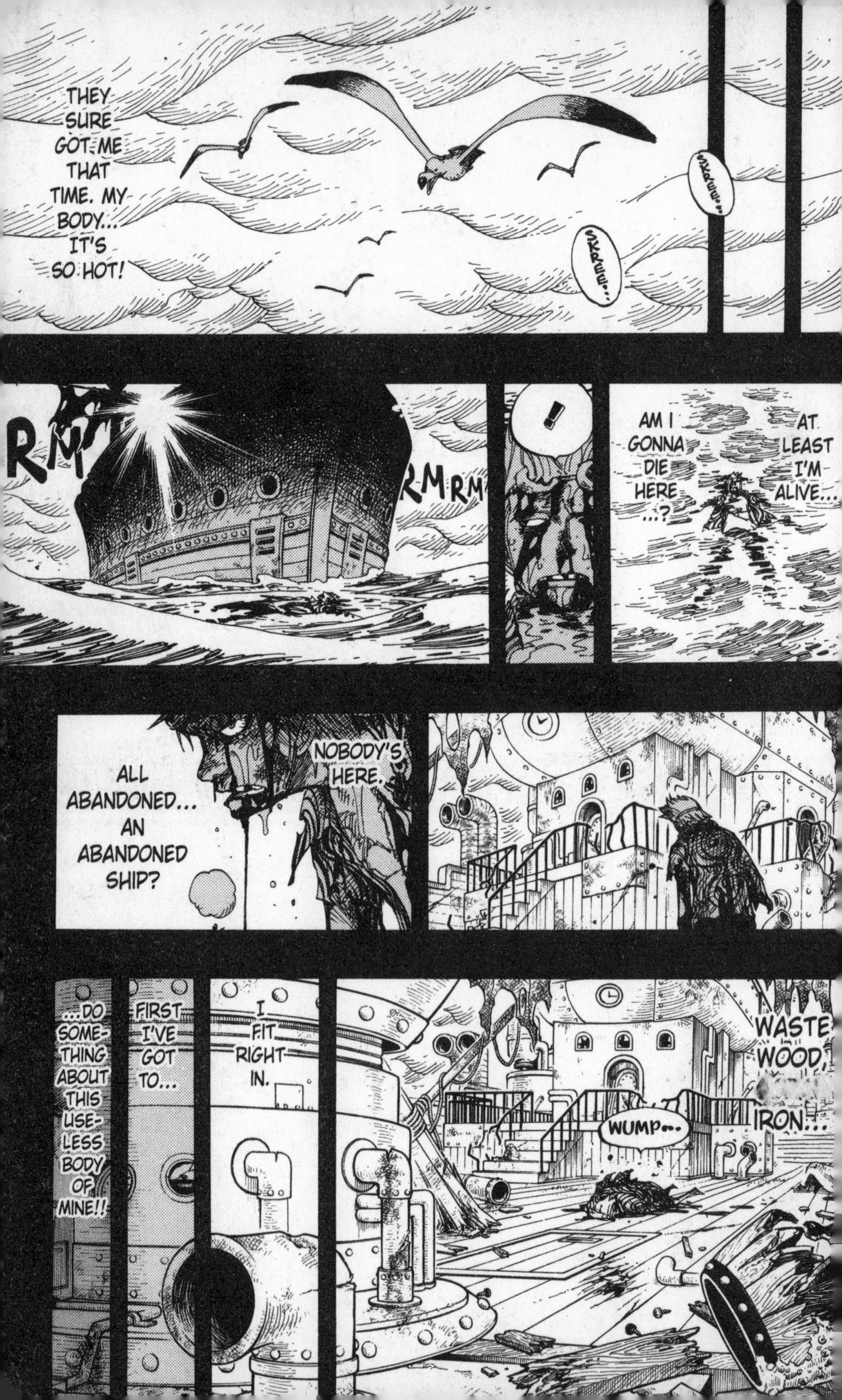
SKREEE...
SKREE...
THEY SURE GOT ME THAT TIME. MY BODY... IT'S SO HOT!
AT LEAST I'M ALIVE...
AM I GONNA DIE HERE ...?
!
RMRM
RM
NOBODY'S HERE.
ALL ABANDONED... AN ABANDONED SHIP?
WASTE WOOD,
IRON...!
WUMP...
I FIT RIGHT IN.
FIRST I'VE GOT TO...
...DO SOMETHING ABOUT THIS USELESS BODY OF MINE!!

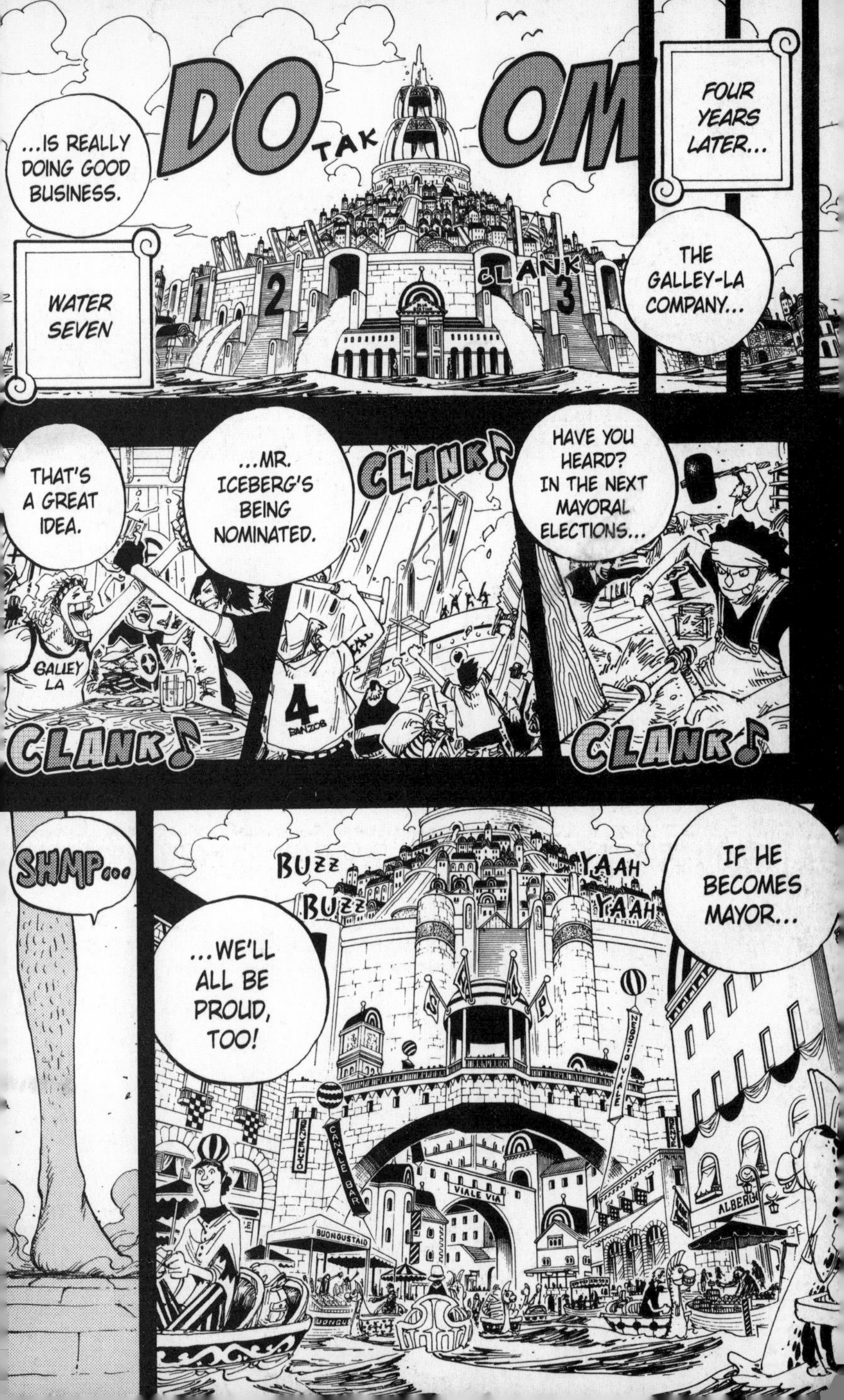
FOUR YEARS LATER...
THE GALLEY-LA COMPANY...
DO OM
TAK
CLANK
1 2 3
...IS REALLY DOING GOOD BUSINESS.
WATER SEVEN
HAVE YOU HEARD? IN THE NEXT MAYORAL ELECTIONS...
CLANK♪
CLANK♪
...MR. ICEBERG'S BEING NOMINATED.
4
THAT'S A GREAT IDEA.
GALLEY LA
CLANK♪
IF HE BECOMES MAYOR...
YAAH YAAH
BUZZ BUZZ
...WE'LL ALL BE PROUD, TOO!
NEGOZIO VIALE
CANALE BAR
VIALE VIA
BUONGUSTAIO
ALBERGO
SHMP...

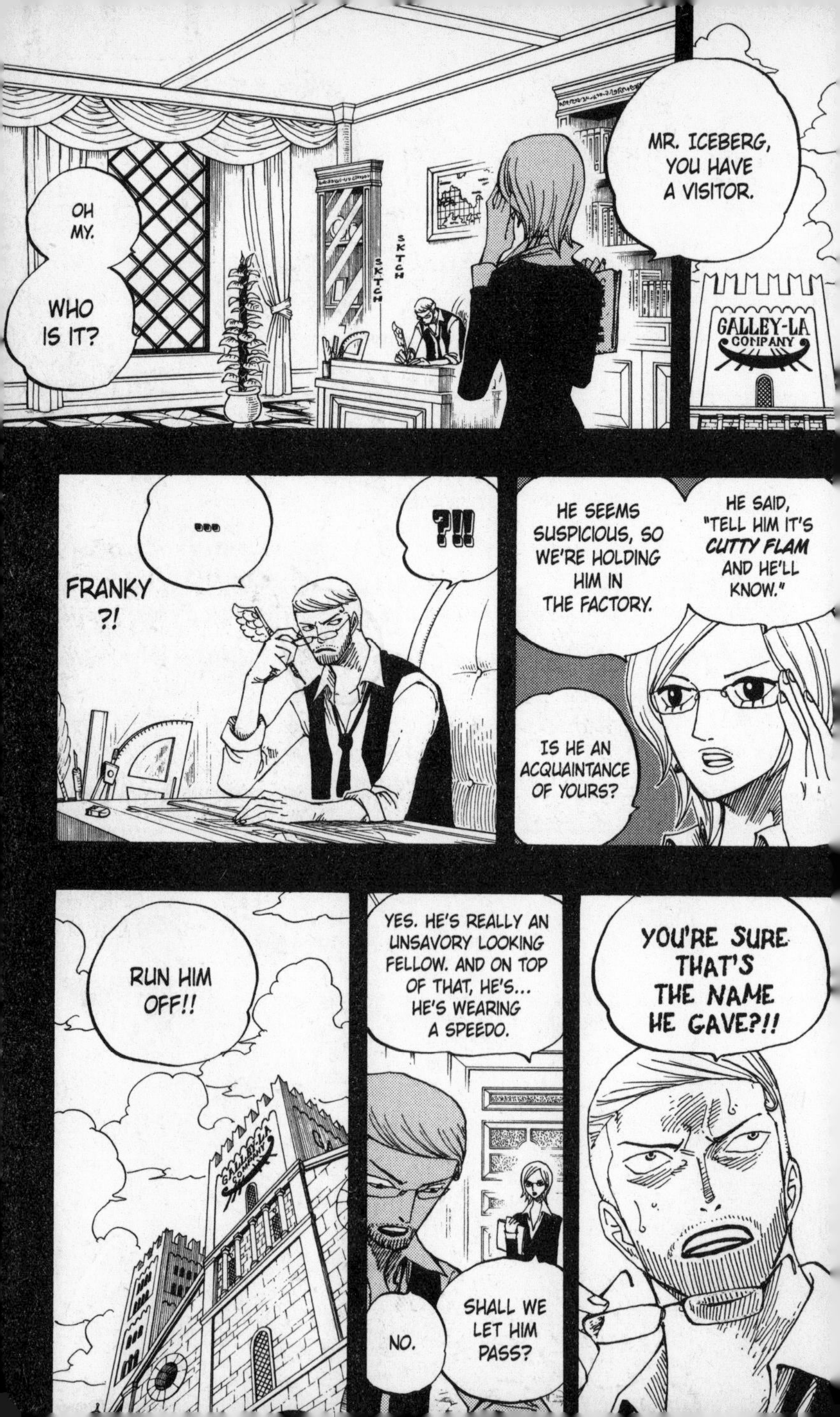
MR. ICEBERG, YOU HAVE A VISITOR.
SKTCH
SKTCH
GALLEY-LA COMPANY
OH MY.
WHO IS IT?
HE SAID, "TELL HIM IT'S *CUTTY FLAM* AND HE'LL KNOW."
HE SEEMS SUSPICIOUS, SO WE'RE HOLDING HIM IN THE FACTORY.
IS HE AN ACQUAINTANCE OF YOURS?
?!!
...
FRANKY ?!
YOU'RE SURE THAT'S THE NAME HE GAVE?!!
YES. HE'S REALLY AN UNSAVORY LOOKING FELLOW. AND ON TOP OF THAT, HE'S... HE'S WEARING A SPEEDO.
SHALL WE LET HIM PASS?
NO.
RUN HIM OFF!!
GALLEY-LA COMPANY

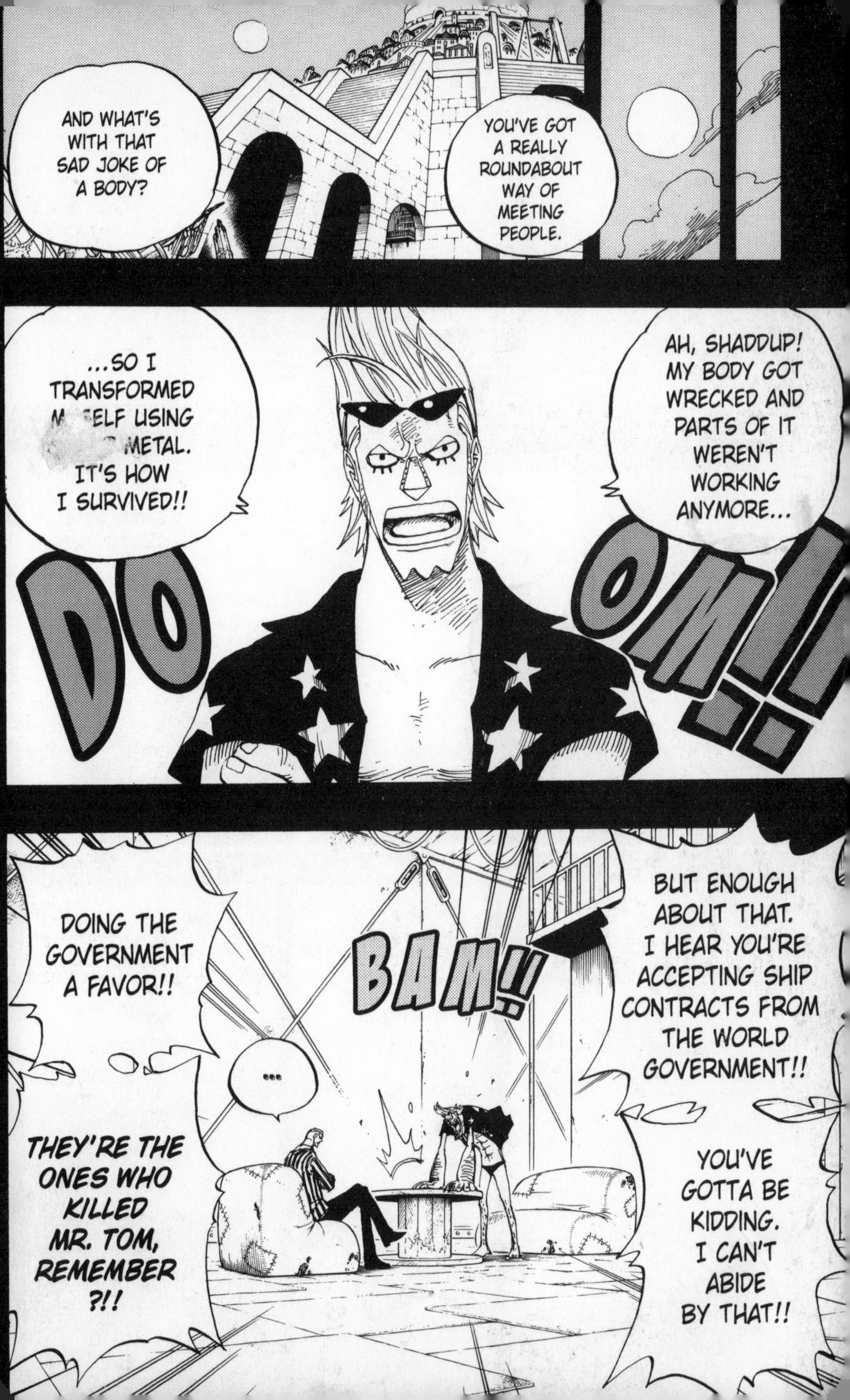
YOU'VE GOT A REALLY ROUNDABOUT WAY OF MEETING PEOPLE.
AND WHAT'S WITH THAT SAD JOKE OF A BODY?
AH, SHADDUP! MY BODY GOT WRECKED AND PARTS OF IT WEREN'T WORKING ANYMORE...
...SO I TRANSFORMED M ELF USING METAL. IT'S HOW I SURVIVED!!
DO
OM!!
BUT ENOUGH ABOUT THAT. I HEAR YOU'RE ACCEPTING SHIP CONTRACTS FROM THE WORLD GOVERNMENT!!
DOING THE GOVERNMENT A FAVOR!!
BAM!!
...
YOU'VE GOTTA BE KIDDING. I CAN'T ABIDE BY THAT!!
THEY'RE THE ONES WHO KILLED MR. TOM, REMEMBER?!!

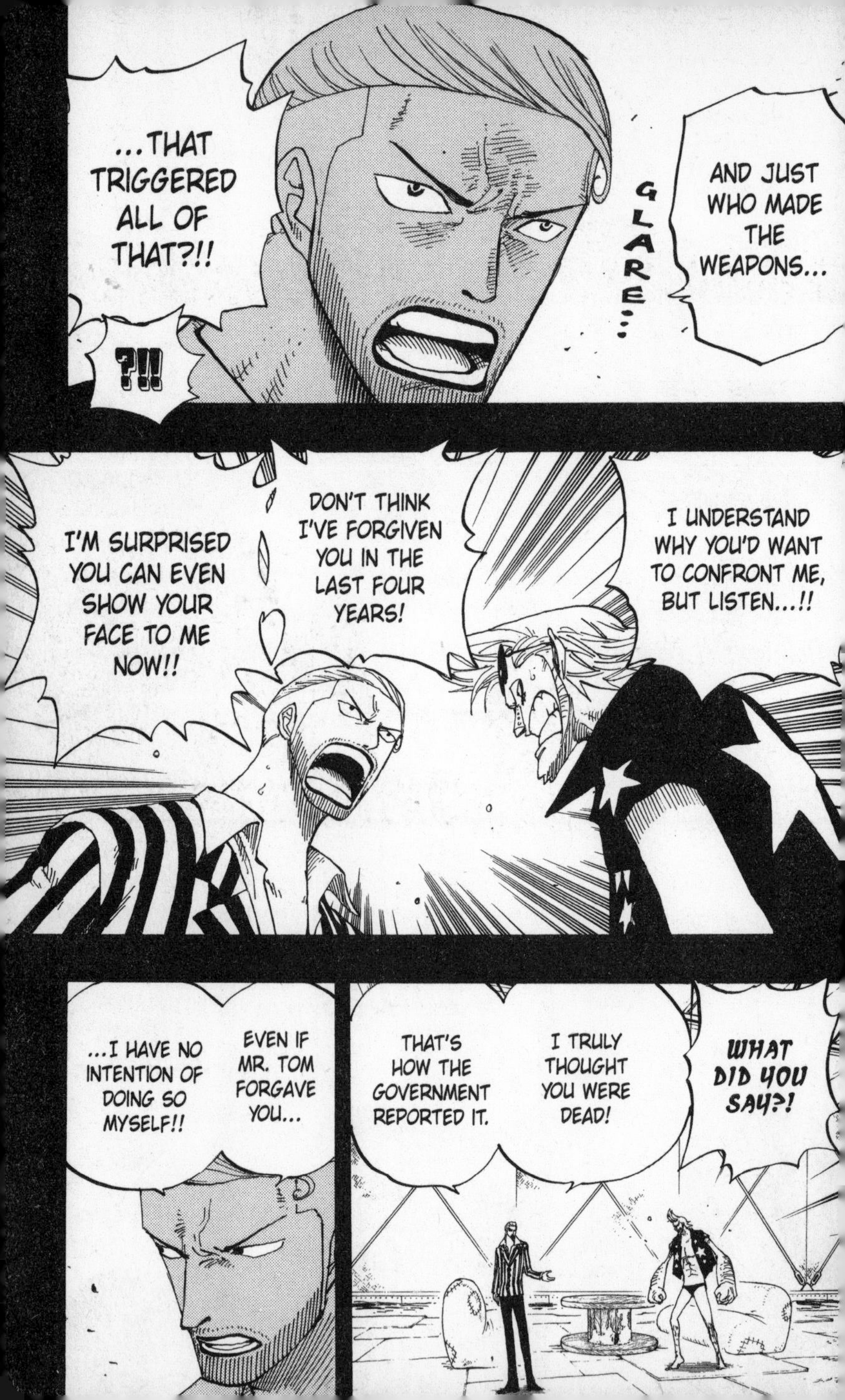
AND JUST WHO MADE THE WEAPONS...
GLARE...
...THAT TRIGGERED ALL OF THAT?!!
?!!
I UNDERSTAND WHY YOU'D WANT TO CONFRONT ME, BUT LISTEN...!!
DON'T THINK I'VE FORGIVEN YOU IN THE LAST FOUR YEARS!
I'M SURPRISED YOU CAN EVEN SHOW YOUR FACE TO ME NOW!!
WHAT DID YOU SAY?!
I TRULY THOUGHT YOU WERE DEAD!
THAT'S HOW THE GOVERNMENT REPORTED IT.
EVEN IF MR. TOM FORGAVE YOU...
...I HAVE NO INTENTION OF DOING SO MYSELF!!

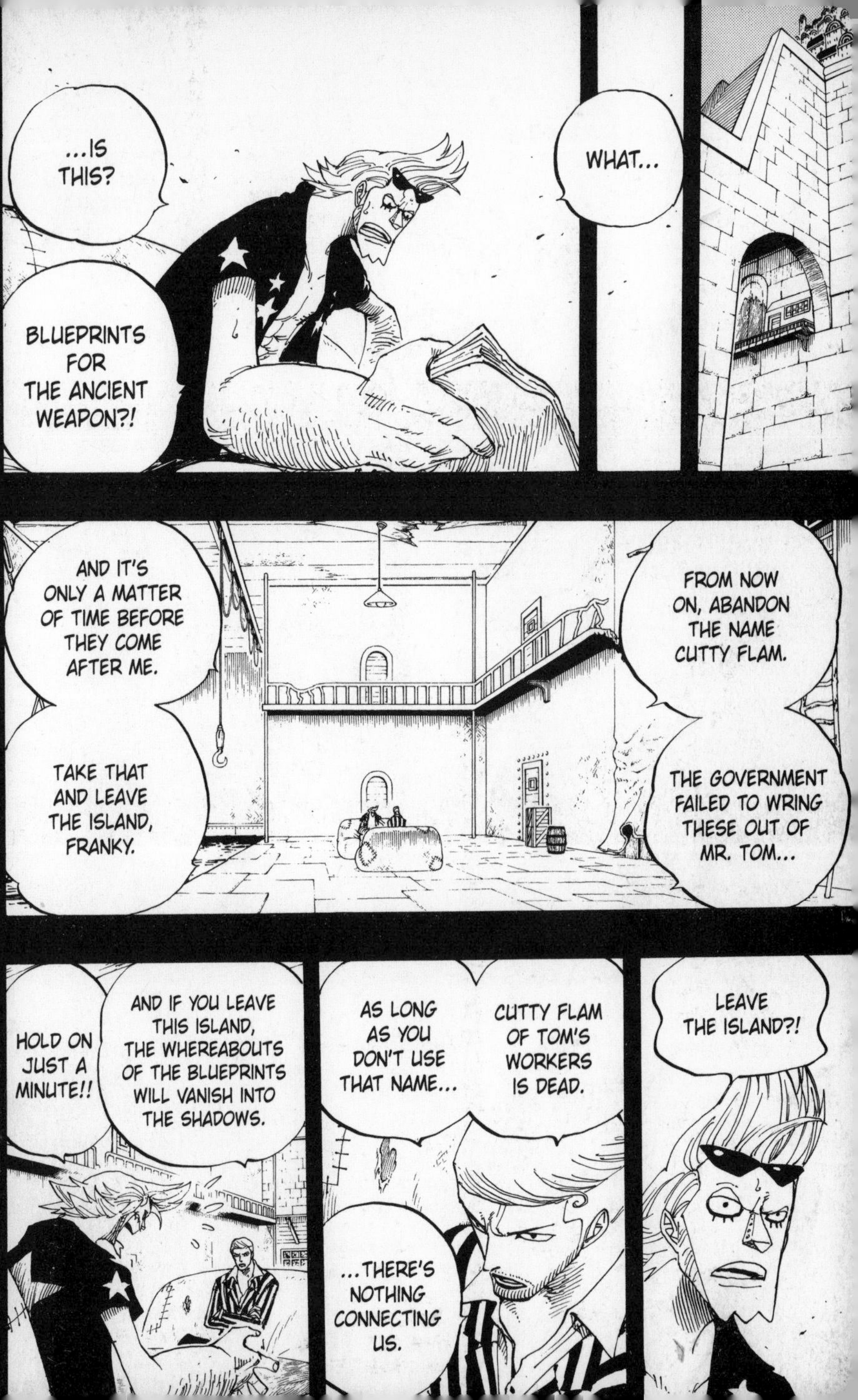
WHAT...
...IS THIS?
BLUEPRINTS FOR THE ANCIENT WEAPON?!
FROM NOW ON, ABANDON THE NAME CUTTY FLAM.
THE GOVERNMENT FAILED TO WRING THESE OUT OF MR. TOM...
AND IT'S ONLY A MATTER OF TIME BEFORE THEY COME AFTER ME.
TAKE THAT AND LEAVE THE ISLAND, FRANKY.
LEAVE THE ISLAND?!
CUTTY FLAM OF TOM'S WORKERS IS DEAD.
AS LONG AS YOU DON'T USE THAT NAME...
...THERE'S NOTHING CONNECTING US.
AND IF YOU LEAVE THIS ISLAND, THE WHEREABOUTS OF THE BLUEPRINTS WILL VANISH INTO THE SHADOWS.
HOLD ON JUST A MINUTE!!

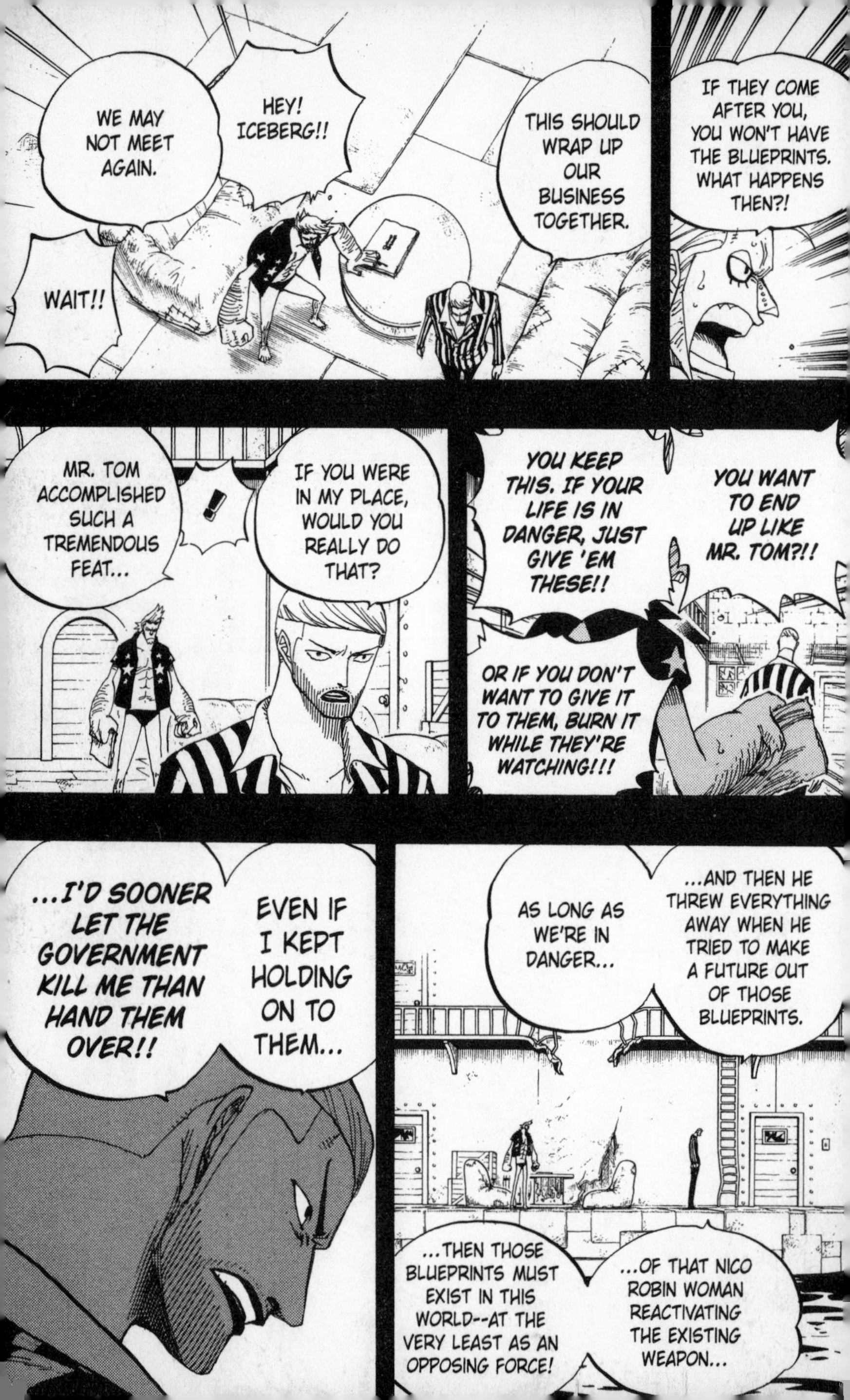
IF THEY COME AFTER YOU, YOU WON'T HAVE THE BLUEPRINTS. WHAT HAPPENS THEN?!
THIS SHOULD WRAP UP OUR BUSINESS TOGETHER.
HEY! ICEBERG!!
WE MAY NOT MEET AGAIN.
WAIT!!
YOU WANT TO END UP LIKE MR. TOM?!!
YOU KEEP THIS. IF YOUR LIFE IS IN DANGER, JUST GIVE 'EM THESE!!
OR IF YOU DON'T WANT TO GIVE IT TO THEM, BURN IT WHILE THEY'RE WATCHING!!!
IF YOU WERE IN MY PLACE, WOULD YOU REALLY DO THAT?
!
MR. TOM ACCOMPLISHED SUCH A TREMENDOUS FEAT...
...AND THEN HE THREW EVERYTHING AWAY WHEN HE TRIED TO MAKE A FUTURE OUT OF THOSE BLUEPRINTS.
AS LONG AS WE'RE IN DANGER...
...OF THAT NICO ROBIN WOMAN REACTIVATING THE EXISTING WEAPON...
...THEN THOSE BLUEPRINTS MUST EXIST IN THIS WORLD--AT THE VERY LEAST AS AN OPPOSING FORCE!
EVEN IF I KEPT HOLDING ON TO THEM...
...I'D SOONER LET THE GOVERNMENT KILL ME THAN HAND THEM OVER!!

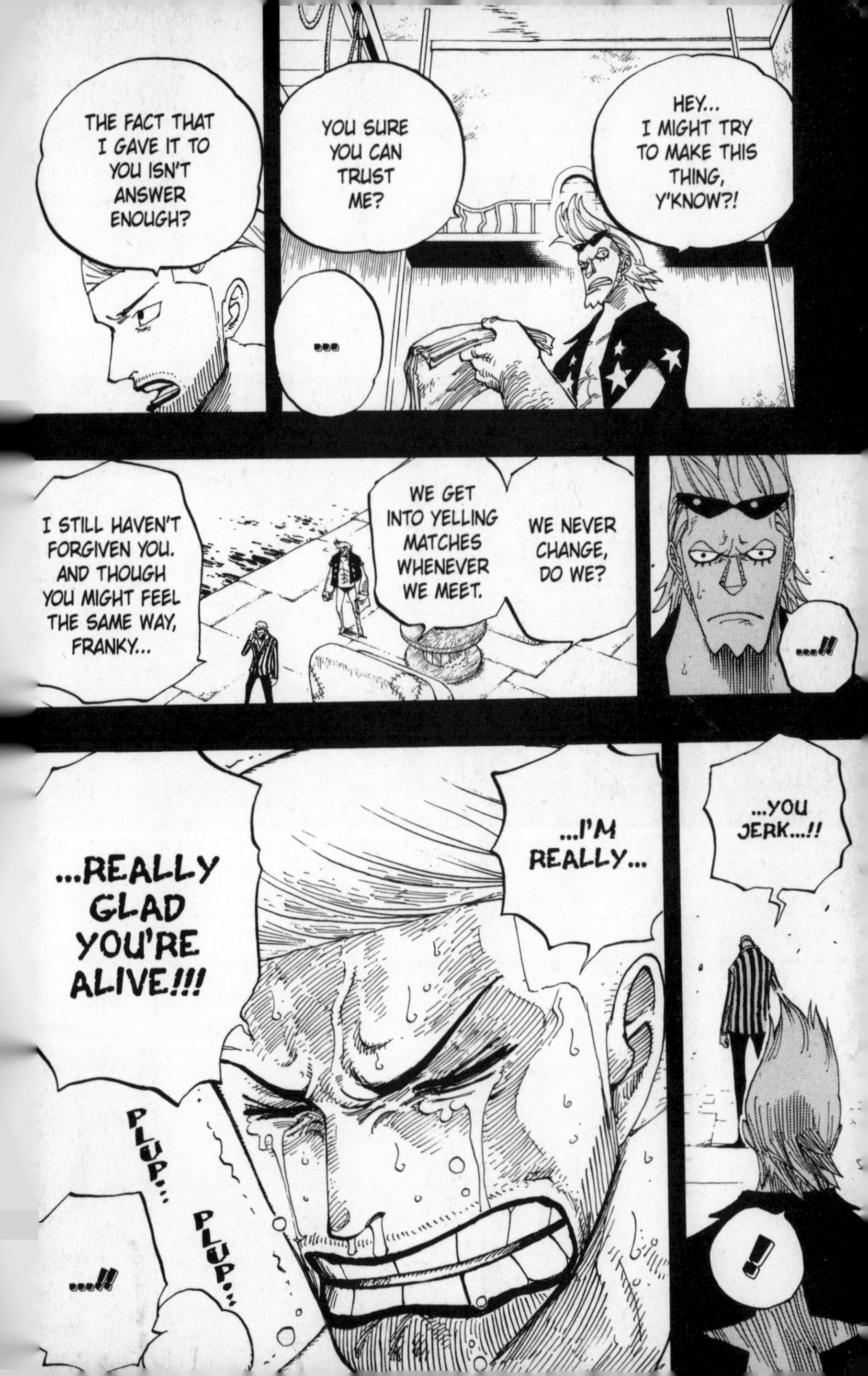
HEY... I MIGHT TRY TO MAKE THIS THING, Y'KNOW?!
YOU SURE YOU CAN TRUST ME?
...
THE FACT THAT I GAVE IT TO YOU ISN'T ANSWER ENOUGH?
...!!
WE NEVER CHANGE, DO WE?
WE GET INTO YELLING MATCHES WHENEVER WE MEET.
I STILL HAVEN'T FORGIVEN YOU. AND THOUGH YOU MIGHT FEEL THE SAME WAY, FRANKY...
...YOU JERK...!!
!
...I'M REALLY...
...REALLY GLAD YOU'RE ALIVE!!!
PLUP...
PLUP...
...!!

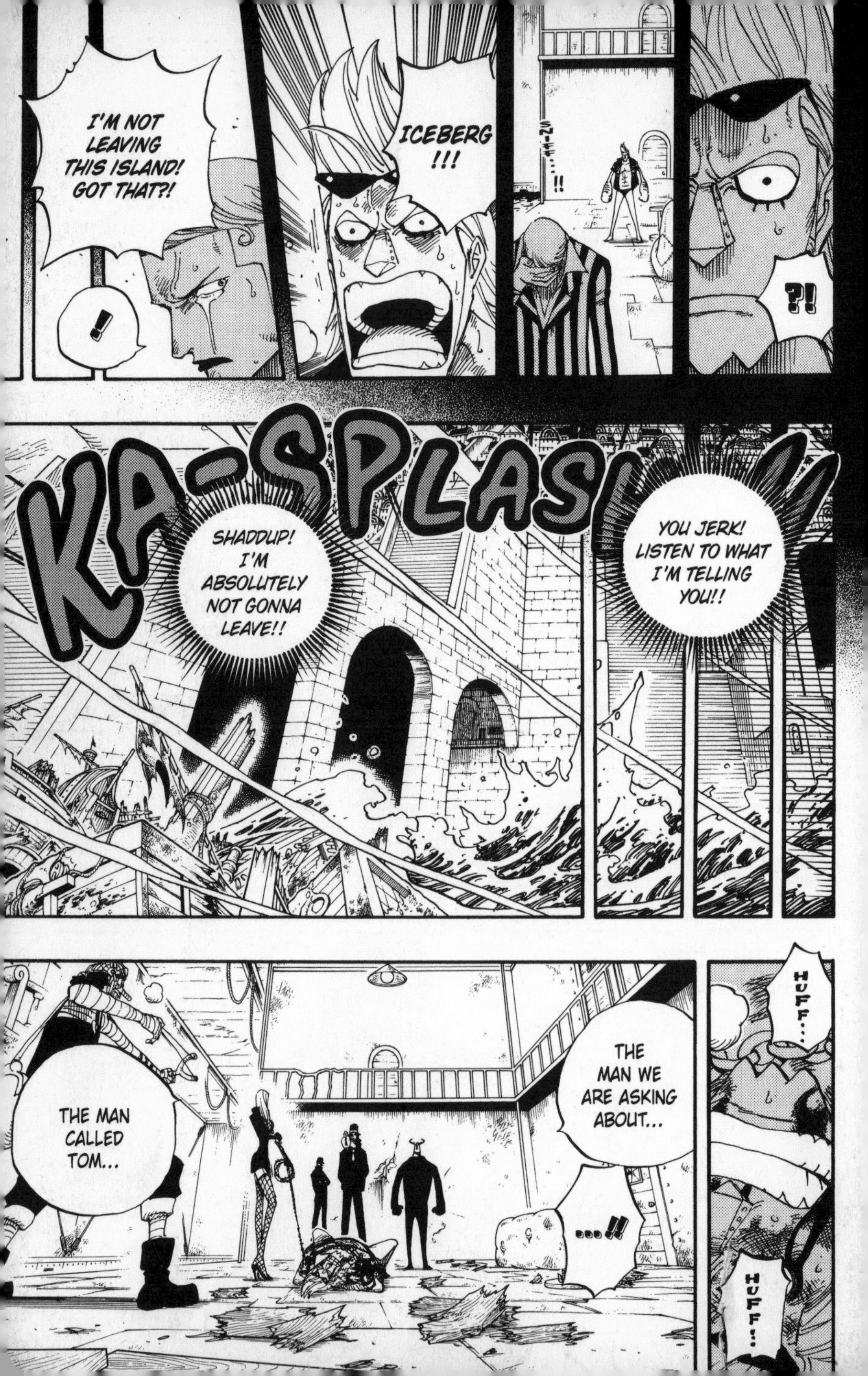

?!
SNIFF...!!
ICEBERG!!!
I'M NOT LEAVING THIS ISLAND! GOT THAT?!
!
KA-SPLASH
YOU JERK! LISTEN TO WHAT I'M TELLING YOU!!
SHADDUP! I'M ABSOLUTELY NOT GONNA LEAVE!!
HUFF...
HUFF!!
THE MAN WE ARE ASKING ABOUT...
...!!
THE MAN CALLED TOM...

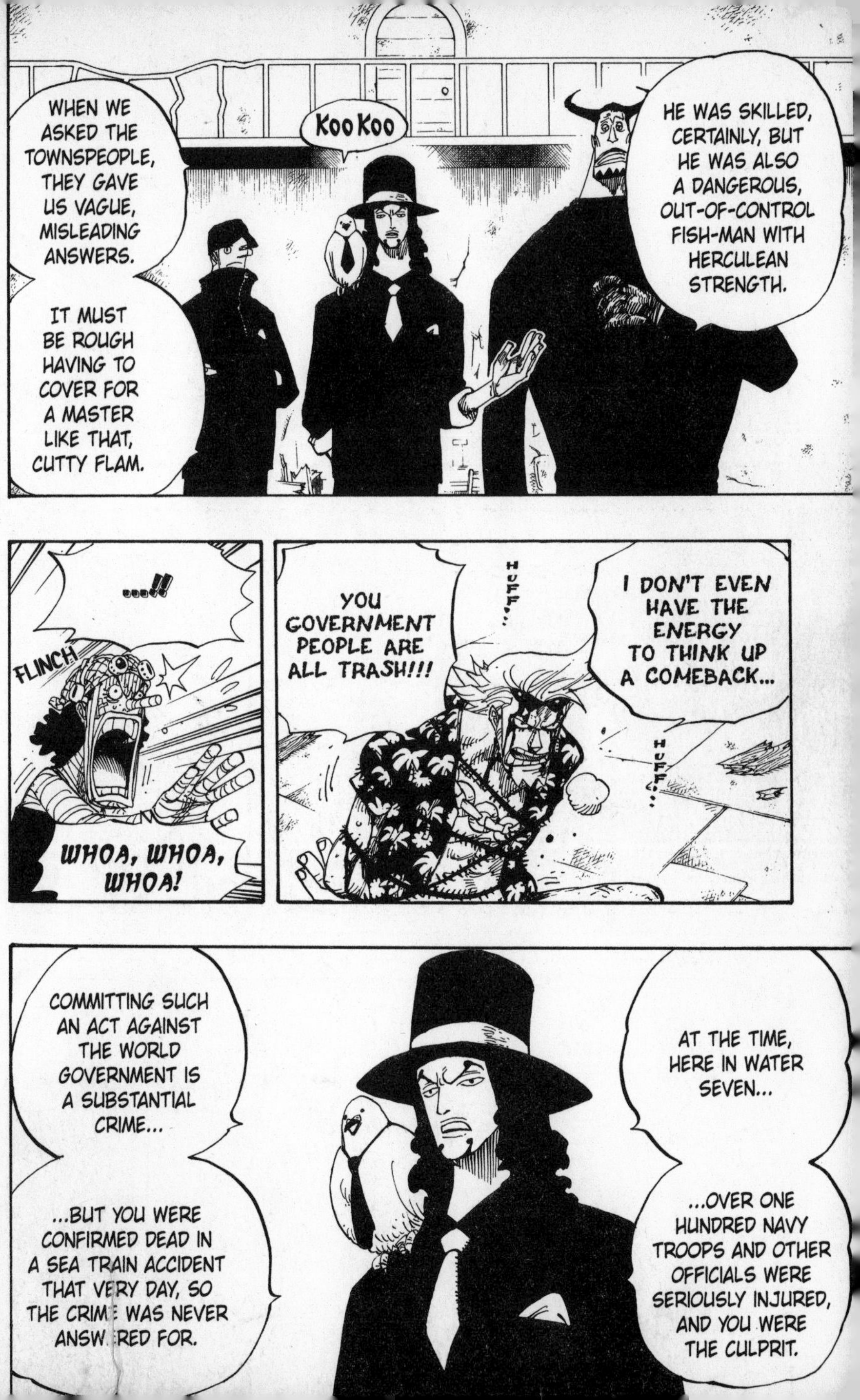
HE WAS SKILLED, CERTAINLY, BUT HE WAS ALSO A DANGEROUS, OUT-OF-CONTROL FISH-MAN WITH HERCULEAN STRENGTH.
KOO KOO
WHEN WE ASKED THE TOWNSPEOPLE, THEY GAVE US VAGUE, MISLEADING ANSWERS.
IT MUST BE ROUGH HAVING TO COVER FOR A MASTER LIKE THAT, CUTTY FLAM.
I DON'T EVEN HAVE THE ENERGY TO THINK UP A COMEBACK...
HUFF...
YOU GOVERNMENT PEOPLE ARE ALL TRASH!!!
HUFF...
...!!
FLINCH
WHOA, WHOA, WHOA!
AT THE TIME, HERE IN WATER SEVEN...
...OVER ONE HUNDRED NAVY TROOPS AND OTHER OFFICIALS WERE SERIOUSLY INJURED, AND YOU WERE THE CULPRIT.
COMMITTING SUCH AN ACT AGAINST THE WORLD GOVERNMENT IS A SUBSTANTIAL CRIME...
...BUT YOU WERE CONFIRMED DEAD IN A SEA TRAIN ACCIDENT THAT VERY DAY, SO THE CRIME WAS NEVER ANSWERED FOR.

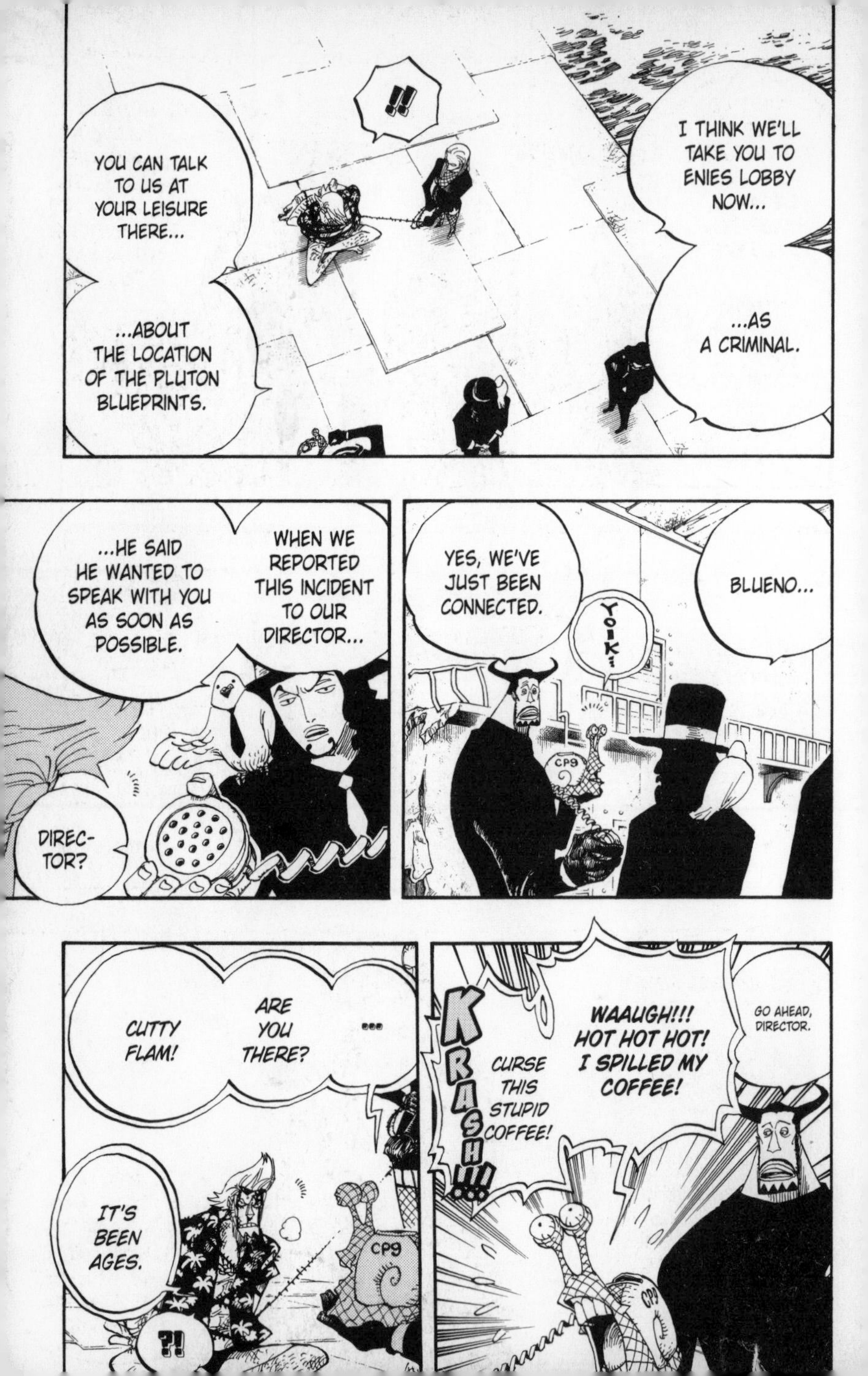
I THINK WE'LL TAKE YOU TO ENIES LOBBY NOW...
...AS A CRIMINAL.
!!
YOU CAN TALK TO US AT YOUR LEISURE THERE...
...ABOUT THE LOCATION OF THE PLUTON BLUEPRINTS.
BLUENO...
YES, WE'VE JUST BEEN CONNECTED.
YOIK!
WHEN WE REPORTED THIS INCIDENT TO OUR DIRECTOR...
...HE SAID HE WANTED TO SPEAK WITH YOU AS SOON AS POSSIBLE.
DIREC-TOR?
GO AHEAD, DIRECTOR.
WAAUGH!!! HOT HOT HOT! I SPILLED MY COFFEE!
CURSE THIS STUPID COFFEE!
KRASH!!!
...
ARE YOU THERE?
CUTTY FLAM!
IT'S BEEN AGES.
?!

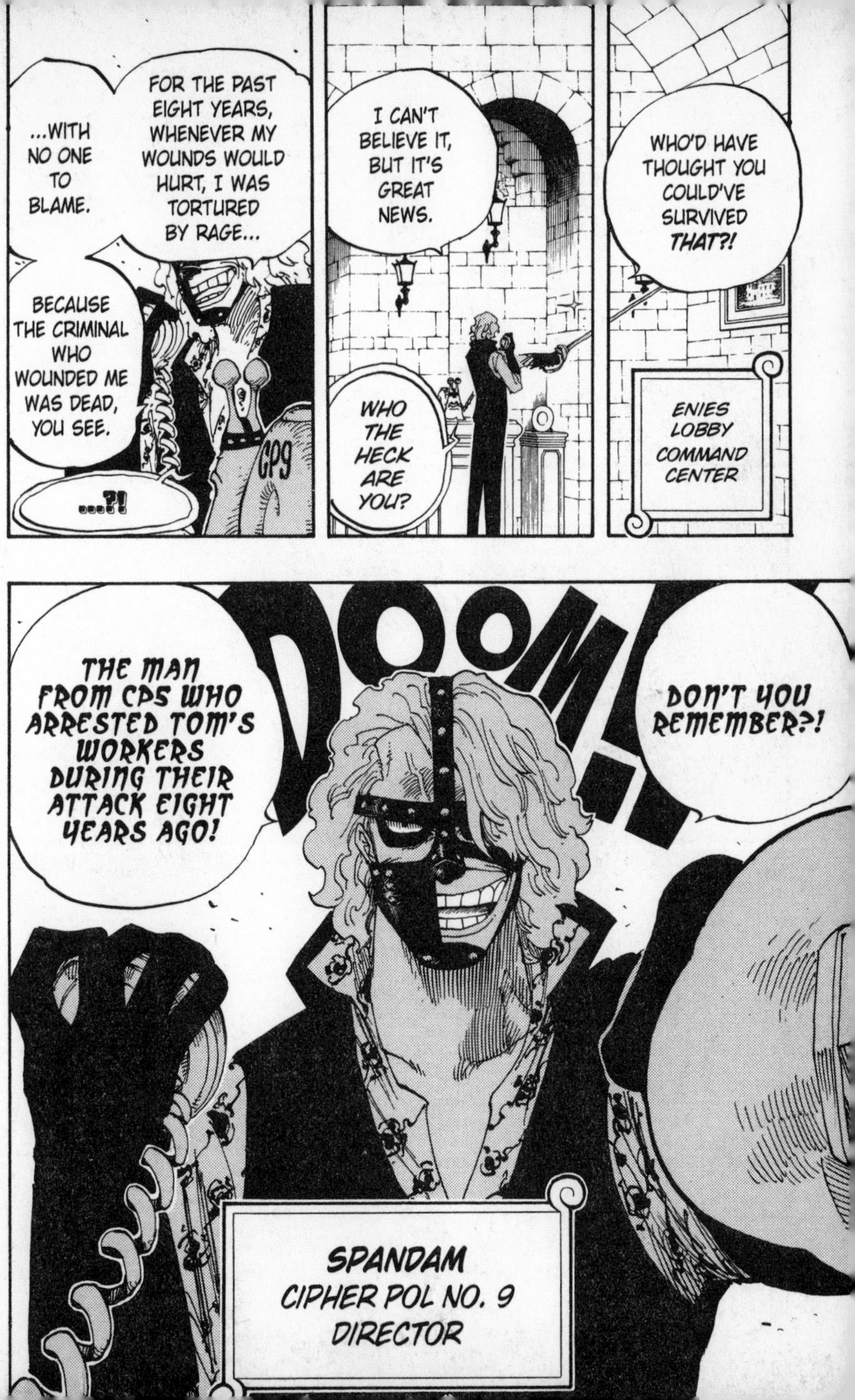
WHO'D HAVE THOUGHT YOU COULD'VE SURVIVED THAT?!
ENIES LOBBY COMMAND CENTER
I CAN'T BELIEVE IT, BUT IT'S GREAT NEWS.
WHO THE HECK ARE YOU?
FOR THE PAST EIGHT YEARS, WHENEVER MY WOUNDS WOULD HURT, I WAS TORTURED BY RAGE...
...WITH NO ONE TO BLAME.
BECAUSE THE CRIMINAL WHO WOUNDED ME WAS DEAD, YOU SEE.
CP9
...?!
DOOM!!
DON'T YOU REMEMBER?!
THE MAN FROM CP5 WHO ARRESTED TOM'S WORKERS DURING THEIR ATTACK EIGHT YEARS AGO!
SPANDAM
CIPHER POL NO. 9
DIRECTOR

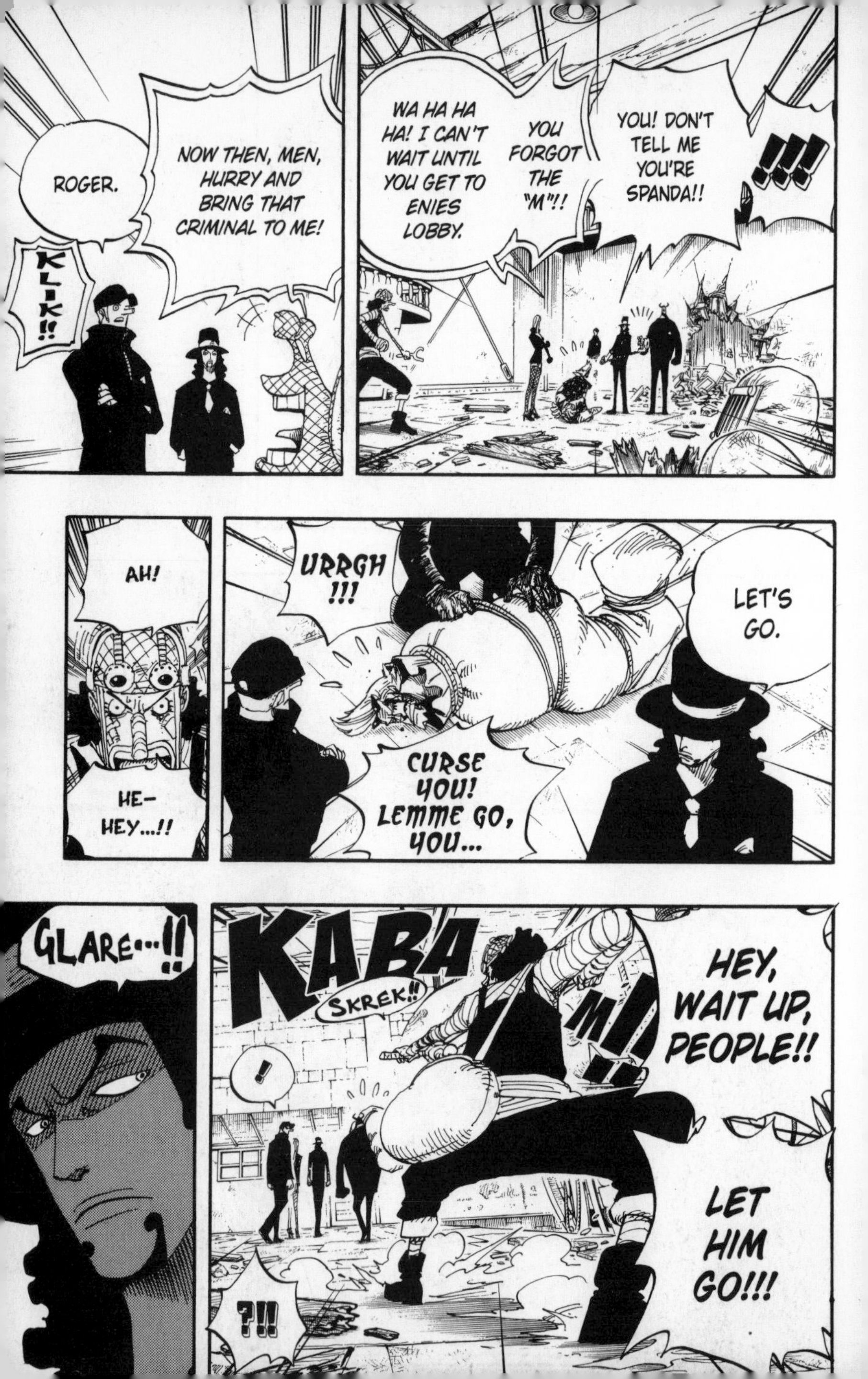
!!!
YOU! DON'T TELL ME YOU'RE SPANDA!!
YOU FORGOT THE "M"!!
WA HA HA HA! I CAN'T WAIT UNTIL YOU GET TO ENIES LOBBY.
NOW THEN, MEN, HURRY AND BRING THAT CRIMINAL TO ME!
ROGER.
KLIK!!
LET'S GO.
URRGH!!!
CURSE YOU! LEMME GO, YOU...
AH!
HE-HEY...!!
HEY, WAIT UP, PEOPLE!!
KABAM!!
SKREK!!
!
LET HIM GO!!!
?!!
GLARE...!!

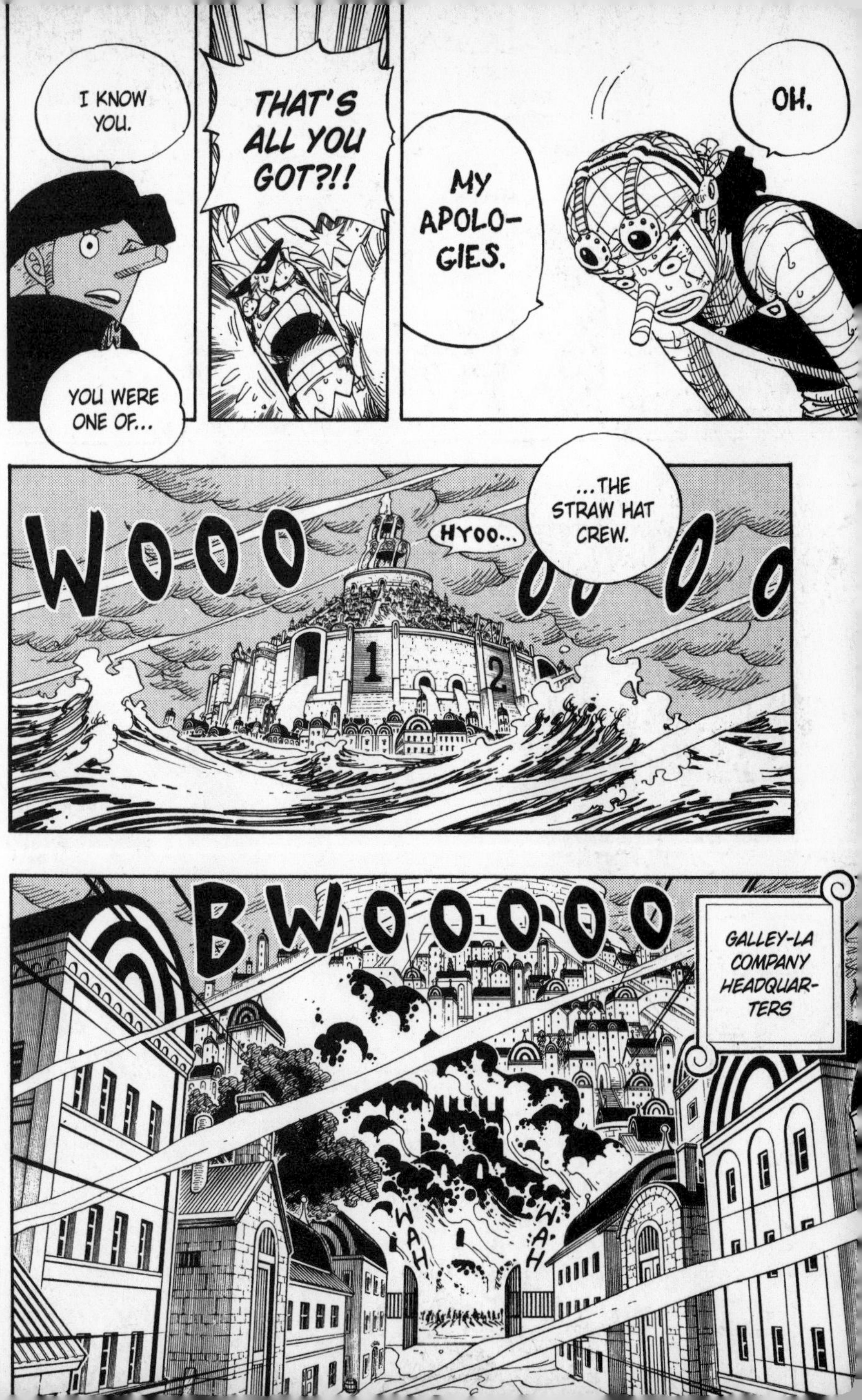
OH.
MY APOLO-GIES.
THAT'S ALL YOU GOT?!!
I KNOW YOU.
YOU WERE ONE OF...
...THE STRAW HAT CREW.
HYOO...
WOOOOOOO
GALLEY-LA COMPANY HEADQUAR-TERS
BWOOOOOO
WAH
WAH

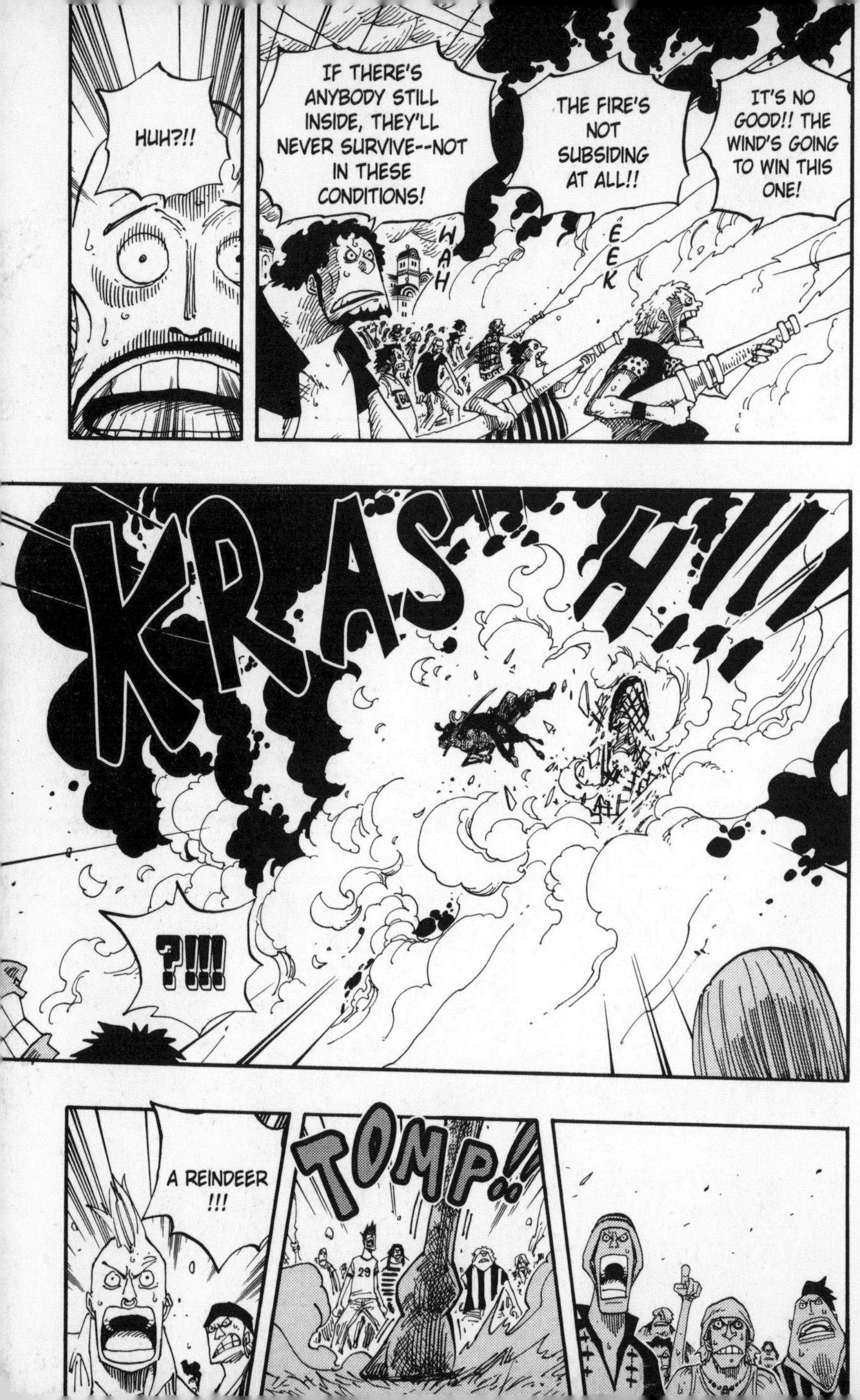
IT'S NO GOOD!! THE WIND'S GOING TO WIN THIS ONE!
THE FIRE'S NOT SUBSIDING AT ALL!!
EEEK
IF THERE'S ANYBODY STILL INSIDE, THEY'LL NEVER SURVIVE--NOT IN THESE CONDITIONS!
WAH
HUH?!!
KRASH!!!
?!!!
TOMP!!
A REINDEER !!!

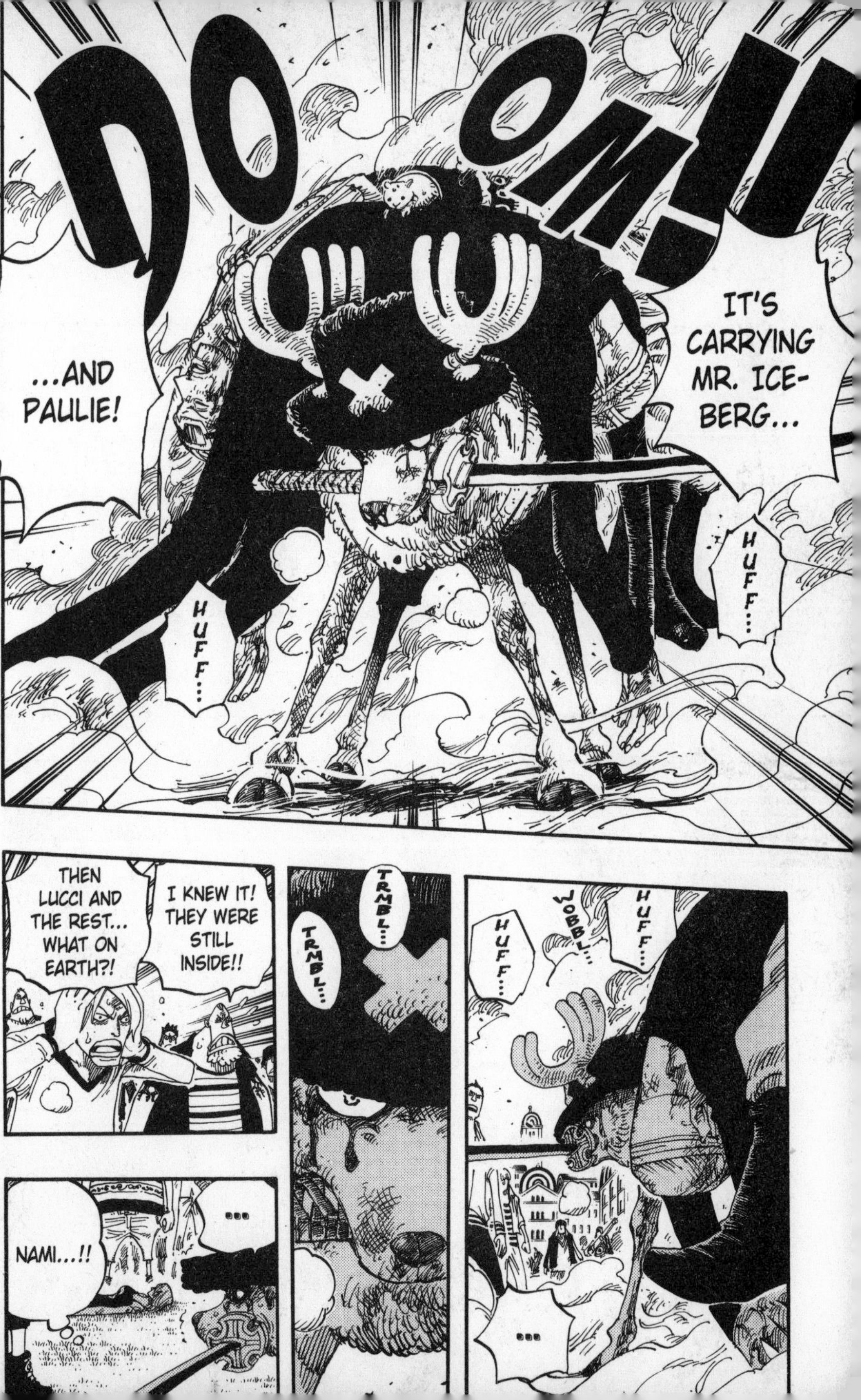
DO-OM!!
IT'S CARRYING MR. ICEBERG...
...AND PAULIE!
HUFF HUFF...
HUFF HUFF...
HUFF...
WOBBL...
HUFF...
...
TRMBL...
TRMBL...
I KNEW IT! THEY WERE STILL INSIDE!!
THEN LUCCI AND THE REST... WHAT ON EARTH?!
...
NAMI...!!

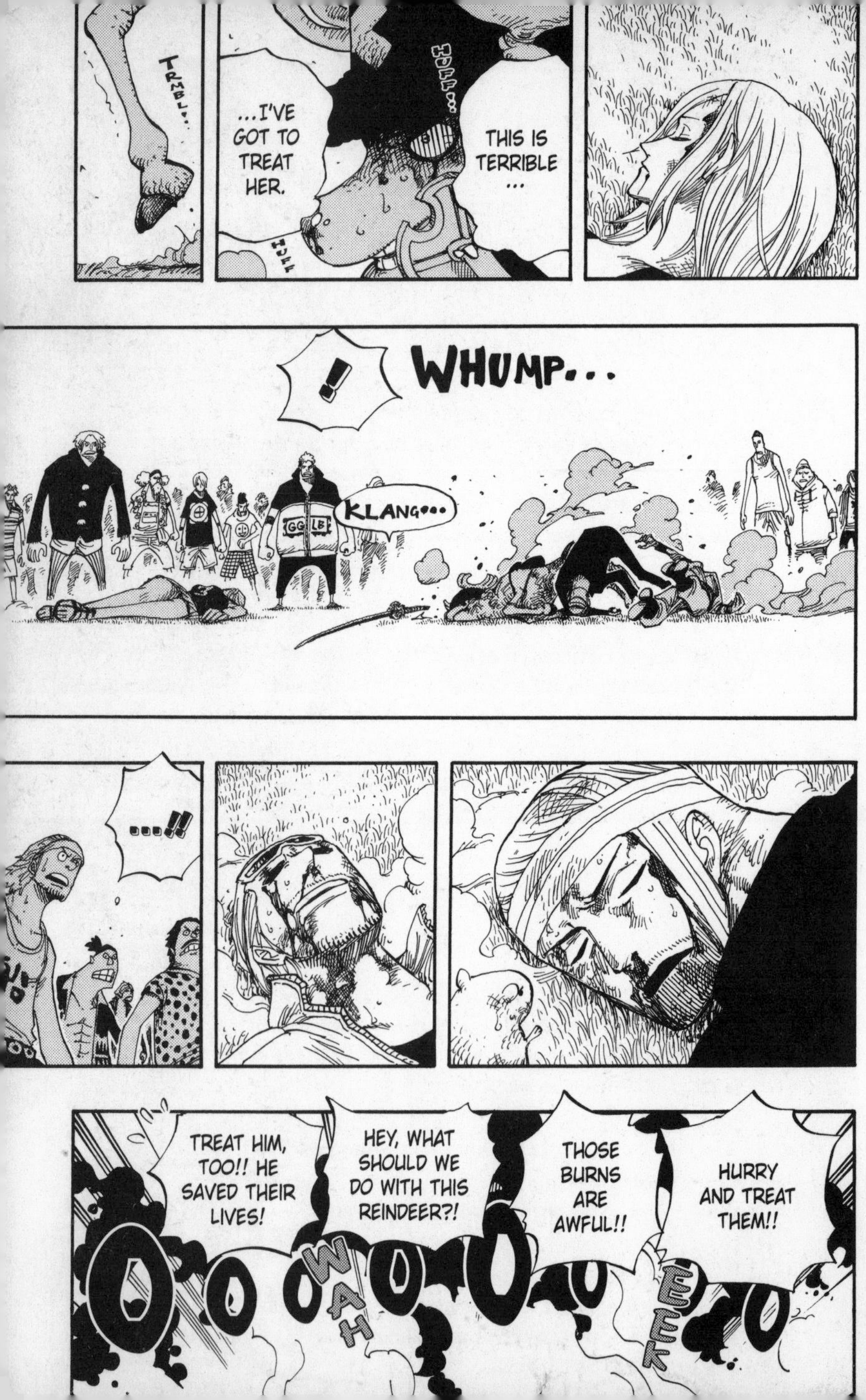
HUFF...
THIS IS TERRIBLE ...
...I'VE GOT TO TREAT HER.
HUFF
TRMBL...
WHUMP...
!
KLANG...
...!!
HURRY AND TREAT THEM!!
THOSE BURNS ARE AWFUL!!
EEK
HEY, WHAT SHOULD WE DO WITH THIS REINDEER?!
TREAT HIM, TOO!! HE SAVED THEIR LIVES!
WAH

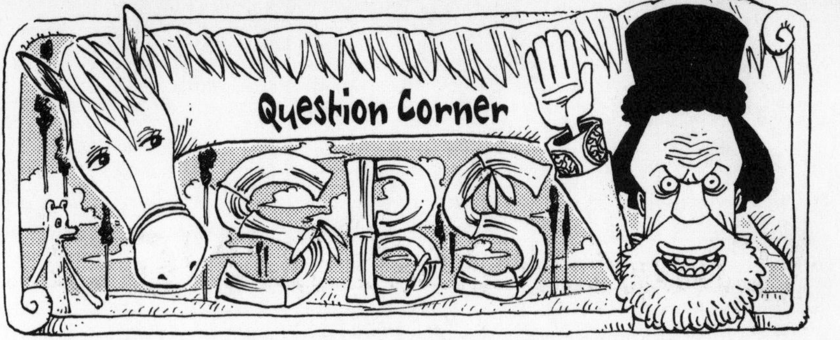
Question Corner
SBS

Oda: Hello, All. Everybody else always hijacks this corner, but in this volume I've managed to keep hold on my place as creator! (Applause, applause, applause.) That means lining up at the Question Corner site all last night with a sack lunch was worth it. And the rice balls were filled with tuna, my absolute favorite. It was so incredibly yummy. Oh, hurry up and start, you say? Just get on with it? Right, okay then, sorry to have kept you waiting. The S (Silly) B (Bear) S (Says "excuse me") corner is starting! ← I've mistaken the meaning.

Reader: Hello, Oda Sensei! I just thought of something: It's about the Door-Door Fruit. If Sanji ate the Door-Door Fruit, Nami could never take a bath again, could she? And with that, please keep up all the good work.☆

--KIE

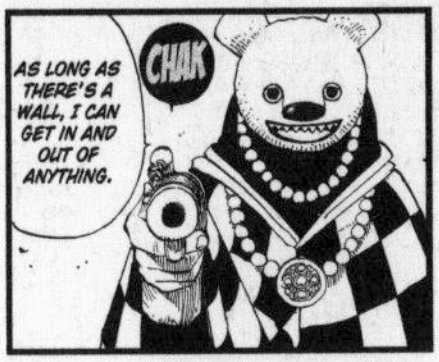
CHAK
AS LONG AS THERE'S A WALL, I CAN GET IN AND OUT OF ANYTHING.
The power of the Door-Door Fruit.

Oda: You're completely right. That'd be the end of the world as we know it. He'd be able to spy on the baths of all the women in the world. Agh, knock on wood, knock on wood!

Reader: The guy in the seat behind me keeps firing the Gum-Gum Pistol. What should I do about it??

--Usopp Pirate Crew Navigator

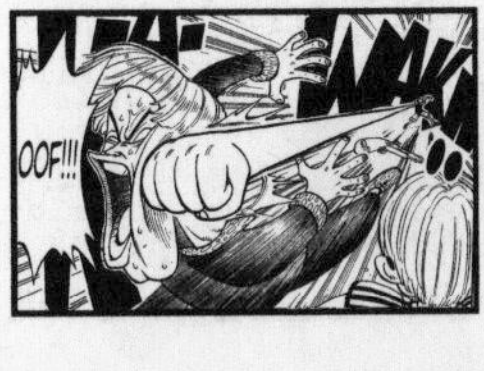
OOF!!!

Oda: That's definitely a problem. But that guy's Luffy, no mistake, so... give him some meat, and I think he'll calm down.

Chapter 359: BINGO

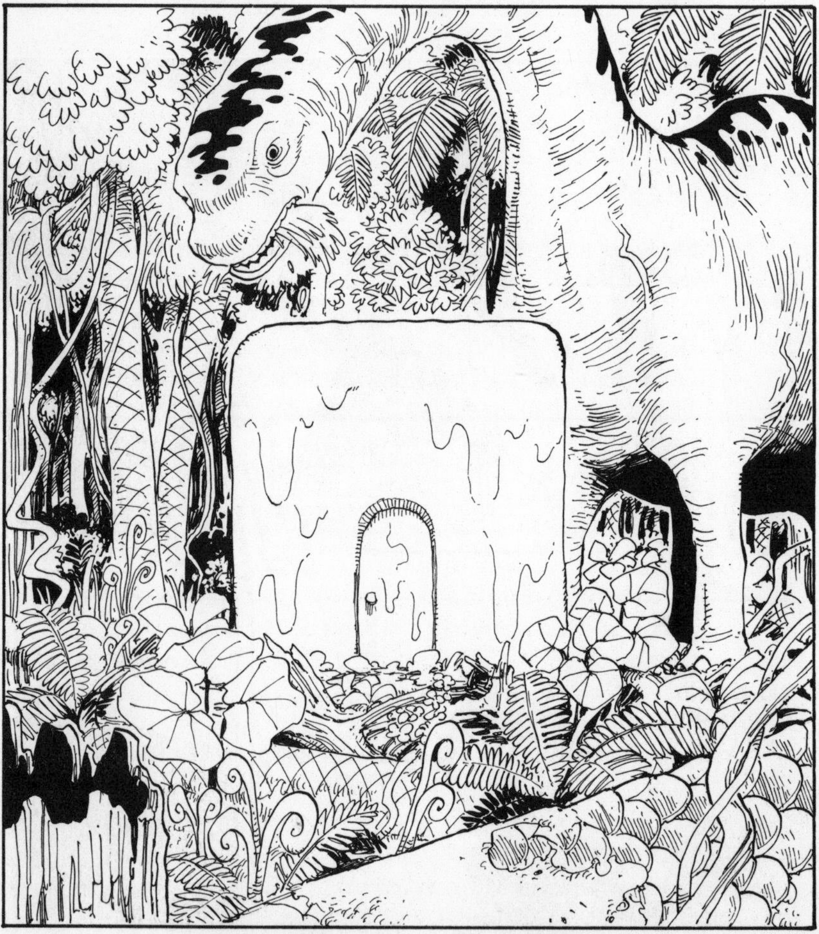

LIMITED–RUN SERIES NO. 8:
"THE HOUSE IN THE JUNGLE"

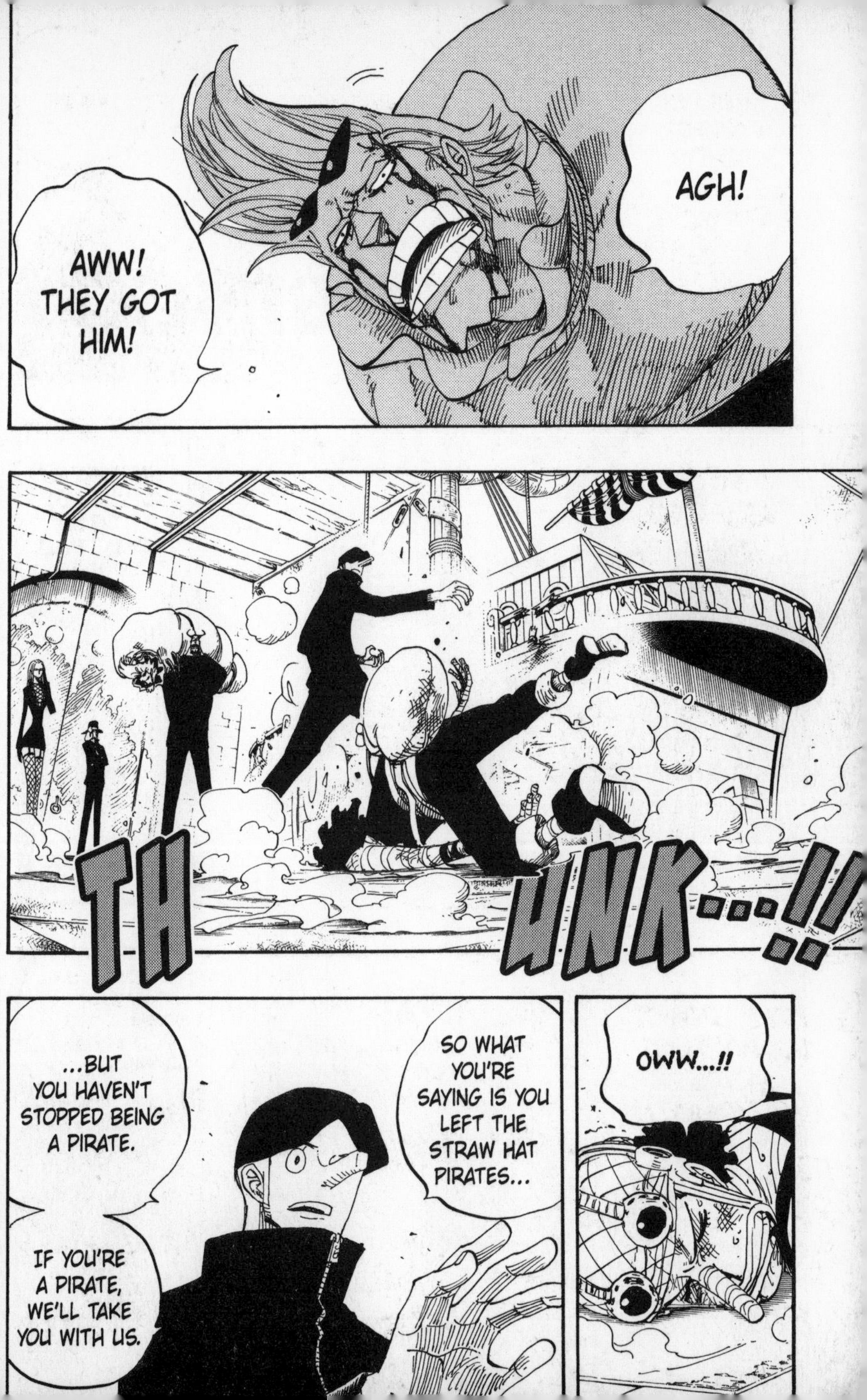
AGH!
AWW! THEY GOT HIM!
THUNK...!!
OWW...!!
SO WHAT YOU'RE SAYING IS YOU LEFT THE STRAW HAT PIRATES...
...BUT YOU HAVEN'T STOPPED BEING A PIRATE.
IF YOU'RE A PIRATE, WE'LL TAKE YOU WITH US.

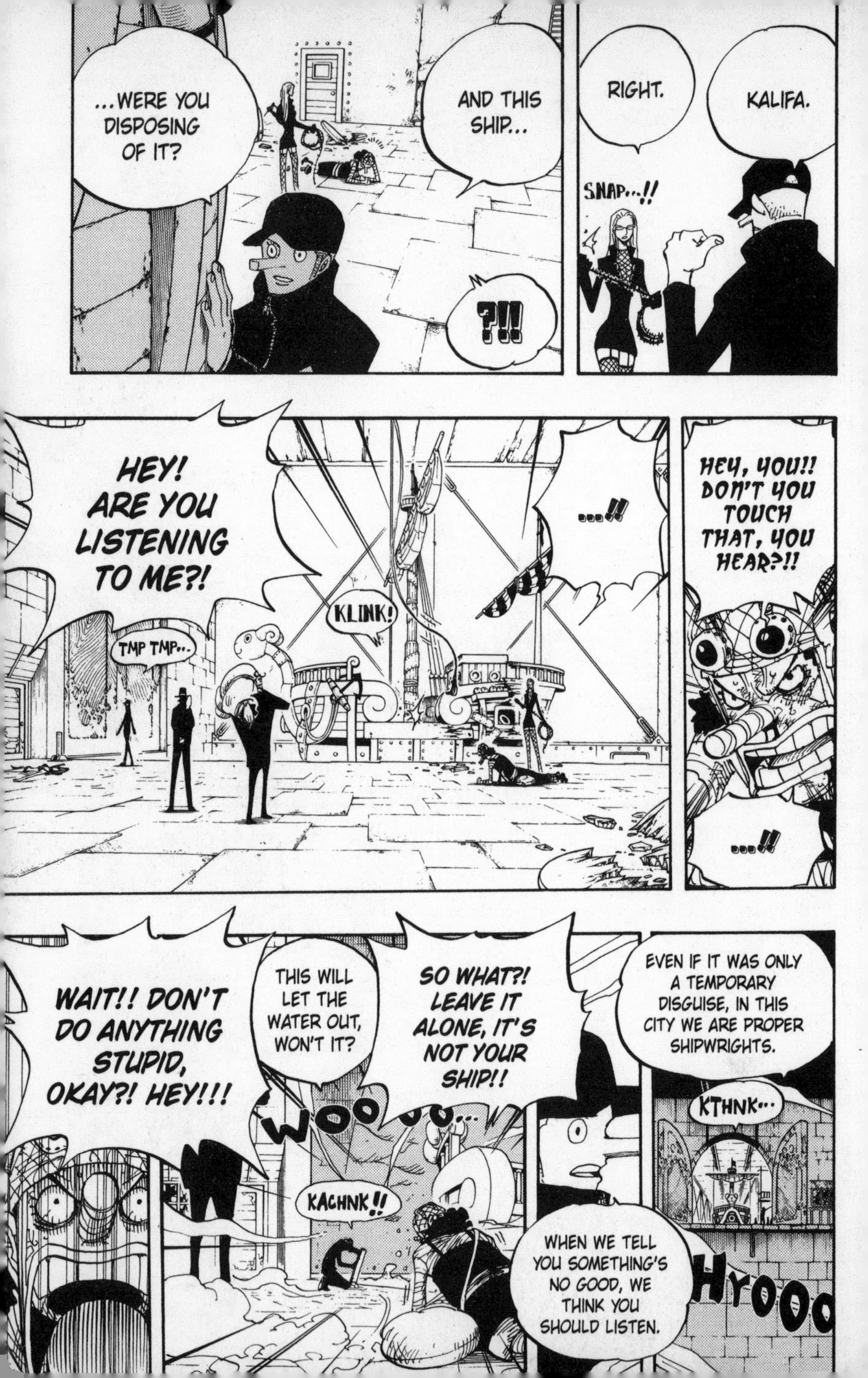
KALIFA.
RIGHT.
SNAP...!!
AND THIS SHIP...
...WERE YOU DISPOSING OF IT?
?!!
HEY, YOU!! DON'T YOU TOUCH THAT, YOU HEAR?!!
...!!
...!!
HEY! ARE YOU LISTENING TO ME?!
KLINK!
TMP TMP...
EVEN IF IT WAS ONLY A TEMPORARY DISGUISE, IN THIS CITY WE ARE PROPER SHIPWRIGHTS.
KTHNK...
WHEN WE TELL YOU SOMETHING'S NO GOOD, WE THINK YOU SHOULD LISTEN.
HYOOO
SO WHAT?! LEAVE IT ALONE, IT'S NOT YOUR SHIP!!
THIS WILL LET THE WATER OUT, WON'T IT?
WAIT!! DON'T DO ANYTHING STUPID, OKAY?! HEY!!!
WOOOO...
KACHNK!!

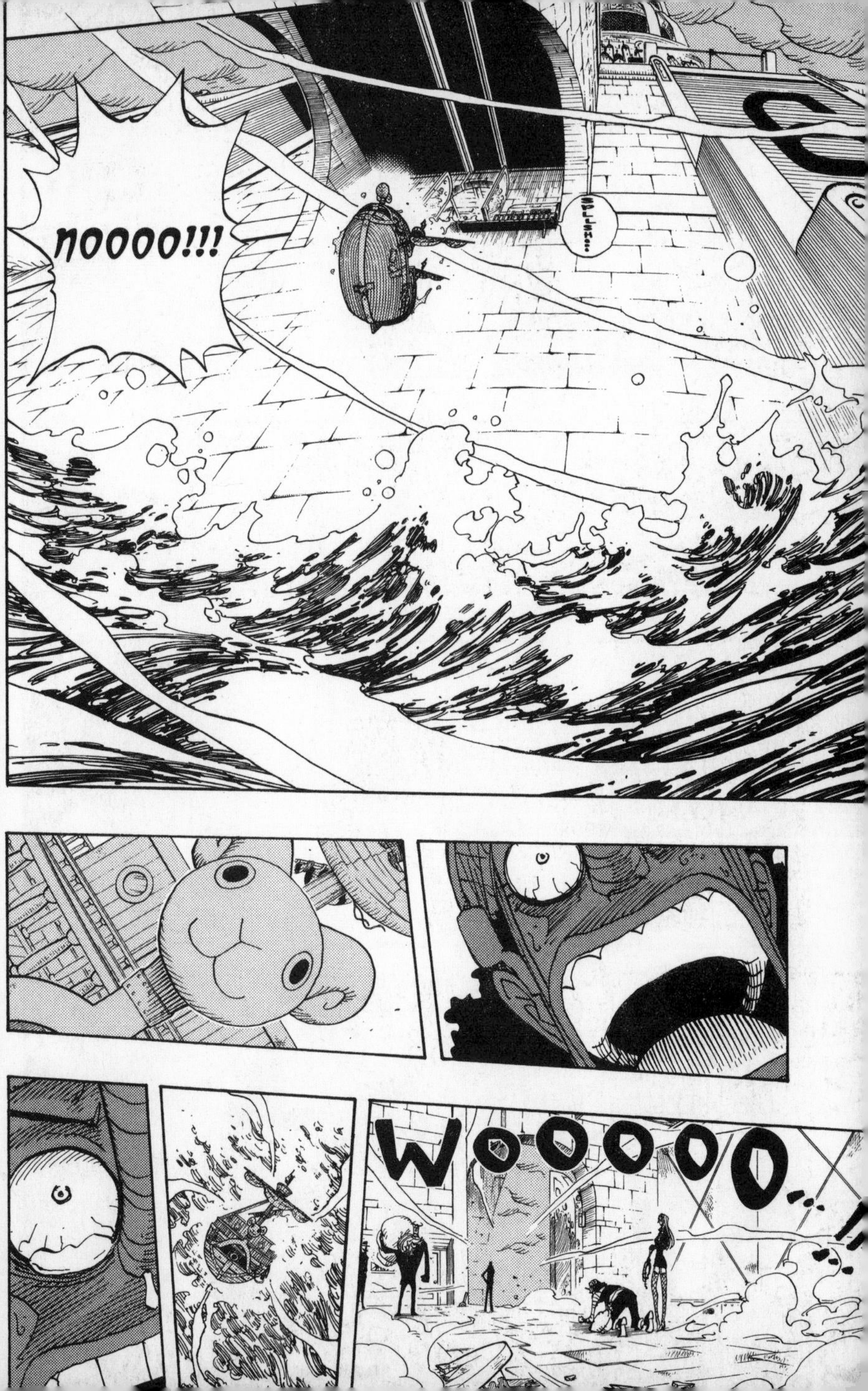
SPLISH...
NOOOO!!!
WOOOOO...!!

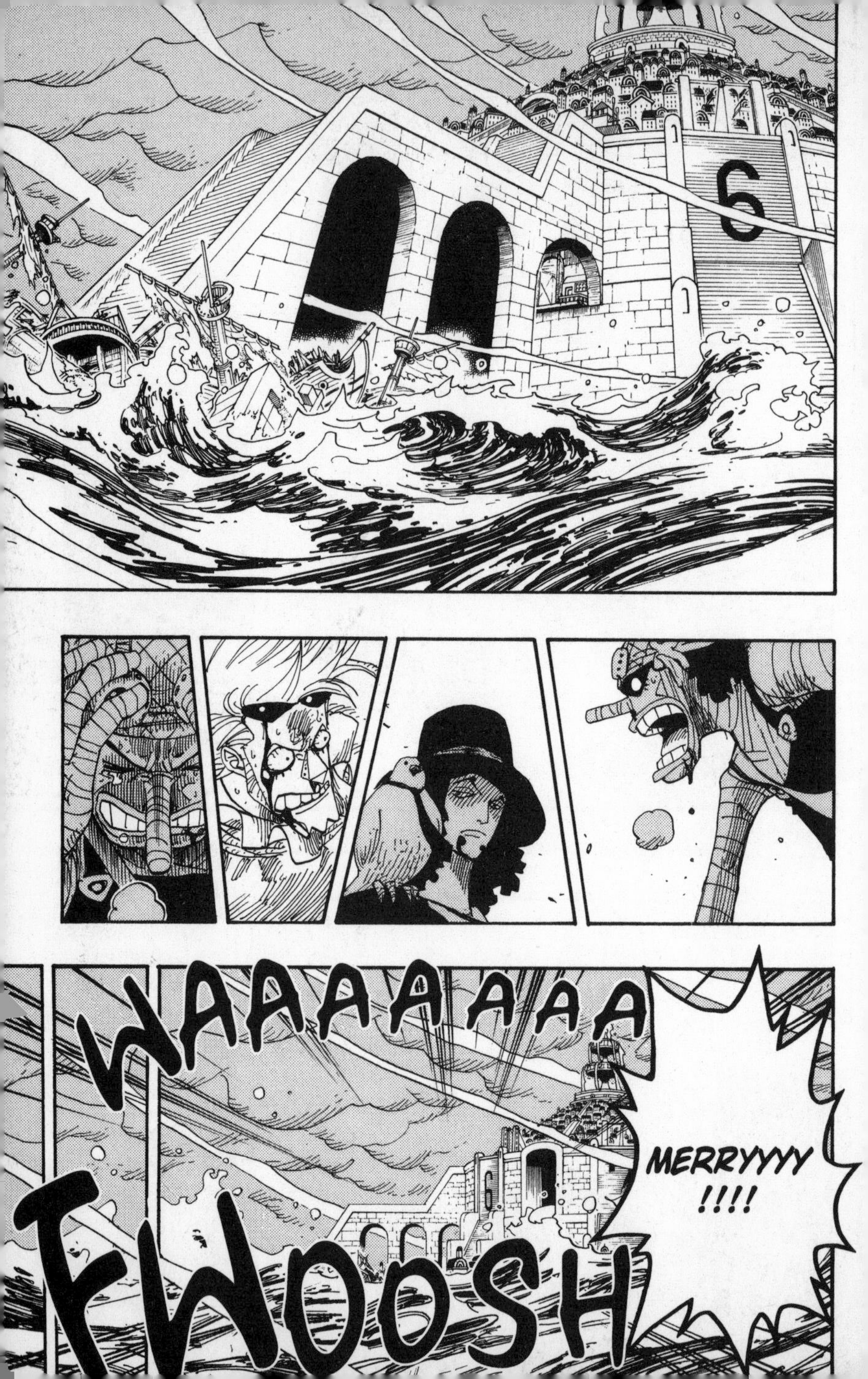
MERRYYYY
!!!!
WAAAAAAAA
FWOOSH

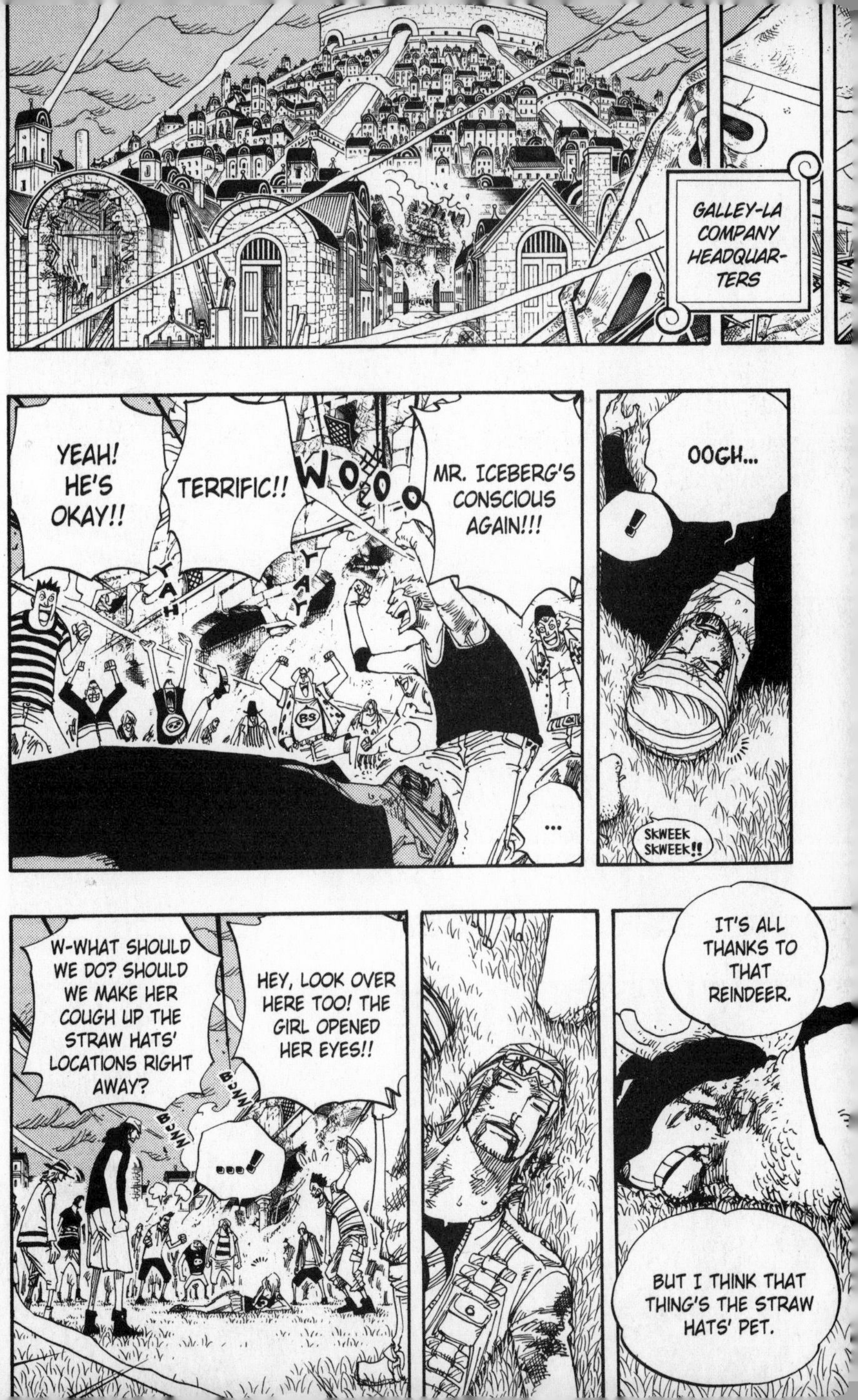
GALLEY-LA COMPANY HEADQUARTERS
OOGH...
!
SKWEEK SKWEEK!!
MR. ICEBERG'S CONSCIOUS AGAIN!!!
WOOO
TERRIFIC!!
YEAH! HE'S OKAY!!
YAY
YAH
...
IT'S ALL THANKS TO THAT REINDEER.
BUT I THINK THAT THING'S THE STRAW HATS' PET.
HEY, LOOK OVER HERE TOO! THE GIRL OPENED HER EYES!!
BUNN
W-WHAT SHOULD WE DO? SHOULD WE MAKE HER COUGH UP THE STRAW HATS' LOCATIONS RIGHT AWAY?
BUNN
...!

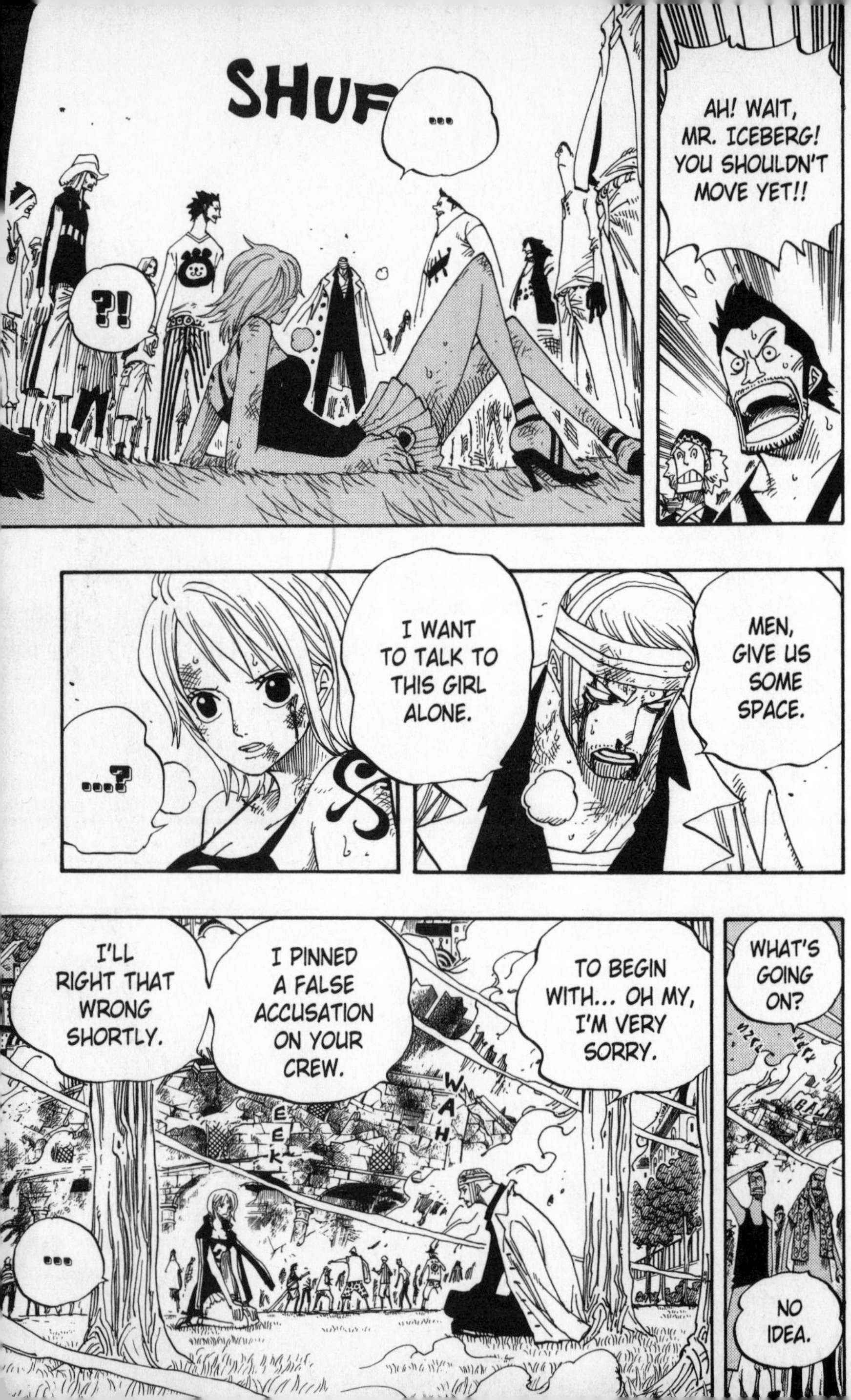
AH! WAIT, MR. ICEBERG! YOU SHOULDN'T MOVE YET!!
SHUF
...
?!
MEN, GIVE US SOME SPACE.
I WANT TO TALK TO THIS GIRL ALONE.
...?
WHAT'S GOING ON?
NO IDEA.
TO BEGIN WITH... OH MY, I'M VERY SORRY.
WAH
I PINNED A FALSE ACCUSATION ON YOUR CREW.
EEK
I'LL RIGHT THAT WRONG SHORTLY.
...

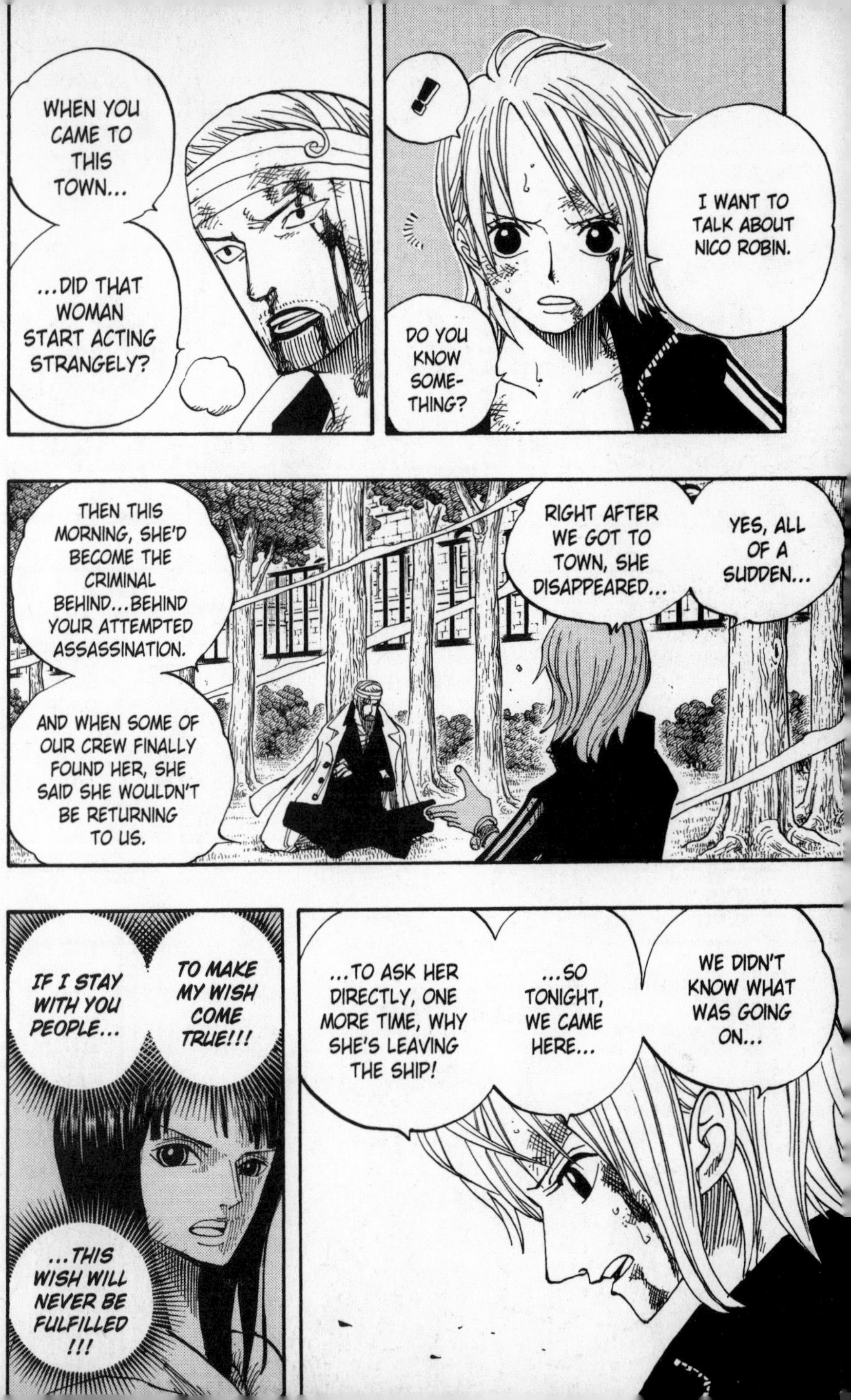
!
I WANT TO TALK ABOUT NICO ROBIN.
DO YOU KNOW SOMETHING?
WHEN YOU CAME TO THIS TOWN...
...DID THAT WOMAN START ACTING STRANGELY?
YES, ALL OF A SUDDEN...
RIGHT AFTER WE GOT TO TOWN, SHE DISAPPEARED...
THEN THIS MORNING, SHE'D BECOME THE CRIMINAL BEHIND...BEHIND YOUR ATTEMPTED ASSASSINATION.
AND WHEN SOME OF OUR CREW FINALLY FOUND HER, SHE SAID SHE WOULDN'T BE RETURNING TO US.
WE DIDN'T KNOW WHAT WAS GOING ON...
...SO TONIGHT, WE CAME HERE...
...TO ASK HER DIRECTLY, ONE MORE TIME, WHY SHE'S LEAVING THE SHIP!
TO MAKE MY WISH COME TRUE!!!
IF I STAY WITH YOU PEOPLE...
...THIS WISH WILL NEVER BE FULFILLED!!!

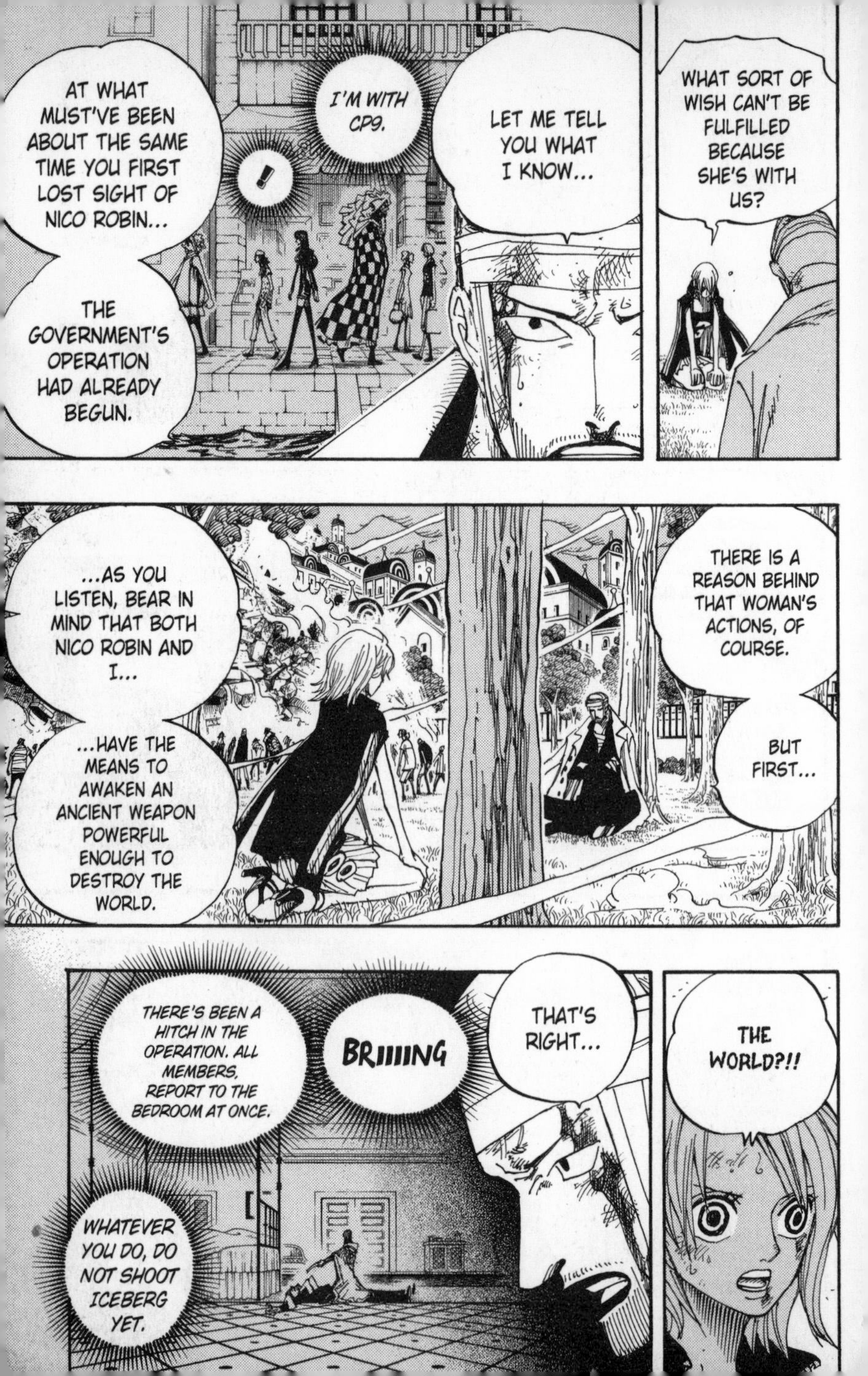
WHAT SORT OF WISH CAN'T BE FULFILLED BECAUSE SHE'S WITH US?
LET ME TELL YOU WHAT I KNOW...
I'M WITH CP9.
!
AT WHAT MUST'VE BEEN ABOUT THE SAME TIME YOU FIRST LOST SIGHT OF NICO ROBIN...
THE GOVERNMENT'S OPERATION HAD ALREADY BEGUN.
THERE IS A REASON BEHIND THAT WOMAN'S ACTIONS, OF COURSE.
BUT FIRST...
...AS YOU LISTEN, BEAR IN MIND THAT BOTH NICO ROBIN AND I...
...HAVE THE MEANS TO AWAKEN AN ANCIENT WEAPON POWERFUL ENOUGH TO DESTROY THE WORLD.
THE WORLD?!!
THAT'S RIGHT...
BRIIIING
THERE'S BEEN A HITCH IN THE OPERATION. ALL MEMBERS, REPORT TO THE BEDROOM AT ONCE.
WHATEVER YOU DO, DO NOT SHOOT ICEBERG YET.

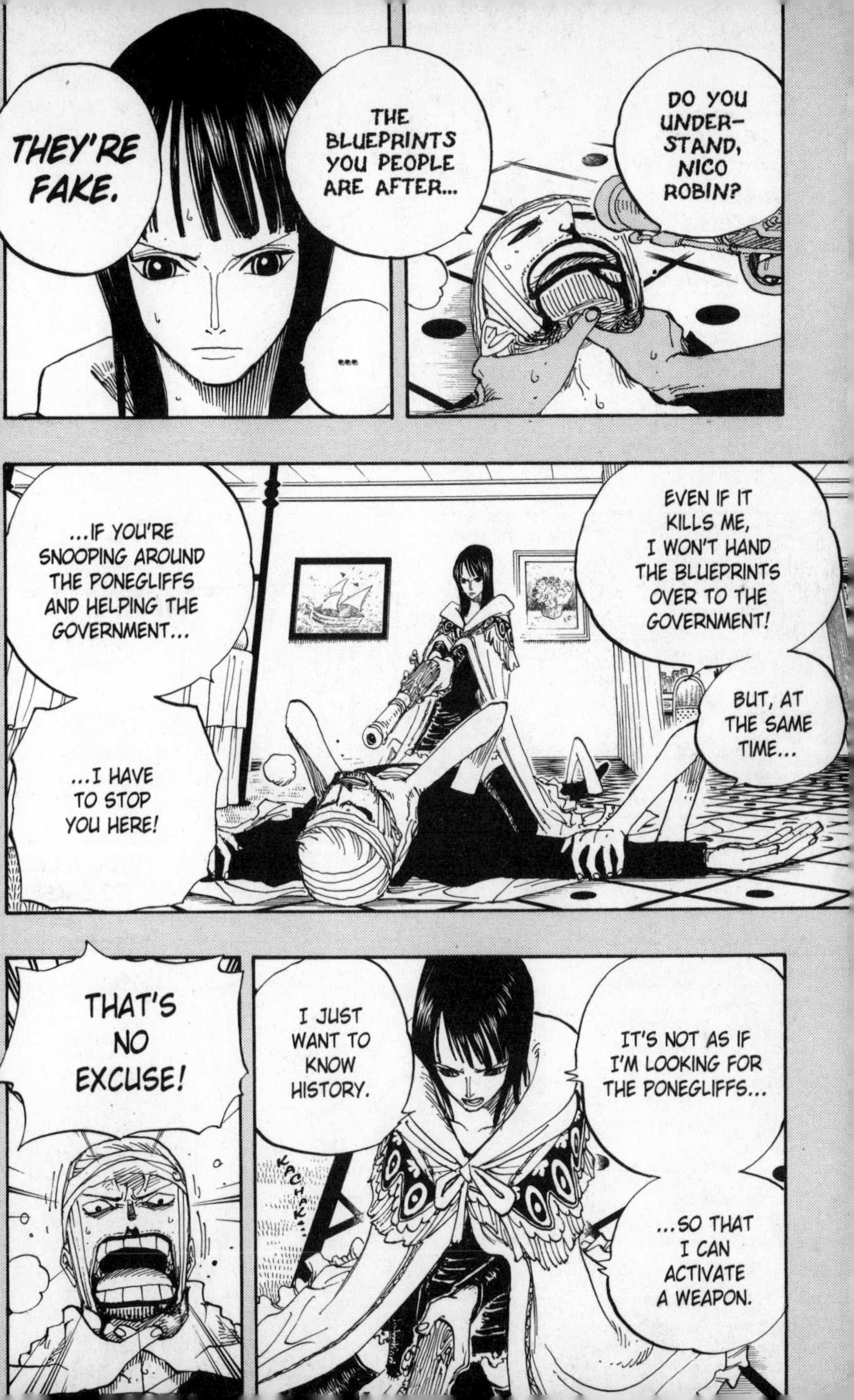
DO YOU UNDER-STAND, NICO ROBIN?
THE BLUEPRINTS YOU PEOPLE ARE AFTER...
THEY'RE FAKE.
...
EVEN IF IT KILLS ME, I WON'T HAND THE BLUEPRINTS OVER TO THE GOVERNMENT!
BUT, AT THE SAME TIME...
...IF YOU'RE SNOOPING AROUND THE PONEGLIFFS AND HELPING THE GOVERNMENT...
...I HAVE TO STOP YOU HERE!
IT'S NOT AS IF I'M LOOKING FOR THE PONEGLIFFS...
...SO THAT I CAN ACTIVATE A WEAPON.
I JUST WANT TO KNOW HISTORY.
KACHAK
THAT'S NO EXCUSE!

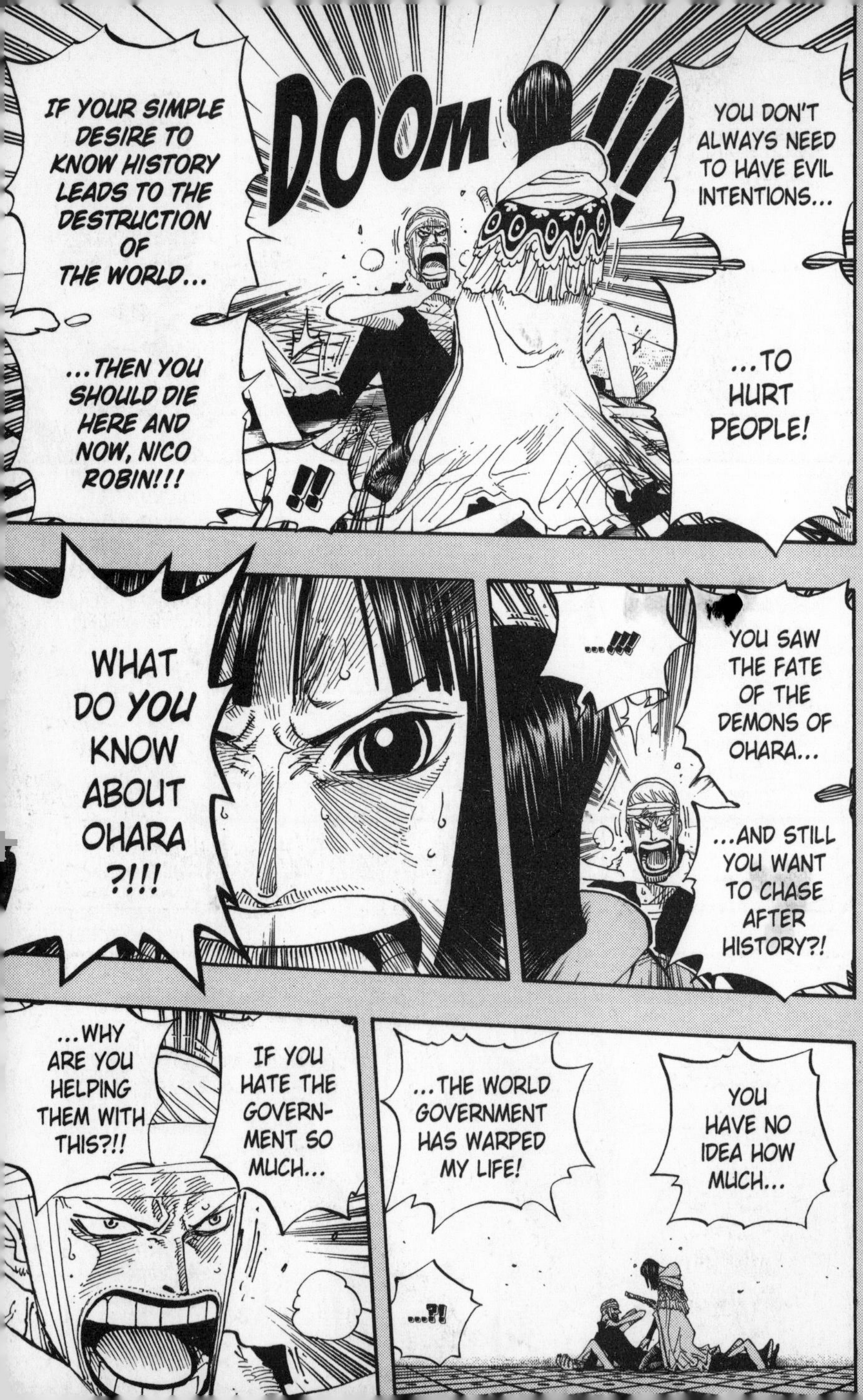
YOU DON'T ALWAYS NEED TO HAVE EVIL INTENTIONS...
...TO HURT PEOPLE!
DOOM!!
IF YOUR SIMPLE DESIRE TO KNOW HISTORY LEADS TO THE DESTRUCTION OF THE WORLD...
...THEN YOU SHOULD DIE HERE AND NOW, NICO ROBIN!!!
!!
...!!!
YOU SAW THE FATE OF THE DEMONS OF OHARA...
...AND STILL YOU WANT TO CHASE AFTER HISTORY?!
WHAT DO YOU KNOW ABOUT OHARA?!!!
YOU HAVE NO IDEA HOW MUCH...
...THE WORLD GOVERNMENT HAS WARPED MY LIFE!
...?!
IF YOU HATE THE GOVERNMENT SO MUCH...
...WHY ARE YOU HELPING THEM WITH THIS?!!

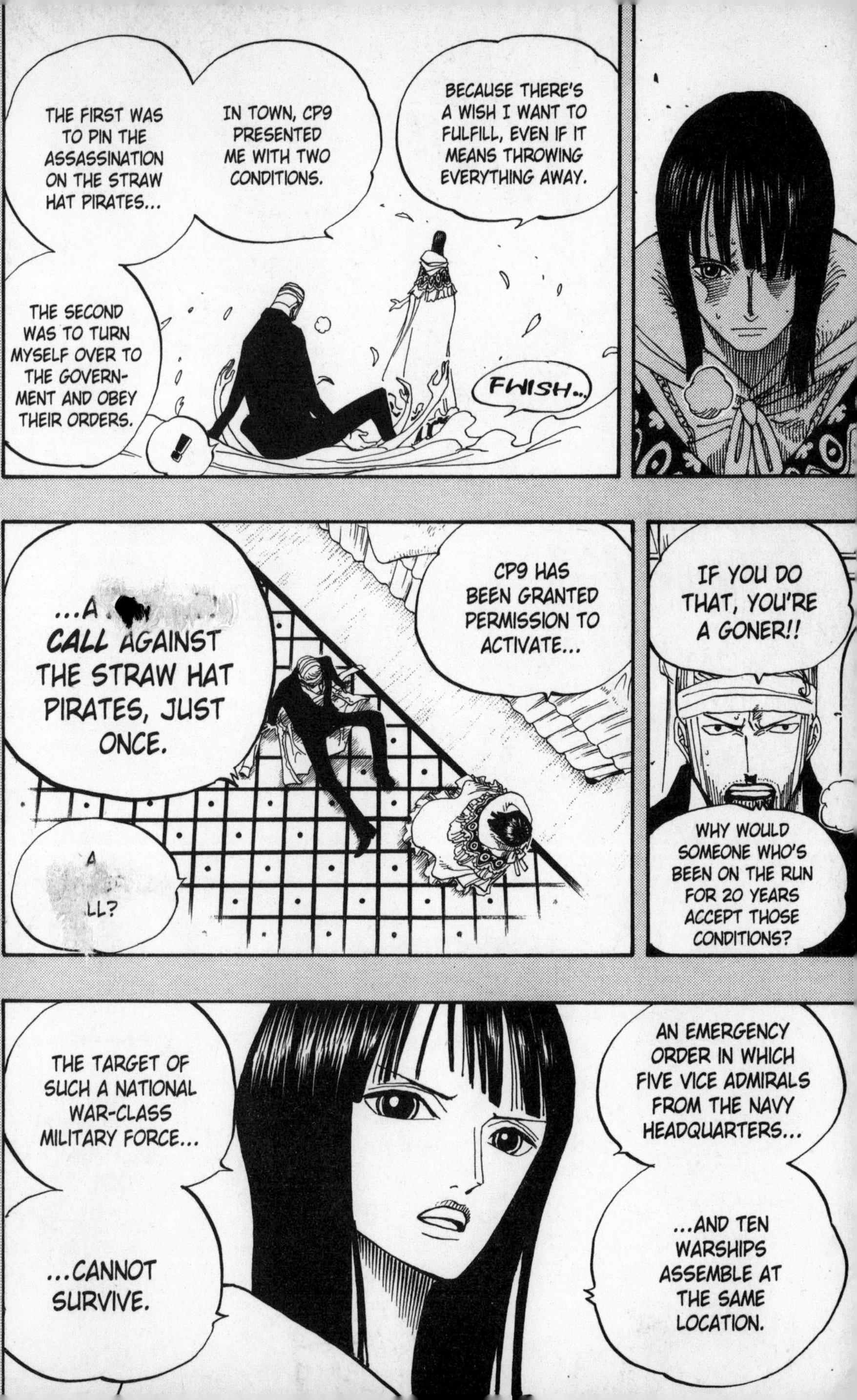
BECAUSE THERE'S A WISH I WANT TO FULFILL, EVEN IF IT MEANS THROWING EVERYTHING AWAY.
IN TOWN, CP9 PRESENTED ME WITH TWO CONDITIONS.
THE FIRST WAS TO PIN THE ASSASSINATION ON THE STRAW HAT PIRATES...
FWISH...
THE SECOND WAS TO TURN MYSELF OVER TO THE GOVERN-MENT AND OBEY THEIR ORDERS.
!
IF YOU DO THAT, YOU'RE A GONER!!
WHY WOULD SOMEONE WHO'S BEEN ON THE RUN FOR 20 YEARS ACCEPT THOSE CONDITIONS?
CP9 HAS BEEN GRANTED PERMISSION TO ACTIVATE...
...A CALL AGAINST THE STRAW HAT PIRATES, JUST ONCE.
A LL?
AN EMERGENCY ORDER IN WHICH FIVE VICE ADMIRALS FROM THE NAVY HEADQUARTERS...
...AND TEN WARSHIPS ASSEMBLE AT THE SAME LOCATION.
THE TARGET OF SUCH A NATIONAL WAR-CLASS MILITARY FORCE...
...CANNOT SURVIVE.

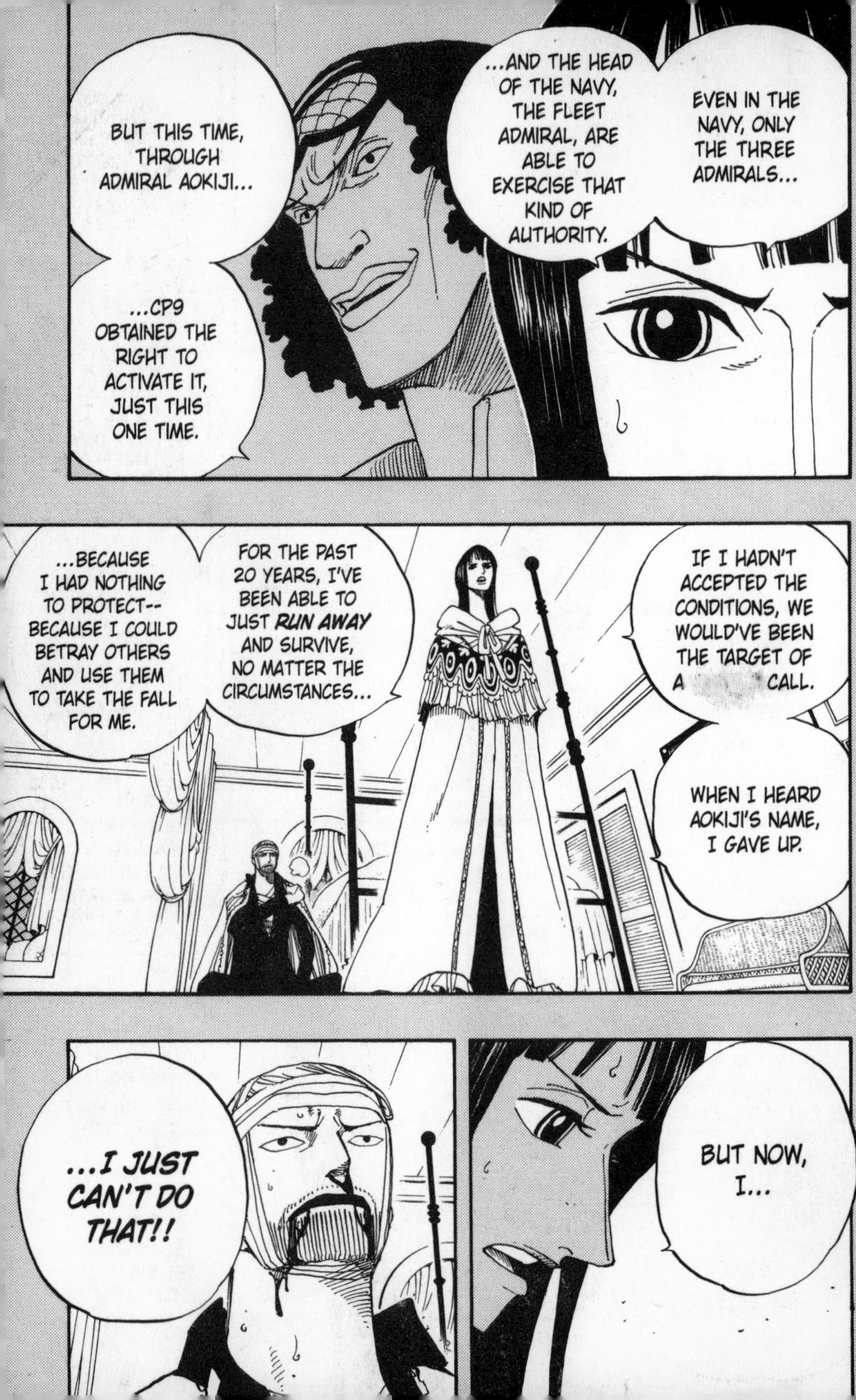
EVEN IN THE NAVY, ONLY THE THREE ADMIRALS...
...AND THE HEAD OF THE NAVY, THE FLEET ADMIRAL, ARE ABLE TO EXERCISE THAT KIND OF AUTHORITY.
BUT THIS TIME, THROUGH ADMIRAL AOKIJI...
...CP9 OBTAINED THE RIGHT TO ACTIVATE IT, JUST THIS ONE TIME.
IF I HADN'T ACCEPTED THE CONDITIONS, WE WOULD'VE BEEN THE TARGET OF A CALL.
WHEN I HEARD AOKIJI'S NAME, I GAVE UP.
FOR THE PAST 20 YEARS, I'VE BEEN ABLE TO JUST RUN AWAY AND SURVIVE, NO MATTER THE CIRCUMSTANCES...
...BECAUSE I HAD NOTHING TO PROTECT-- BECAUSE I COULD BETRAY OTHERS AND USE THEM TO TAKE THE FALL FOR ME.
BUT NOW, I...
...I JUST CAN'T DO THAT!!

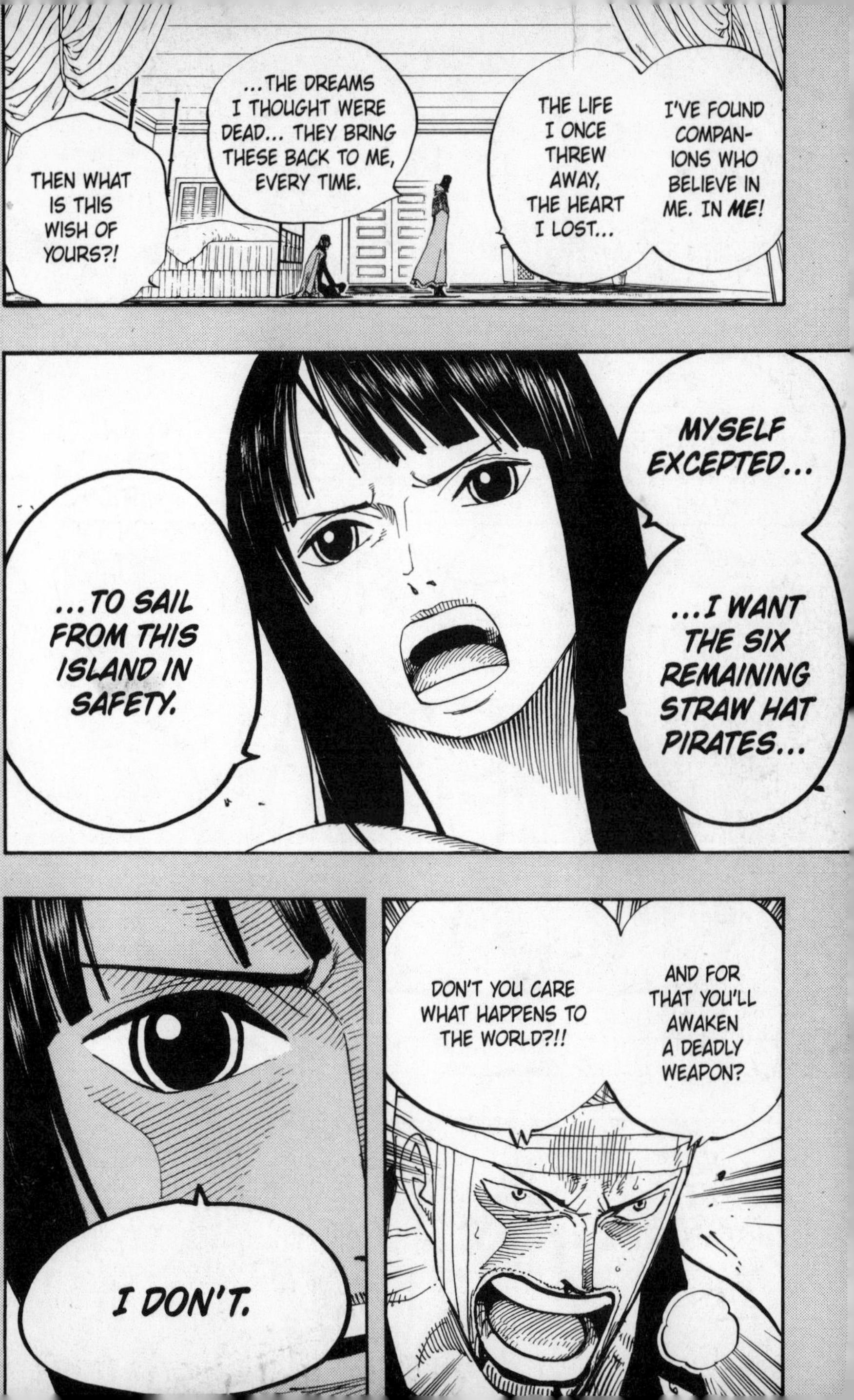
I'VE FOUND COMPANIONS WHO BELIEVE IN ME. IN *ME*!
THE LIFE I ONCE THREW AWAY, THE HEART I LOST...
...THE DREAMS I THOUGHT WERE DEAD... THEY BRING THESE BACK TO ME, EVERY TIME.
THEN WHAT IS THIS WISH OF YOURS?!
MYSELF EXCEPTED...
...I WANT THE SIX REMAINING STRAW HAT PIRATES...
...TO SAIL FROM THIS ISLAND IN SAFETY.
AND FOR THAT YOU'LL AWAKEN A DEADLY WEAPON?
DON'T YOU CARE WHAT HAPPENS TO THE WORLD?!!
I DON'T.

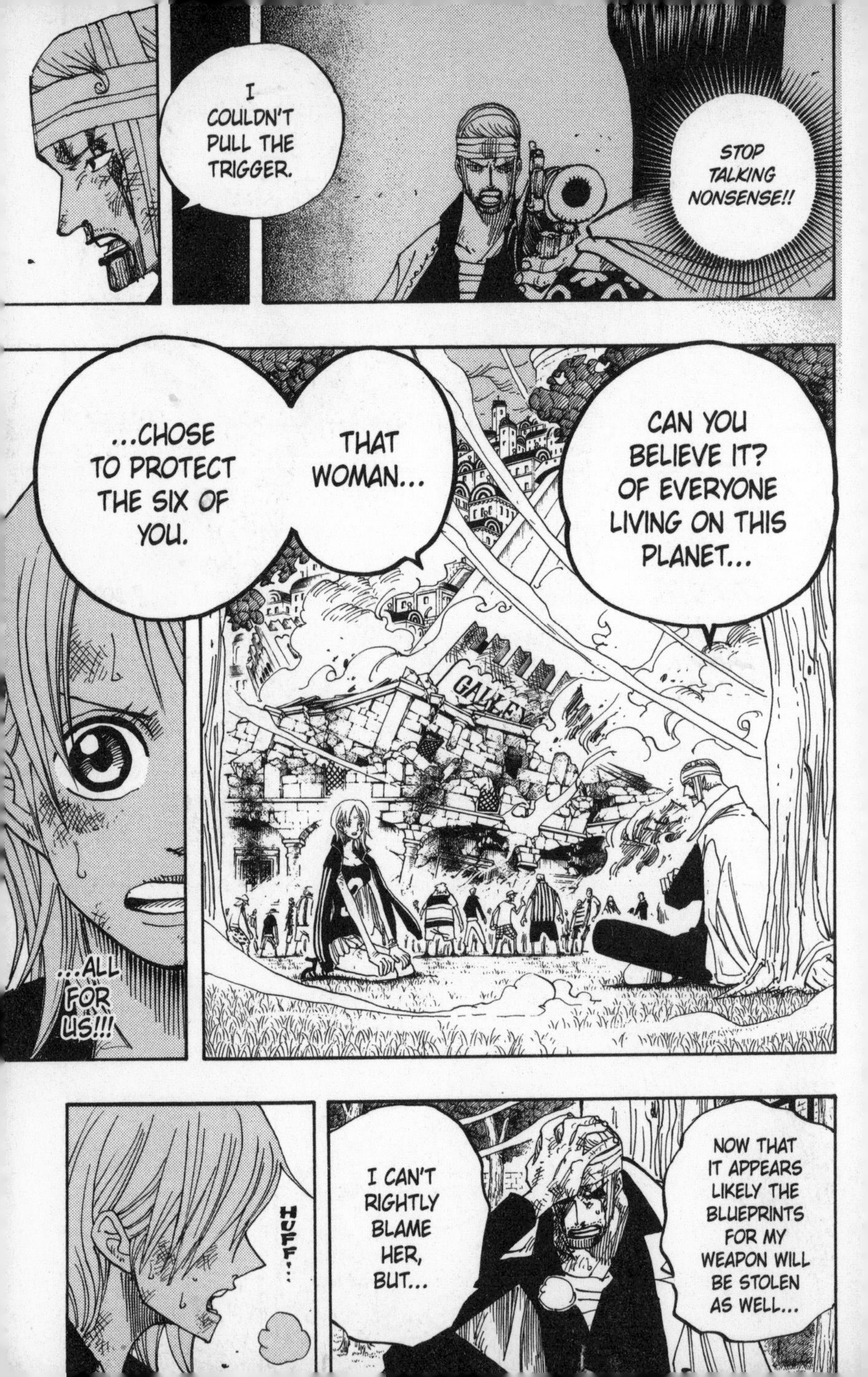
STOP TALKING NONSENSE!!
I COULDN'T PULL THE TRIGGER.
CAN YOU BELIEVE IT? OF EVERYONE LIVING ON THIS PLANET...
THAT WOMAN...
...CHOSE TO PROTECT THE SIX OF YOU.
...ALL FOR US!!!
NOW THAT IT APPEARS LIKELY THE BLUEPRINTS FOR MY WEAPON WILL BE STOLEN AS WELL...
I CAN'T RIGHTLY BLAME HER, BUT...
HUFF!...

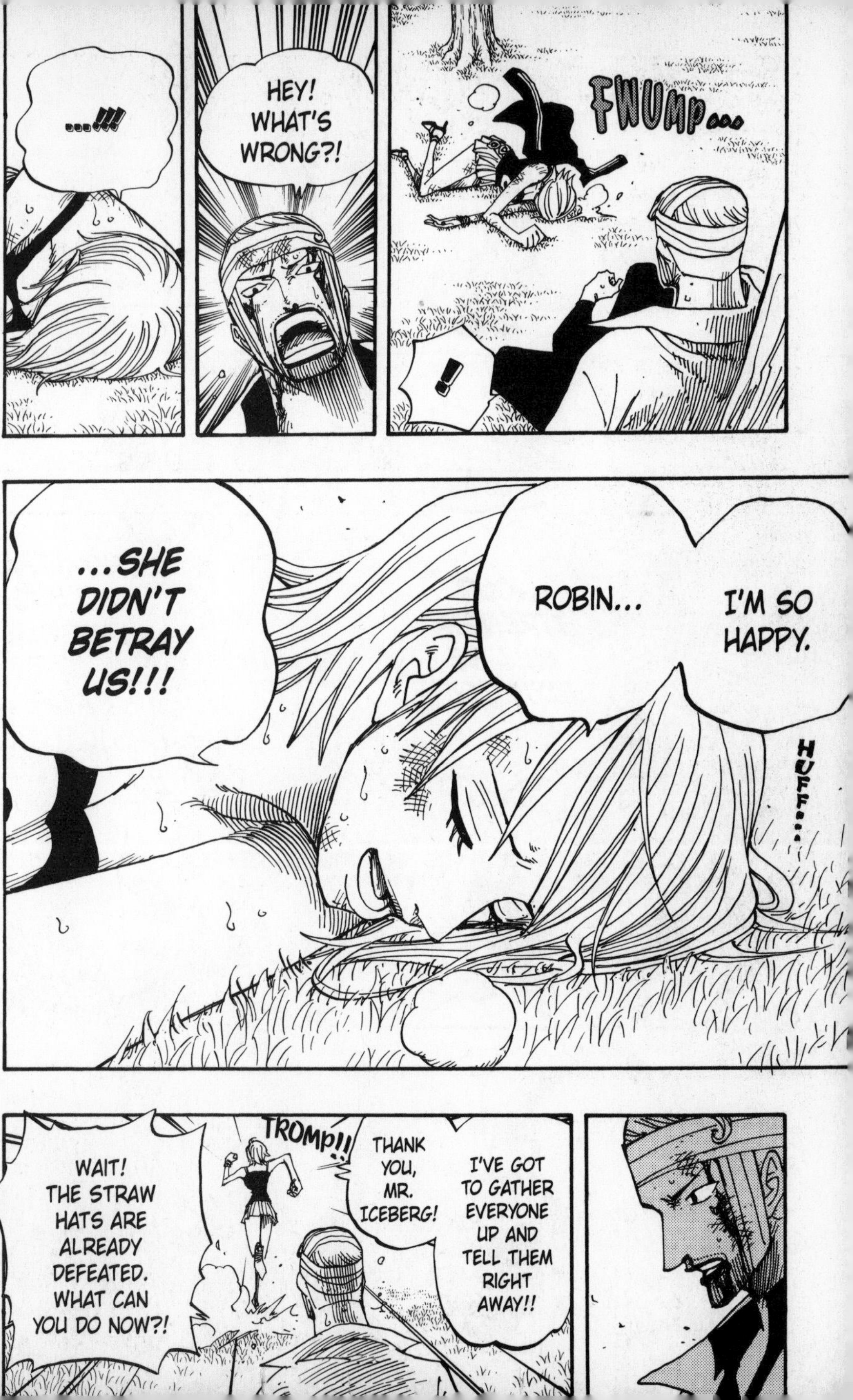
FWUMP...
!
HEY! WHAT'S WRONG?!
...!!!
ROBIN... I'M SO HAPPY.
HUFF...
...SHE DIDN'T BETRAY US!!!
THANK YOU, MR. ICEBERG! I'VE GOT TO GATHER EVERYONE UP AND TELL THEM RIGHT AWAY!!
TROMP!!
WAIT! THE STRAW HATS ARE ALREADY DEFEATED. WHAT CAN YOU DO NOW?!

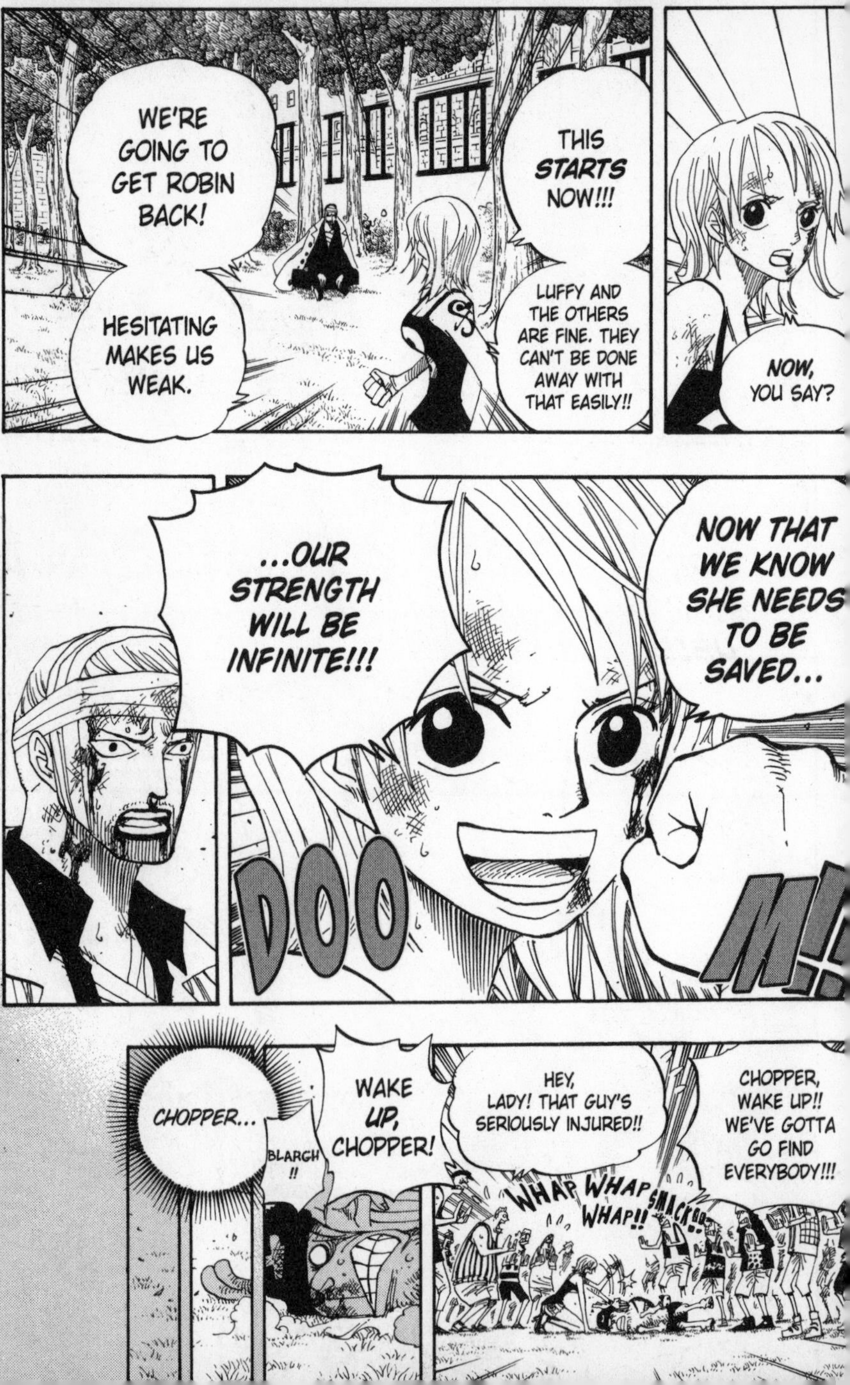
NOW, YOU SAY?
THIS STARTS NOW!!!
LUFFY AND THE OTHERS ARE FINE. THEY CAN'T BE DONE AWAY WITH THAT EASILY!!
WE'RE GOING TO GET ROBIN BACK!
HESITATING MAKES US WEAK.
NOW THAT WE KNOW SHE NEEDS TO BE SAVED...
...OUR STRENGTH WILL BE INFINITE!!!
DOO
M!!
CHOPPER, WAKE UP!! WE'VE GOTTA GO FIND EVERYBODY!!!
HEY, LADY! THAT GUY'S SERIOUSLY INJURED!!
WHAP WHAP WHAP!!
SMACK!!
WAKE UP, CHOPPER!
BLARCH!!
CHOPPER...

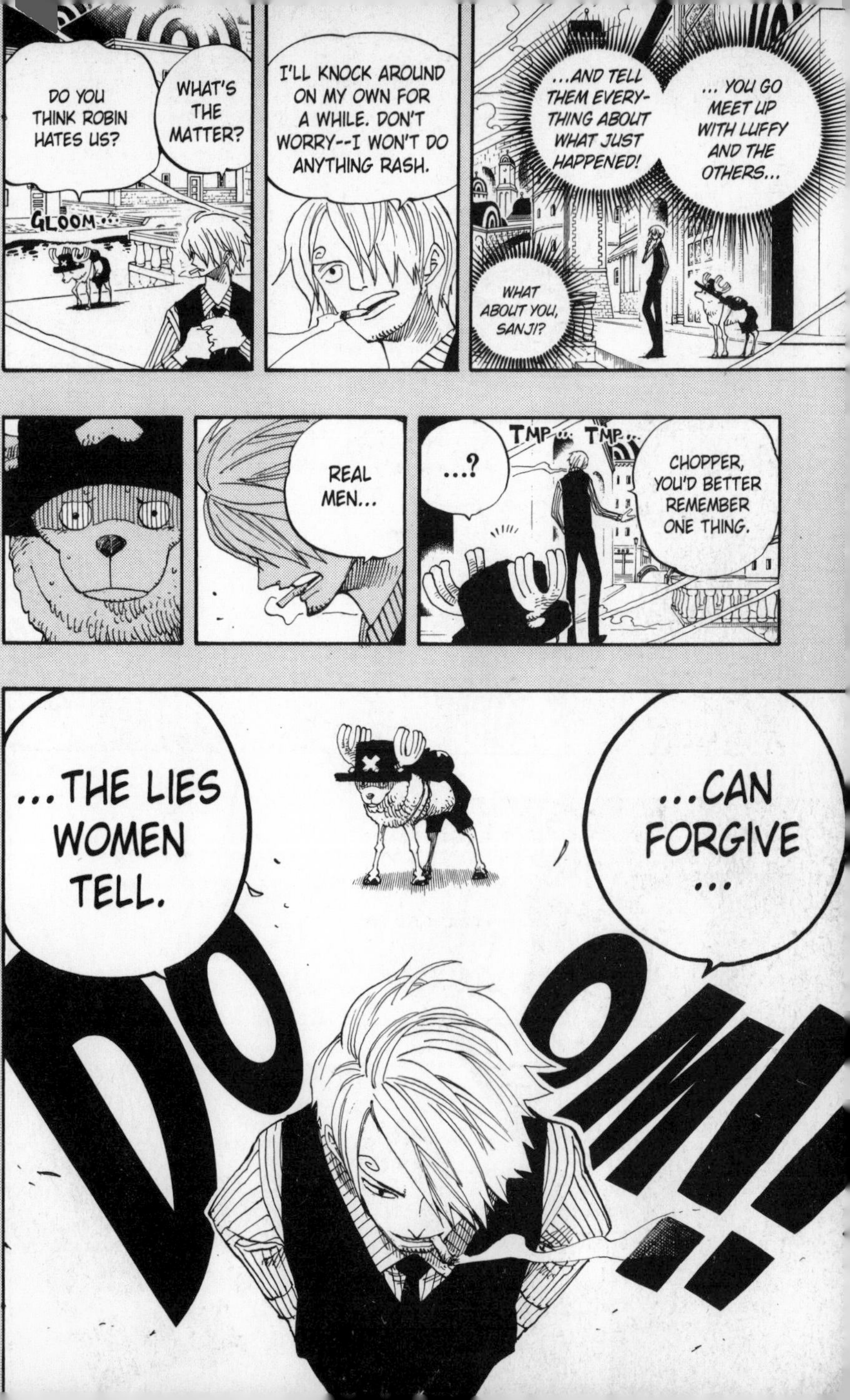
... YOU GO MEET UP WITH LUFFY AND THE OTHERS...
...AND TELL THEM EVERY-THING ABOUT WHAT JUST HAPPENED!
WHAT ABOUT YOU, SANJI?
I'LL KNOCK AROUND ON MY OWN FOR A WHILE. DON'T WORRY--I WON'T DO ANYTHING RASH.
WHAT'S THE MATTER?
DO YOU THINK ROBIN HATES US?
GLOOM...
TMP... TMP...
CHOPPER, YOU'D BETTER REMEMBER ONE THING.
...?
REAL MEN...
...CAN FORGIVE...
...THE LIES WOMEN TELL.
DOOM!!

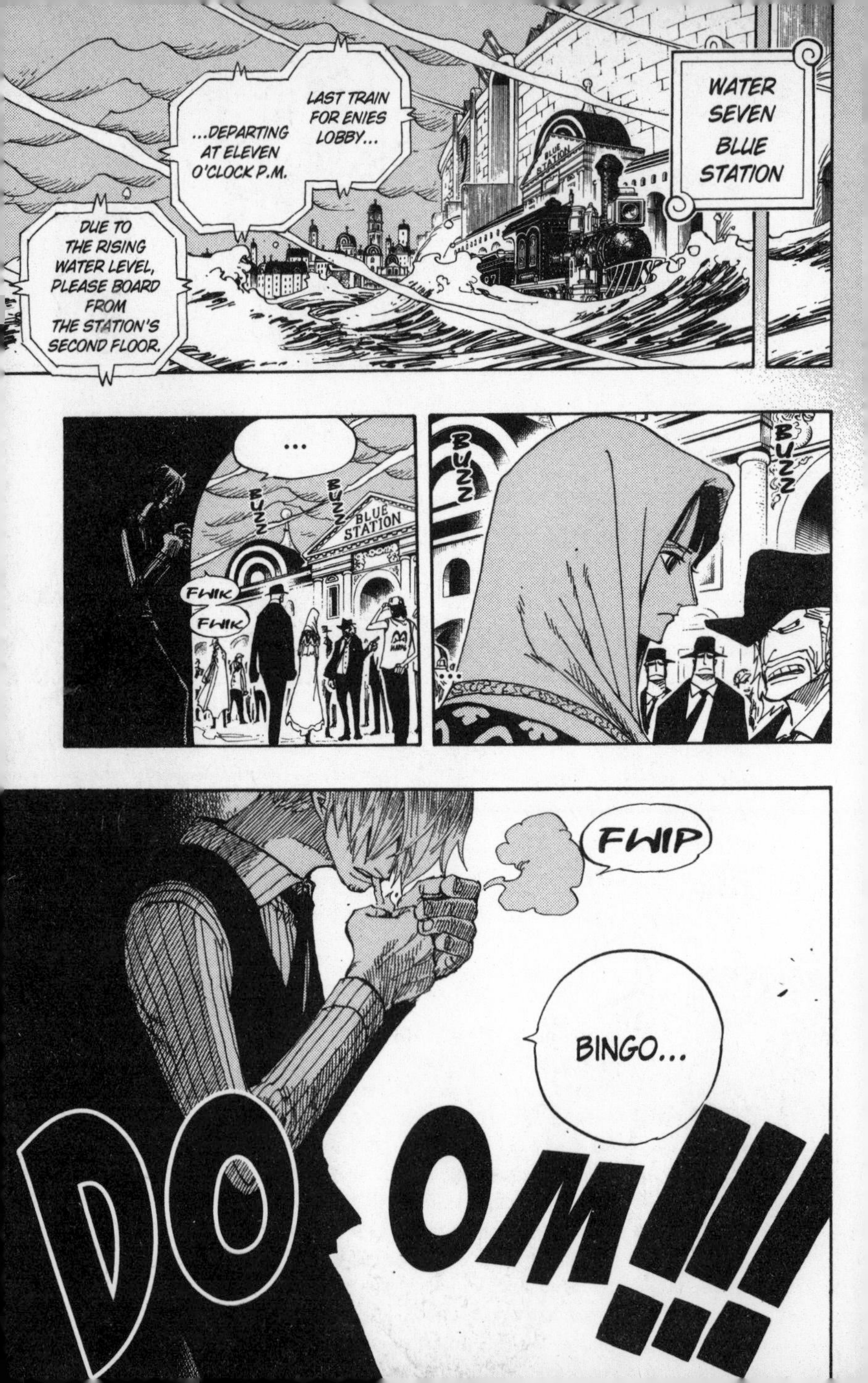
WATER SEVEN BLUE STATION
BLUE STATION
LAST TRAIN FOR ENIES LOBBY...
...DEPARTING AT ELEVEN O'CLOCK P.M.
DUE TO THE RISING WATER LEVEL, PLEASE BOARD FROM THE STATION'S SECOND FLOOR.
BUZZ
BUZZ
...
BUZZ
BUZZ
BLUE STATION
FWIK
FWIK
FWIP
BINGO...
DOOM!!!

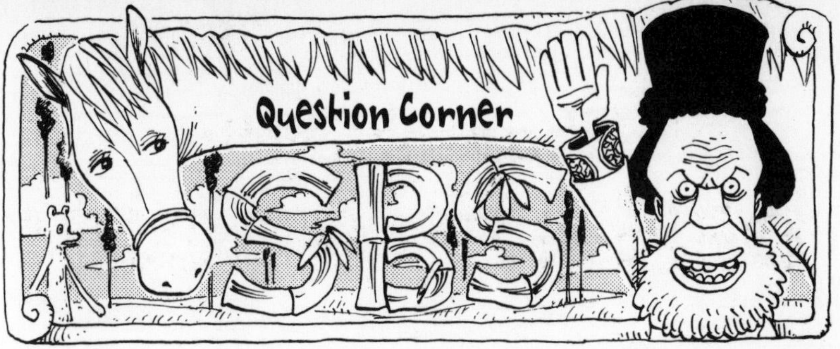
Question Corner
SBS

Reader: Oda Sensei! I've got a friend who tells me, "I saw Oda Sensei!" (via email) Apparently, you were standing by the magazine rack in a convenience store, perusing a dirty magazine. Well, don't worry about it. I always figured you were that kinda guy. ♡ Heh heh heh... That's probably how you research Nami's physique, right?!

--Rude Kid Uier

Oda: How rude!! As if I'd just stand around in the store reading magazines like that!! How uncouth! I'd **buy** 'em!!

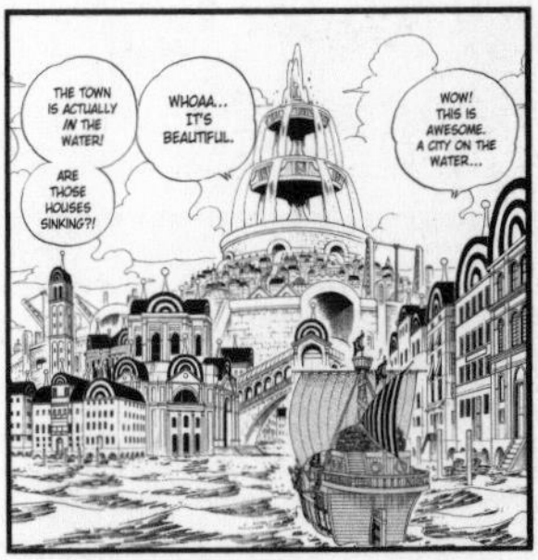
WOW! THIS IS AWESOME. A CITY ON THE WATER...
WHOAA... IT'S BEAUTIFUL.
THE TOWN IS ACTUALLY *IN* THE WATER!
ARE THOSE HOUSES SINKING?!

Reader: Hello, Oda Sensei! A question, right off the bat: A while ago on TV, there was a program about "Venezia, the city of water, where there is a high tide called Aqua Alta, when the townspeople all have to wear boots"! Did you maybe model Water Seven's Aqua Laguna on this?

--I Love *One Piece*

Oda: There was a show on that topic, apparently, and for a little while I got a ton of questions about this from readers... "Maybe you were watching TV and got carried away by that Aqua Alta show?" You're right. Venezia is an Italian city known as the City of Water, so I used it as a model for the setting in this series. Still... Well, as you all know, it makes things more realistic to include the city's trials as well as its beauty, so, although it's done in a very manga style, I've included that in the action as well. But what happens in the manga couldn't actually happen in real life, so you can rest assured while you travel. I want to go to Venice (← English name), too.

Chapter 360:
DEPARTING SOON

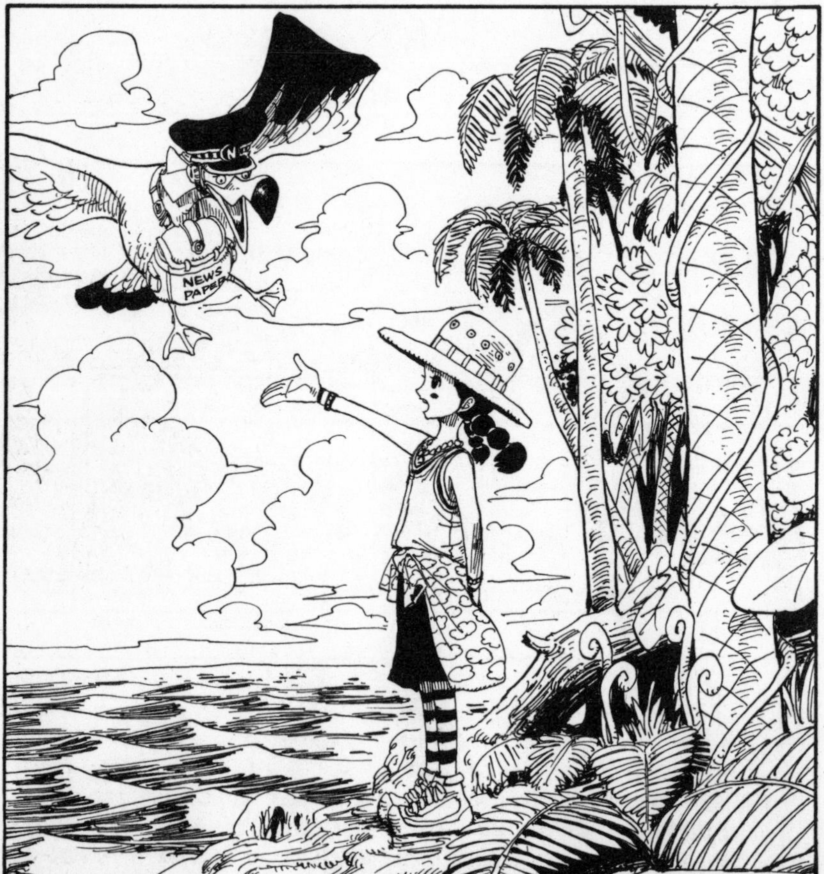
NEWS PAPER

MS. GOLDEN WEEK'S BIG PLAN, A BAROQUE REUNION,
VOL. 2: "NEWSPAPER, PLEASE"

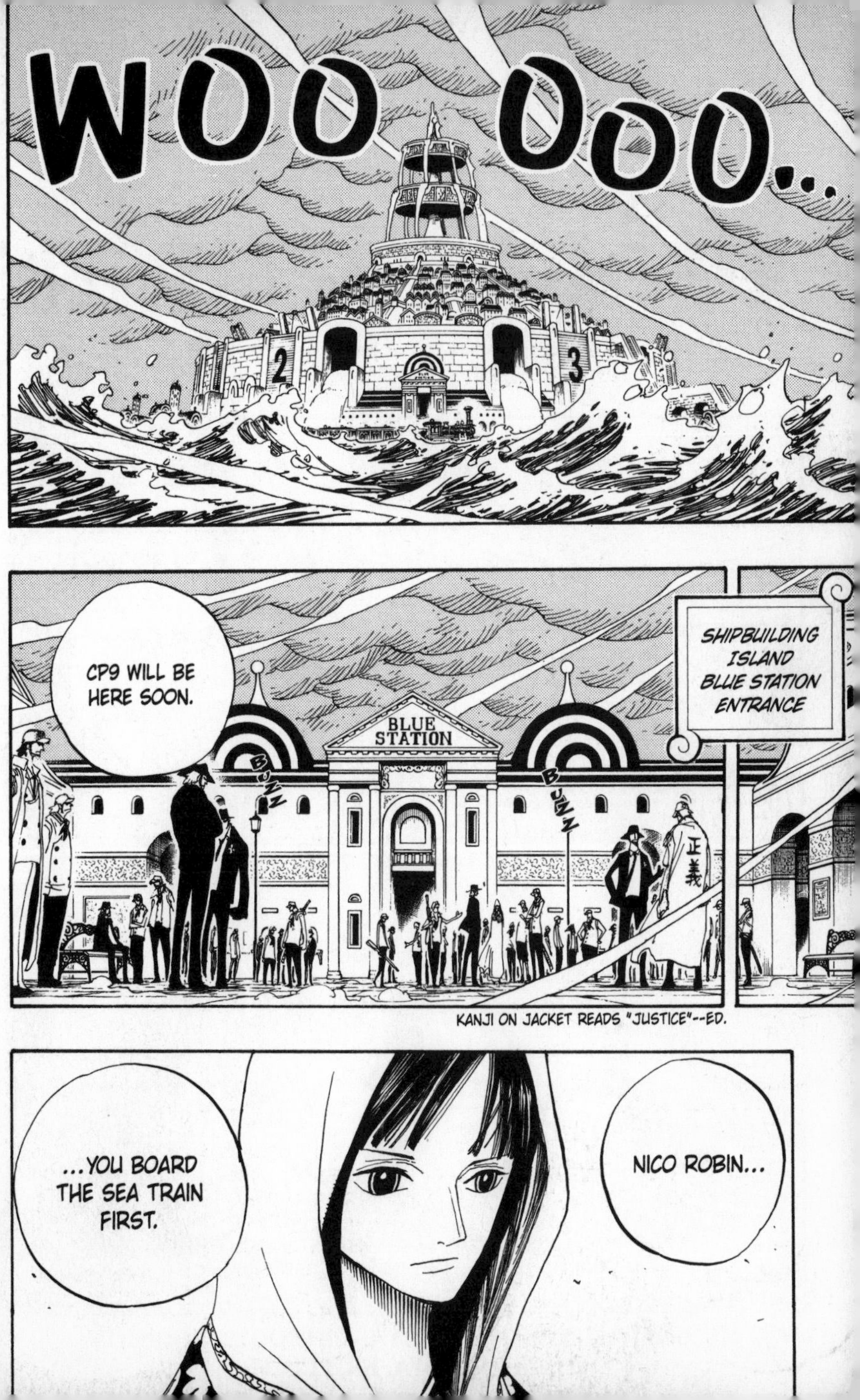
WOOO OOOO...
SHIPBUILDING ISLAND BLUE STATION ENTRANCE
BLUE STATION
BUZZ
BUZZ
CP9 WILL BE HERE SOON.
KANJI ON JACKET READS "JUSTICE"--ED.
NICO ROBIN...
...YOU BOARD THE SEA TRAIN FIRST.

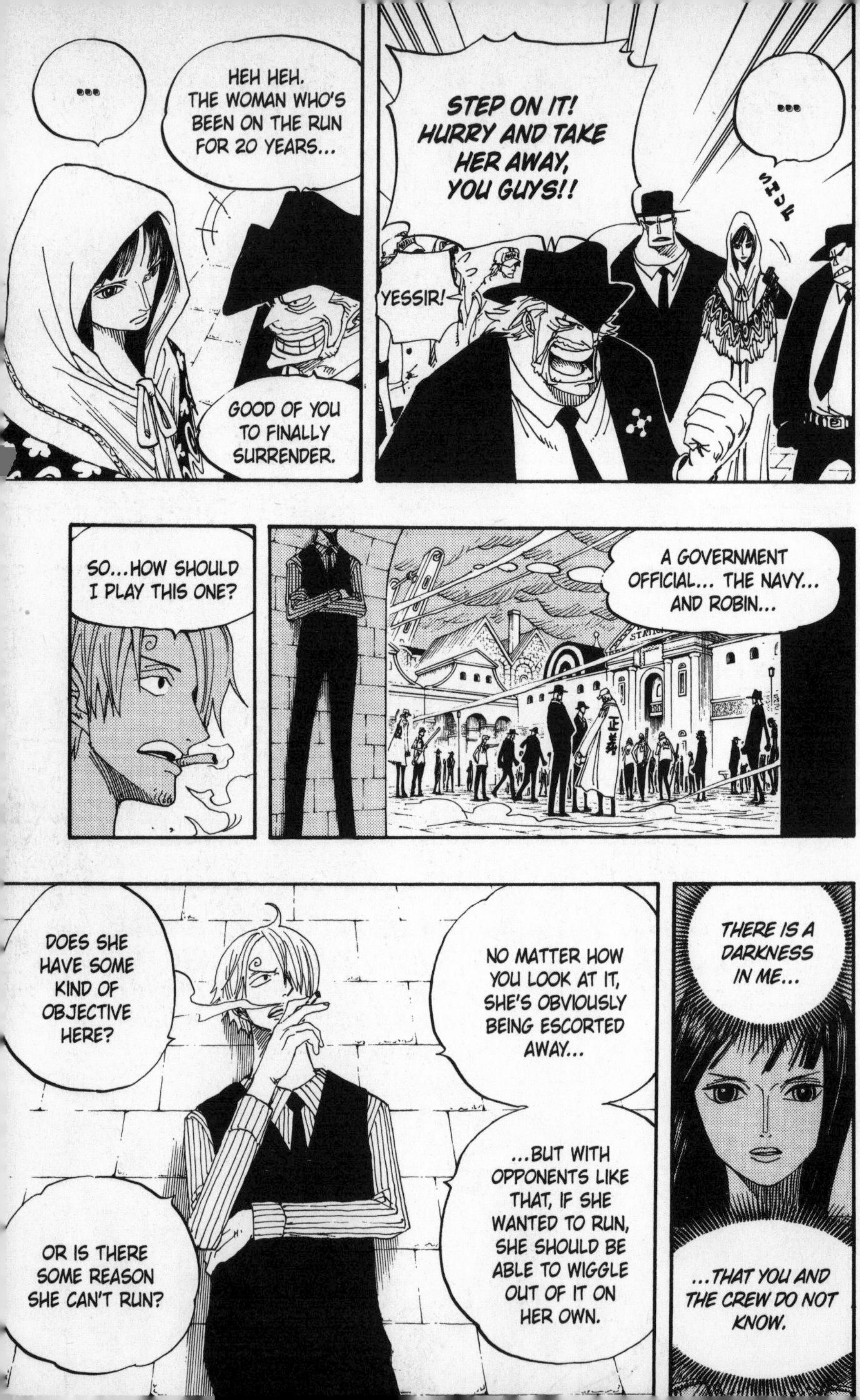
STEP ON IT! HURRY AND TAKE HER AWAY, YOU GUYS!!
...
YESSIR!
HEH HEH. THE WOMAN WHO'S BEEN ON THE RUN FOR 20 YEARS...
...
GOOD OF YOU TO FINALLY SURRENDER.
A GOVERNMENT OFFICIAL... THE NAVY... AND ROBIN...
SO...HOW SHOULD I PLAY THIS ONE?
THERE IS A DARKNESS IN ME...
...THAT YOU AND THE CREW DO NOT KNOW.
NO MATTER HOW YOU LOOK AT IT, SHE'S OBVIOUSLY BEING ESCORTED AWAY...
...BUT WITH OPPONENTS LIKE THAT, IF SHE WANTED TO RUN, SHE SHOULD BE ABLE TO WIGGLE OUT OF IT ON HER OWN.
DOES SHE HAVE SOME KIND OF OBJECTIVE HERE?
OR IS THERE SOME REASON SHE CAN'T RUN?

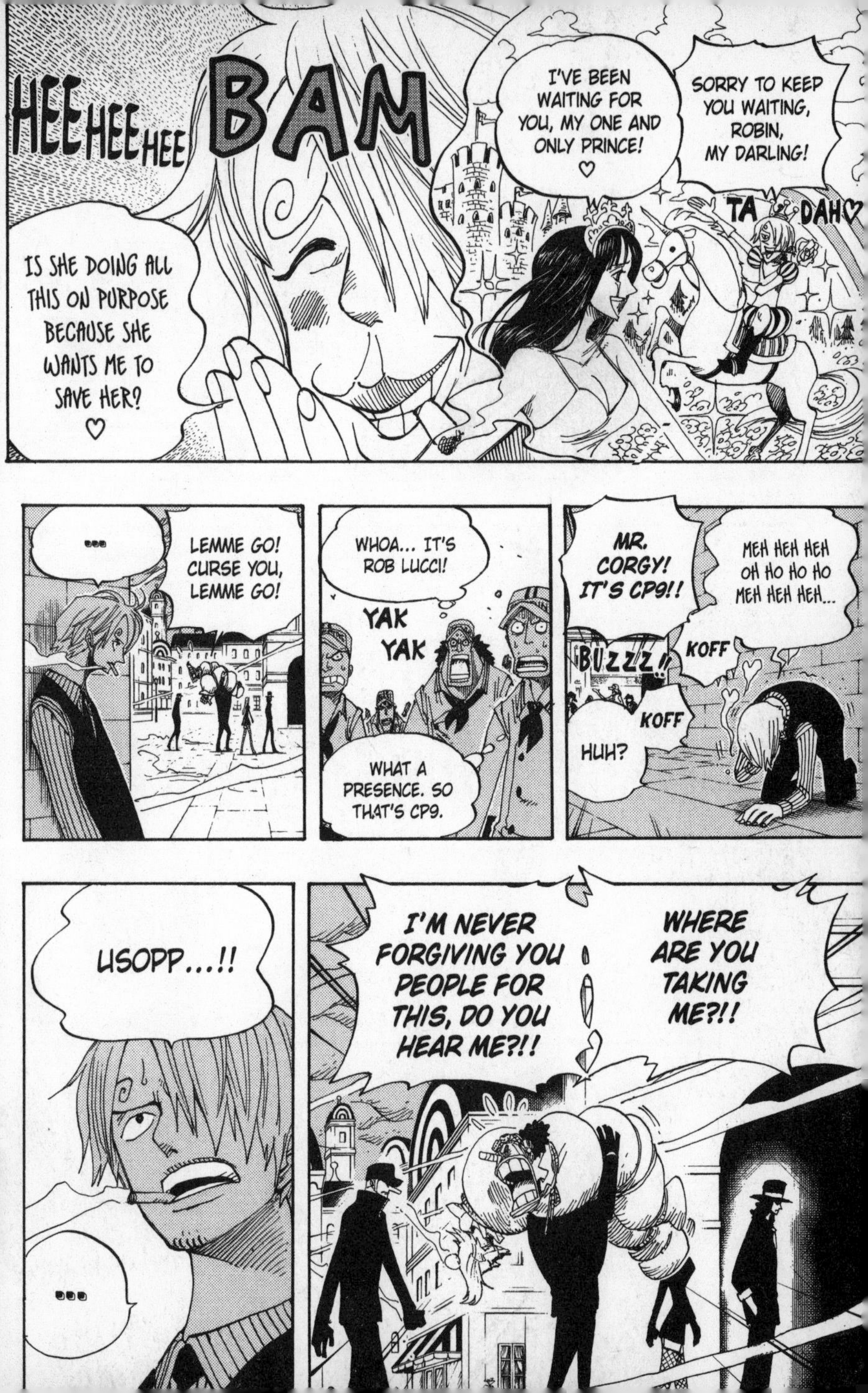
SORRY TO KEEP YOU WAITING, ROBIN, MY DARLING!
I'VE BEEN WAITING FOR YOU, MY ONE AND ONLY PRINCE! ♡
TA DAH♡
BAM
HEE HEE HEE
IS SHE DOING ALL THIS ON PURPOSE BECAUSE SHE WANTS ME TO SAVE HER? ♡
MEH HEH HEH OH HO HO HO MEH HEH HEH...
MR. CORGY! IT'S CP9!!
KOFF
BUZZZ!!
KOFF
HUH?
WHOA... IT'S ROB LUCCI!
YAK YAK
WHAT A PRESENCE. SO THAT'S CP9.
LEMME GO! CURSE YOU, LEMME GO!
...
WHERE ARE YOU TAKING ME?!!
I'M NEVER FORGIVING YOU PEOPLE FOR THIS, DO YOU HEAR ME?!!
USOPP...!!
...

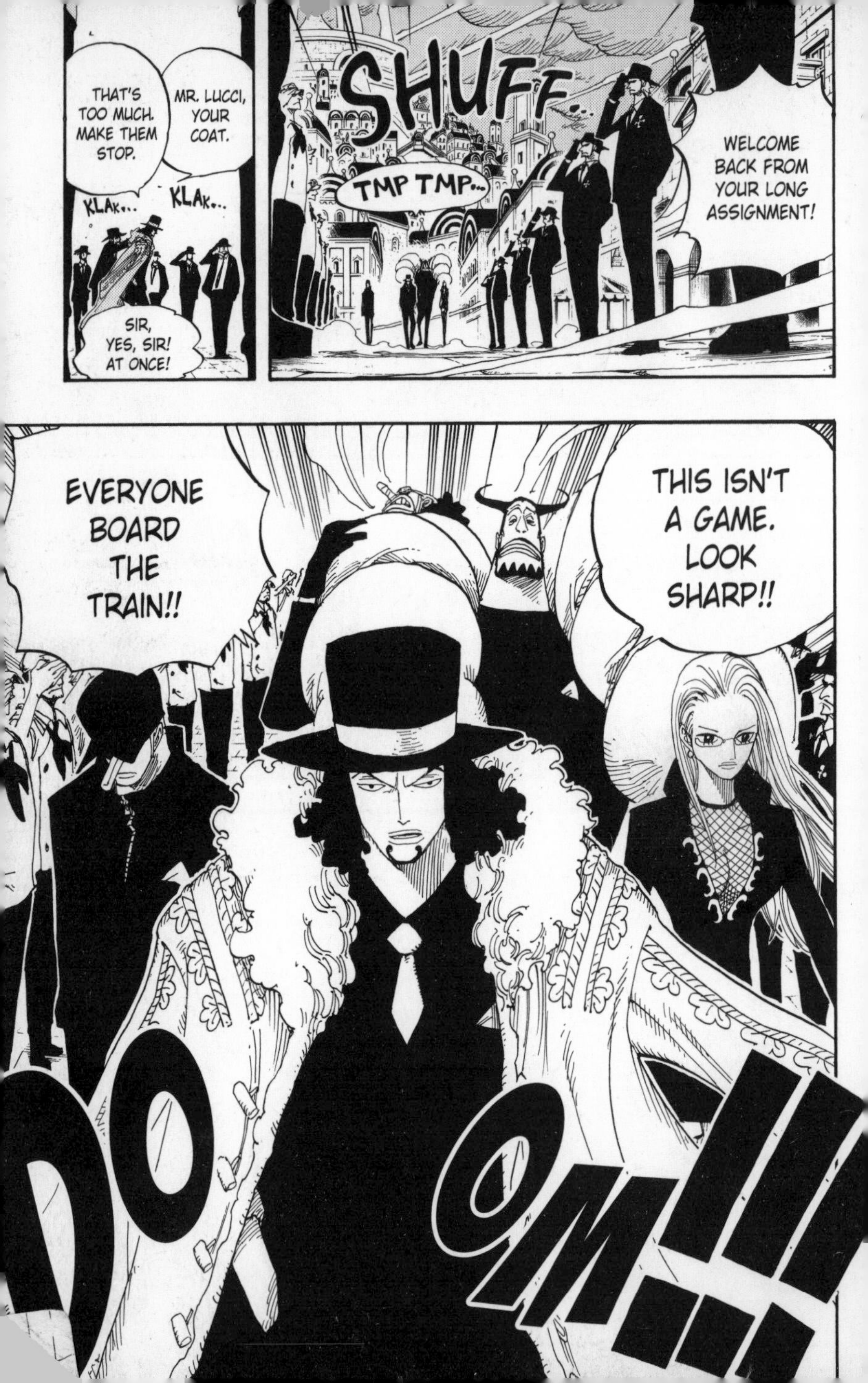
WELCOME BACK FROM YOUR LONG ASSIGNMENT!
SHUFF
TMP TMP...
MR. LUCCI, YOUR COAT.
THAT'S TOO MUCH. MAKE THEM STOP.
KLAK... KLAK...
SIR, YES, SIR! AT ONCE!
THIS ISN'T A GAME. LOOK SHARP!!
EVERYONE BOARD THE TRAIN!!
DOOM!!!...

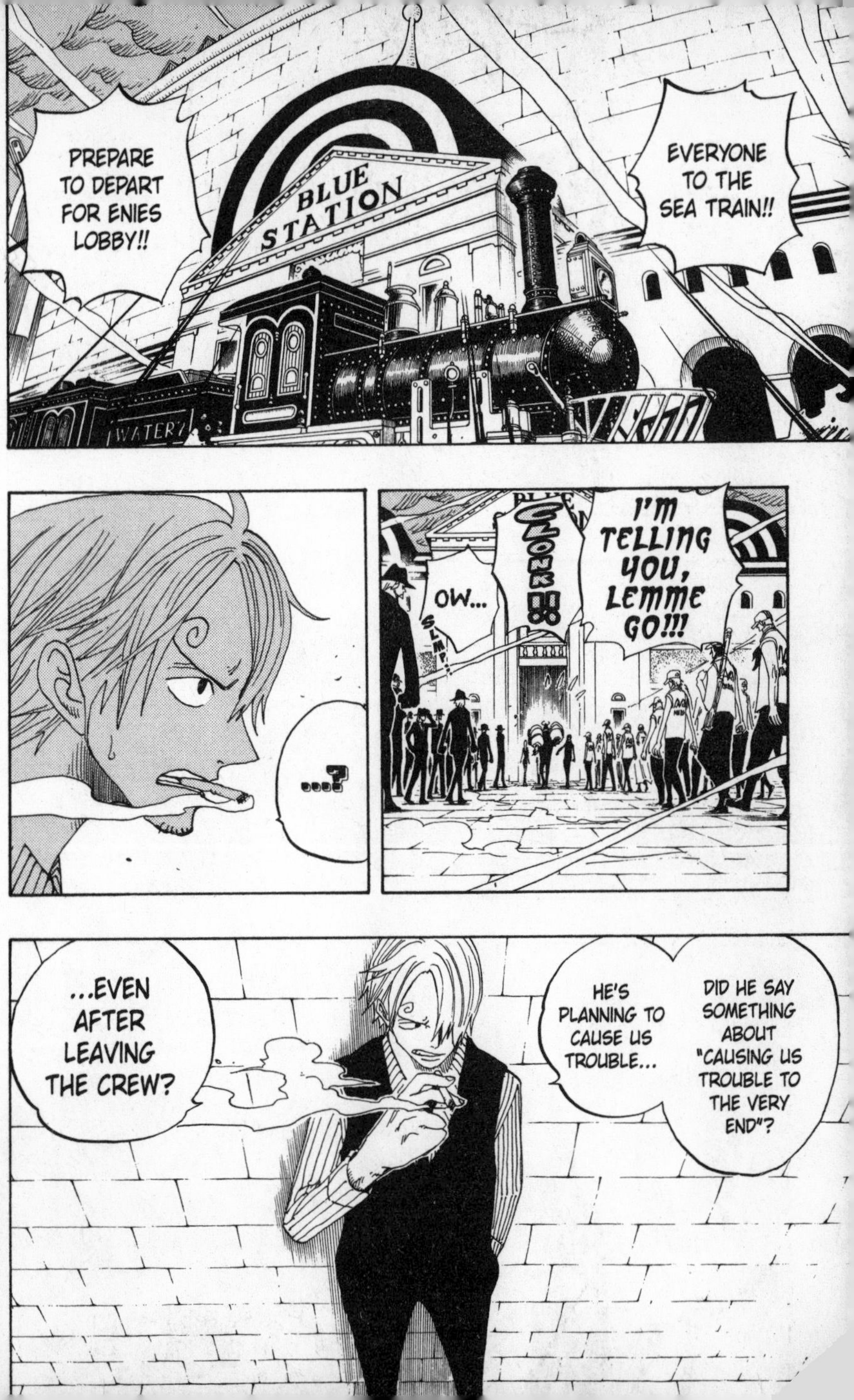
EVERYONE TO THE SEA TRAIN!!
BLUE STATION
PREPARE TO DEPART FOR ENIES LOBBY!!
WATER 7
I'M TELLING YOU, LEMME GO!!!
CLONK!!
OW...
SLMP...
...?
DID HE SAY SOMETHING ABOUT "CAUSING US TROUBLE TO THE VERY END"?
HE'S PLANNING TO CAUSE US TROUBLE...
...EVEN AFTER LEAVING THE CREW?

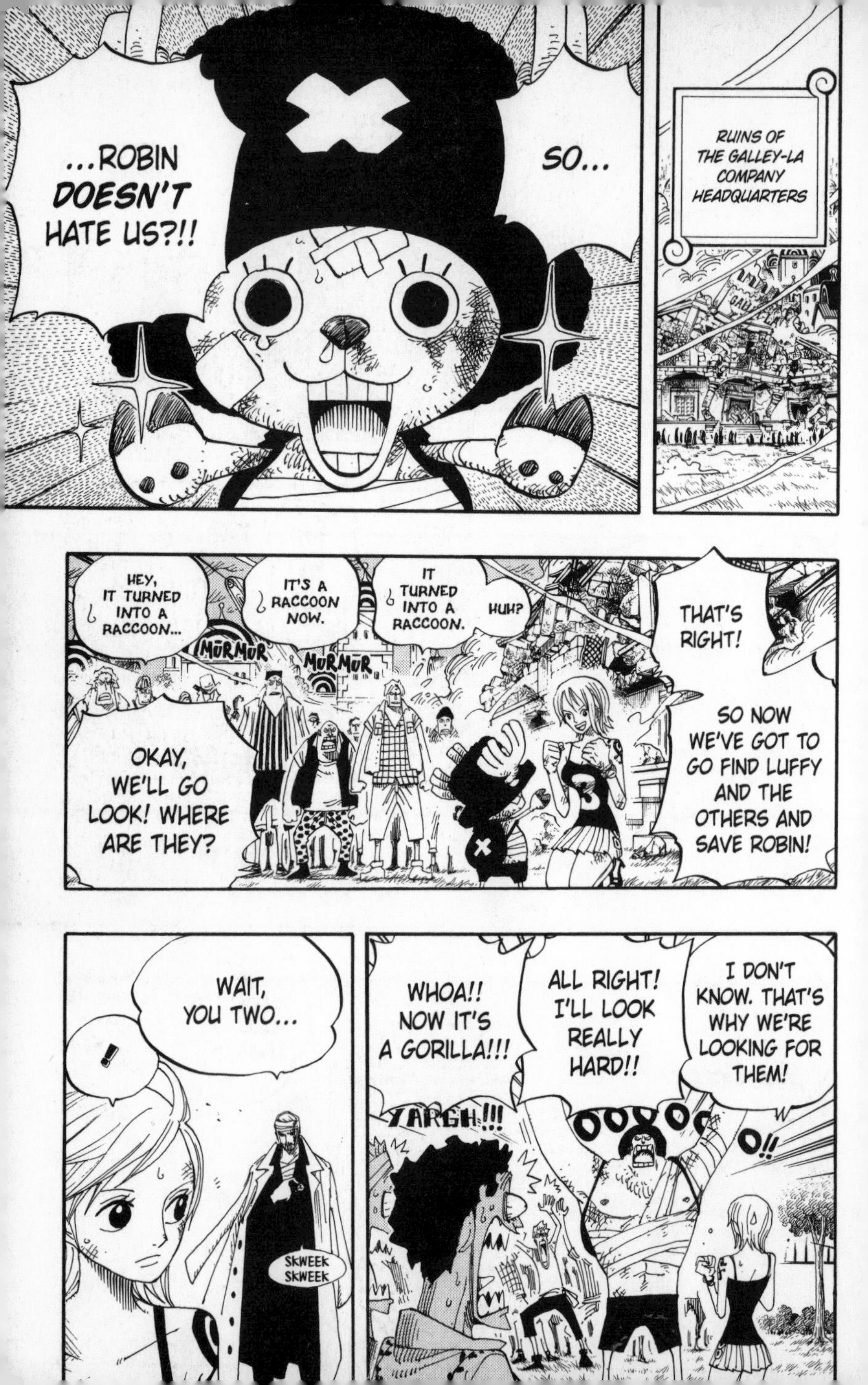
RUINS OF THE GALLEY-LA COMPANY HEADQUARTERS
SO...
...ROBIN DOESN'T HATE US?!!
THAT'S RIGHT!
SO NOW WE'VE GOT TO GO FIND LUFFY AND THE OTHERS AND SAVE ROBIN!
HUH?
IT TURNED INTO A RACCOON.
IT'S A RACCOON NOW.
HEY, IT TURNED INTO A RACCOON...
MURMUR
MURMUR
OKAY, WE'LL GO LOOK! WHERE ARE THEY?
I DON'T KNOW. THAT'S WHY WE'RE LOOKING FOR THEM!
ALL RIGHT! I'LL LOOK REALLY HARD!!
OOOOOO!!
WHOA!! NOW IT'S A GORILLA!!!
YARGH!!!
WAIT, YOU TWO...
!
SKWEEK SKWEEK

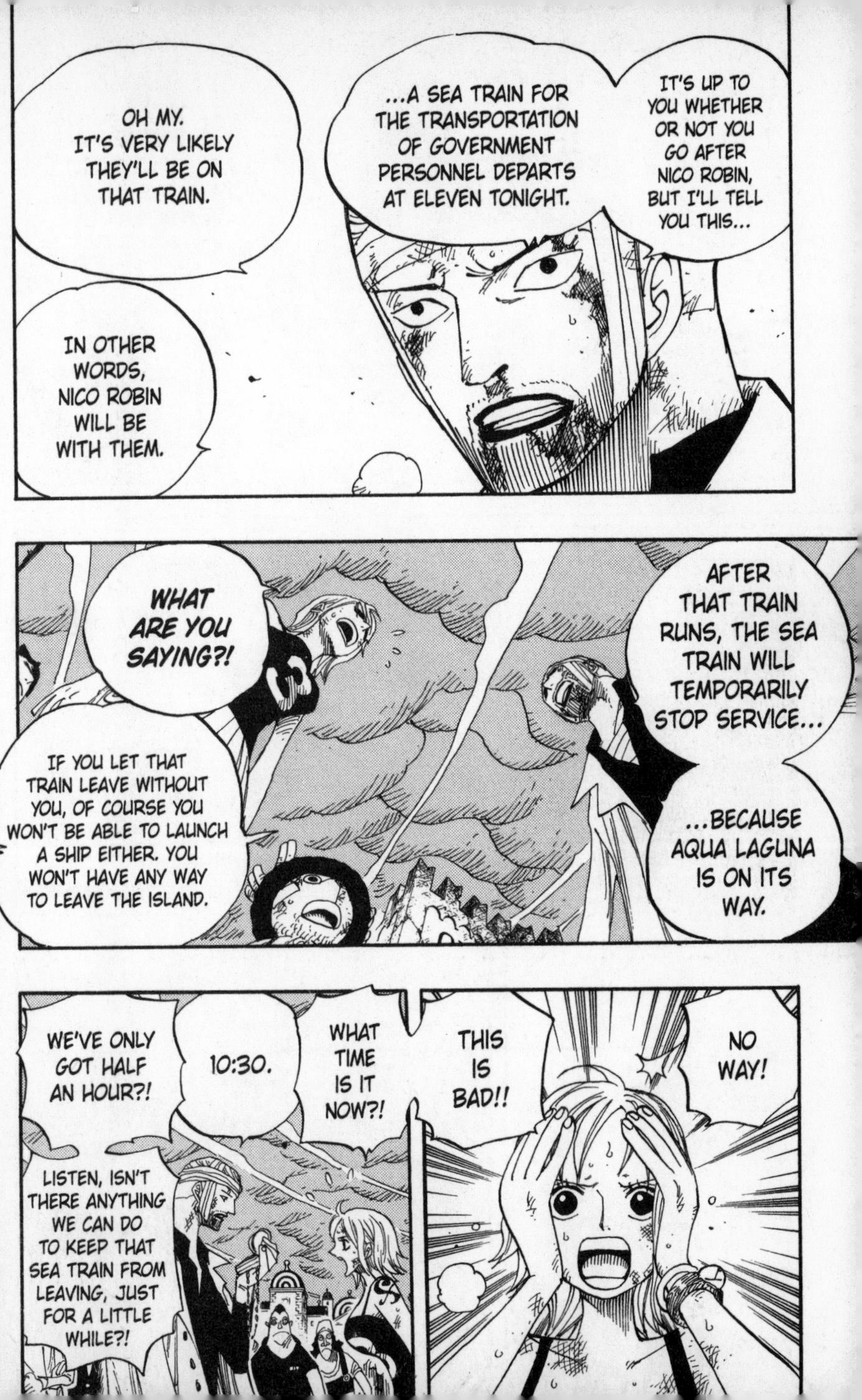
IT'S UP TO YOU WHETHER OR NOT YOU GO AFTER NICO ROBIN, BUT I'LL TELL YOU THIS...
...A SEA TRAIN FOR THE TRANSPORTATION OF GOVERNMENT PERSONNEL DEPARTS AT ELEVEN TONIGHT.
OH MY. IT'S VERY LIKELY THEY'LL BE ON THAT TRAIN.
IN OTHER WORDS, NICO ROBIN WILL BE WITH THEM.
AFTER THAT TRAIN RUNS, THE SEA TRAIN WILL TEMPORARILY STOP SERVICE...
...BECAUSE AQUA LAGUNA IS ON ITS WAY.
WHAT ARE YOU SAYING?!
IF YOU LET THAT TRAIN LEAVE WITHOUT YOU, OF COURSE YOU WON'T BE ABLE TO LAUNCH A SHIP EITHER. YOU WON'T HAVE ANY WAY TO LEAVE THE ISLAND.
NO WAY!
THIS IS BAD!!
WHAT TIME IS IT NOW?!
10:30.
WE'VE ONLY GOT HALF AN HOUR?!
LISTEN, ISN'T THERE ANYTHING WE CAN DO TO KEEP THAT SEA TRAIN FROM LEAVING, JUST FOR A LITTLE WHILE?!

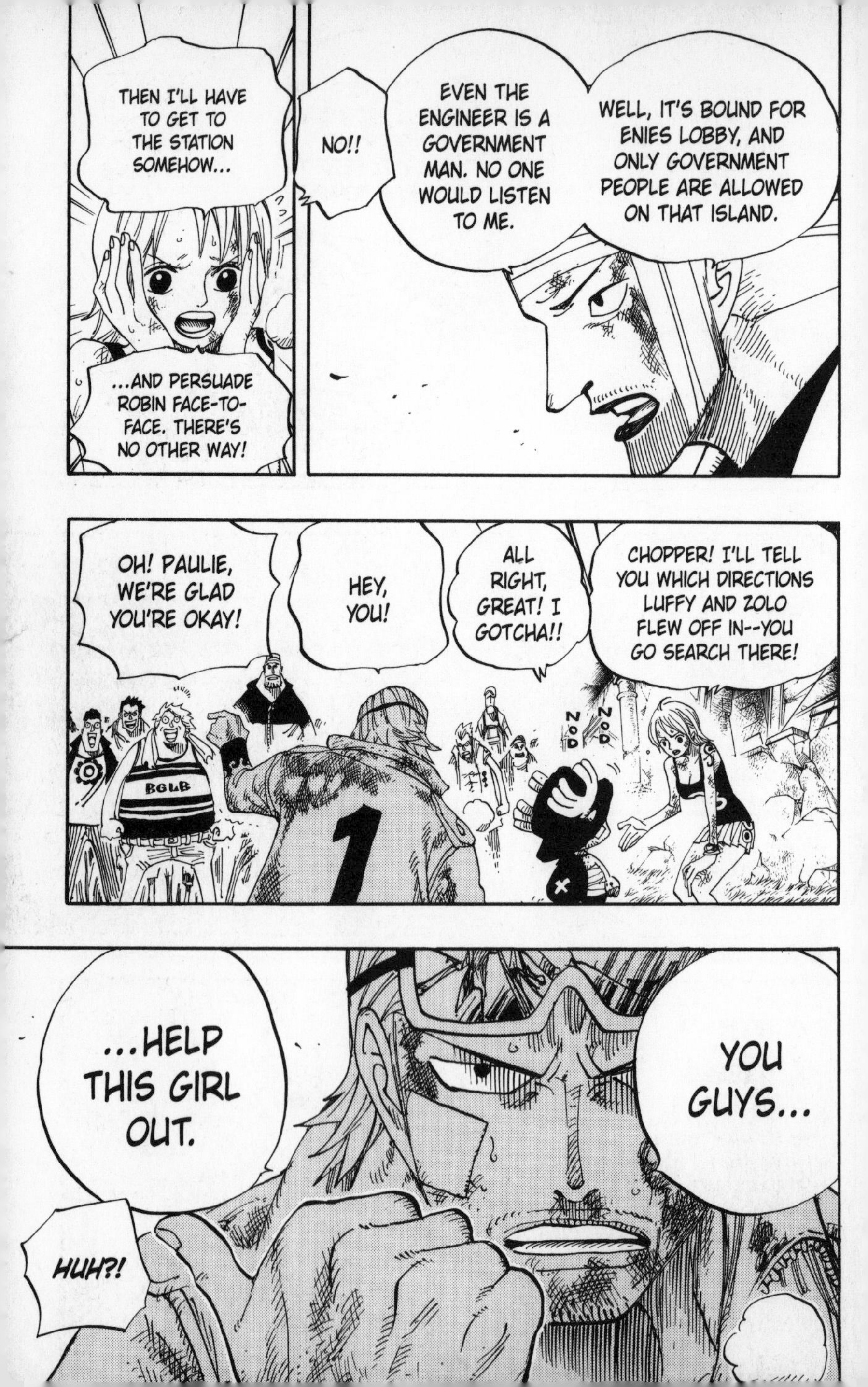
WELL, IT'S BOUND FOR ENIES LOBBY, AND ONLY GOVERNMENT PEOPLE ARE ALLOWED ON THAT ISLAND.
EVEN THE ENGINEER IS A GOVERNMENT MAN. NO ONE WOULD LISTEN TO ME.
NO!!
THEN I'LL HAVE TO GET TO THE STATION SOMEHOW...
...AND PERSUADE ROBIN FACE-TO-FACE. THERE'S NO OTHER WAY!
CHOPPER! I'LL TELL YOU WHICH DIRECTIONS LUFFY AND ZOLO FLEW OFF IN--YOU GO SEARCH THERE!
ALL RIGHT, GREAT! I GOTCHA!!
NOD
NOD
HEY, YOU!
OH! PAULIE, WE'RE GLAD YOU'RE OKAY!
BGLB
YOU GUYS...
...HELP THIS GIRL OUT.
HUH?!

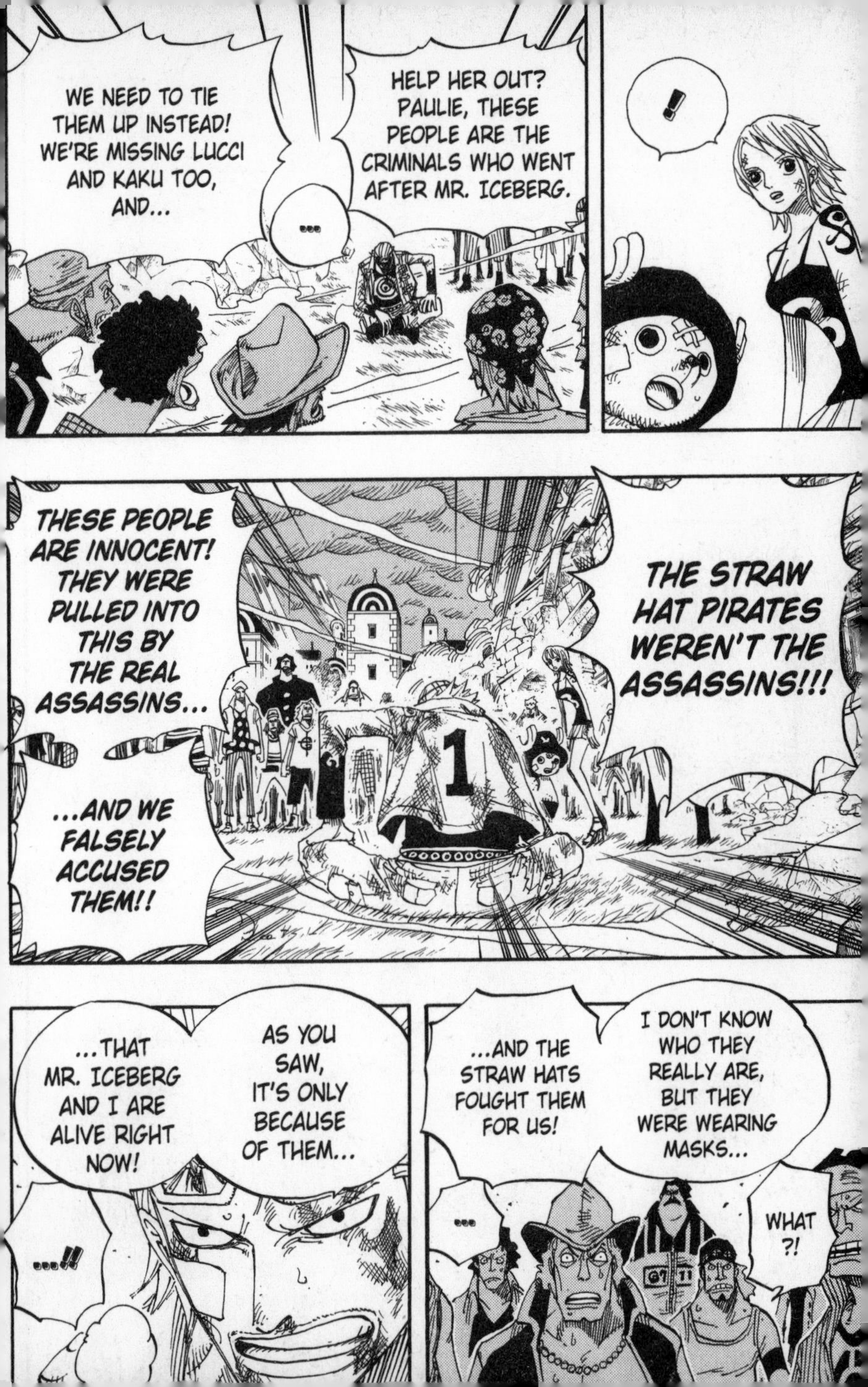
!
HELP HER OUT? PAULIE, THESE PEOPLE ARE THE CRIMINALS WHO WENT AFTER MR. ICEBERG.
WE NEED TO TIE THEM UP INSTEAD! WE'RE MISSING LUCCI AND KAKU TOO, AND...
...
THE STRAW HAT PIRATES WEREN'T THE ASSASSINS!!!
THESE PEOPLE ARE INNOCENT! THEY WERE PULLED INTO THIS BY THE REAL ASSASSINS...
...AND WE FALSELY ACCUSED THEM!!
I DON'T KNOW WHO THEY REALLY ARE, BUT THEY WERE WEARING MASKS...
...AND THE STRAW HATS FOUGHT THEM FOR US!
WHAT?!
...
AS YOU SAW, IT'S ONLY BECAUSE OF THEM...
...THAT MR. ICEBERG AND I ARE ALIVE RIGHT NOW!
...!!

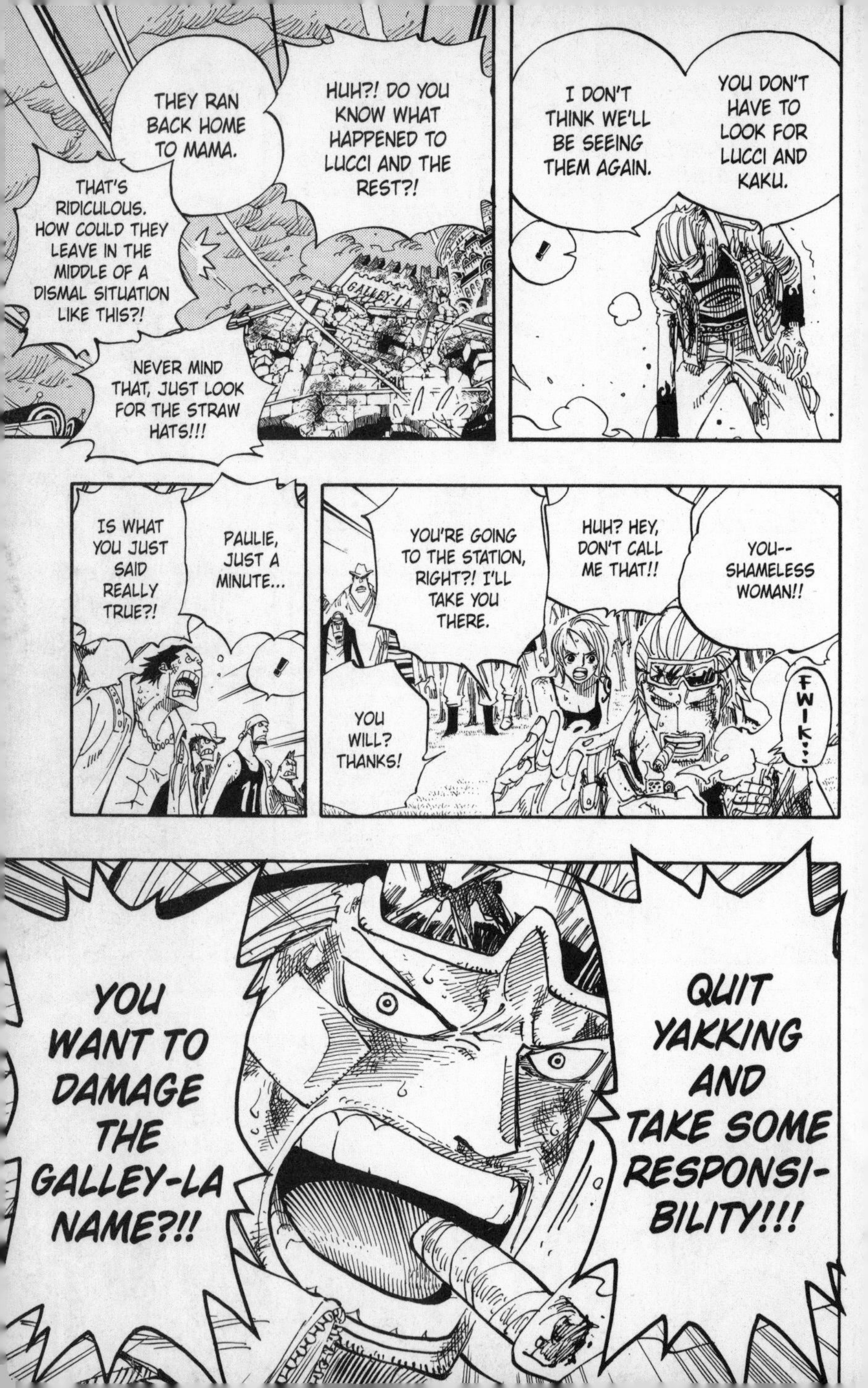
YOU DON'T HAVE TO LOOK FOR LUCCI AND KAKU.
I DON'T THINK WE'LL BE SEEING THEM AGAIN.
!
HUH?! DO YOU KNOW WHAT HAPPENED TO LUCCI AND THE REST?!
THEY RAN BACK HOME TO MAMA.
GALLEY-LA
THAT'S RIDICULOUS. HOW COULD THEY LEAVE IN THE MIDDLE OF A DISMAL SITUATION LIKE THIS?!
NEVER MIND THAT, JUST LOOK FOR THE STRAW HATS!!!
YOU-- SHAMELESS WOMAN!!
FWIK...
HUH? HEY, DON'T CALL ME THAT!!
YOU'RE GOING TO THE STATION, RIGHT?! I'LL TAKE YOU THERE.
YOU WILL? THANKS!
PAULIE, JUST A MINUTE...
IS WHAT YOU JUST SAID REALLY TRUE?!
!
QUIT YAKKING AND TAKE SOME RESPONSI-BILITY!!!
YOU WANT TO DAMAGE THE GALLEY-LA NAME?!!

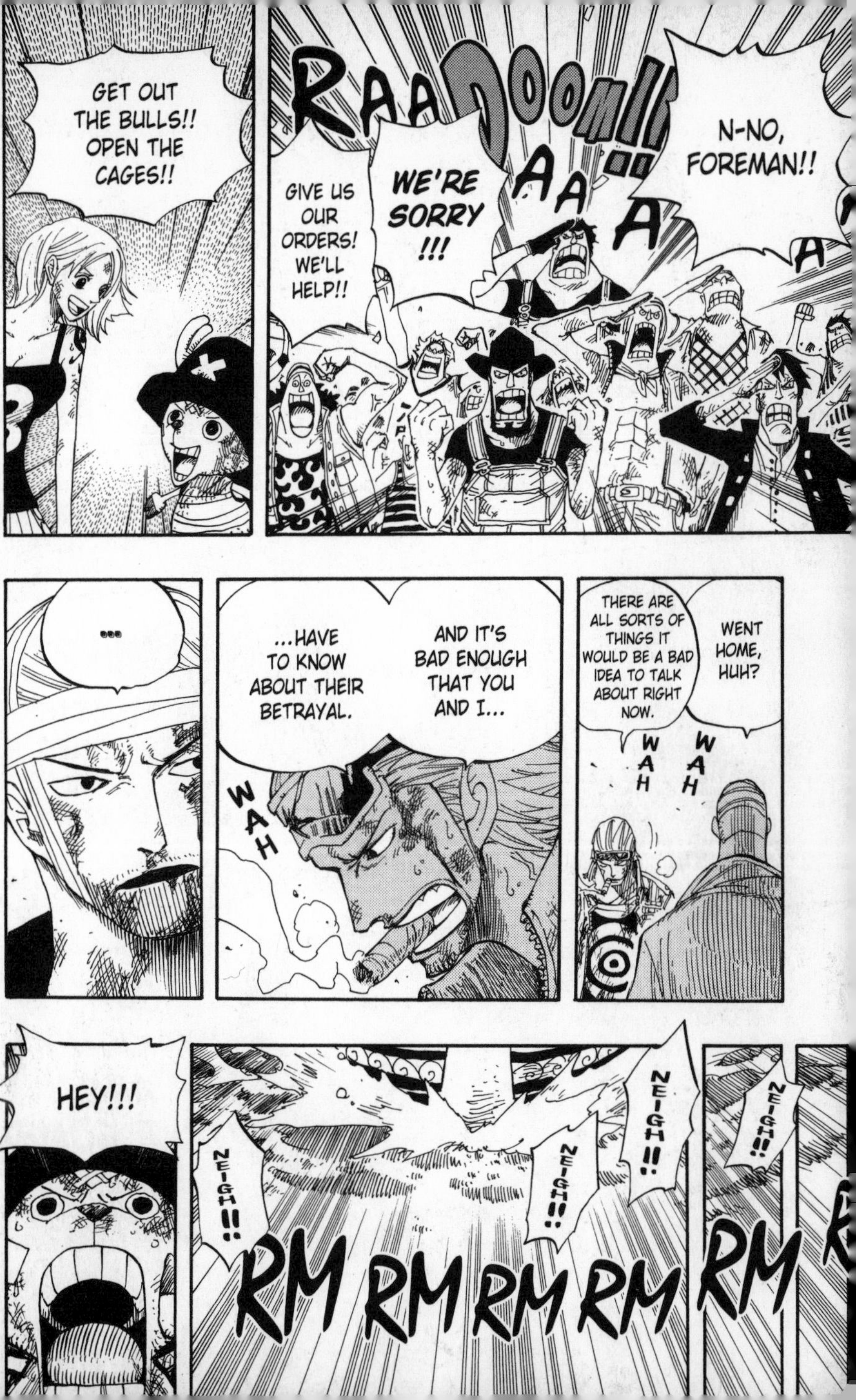
RAADOOM!!
N-NO, FOREMAN!!
AAAA
WE'RE SORRY!!!
GIVE US OUR ORDERS! WE'LL HELP!!
GET OUT THE BULLS!! OPEN THE CAGES!!
WENT HOME, HUH?
THERE ARE ALL SORTS OF THINGS IT WOULD BE A BAD IDEA TO TALK ABOUT RIGHT NOW.
WAH WAH
AND IT'S BAD ENOUGH THAT YOU AND I...
...HAVE TO KNOW ABOUT THEIR BETRAYAL.
WAH
...
NEIGH!!
NEIGH!!
NEIGH!!
NEIGH!!
RM RM RM RM RM RM
HEY!!!

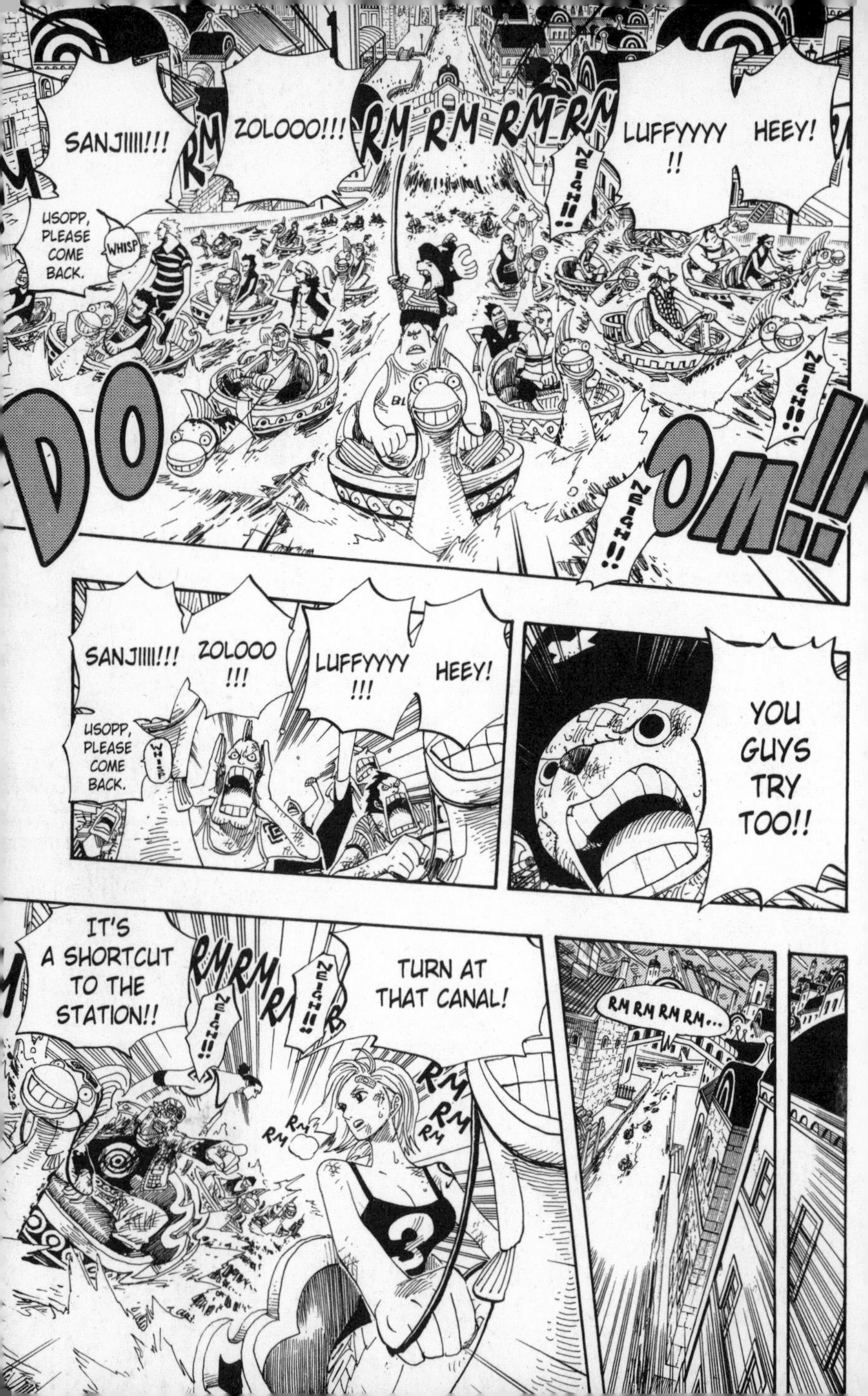
HEEY!
LUFFYYYY !!
NEIGH!!
RM RM RM RM
ZOLOOO!!!
RM
SANJIIII!!!
USOPP, PLEASE COME BACK.
WHISP
NEIGH!!
NEIGH!!
DOOM!!
YOU GUYS TRY TOO!!
HEEY!
LUFFYYYY !!!
ZOLOOO !!!
SANJIIII!!!
USOPP, PLEASE COME BACK.
WHISP
RM RM RM RM...
TURN AT THAT CANAL!
NEIGH!!
RM RM RM
IT'S A SHORTCUT TO THE STATION!!
NEIGH!!
RM RM RM
RM RM

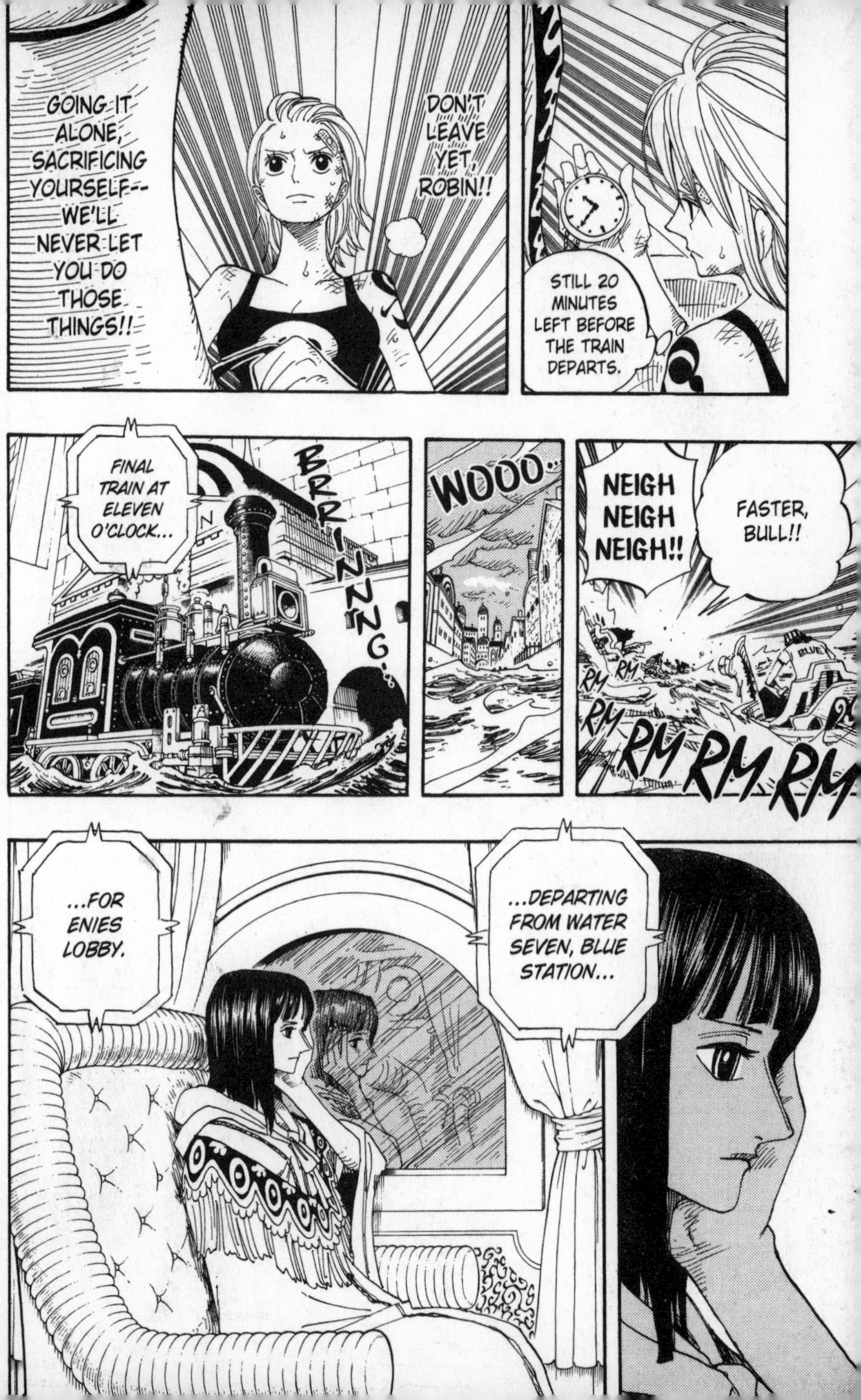
STILL 20 MINUTES LEFT BEFORE THE TRAIN DEPARTS.
DON'T LEAVE YET, ROBIN!!
GOING IT ALONE, SACRIFICING YOURSELF-- WE'LL NEVER LET YOU DO THOSE THINGS!!
FASTER, BULL!!
NEIGH NEIGH NEIGH!!
BLUE
RM RM RM RM RM RM RM
WOOO...
FINAL TRAIN AT ELEVEN O'CLOCK...
BRRRINNNG...
...DEPARTING FROM WATER SEVEN, BLUE STATION...
...FOR ENIES LOBBY.

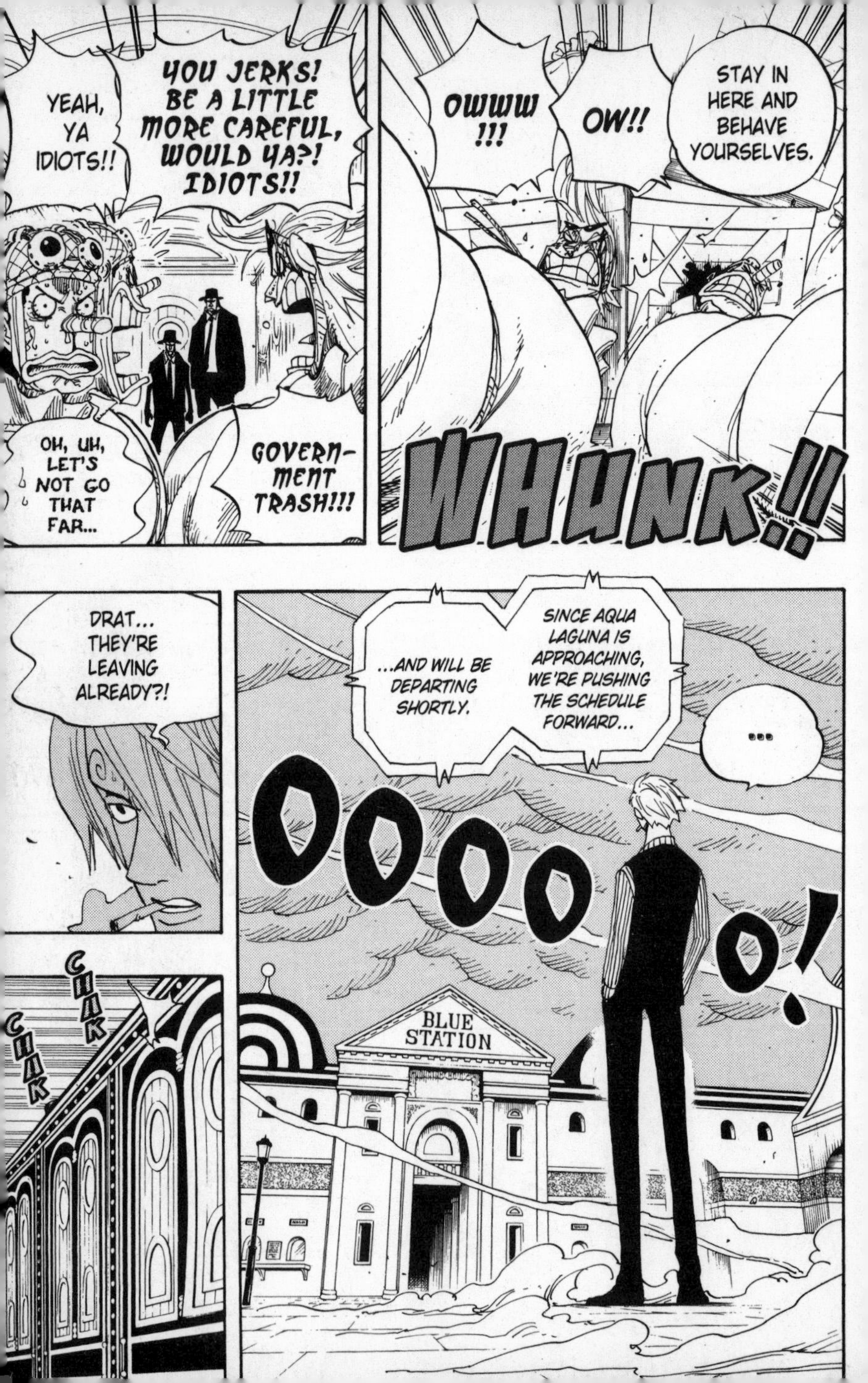
STAY IN HERE AND BEHAVE YOURSELVES.
OW!!
OWWW !!!
WHUNK!!
YOU JERKS! BE A LITTLE MORE CAREFUL, WOULD YA?! IDIOTS!!
YEAH, YA IDIOTS!!
GOVERN-MENT TRASH!!!
OH, UH, LET'S NOT GO THAT FAR...
SINCE AQUA LAGUNA IS APPROACHING, WE'RE PUSHING THE SCHEDULE FORWARD...
...AND WILL BE DEPARTING SHORTLY.
...
OOOOO!
BLUE STATION
DRAT... THEY'RE LEAVING ALREADY?!
CHUK
CHUK

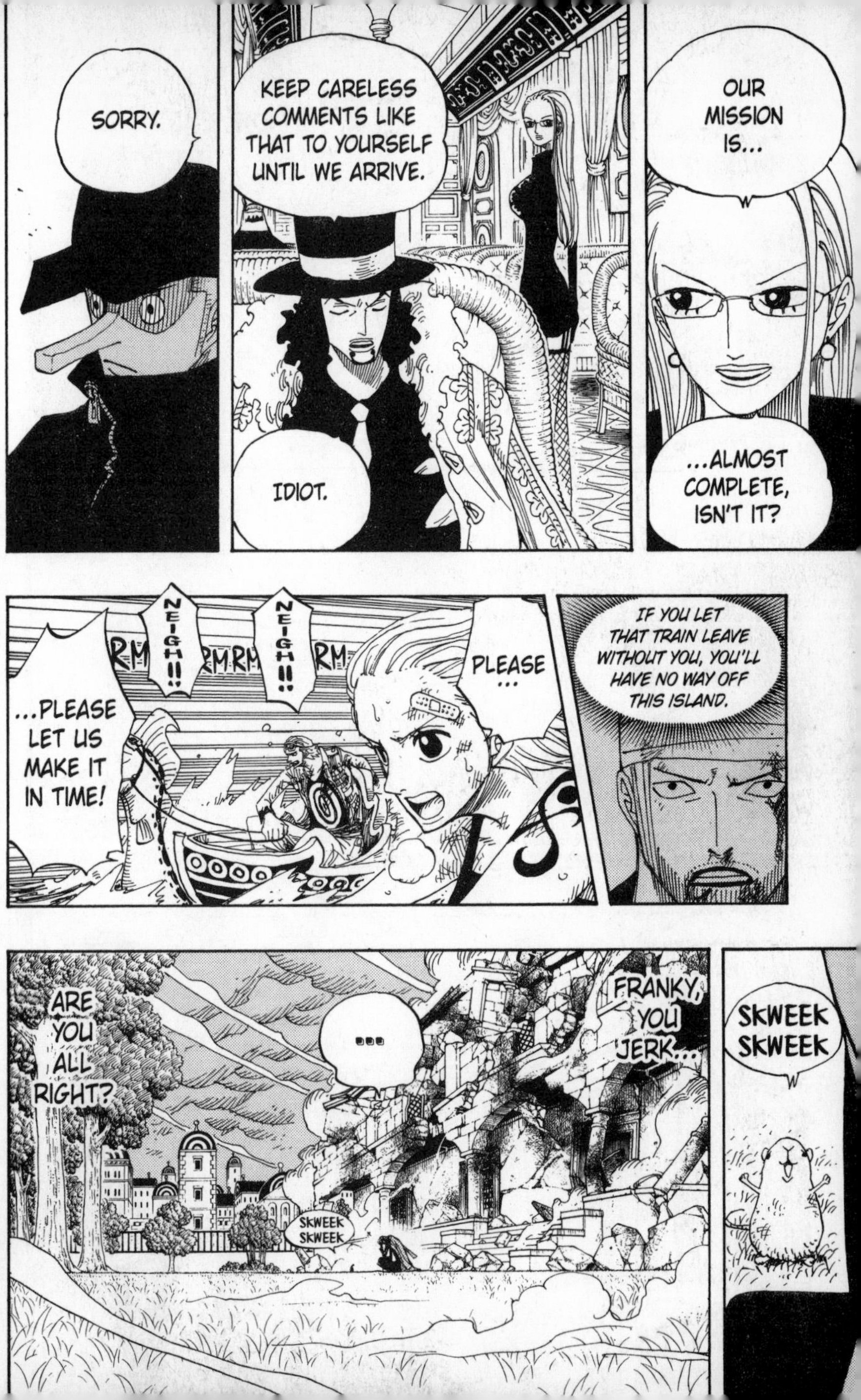
OUR MISSION IS...
...ALMOST COMPLETE, ISN'T IT?
KEEP CARELESS COMMENTS LIKE THAT TO YOURSELF UNTIL WE ARRIVE.
IDIOT.
SORRY.
IF YOU LET THAT TRAIN LEAVE WITHOUT YOU, YOU'LL HAVE NO WAY OFF THIS ISLAND.
PLEASE ...
RM
NEIGH!!
RMRM
NEIGH!!
RM
...PLEASE LET US MAKE IT IN TIME!
SKWEEK SKWEEK
FRANKY, YOU JERK...
...
SKWEEK SKWEEK
ARE YOU ALL RIGHT?

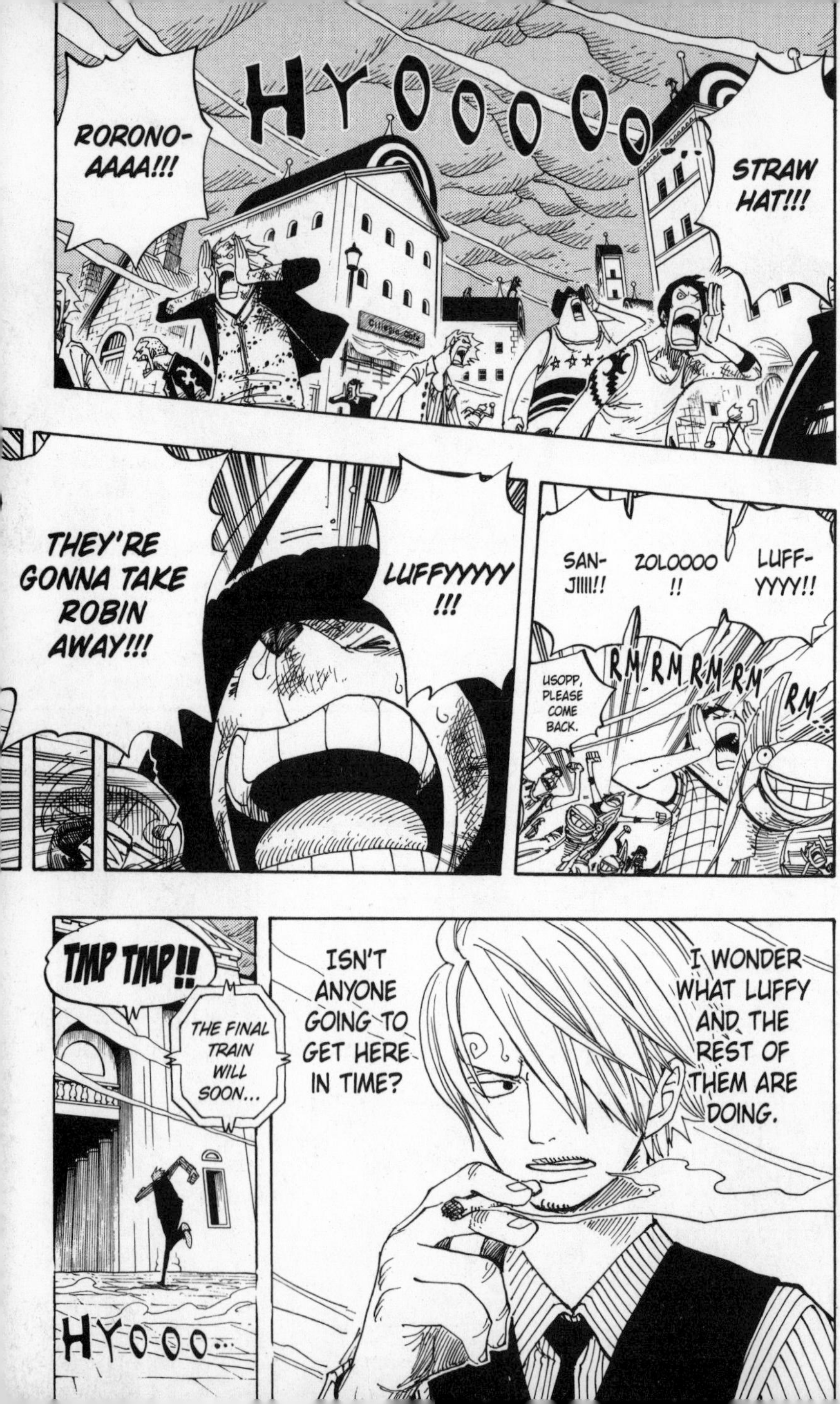
STRAW HAT!!!
HYOOOOO
RORONO-AAAA!!!
LUFF-YYYY!!
ZOLOOOO!!
SAN-JIIII!!
RM RM RM RM RM
USOPP, PLEASE COME BACK.
LUFFYYYYY!!!
THEY'RE GONNA TAKE ROBIN AWAY!!!
I WONDER WHAT LUFFY AND THE REST OF THEM ARE DOING.
ISN'T ANYONE GOING TO GET HERE IN TIME?
TMP TMP!!
THE FINAL TRAIN WILL SOON...
HYOOO...

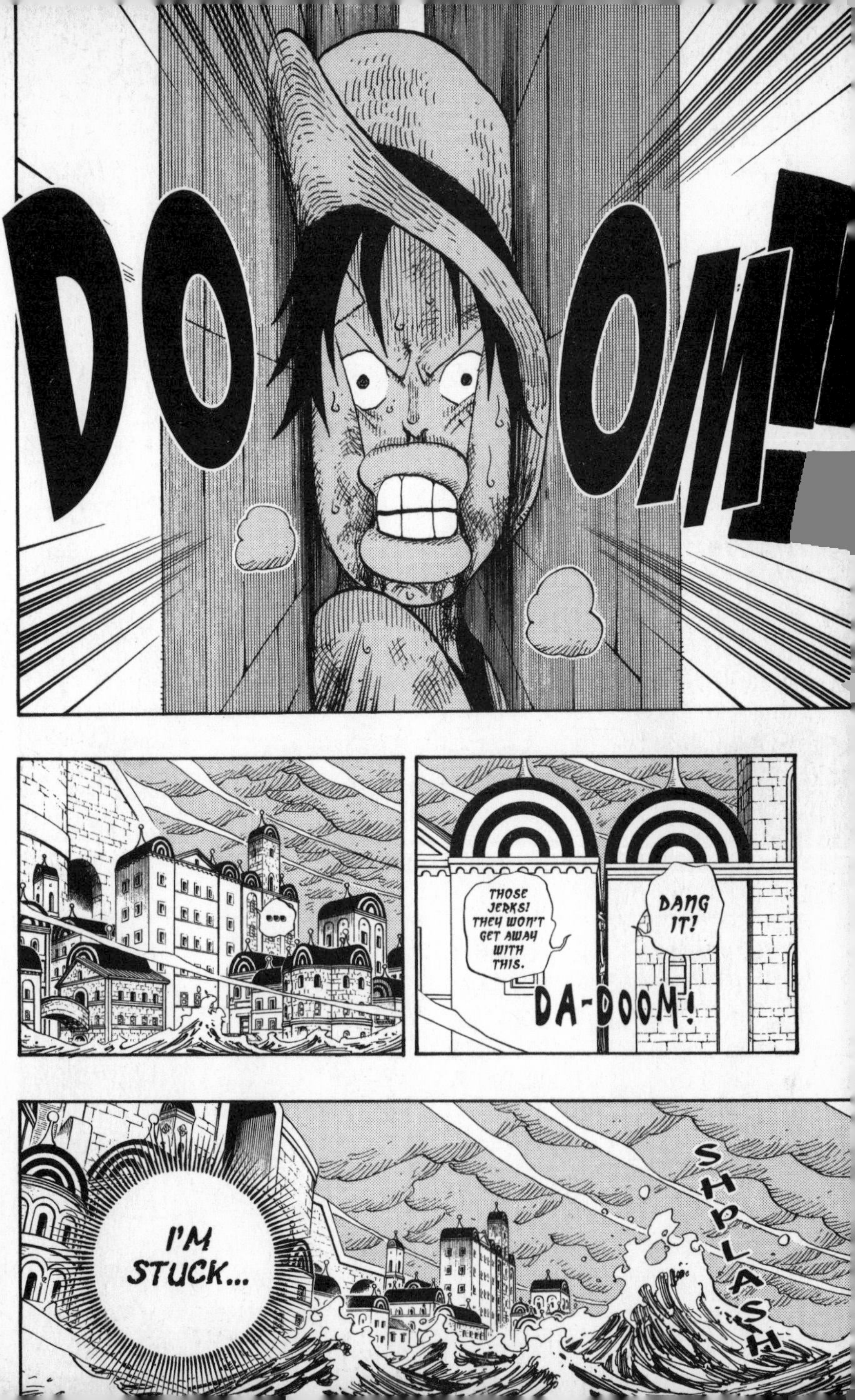
DOOM!!
DANG IT!
THOSE JERKS! THEY WON'T GET AWAY WITH THIS.
DA-DOOM!
...
SHPLASH
I'M STUCK...

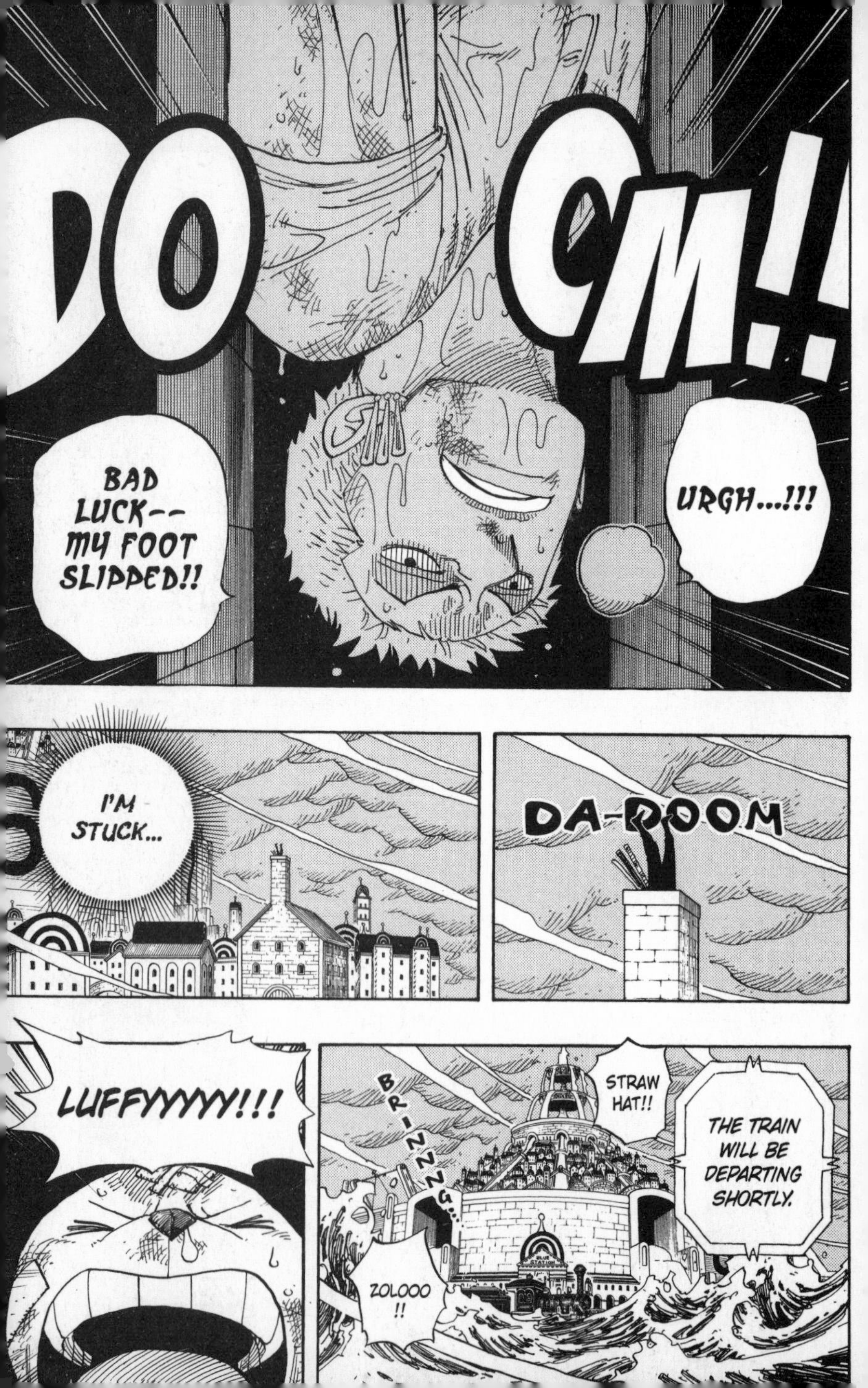
DOOM!!
URGH...!!!
BAD LUCK-- MY FOOT SLIPPED!!
DA-DOOM
I'M STUCK...
THE TRAIN WILL BE DEPARTING SHORTLY.
STRAW HAT!!
BRINNNG...
ZOLOOO !!
LUFFYYYYY!!!

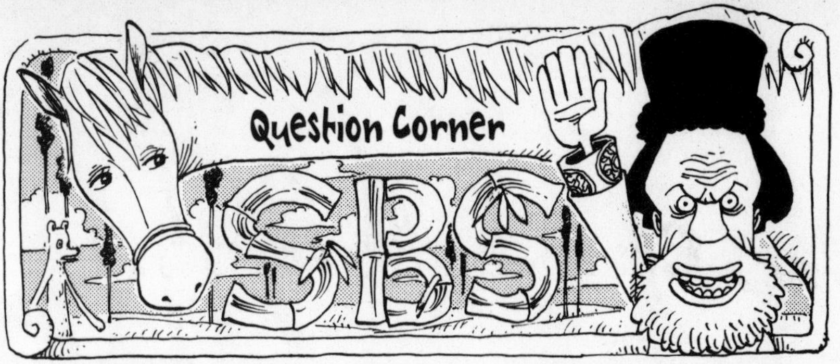
Question Corner
SBS

Reader: It's me! Me, me! Remember me?! Oda Sensei, it's me! I just now got into a traffic accident, and I need two million right away! Will you transfer that over to my account? That--and I had a question: Can lots of people eat the same Devil Fruit? Or can't they? Is that even possible? If that happened, what would happen? 'Kay, thanks for answering!

--Early Years

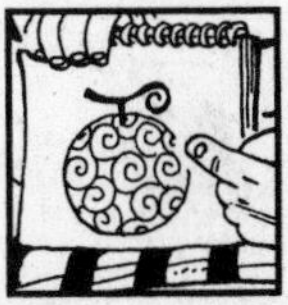

Oda: Huh?! That's terrible! A traffic accident?! All righty, let me just transfer that to you! ...Hey! Would you quit that?! You're trying an "It's me, remember me" fraud?! ※ Right, then, I give that evil fraud an Oda Sliding Chop! Okay, I chopped your shins. Here's your answer. It's not possible for lots of people to divide a fruit and eat it. I get lots of questions like this, but with Devil Fruits, just one bite is enough to give you the ability. And once somebody's bitten into the fruit, it's just a normal, nasty-tasting fruit. Nothing will happen, no matter who eats it. In short, several people can't get abilities from a single fruit.

Reader: There was something I didn't understand, and I want to look into it: What kind of a blowfish is a long-horned cowfish? Mr. Tom is obviously too fat, right?! I would love to see your gorgeous drawing of a blowfish, Ei-chan! Thank you!

--Naomi

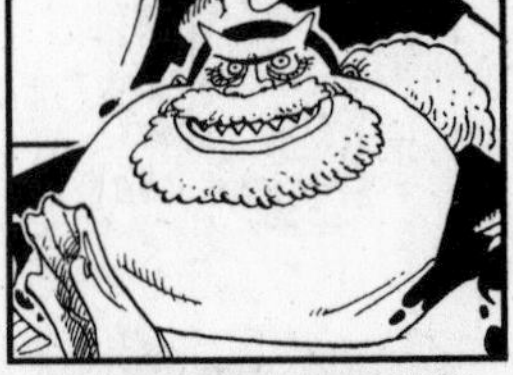

THE LONG-HORNED COWFISH FISH-MAN, TOM

Oda:

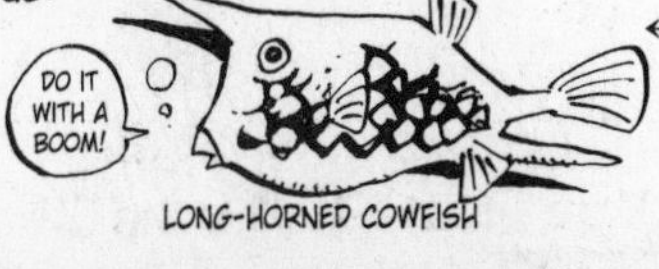
DO IT WITH A BOOM!

LONG-HORNED COWFISH

← Okay. It looks like this. Its skin is poison. (Mr. Tom's isn't.)

(※THE "IT'S ME, REMEMBER ME?" FRAUD IS A CRIME IN JAPAN!!)

Chapter 361: P.S.

**MS. GOLDEN WEEK'S BIG PLAN, A BAROQUE REUNION,
VOL. 3: "BAROQUE WORKS COLLAPSES; I SEE MY COMRADES
FOR THE FIRST TIME"**

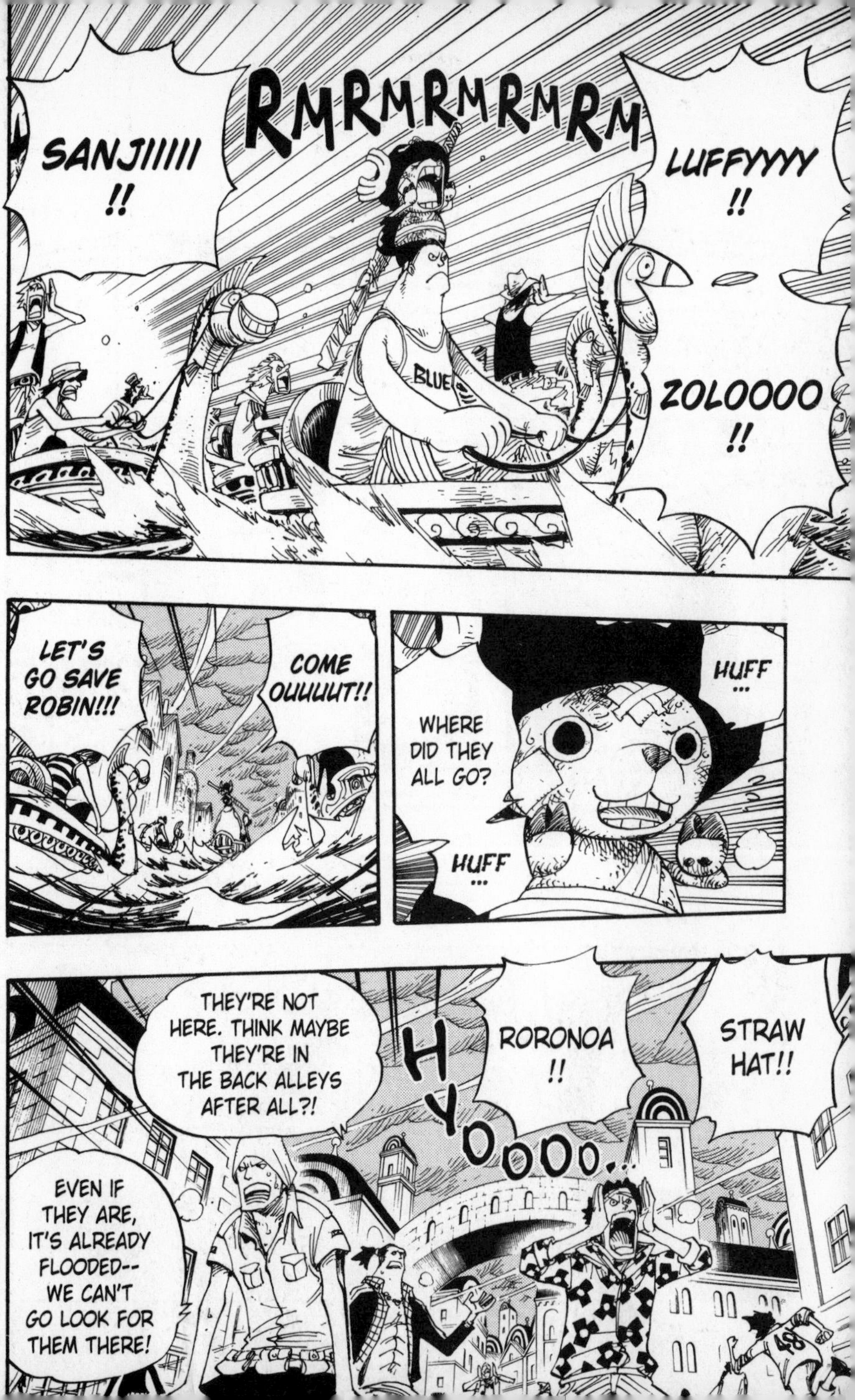
LUFFYYYY!!
ZOLOOOO!!
RMRMRMRMRMRM
SANJIIIII!!
HUFF...
WHERE DID THEY ALL GO?
HUFF...
COME OUUUUT!!
LET'S GO SAVE ROBIN!!!
STRAW HAT!!
RORONOA!!
HYOOOO...
THEY'RE NOT HERE. THINK MAYBE THEY'RE IN THE BACK ALLEYS AFTER ALL?!
EVEN IF THEY ARE, IT'S ALREADY FLOODED-- WE CAN'T GO LOOK FOR THEM THERE!

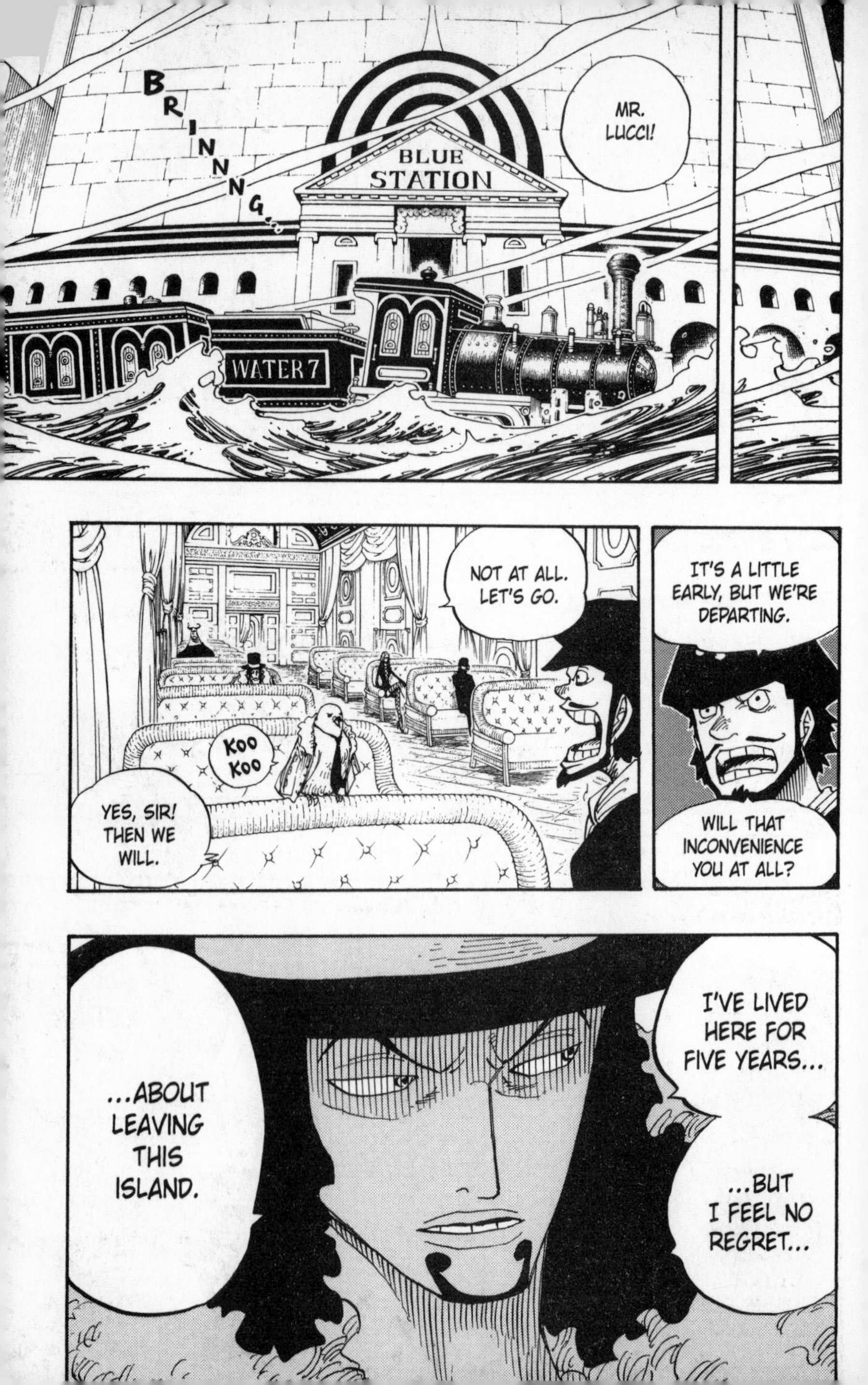
MR. LUCCI!
BRINNNG...
BLUE STATION
WATER 7
IT'S A LITTLE EARLY, BUT WE'RE DEPARTING.
WILL THAT INCONVENIENCE YOU AT ALL?
NOT AT ALL. LET'S GO.
KOO KOO
YES, SIR! THEN WE WILL.
I'VE LIVED HERE FOR FIVE YEARS...
...BUT I FEEL NO REGRET...
...ABOUT LEAVING THIS ISLAND.

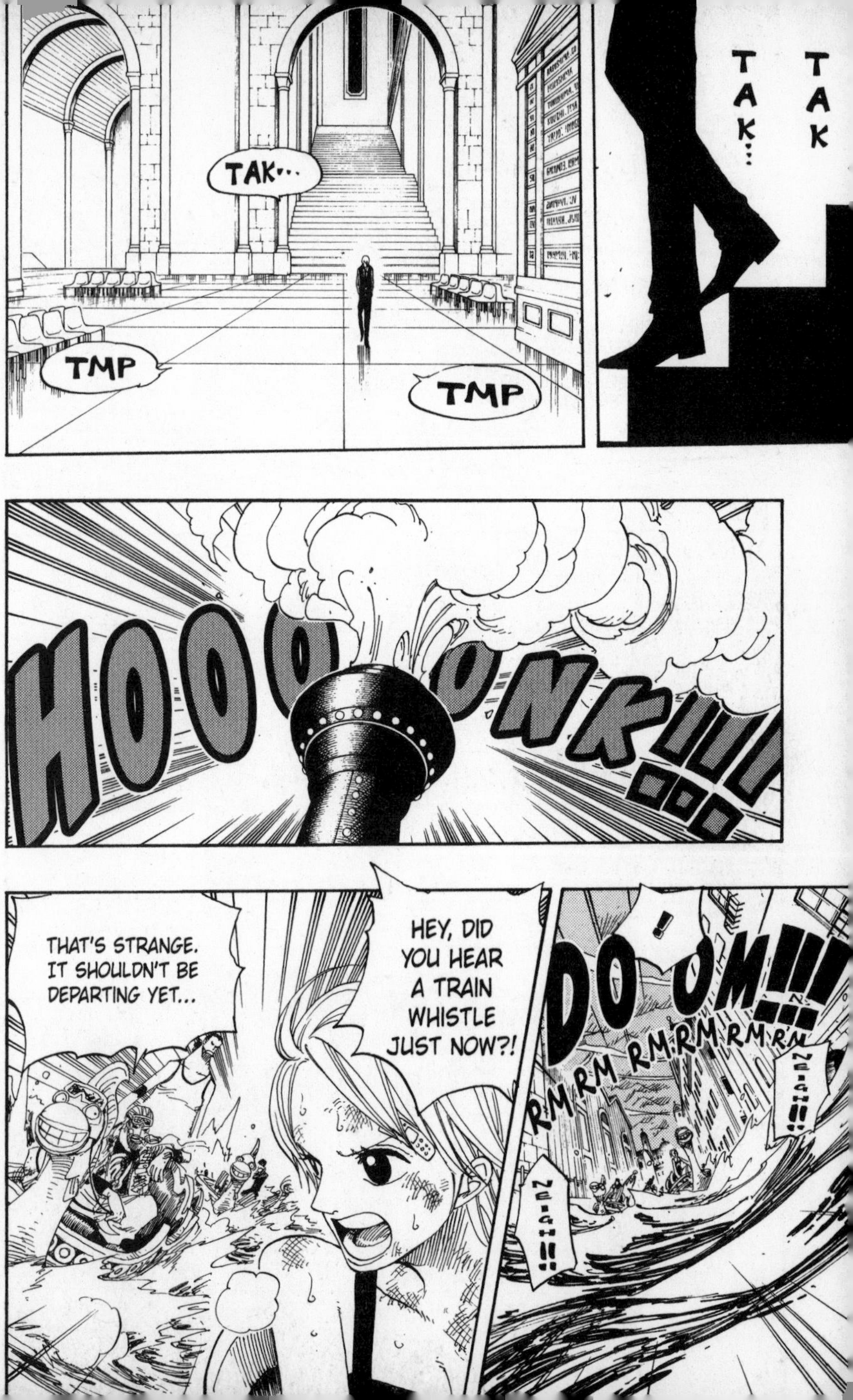
TAK
TAK...
TAK...
TMP
TMP
HOOOONK!!!!
DOOM!!!
RMRM RMRMRMRMRM
NEIGH!!
NEIGH!!
HEY, DID YOU HEAR A TRAIN WHISTLE JUST NOW?!
THAT'S STRANGE. IT SHOULDN'T BE DEPARTING YET...

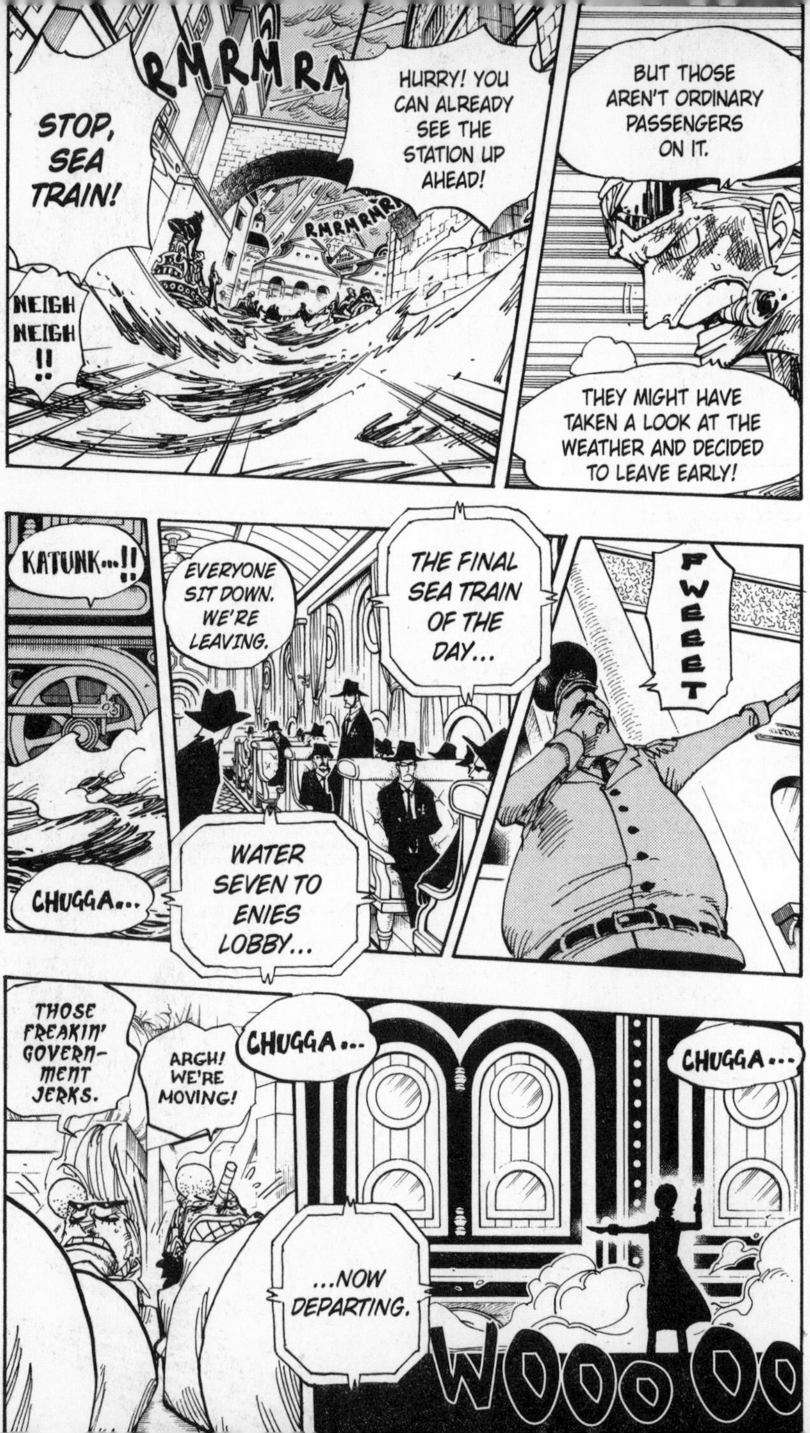
BUT THOSE AREN'T ORDINARY PASSENGERS ON IT.
THEY MIGHT HAVE TAKEN A LOOK AT THE WEATHER AND DECIDED TO LEAVE EARLY!
HURRY! YOU CAN ALREADY SEE THE STATION UP AHEAD!
RMRMRA
RMRMRMR
STOP, SEA TRAIN!
NEIGH NEIGH !!
FWEEET
THE FINAL SEA TRAIN OF THE DAY...
EVERYONE SIT DOWN. WE'RE LEAVING.
WATER SEVEN TO ENIES LOBBY...
KATUNK...!!
CHUGGA...
CHUGGA...
CHUGGA...
ARGH! WE'RE MOVING!
THOSE FREAKIN' GOVERNMENT JERKS.
...NOW DEPARTING.
WOOO OO

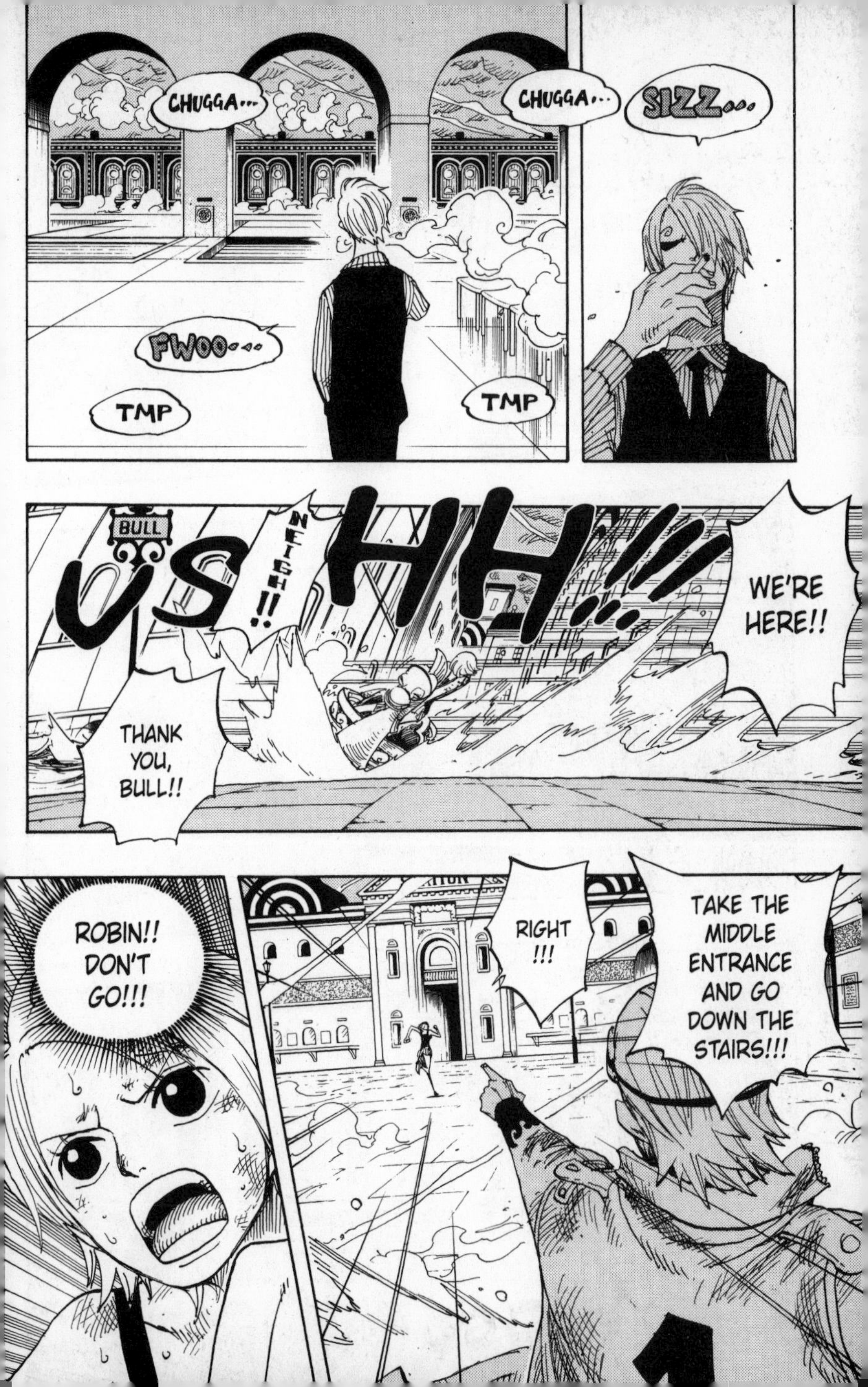
SIZZ...
CHUGGA...
CHUGGA...
FWOO...
TMP
TMP
WE'RE HERE!!
USHH!!!
NEIGH!!
BULL
THANK YOU, BULL!!
TAKE THE MIDDLE ENTRANCE AND GO DOWN THE STAIRS!!!
RIGHT!!!
ROBIN!! DON'T GO!!!

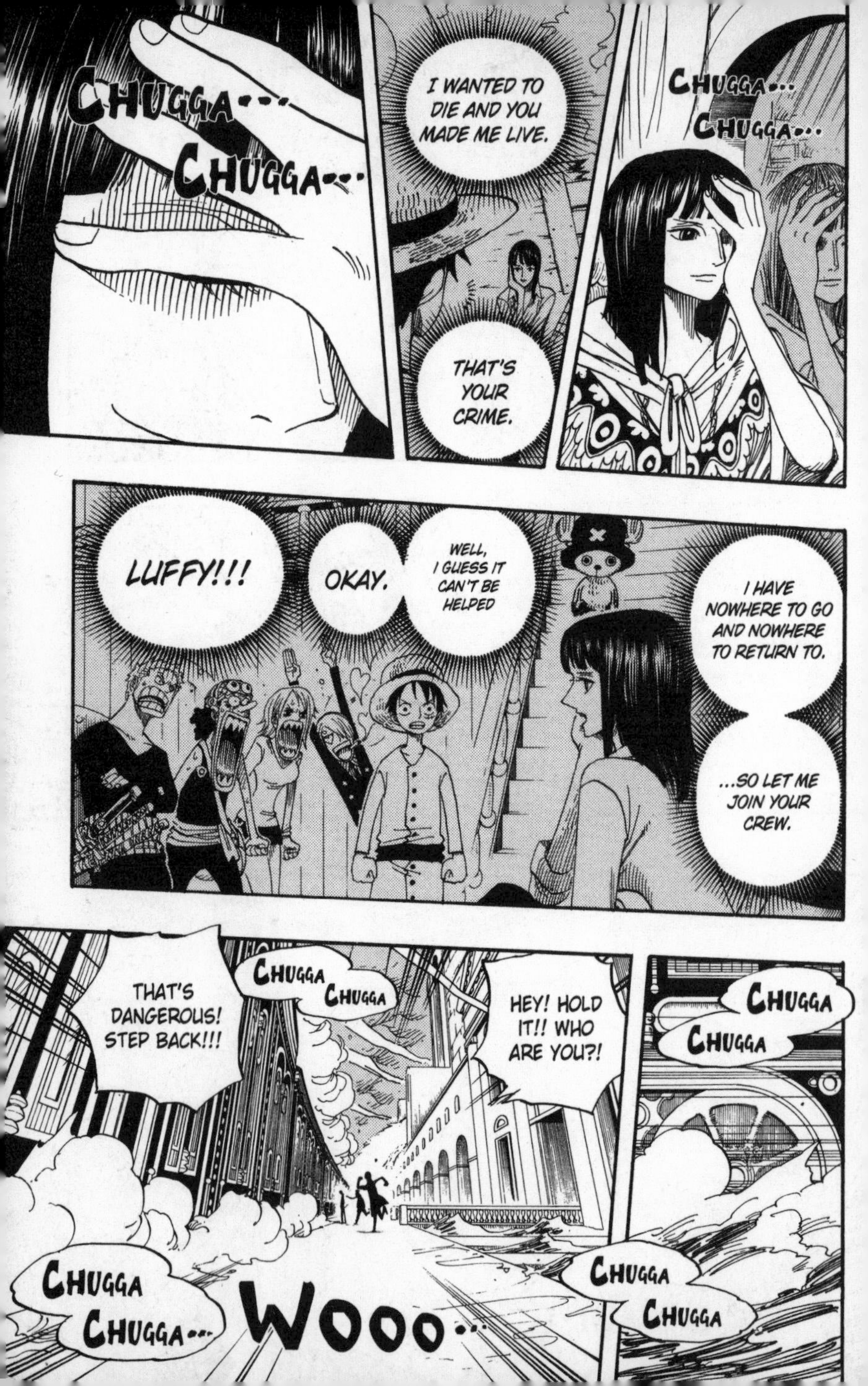
CHUGGA...
CHUGGA...
I WANTED TO DIE AND YOU MADE ME LIVE.
THAT'S YOUR CRIME.
CHUGGA...
CHUGGA...
I HAVE NOWHERE TO GO AND NOWHERE TO RETURN TO.
...SO LET ME JOIN YOUR CREW.
WELL, I GUESS IT CAN'T BE HELPED
OKAY.
LUFFY!!!
CHUGGA
CHUGGA
HEY! HOLD IT!! WHO ARE YOU?!
CHUGGA
CHUGGA
CHUGGA
CHUGGA
THAT'S DANGEROUS! STEP BACK!!!
WOOO...
CHUGGA
CHUGGA...

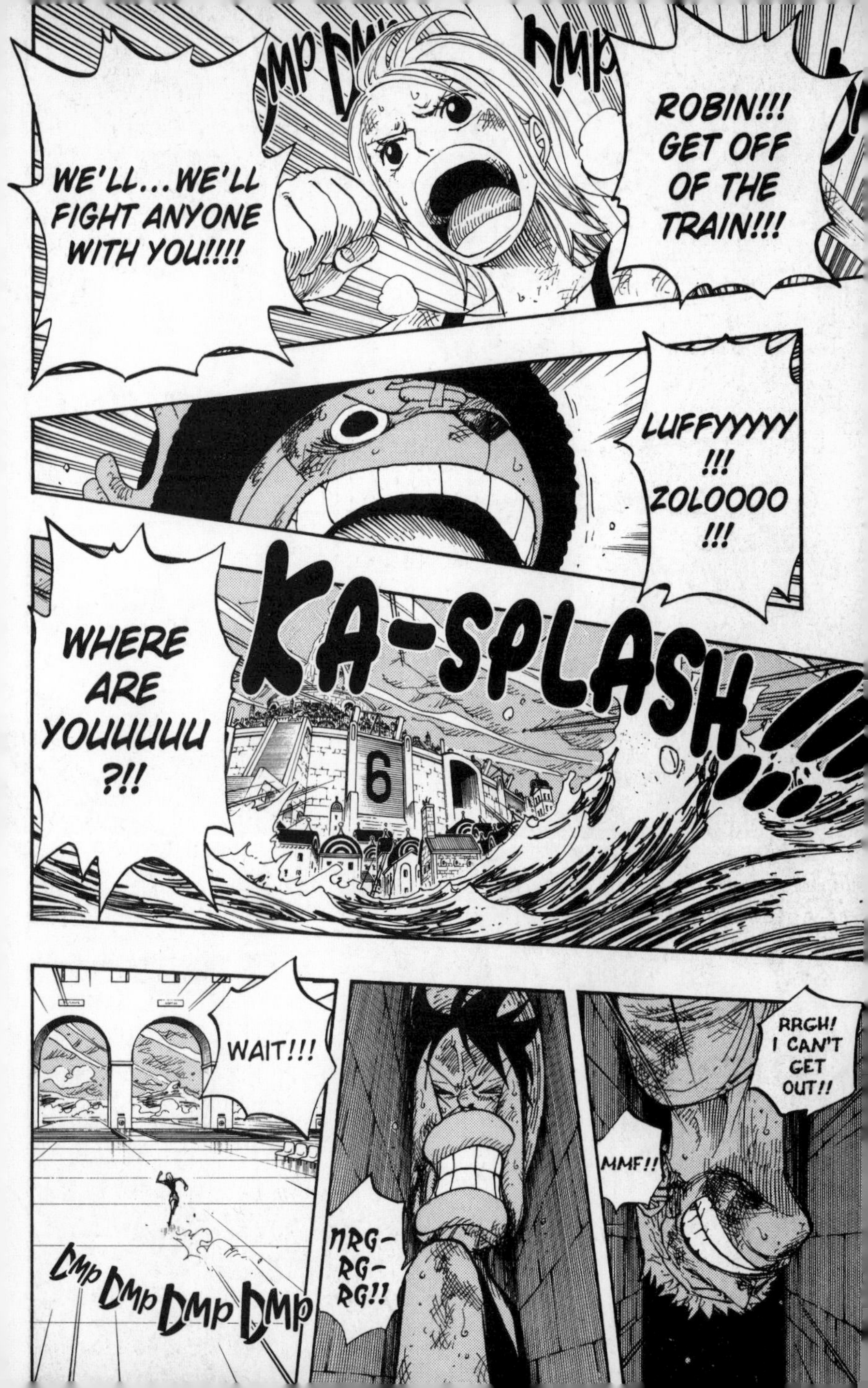
DMP DMP DMP
ROBIN!!! GET OFF OF THE TRAIN!!!
WE'LL...WE'LL FIGHT ANYONE WITH YOU!!!!
LUFFYYYYY!!! ZOLOOOO!!!
KA-SPLASH!!!
6
WHERE ARE YOUUUUUU?!!
RRGH! I CAN'T GET OUT!!
MMF!!
NRG-RG-RG!!
WAIT!!!
DMP DMP DMP DMP

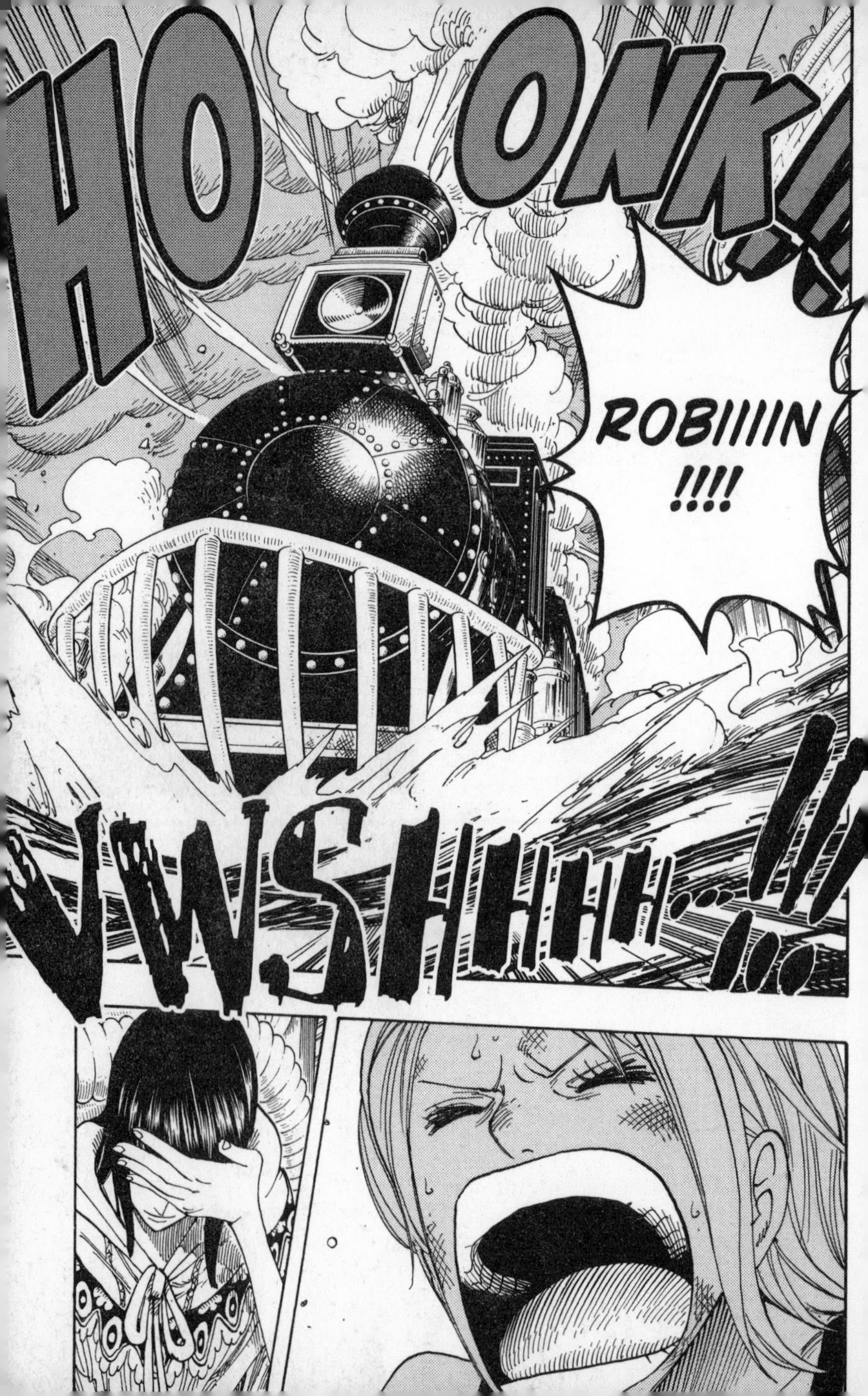
HOOONK!!
ROBIIIIN !!!!
WSHHHH...!!!

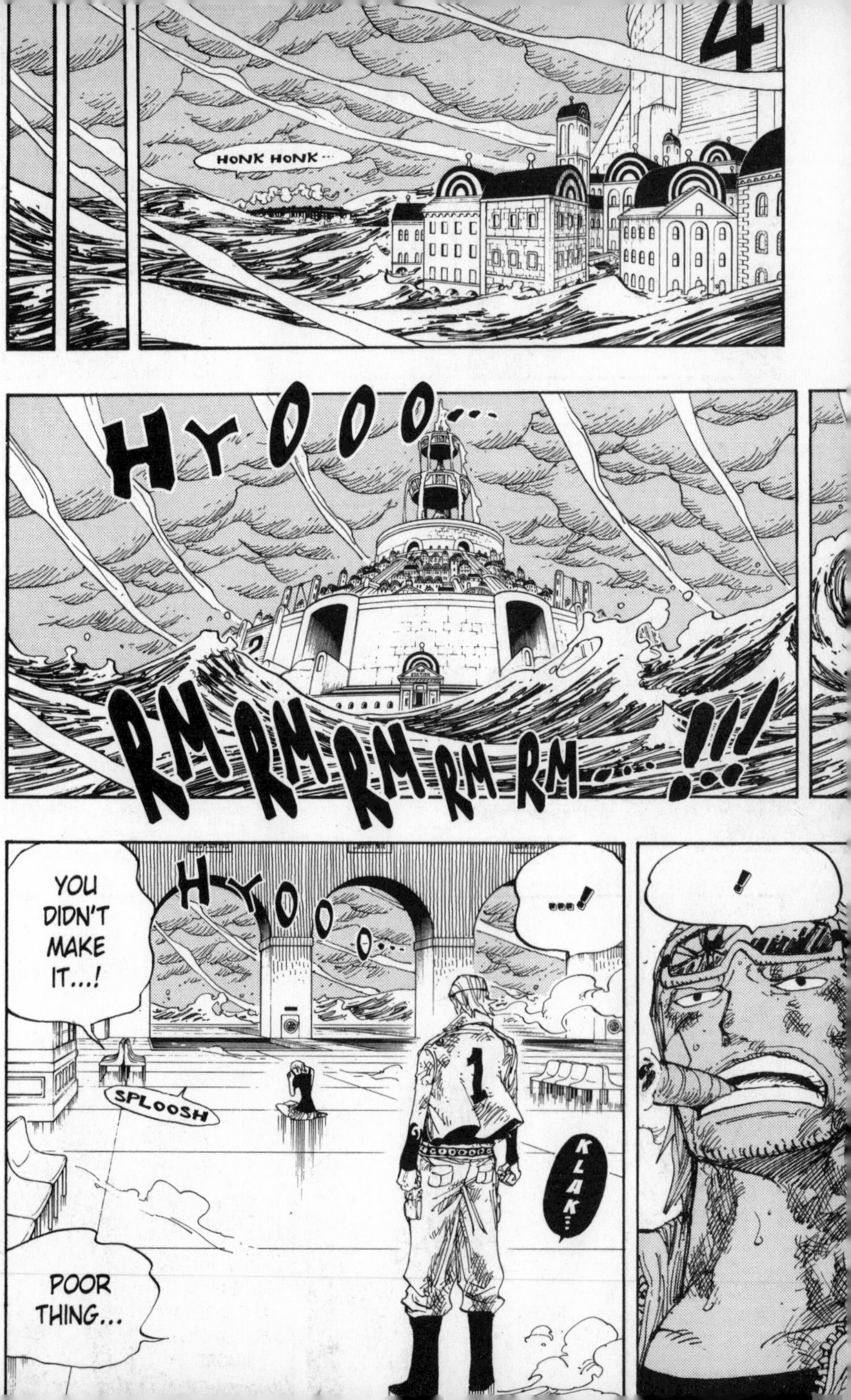

4
HONK HONK...
HYOOO...
RMRMRMRMRM...!!!
!
...!
HYOOO...
YOU DIDN'T MAKE IT...!
SPLOOSH
KLAK...
POOR THING...

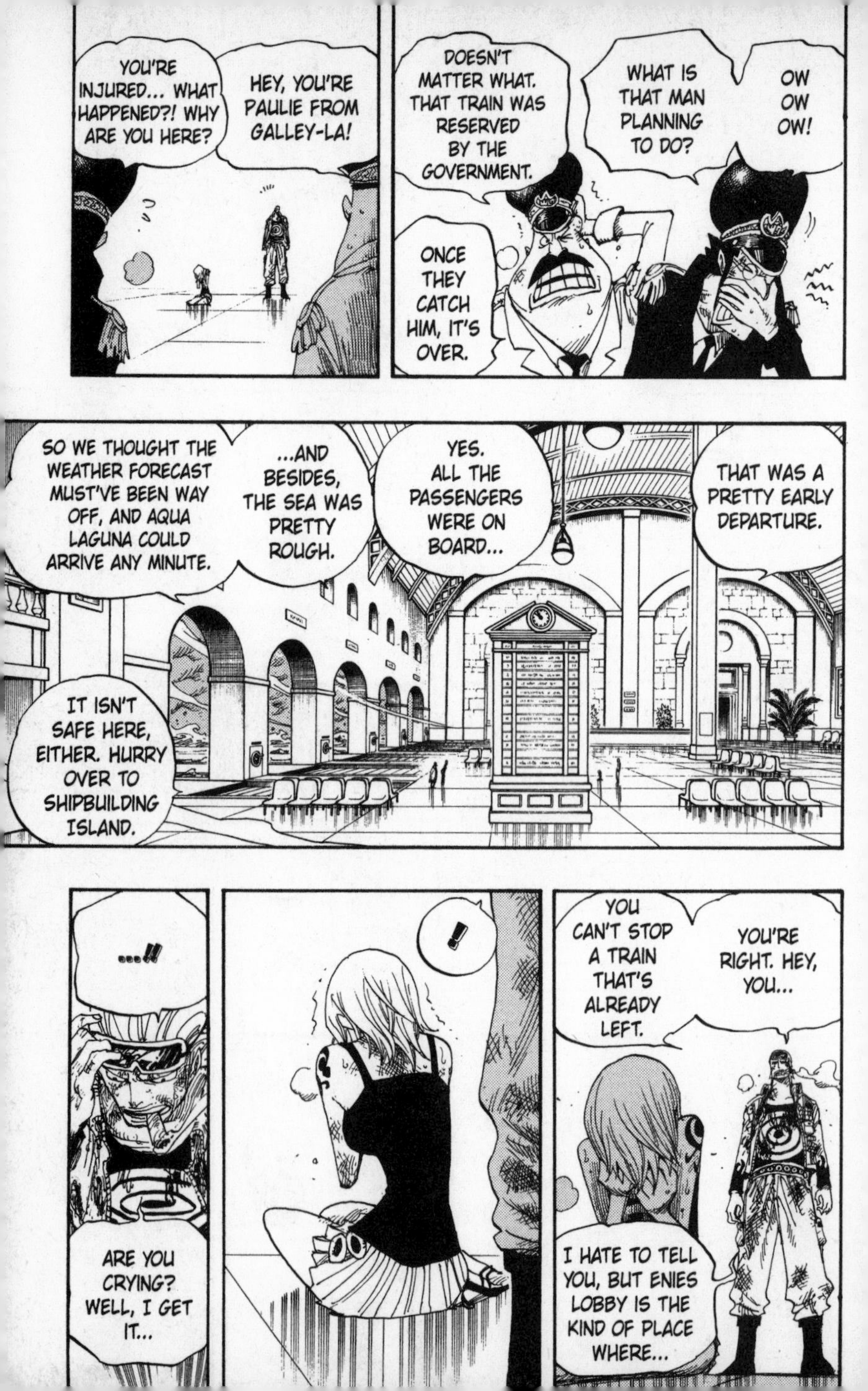
OW OW OW!
WHAT IS THAT MAN PLANNING TO DO?
DOESN'T MATTER WHAT. THAT TRAIN WAS RESERVED BY THE GOVERNMENT.
ONCE THEY CATCH HIM, IT'S OVER.
HEY, YOU'RE PAULIE FROM GALLEY-LA!
YOU'RE INJURED... WHAT HAPPENED?! WHY ARE YOU HERE?
THAT WAS A PRETTY EARLY DEPARTURE.
YES. ALL THE PASSENGERS WERE ON BOARD...
...AND BESIDES, THE SEA WAS PRETTY ROUGH.
SO WE THOUGHT THE WEATHER FORECAST MUST'VE BEEN WAY OFF, AND AQUA LAGUNA COULD ARRIVE ANY MINUTE.
IT ISN'T SAFE HERE, EITHER. HURRY OVER TO SHIPBUILDING ISLAND.
YOU CAN'T STOP A TRAIN THAT'S ALREADY LEFT.
YOU'RE RIGHT. HEY, YOU...
I HATE TO TELL YOU, BUT ENIES LOBBY IS THE KIND OF PLACE WHERE...
!
...!!
ARE YOU CRYING? WELL, I GET IT...

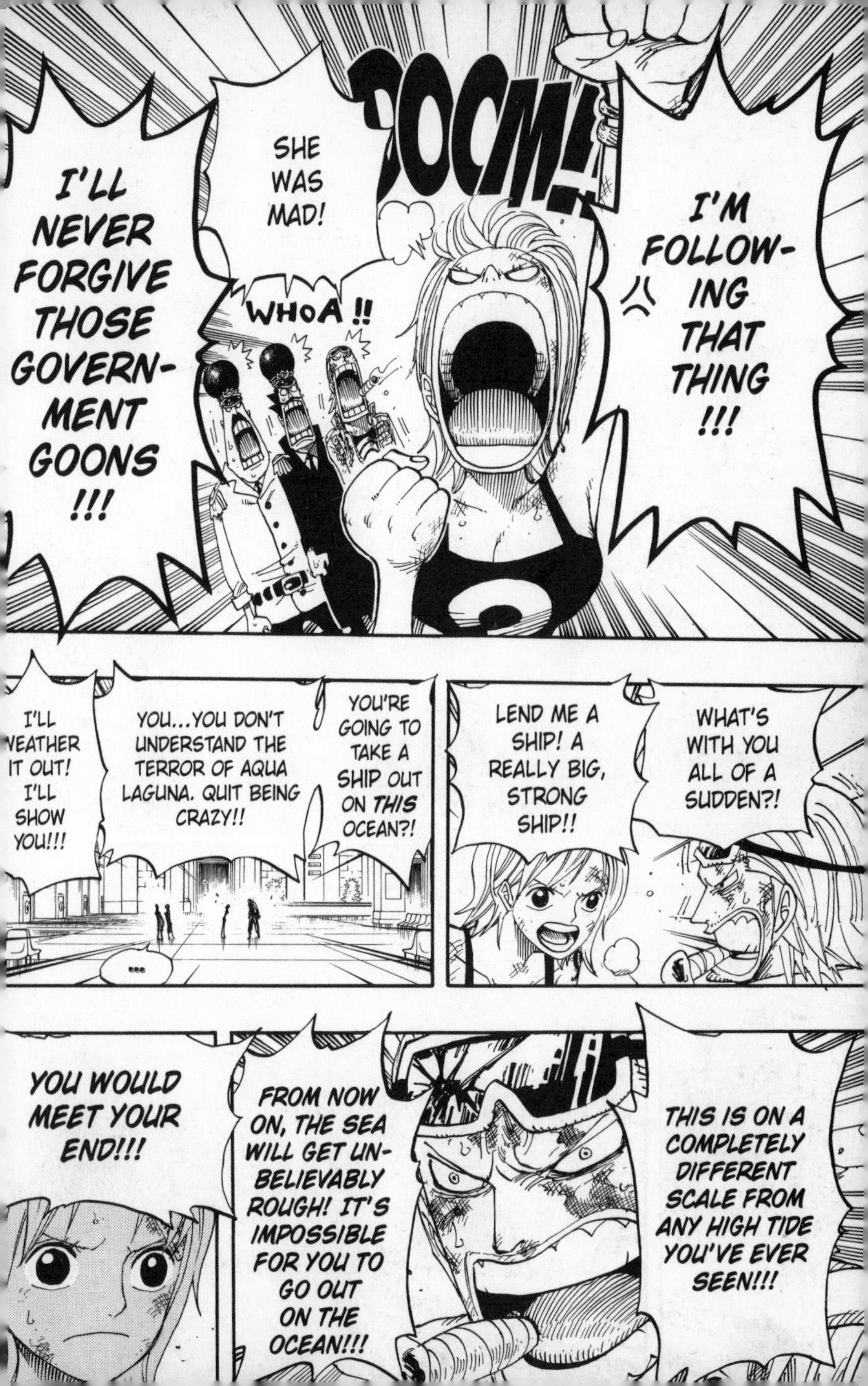

I'M FOLLOWING THAT THING!!!
DOOM!!
SHE WAS MAD!
WHOA!!
I'LL NEVER FORGIVE THOSE GOVERNMENT GOONS!!!
WHAT'S WITH YOU ALL OF A SUDDEN?!
LEND ME A SHIP! A REALLY BIG, STRONG SHIP!!
YOU'RE GOING TO TAKE A SHIP OUT ON *THIS* OCEAN?!
YOU...YOU DON'T UNDERSTAND THE TERROR OF AQUA LAGUNA. QUIT BEING CRAZY!!
I'LL WEATHER IT OUT! I'LL SHOW YOU!!!
...
THIS IS ON A COMPLETELY DIFFERENT SCALE FROM ANY HIGH TIDE YOU'VE EVER SEEN!!!
FROM NOW ON, THE SEA WILL GET UNBELIEVABLY ROUGH! IT'S IMPOSSIBLE FOR YOU TO GO OUT ON THE OCEAN!!!
YOU WOULD MEET YOUR END!!!

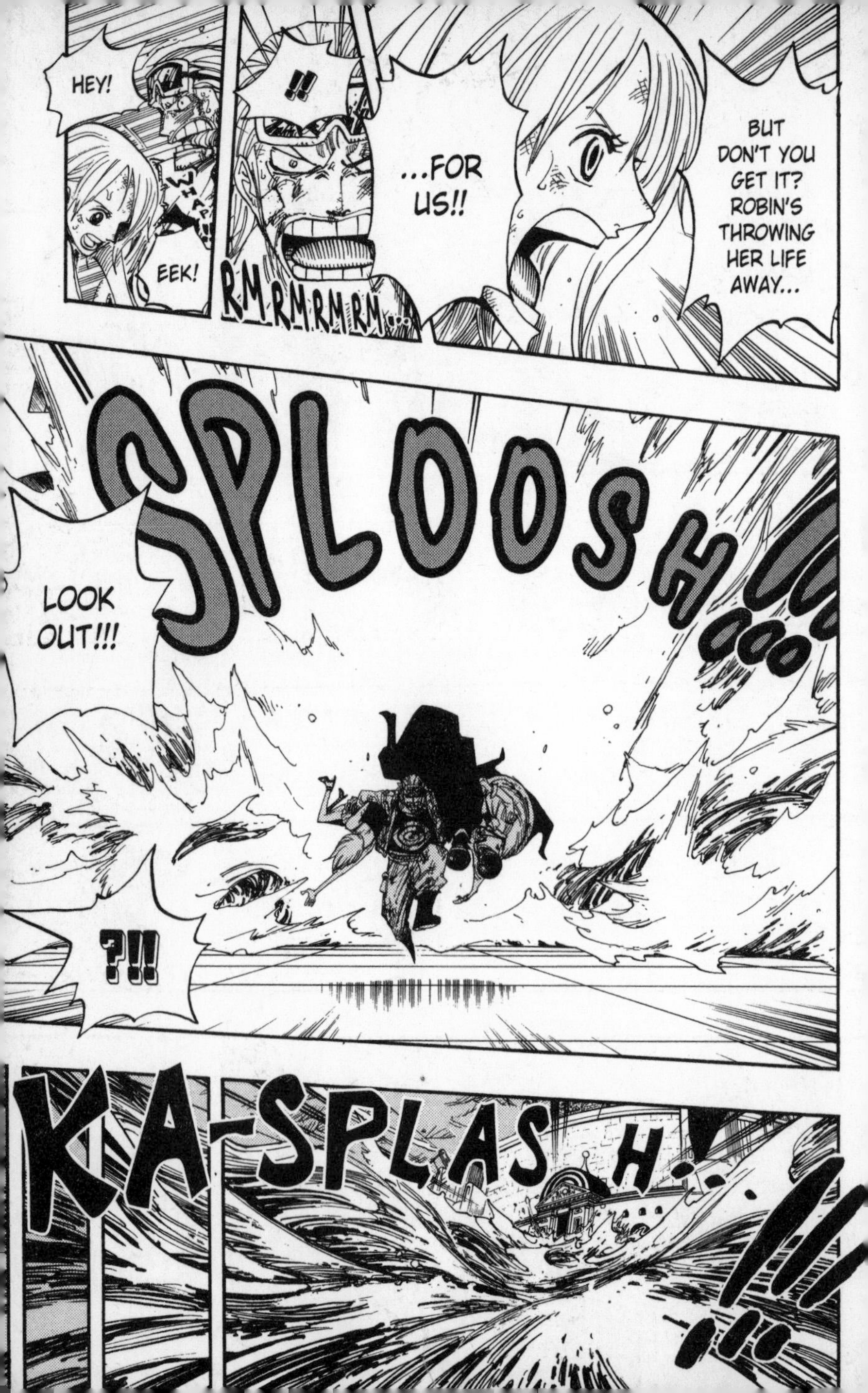
BUT DON'T YOU GET IT? ROBIN'S THROWING HER LIFE AWAY...
...FOR US!!
!!
RMRMRMRM...
HEY!
WHAP!!
EEK!
SPLOOSH...!!!
LOOK OUT!!!
?!!
KA-SPLASH...!!!

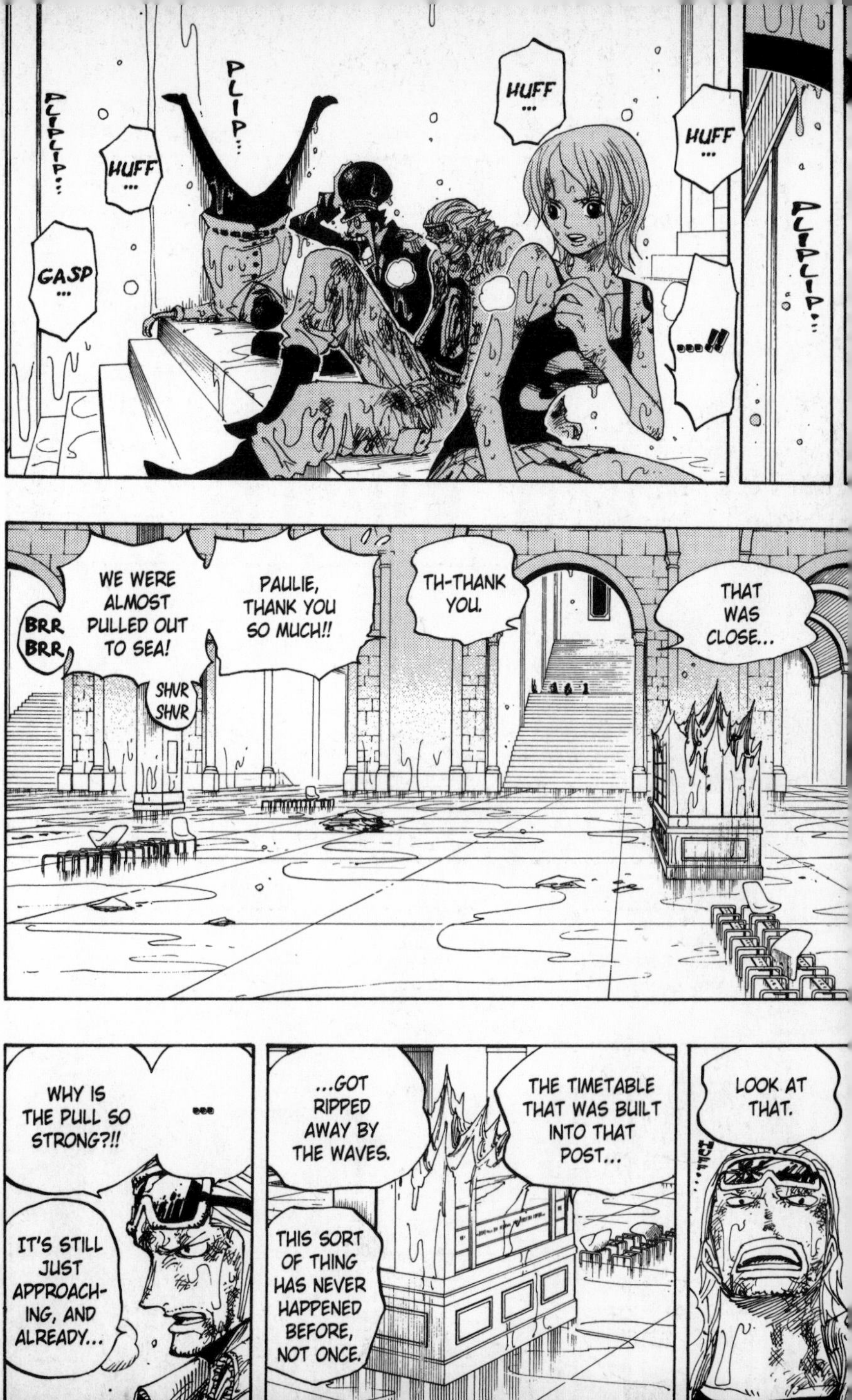
HUFF...
PLIPLIP...
HUFF...
...!!
PLIP...
PLIPLIP...
HUFF...
GASP...
THAT WAS CLOSE...
TH-THANK YOU.
PAULIE, THANK YOU SO MUCH!!
WE WERE ALMOST PULLED OUT TO SEA!
BRR BRR
SHUR SHUR
LOOK AT THAT.
HUFF...
THE TIMETABLE THAT WAS BUILT INTO THAT POST...
...GOT RIPPED AWAY BY THE WAVES.
THIS SORT OF THING HAS NEVER HAPPENED BEFORE, NOT ONCE.
...
WHY IS THE PULL SO STRONG?!!
IT'S STILL JUST APPROACHING, AND ALREADY...

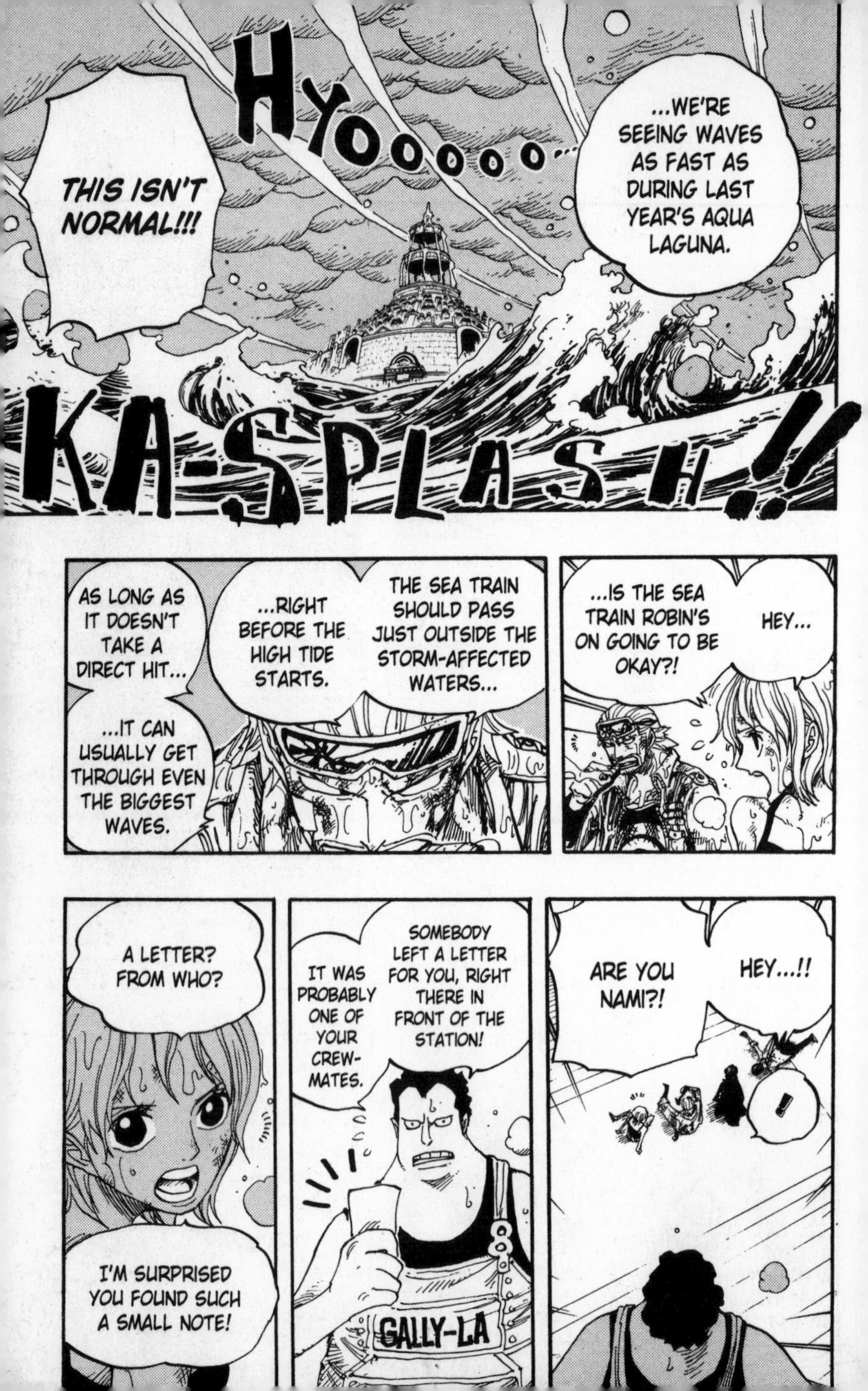
...WE'RE SEEING WAVES AS FAST AS DURING LAST YEAR'S AQUA LAGUNA.
HYOOOOO...
THIS ISN'T NORMAL!!!
KA-SPLASH!!
HEY...
...IS THE SEA TRAIN ROBIN'S ON GOING TO BE OKAY?!
THE SEA TRAIN SHOULD PASS JUST OUTSIDE THE STORM-AFFECTED WATERS...
...RIGHT BEFORE THE HIGH TIDE STARTS.
AS LONG AS IT DOESN'T TAKE A DIRECT HIT...
...IT CAN USUALLY GET THROUGH EVEN THE BIGGEST WAVES.
HEY...!!
ARE YOU NAMI?!
!
SOMEBODY LEFT A LETTER FOR YOU, RIGHT THERE IN FRONT OF THE STATION!
IT WAS PROBABLY ONE OF YOUR CREW-MATES.
GALLY-LA
A LETTER? FROM WHO?
I'M SURPRISED YOU FOUND SUCH A SMALL NOTE!

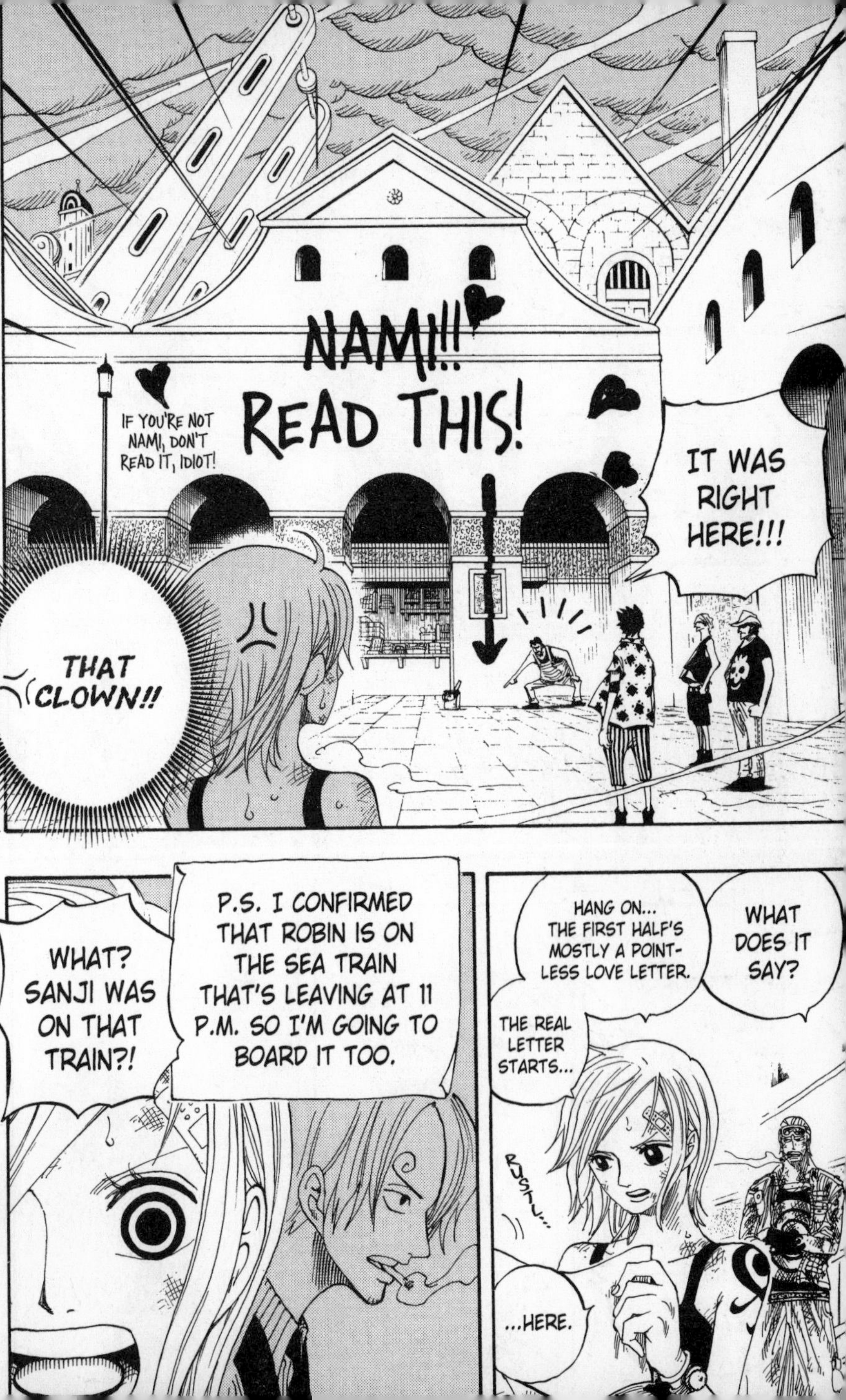
IT WAS RIGHT HERE!!!
NAMI!! READ THIS!
IF YOU'RE NOT NAMI, DON'T READ IT, IDIOT!
THAT CLOWN!!
WHAT DOES IT SAY?
HANG ON... THE FIRST HALF'S MOSTLY A POINT-LESS LOVE LETTER.
THE REAL LETTER STARTS...
RUSTL...
...HERE.
P.S. I CONFIRMED THAT ROBIN IS ON THE SEA TRAIN THAT'S LEAVING AT 11 P.M. SO I'M GOING TO BOARD IT TOO.
WHAT? SANJI WAS ON THAT TRAIN?!

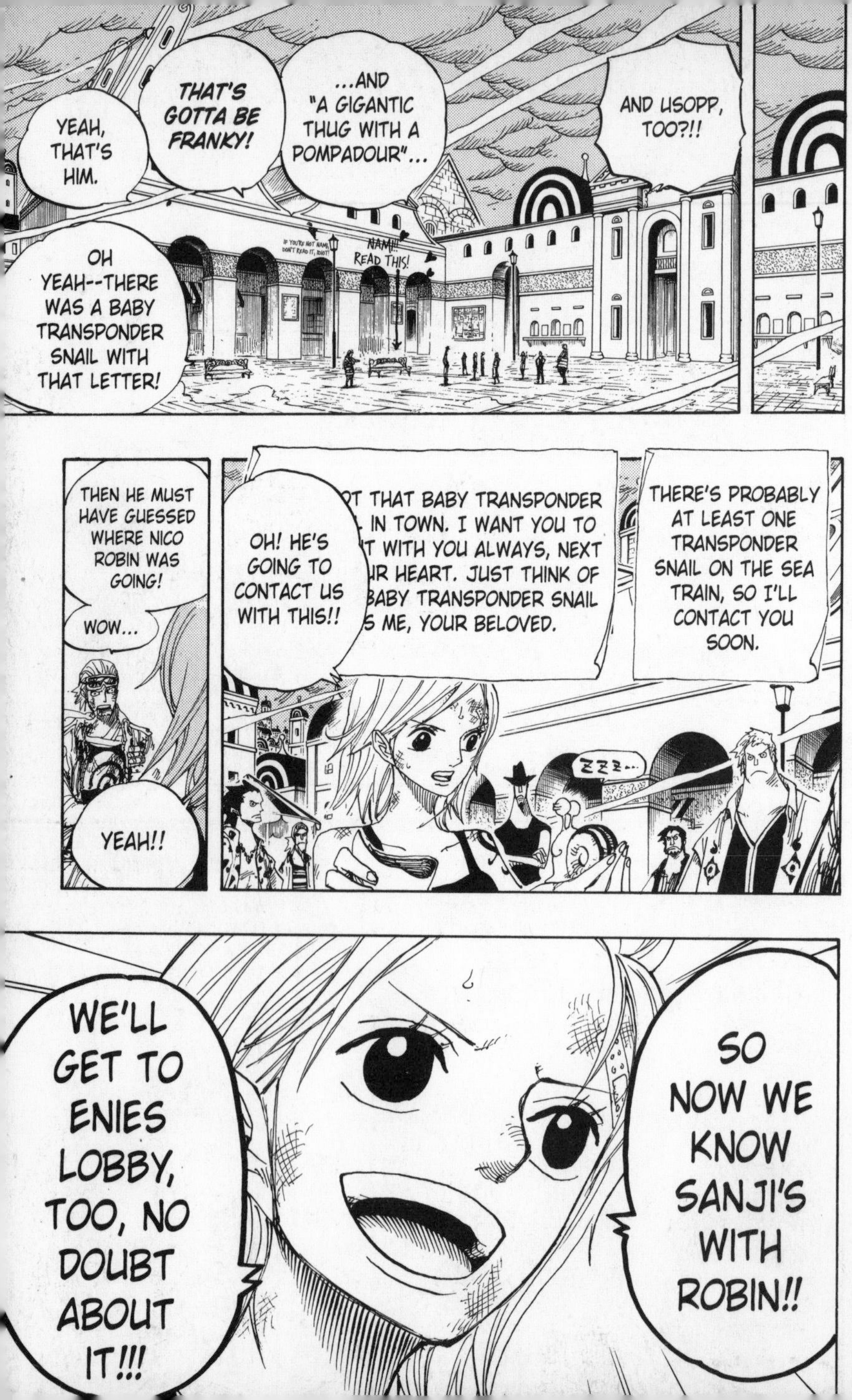
AND USOPP, TOO?!!
...AND "A GIGANTIC THUG WITH A POMPADOUR"...
THAT'S GOTTA BE FRANKY!
YEAH, THAT'S HIM.
NAMI!! READ THIS!
IF YOU'RE NOT NAMI, DON'T READ IT, IDIOT!
OH YEAH--THERE WAS A BABY TRANSPONDER SNAIL WITH THAT LETTER!
OT THAT BABY TRANSPONDER
IN TOWN. I WANT YOU TO
T WITH YOU ALWAYS, NEXT
UR HEART. JUST THINK OF
BABY TRANSPONDER SNAIL
S ME, YOUR BELOVED.
THERE'S PROBABLY AT LEAST ONE TRANSPONDER SNAIL ON THE SEA TRAIN, SO I'LL CONTACT YOU SOON.
OH! HE'S GOING TO CONTACT US WITH THIS!!
ZZZ...
THEN HE MUST HAVE GUESSED WHERE NICO ROBIN WAS GOING!
WOW...
YEAH!!
SO NOW WE KNOW SANJI'S WITH ROBIN!!
WE'LL GET TO ENIES LOBBY, TOO, NO DOUBT ABOUT IT!!!

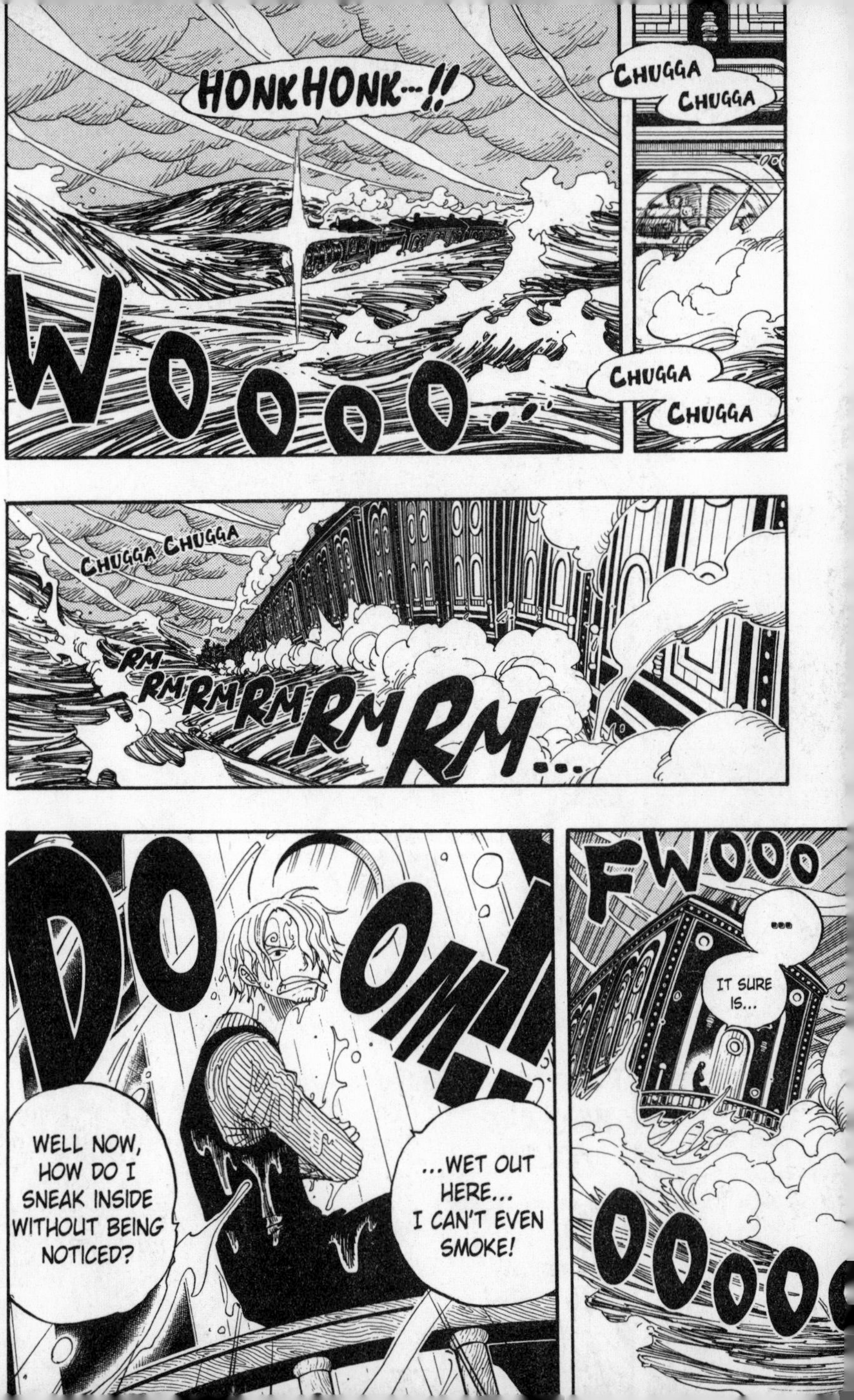
CHUGGA CHUGGA
CHUGGA CHUGGA
HONKHONK...!!
WOOOOO...
CHUGGA CHUGGA
RM RM RM RM RMRM...
FWOOO
...
IT SURE IS...
OOOOO
DOOM!!
...WET OUT HERE... I CAN'T EVEN SMOKE!
WELL NOW, HOW DO I SNEAK INSIDE WITHOUT BEING NOTICED?

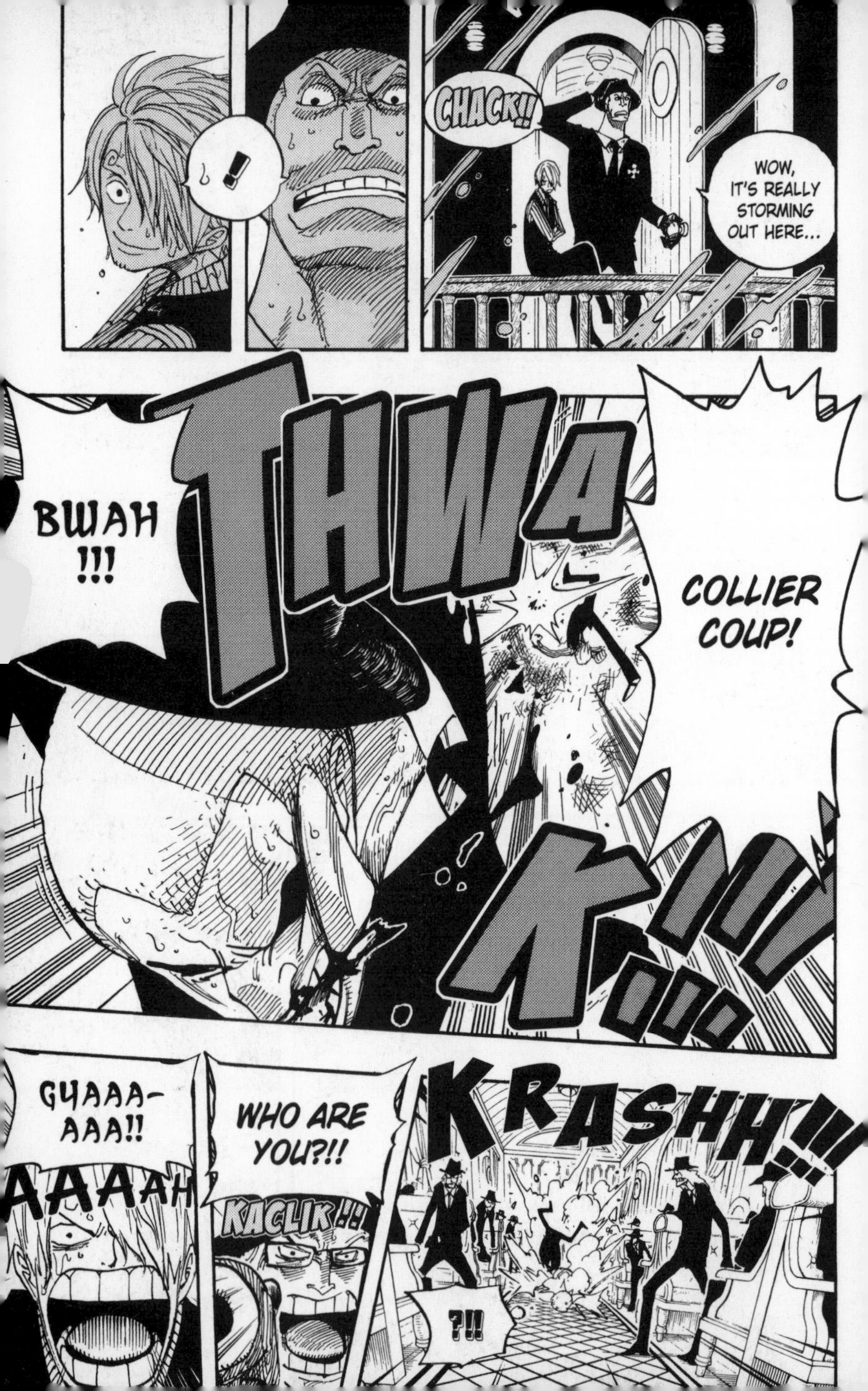
CHACK!!
WOW, IT'S REALLY STORMING OUT HERE...
!
COLLIER COUP!
THWACK!!!
BWAH !!!
KRASHH!!!
?!!
WHO ARE YOU?!!
KACLIK!!
GYAAA-AAA!!
AAAAAH

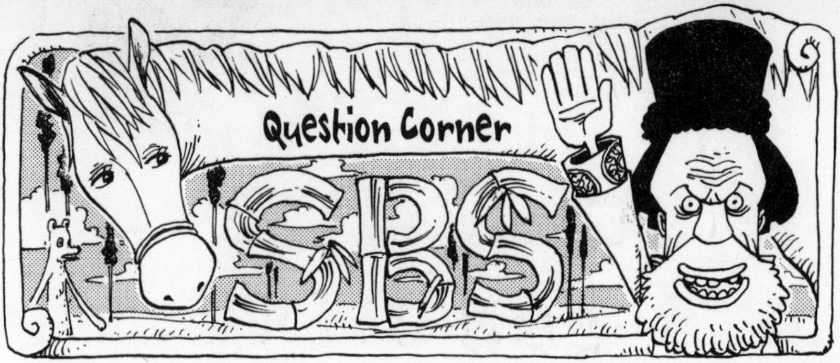
Question Corner
SBS

Reader: Oda Sensei, hello! I noticed this a while ago when I was watching the subtitles on a pirate movie on DVD: the actors said "go to Davy Jones's locker," when the subtitles were saying something like "drown at sea." But were they referring to the Davy from "Davy Back"?! Was Davy Jones an actual pirate? Please tell me.

--Tadokoro

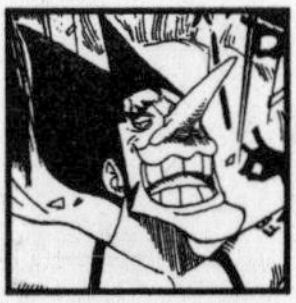

DAVY JONES

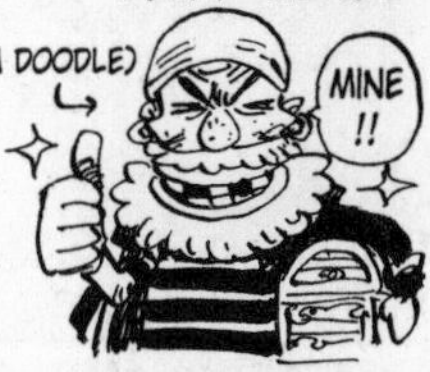
(RANDOM DOODLE)
MINE !!

Oda: Hmm, to start with, the words "Davy Back" don't exist even in legend. The DBF (Davy Back Fight) is a game that exists only in the world of One Piece. But as for Davy Jones's Locker, it's a legend that's been famous among sailors for a long, long time. (Nico Robin also told the story in vol. 33.) There are several different versions, but basically it goes like this: There once was a lying, no-good pirate named Davy Jones. He was a greedy fellow famous for shutting his crewmates' belongings and treasure and such into his own locker. Even for a pirate he was a bad guy, and one day the devil cursed him to live forever on the ocean floor. Since that time, whenever ships, sailors or treasure sink into the sea, they end up shut in his locker on the ocean floor, and never seen again. That's the legend.
Example of usage among pirates: "Let's throw 'im into Davy Jones's Locker!"
Meaning: "Let's kill him by sinking him in the deep sea!"

Chapter 362:
EBB TIDE

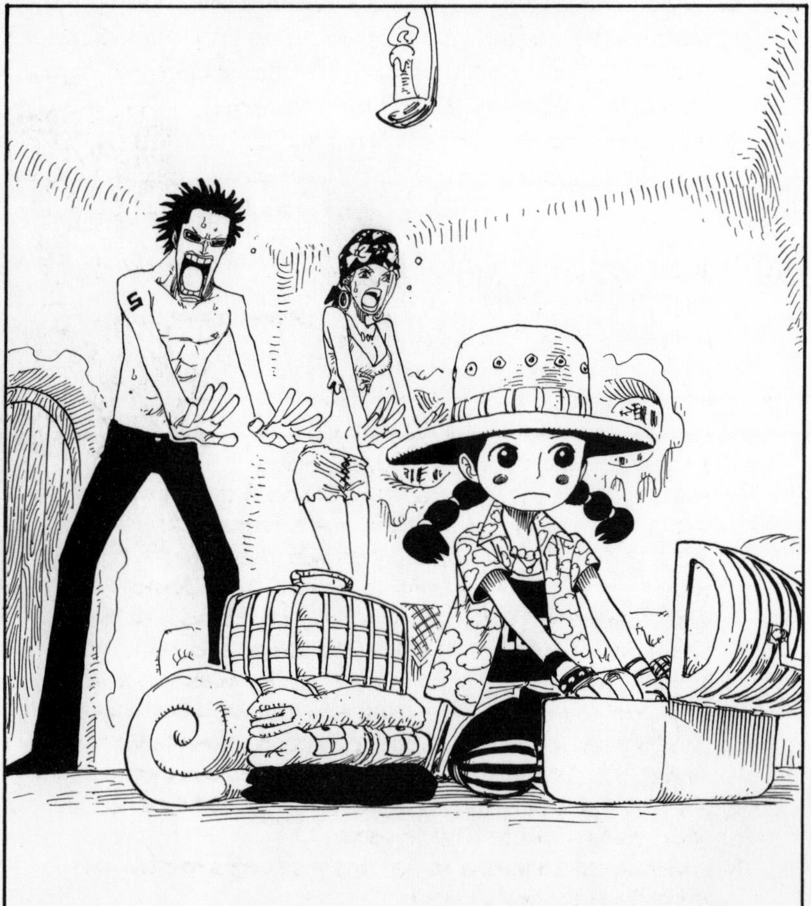

MS. GOLDEN WEEK'S BIG PLAN, A BAROQUE REUNION, VOL. 4:
"LET'S GO TO THE PRISON"

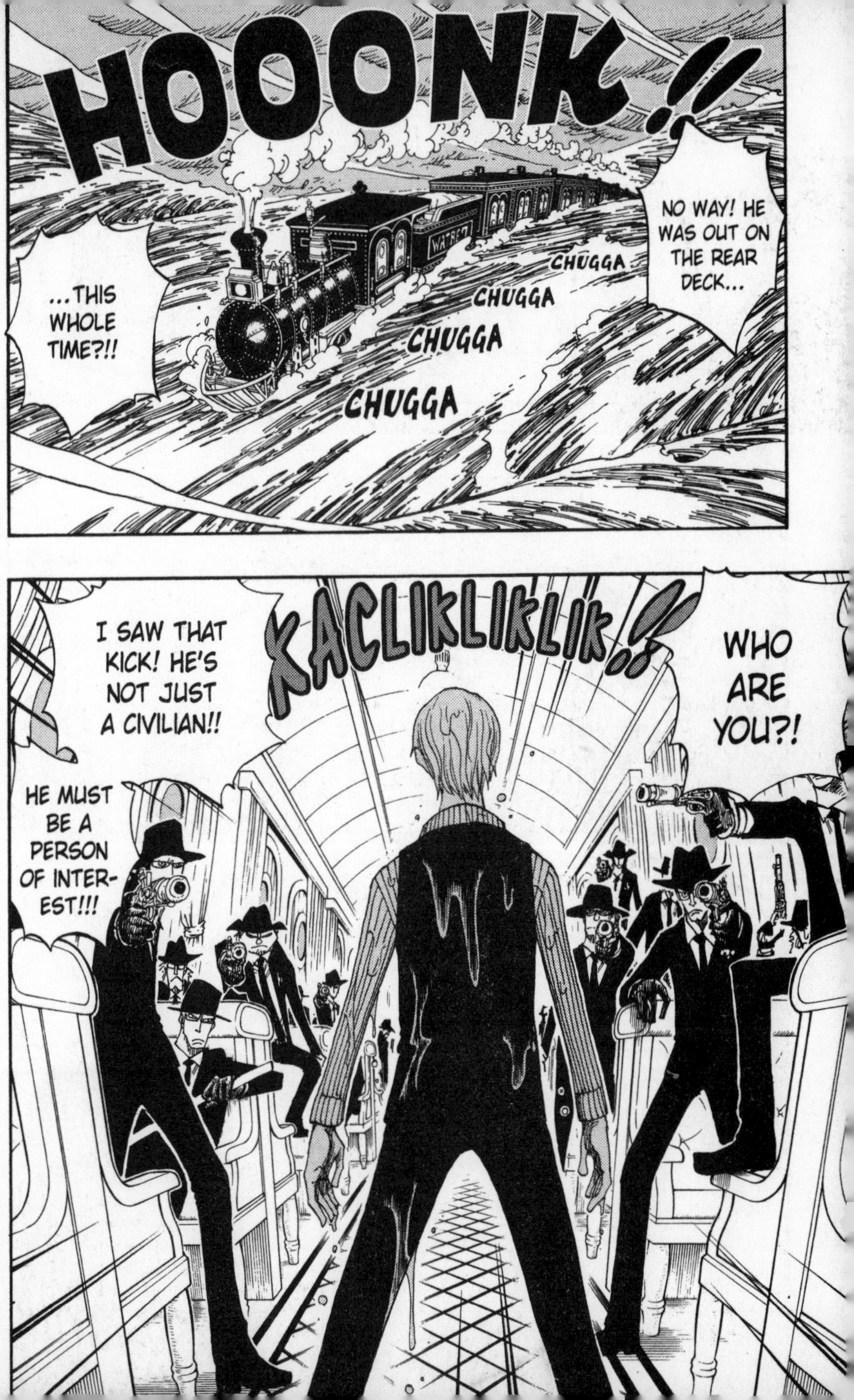
HOOONK!!
NO WAY! HE WAS OUT ON THE REAR DECK...
...THIS WHOLE TIME?!!
CHUGGA
CHUGGA
CHUGGA
CHUGGA
WHO ARE YOU?!
KACLIKLIKLIK!!
I SAW THAT KICK! HE'S NOT JUST A CIVILIAN!!
HE MUST BE A PERSON OF INTER-EST!!!

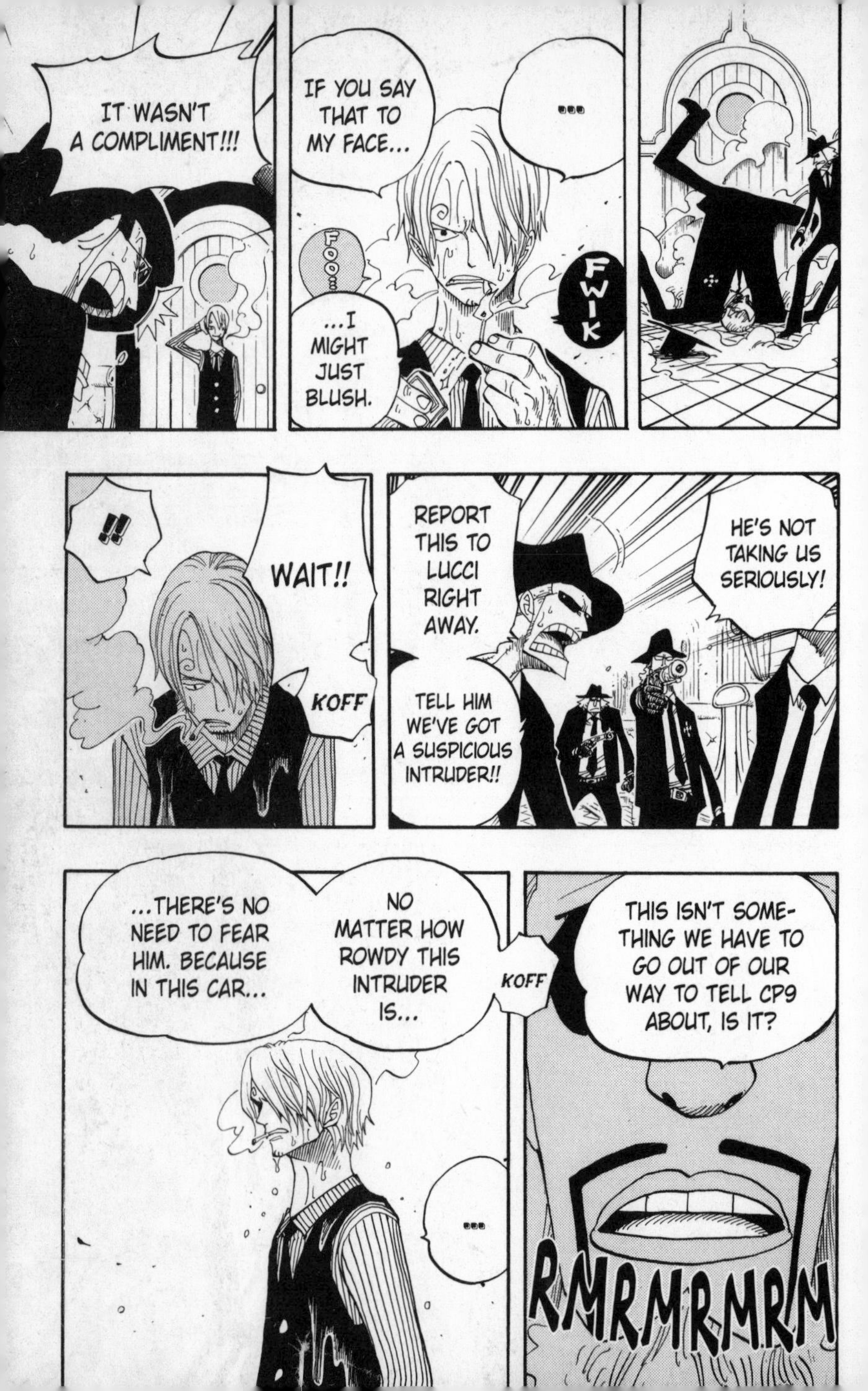
...
IF YOU SAY THAT TO MY FACE...
FWIK
FOO...
...I MIGHT JUST BLUSH.
IT WASN'T A COMPLIMENT!!!
HE'S NOT TAKING US SERIOUSLY!
REPORT THIS TO LUCCI RIGHT AWAY.
TELL HIM WE'VE GOT A SUSPICIOUS INTRUDER!!
WAIT!!
!!
KOFF
THIS ISN'T SOME-THING WE HAVE TO GO OUT OF OUR WAY TO TELL CP9 ABOUT, IS IT?
RMRMRMRM
KOFF
NO MATTER HOW ROWDY THIS INTRUDER IS...
...THERE'S NO NEED TO FEAR HIM. BECAUSE IN THIS CAR...
...

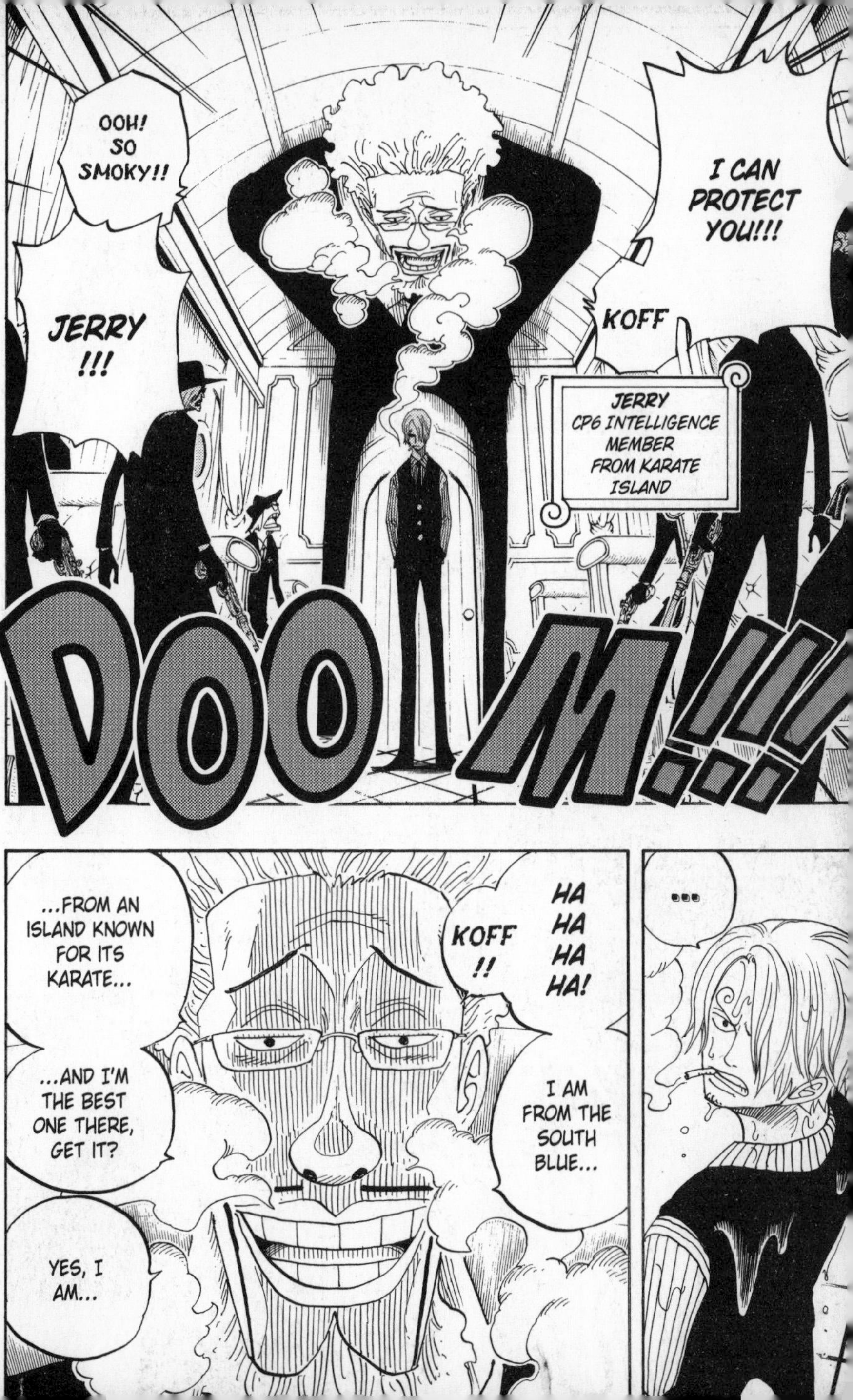
I CAN PROTECT YOU!!!
OOH! SO SMOKY!!
KOFF
JERRY !!!
JERRY
CP6 INTELLIGENCE
MEMBER
FROM KARATE
ISLAND
DOOM!!!
...
HA HA HA HA!
KOFF !!
I AM FROM THE SOUTH BLUE...
...FROM AN ISLAND KNOWN FOR ITS KARATE...
...AND I'M THE BEST ONE THERE, GET IT?
YES, I AM...

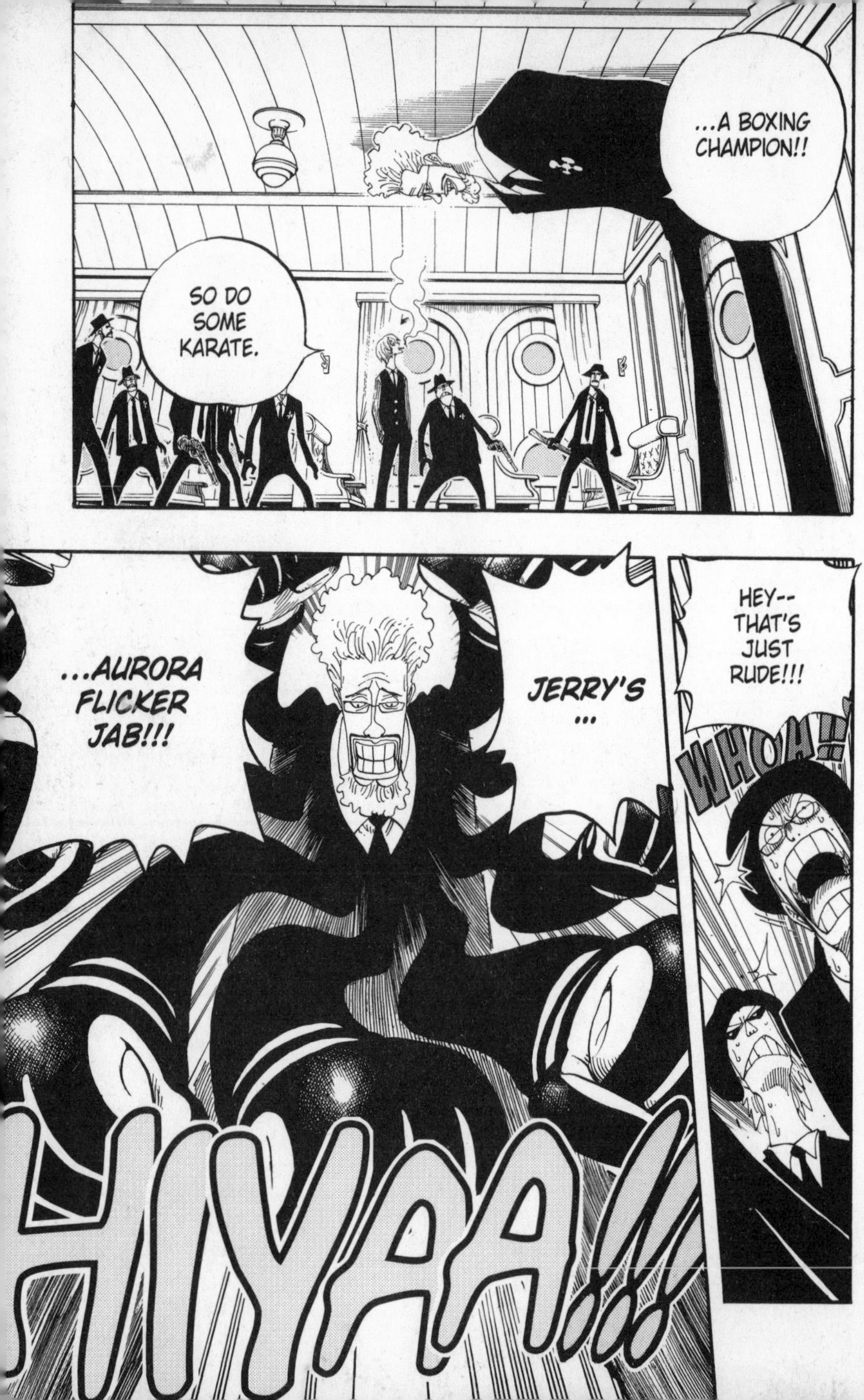
...A BOXING CHAMPION!!
SO DO SOME KARATE.
HEY-- THAT'S JUST RUDE!!!
WHOA!!
JERRY'S ...
...AURORA FLICKER JAB!!!
HIYAA!!

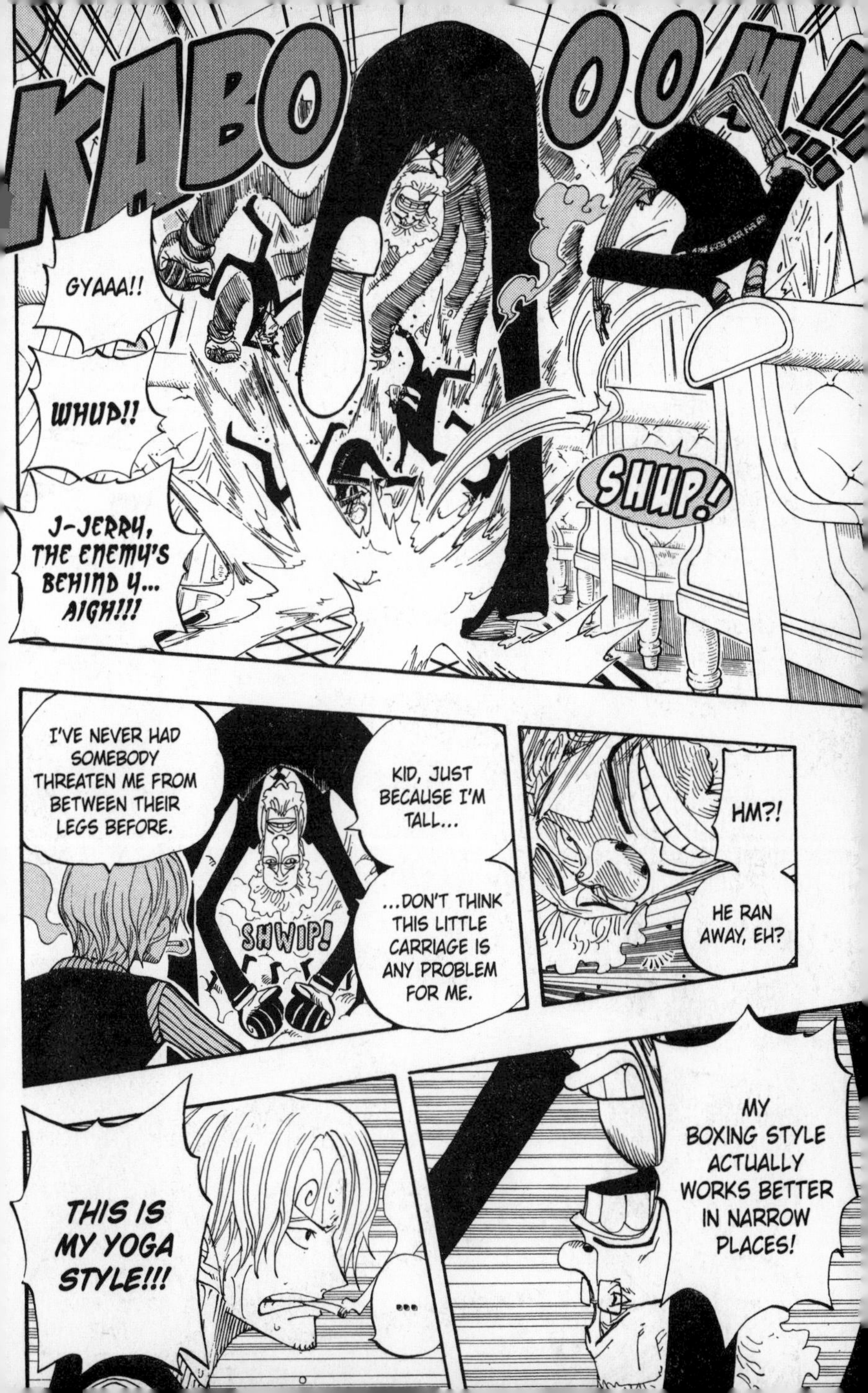
KABOOOM!!
SHUP!
GYAAA!!
WHUP!!
J-JERRY, THE ENEMY'S BEHIND Y... AIGH!!!
HM?!
HE RAN AWAY, EH?
KID, JUST BECAUSE I'M TALL...
...DON'T THINK THIS LITTLE CARRIAGE IS ANY PROBLEM FOR ME.
SHWIP!
I'VE NEVER HAD SOMEBODY THREATEN ME FROM BETWEEN THEIR LEGS BEFORE.
MY BOXING STYLE ACTUALLY WORKS BETTER IN NARROW PLACES!
THIS IS MY YOGA STYLE!!!
...

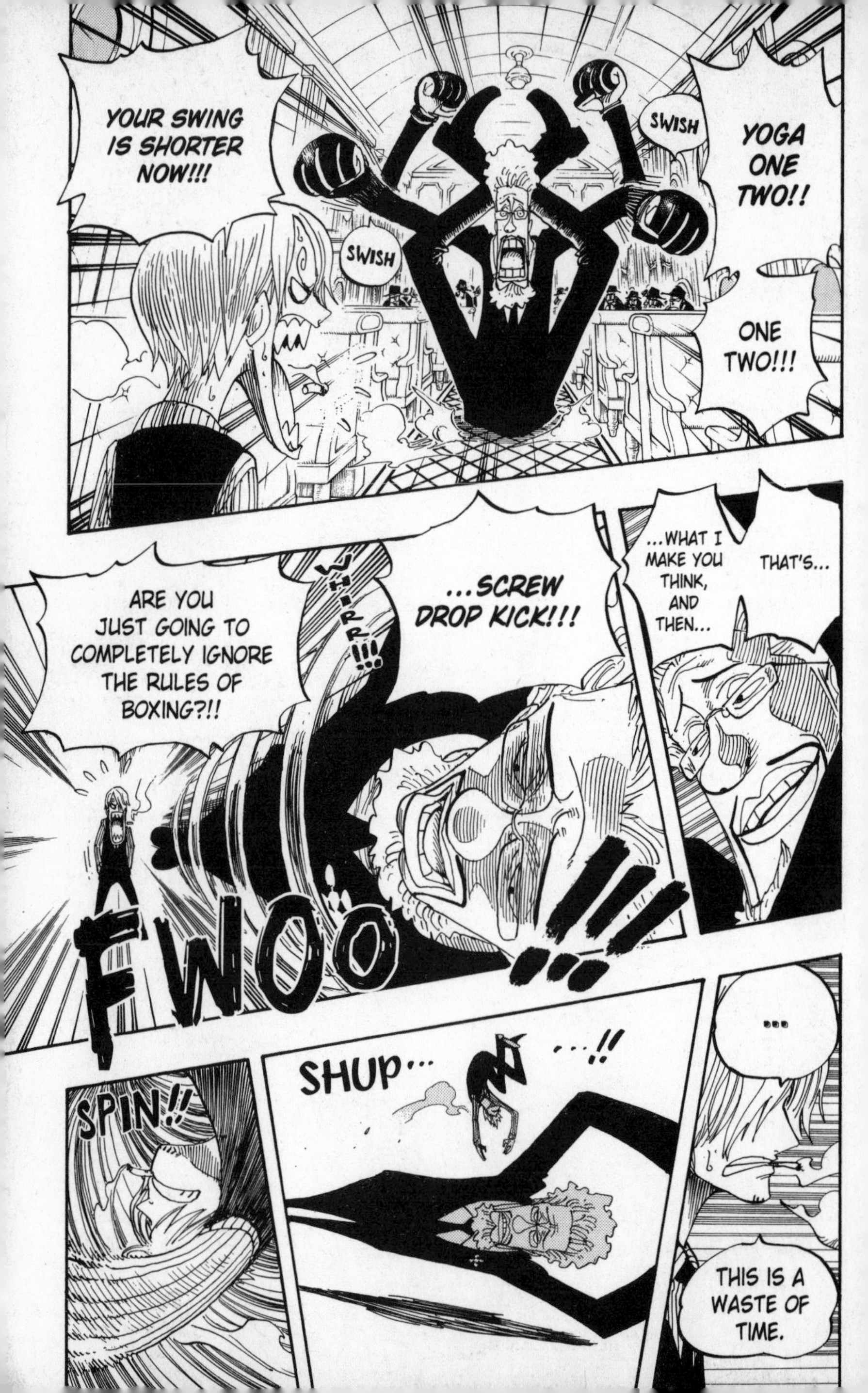

YOGA ONE TWO!!
SWISH
YOUR SWING IS SHORTER NOW!!!
SWISH
ONE TWO!!!
THAT'S...
...WHAT I MAKE YOU THINK, AND THEN...
...SCREW DROP KICK!!!
WHIRR!!!
ARE YOU JUST GOING TO COMPLETELY IGNORE THE RULES OF BOXING?!!
FWOO!!!
...
THIS IS A WASTE OF TIME.
...!!
SHUP...
SPIN!!

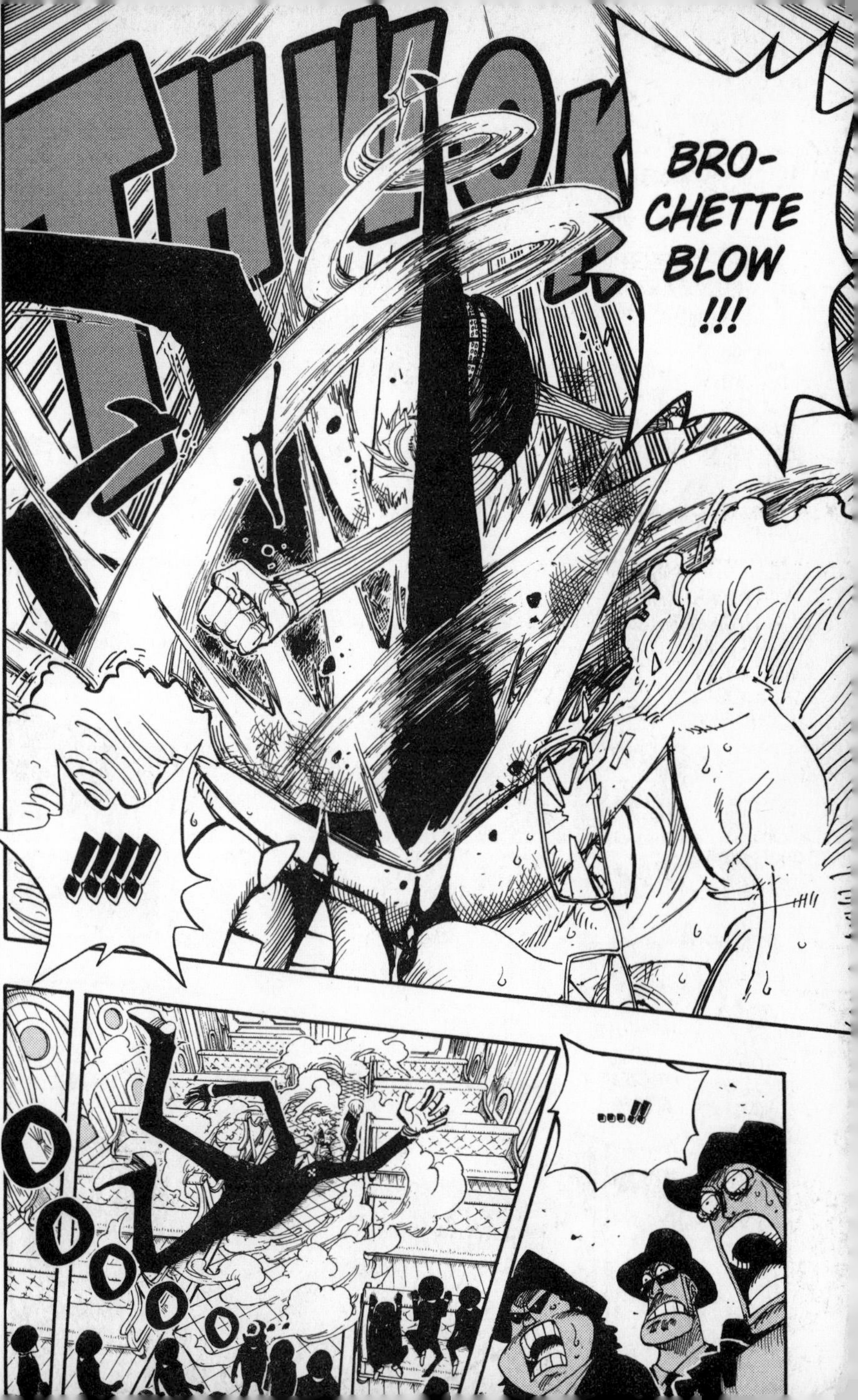
BRO-
CHETTE
BLOW
!!!
THWOK
!!!!
...!!

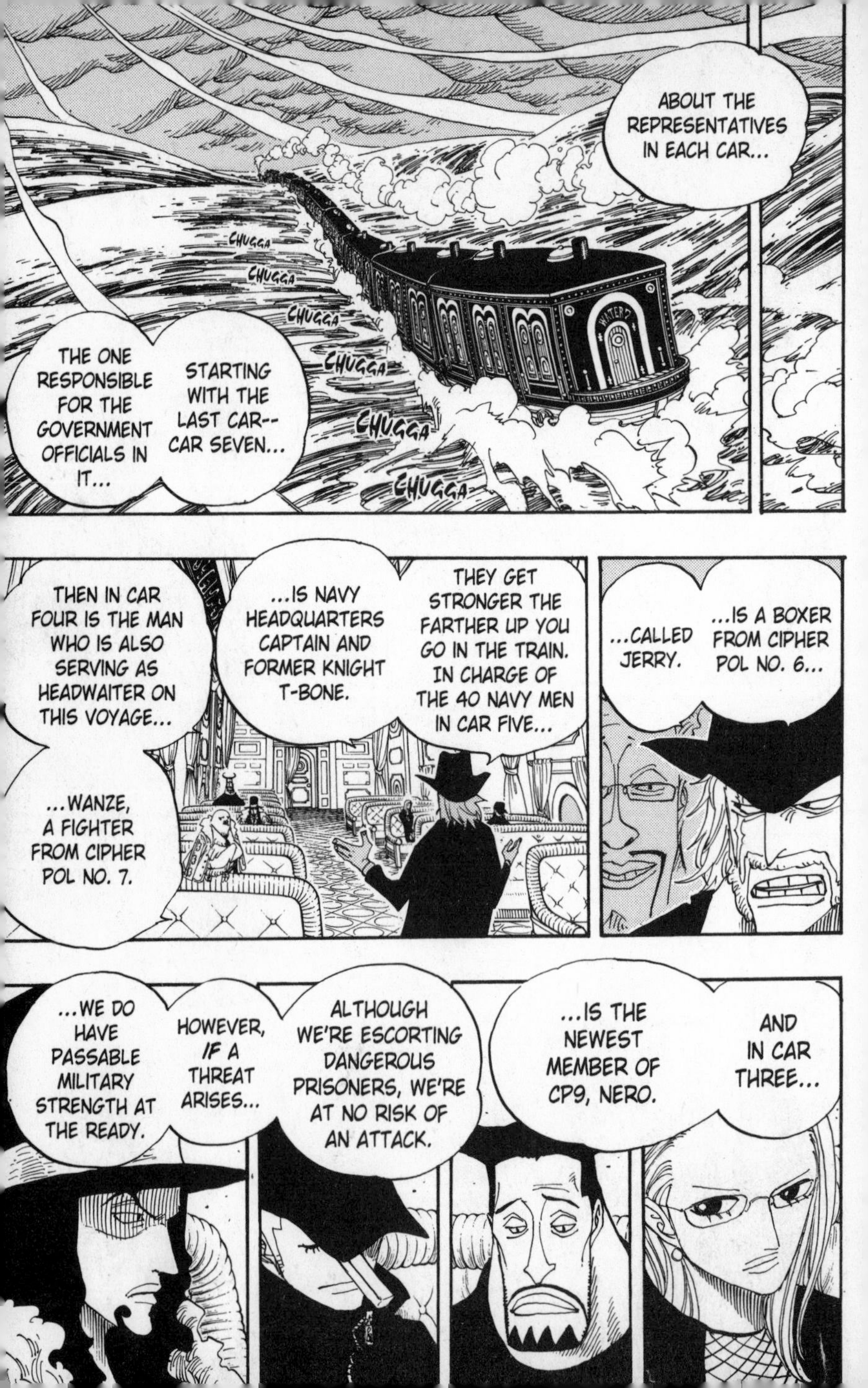
ABOUT THE REPRESENTATIVES IN EACH CAR...
CHUGGA
CHUGGA
CHUGGA
CHUGGA
CHUGGA
CHUGGA
STARTING WITH THE LAST CAR-- CAR SEVEN...
THE ONE RESPONSIBLE FOR THE GOVERNMENT OFFICIALS IN IT...
...IS A BOXER FROM CIPHER POL NO. 6...
...CALLED JERRY.
THEY GET STRONGER THE FARTHER UP YOU GO IN THE TRAIN. IN CHARGE OF THE 40 NAVY MEN IN CAR FIVE...
...IS NAVY HEADQUARTERS CAPTAIN AND FORMER KNIGHT T-BONE.
THEN IN CAR FOUR IS THE MAN WHO IS ALSO SERVING AS HEADWAITER ON THIS VOYAGE...
...WANZE, A FIGHTER FROM CIPHER POL NO. 7.
AND IN CAR THREE...
...IS THE NEWEST MEMBER OF CP9, NERO.
ALTHOUGH WE'RE ESCORTING DANGEROUS PRISONERS, WE'RE AT NO RISK OF AN ATTACK.
HOWEVER, *IF* A THREAT ARISES...
...WE DO HAVE PASSABLE MILITARY STRENGTH AT THE READY.

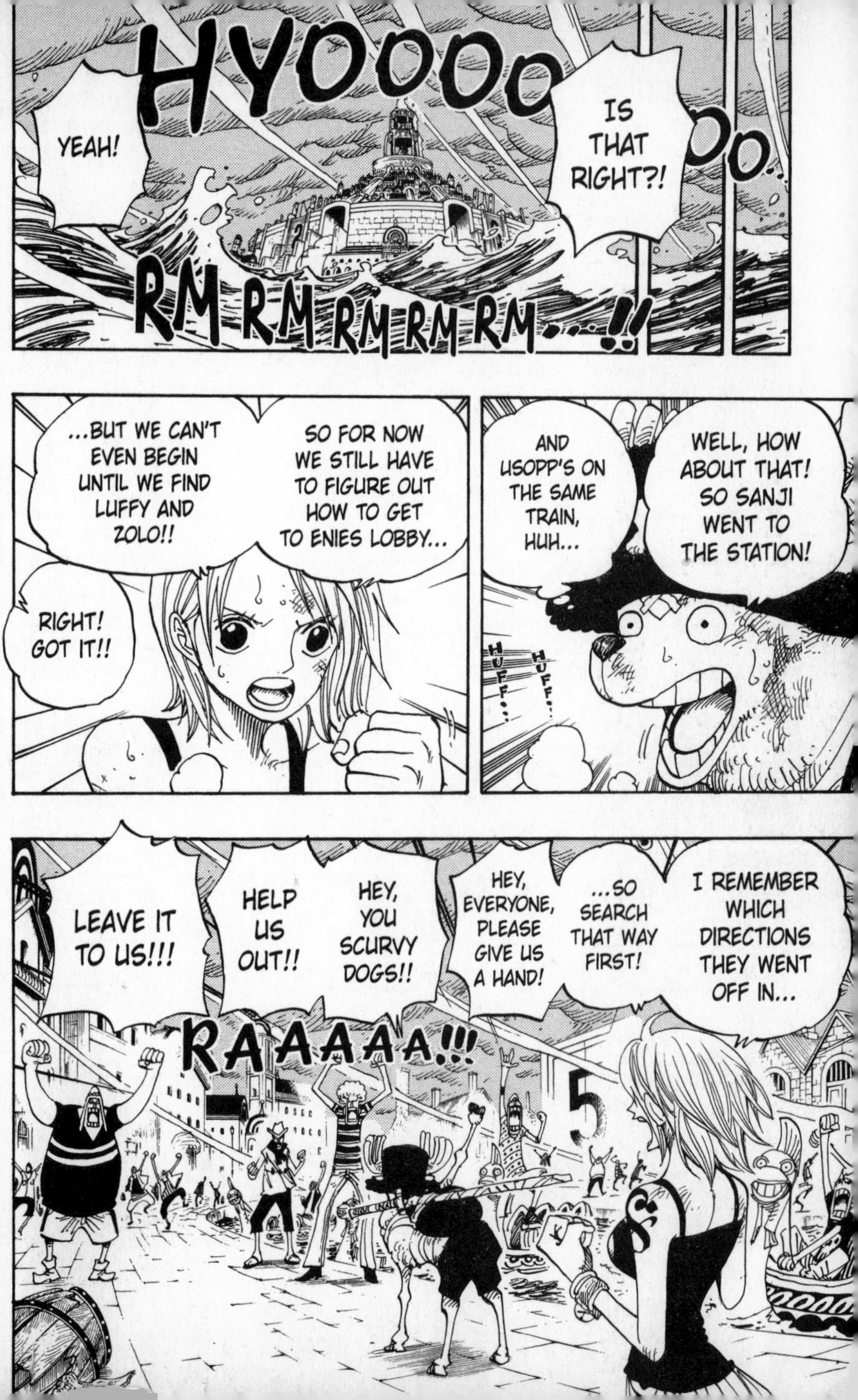
HYOOOOOO...
IS THAT RIGHT?!
YEAH!
RM RM RM RM RM...!!
WELL, HOW ABOUT THAT! SO SANJI WENT TO THE STATION!
AND USOPP'S ON THE SAME TRAIN, HUH...
HUFF...
HUFF...
SO FOR NOW WE STILL HAVE TO FIGURE OUT HOW TO GET TO ENIES LOBBY...
...BUT WE CAN'T EVEN BEGIN UNTIL WE FIND LUFFY AND ZOLO!!
RIGHT! GOT IT!!
I REMEMBER WHICH DIRECTIONS THEY WENT OFF IN...
...SO SEARCH THAT WAY FIRST!
HEY, EVERYONE, PLEASE GIVE US A HAND!
HEY, YOU SCURVY DOGS!!
HELP US OUT!!
LEAVE IT TO US!!!
RAAAAA!!!
5

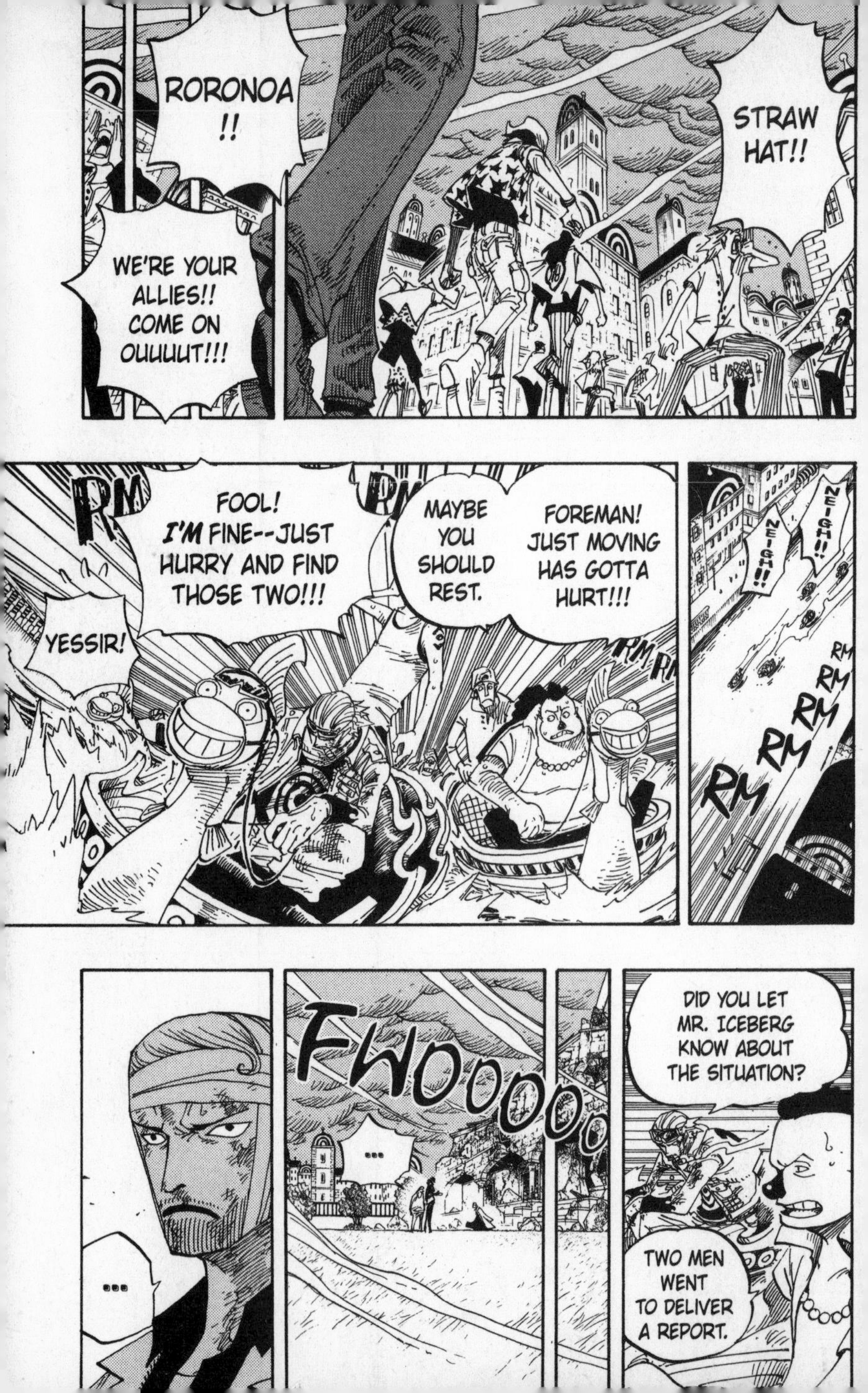
STRAW HAT!!
RORONOA !!
WE'RE YOUR ALLIES!! COME ON OUUUUT!!!
NEIGH!!
NEIGH!!
RM RM RM RM RM
FOREMAN! JUST MOVING HAS GOTTA HURT!!!
MAYBE YOU SHOULD REST.
RM RM
FOOL! *I'M* FINE--JUST HURRY AND FIND THOSE TWO!!!
RM
YESSIR!
RM
DID YOU LET MR. ICEBERG KNOW ABOUT THE SITUATION?
TWO MEN WENT TO DELIVER A REPORT.
FWOOOOOO
...
...

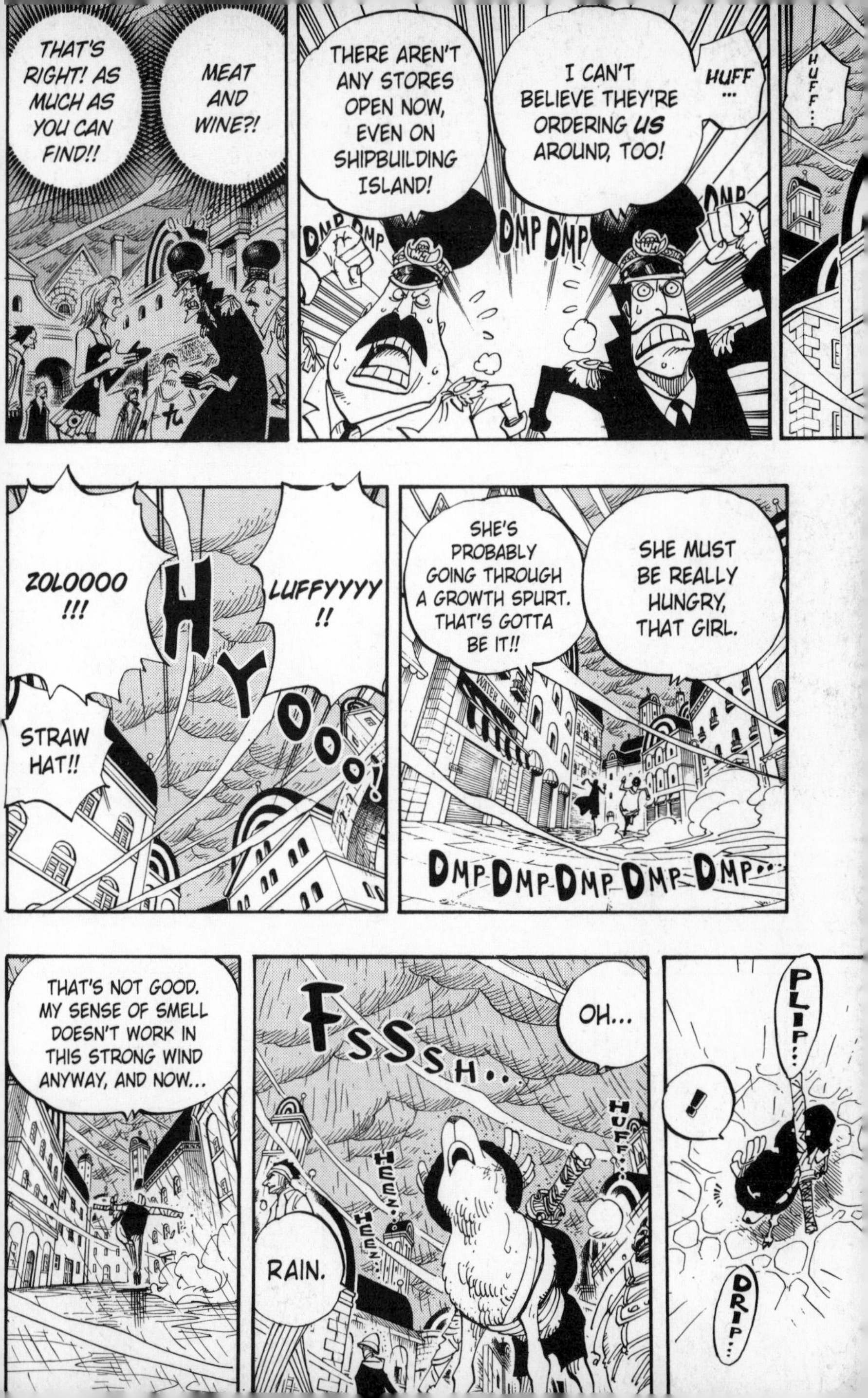
HUFF...
HUFF...
I CAN'T BELIEVE THEY'RE ORDERING US AROUND, TOO!
THERE AREN'T ANY STORES OPEN NOW, EVEN ON SHIPBUILDING ISLAND!
DMP
DMP DMP
DMP DMP
MEAT AND WINE?!
THAT'S RIGHT! AS MUCH AS YOU CAN FIND!!
SHE MUST BE REALLY HUNGRY, THAT GIRL.
SHE'S PROBABLY GOING THROUGH A GROWTH SPURT. THAT'S GOTTA BE IT!!
DMP DMP DMP DMP DMP...
LUFFYYYY !!
HYOOO!
ZOLOOOO !!!
STRAW HAT!!
PLIP...
!
DRIP...
OH...
FSSSH..
HUFF...
HEEZ...
HEEZ...
RAIN.
THAT'S NOT GOOD. MY SENSE OF SMELL DOESN'T WORK IN THIS STRONG WIND ANYWAY, AND NOW...

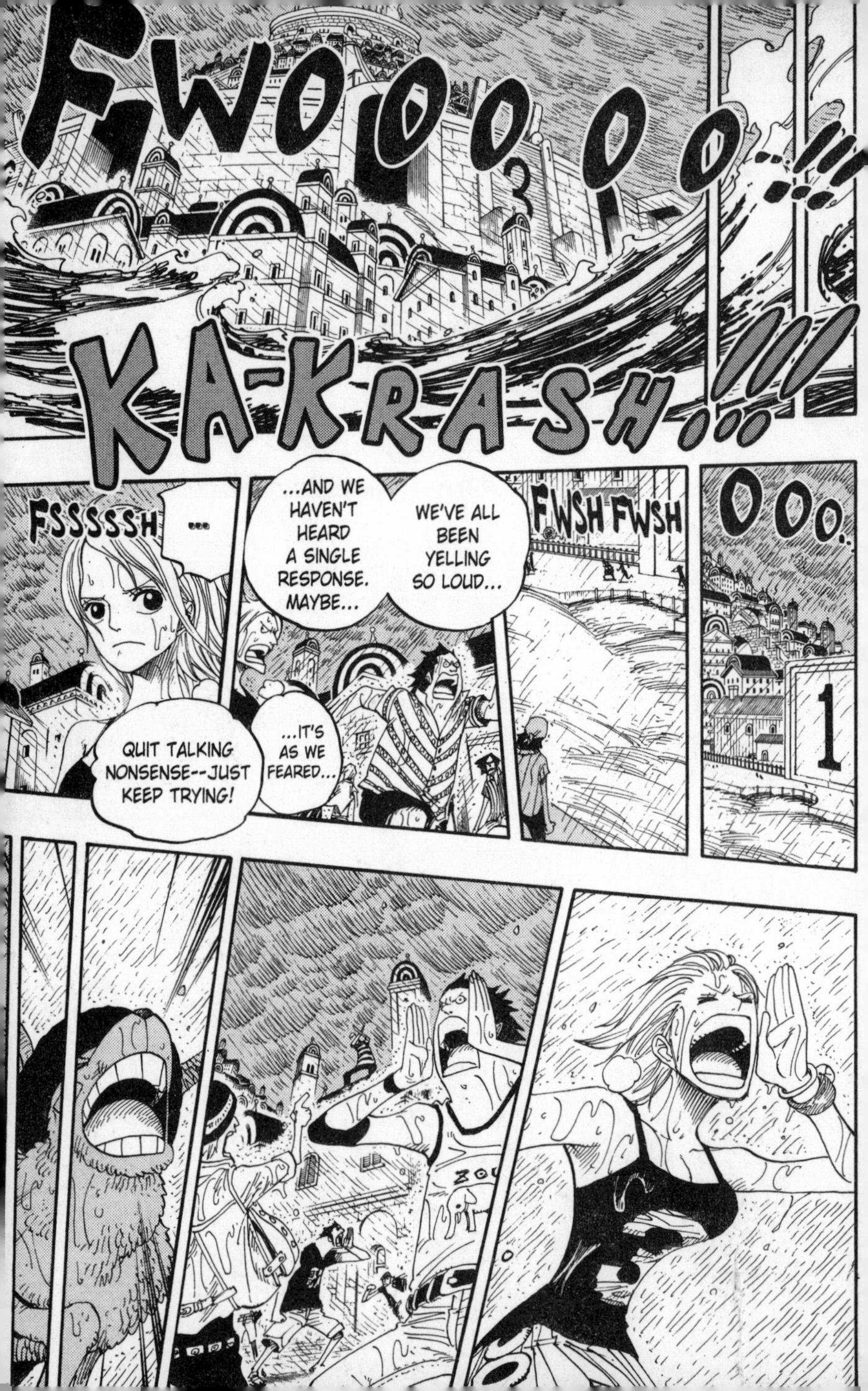
FWOOOOO...!!!
KA-KRASH...!!!
OOO..
1
FWSH FWSH
WE'VE ALL BEEN YELLING SO LOUD...
...AND WE HAVEN'T HEARD A SINGLE RESPONSE. MAYBE...
...IT'S AS WE FEARED...
FSSSSSH
...
QUIT TALKING NONSENSE--JUST KEEP TRYING!

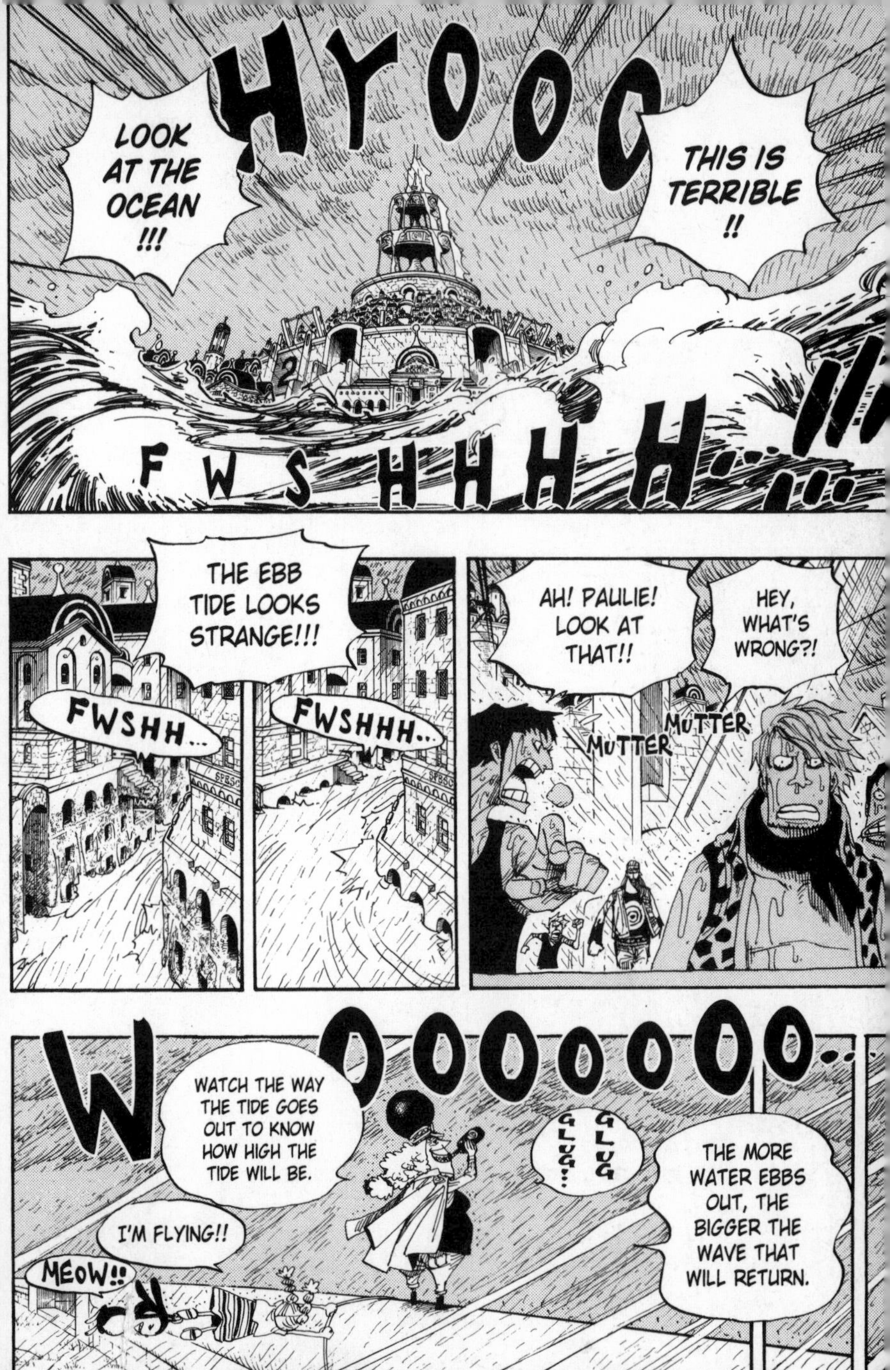
THIS IS TERRIBLE!!
HYOOO
LOOK AT THE OCEAN!!!
FWSHHHH...!!!
HEY, WHAT'S WRONG?!
AH! PAULIE! LOOK AT THAT!!
MUTTER
MUTTER
THE EBB TIDE LOOKS STRANGE!!!
FWSHHH...
FWSHH...
WOOOOOOO...
THE MORE WATER EBBS OUT, THE BIGGER THE WAVE THAT WILL RETURN.
GLUG
GLUG...
WATCH THE WAY THE TIDE GOES OUT TO KNOW HOW HIGH THE TIDE WILL BE.
I'M FLYING!!
MEOW!!

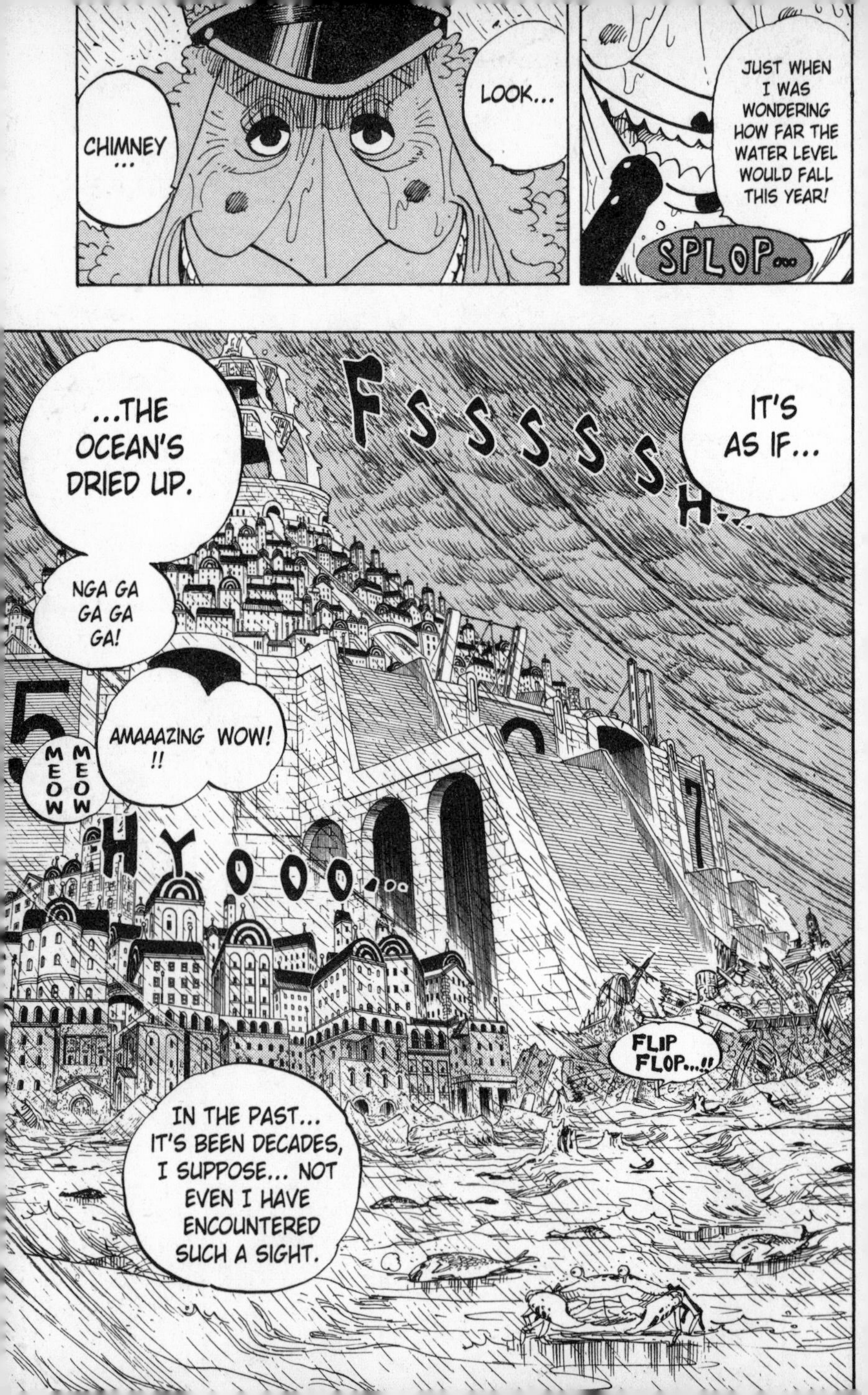

JUST WHEN I WAS WONDERING HOW FAR THE WATER LEVEL WOULD FALL THIS YEAR!
SPLOP...
LOOK...
CHIMNEY...
IT'S AS IF...
FSSSSSH...
...THE OCEAN'S DRIED UP.
NGA GA GA GA GA!
WOW!
AMAAAZING!!
MEOW
MEOW
7
5
HYOOO...
FLIP FLOP...!!
IN THE PAST... IT'S BEEN DECADES, I SUPPOSE... NOT EVEN I HAVE ENCOUNTERED SUCH A SIGHT.

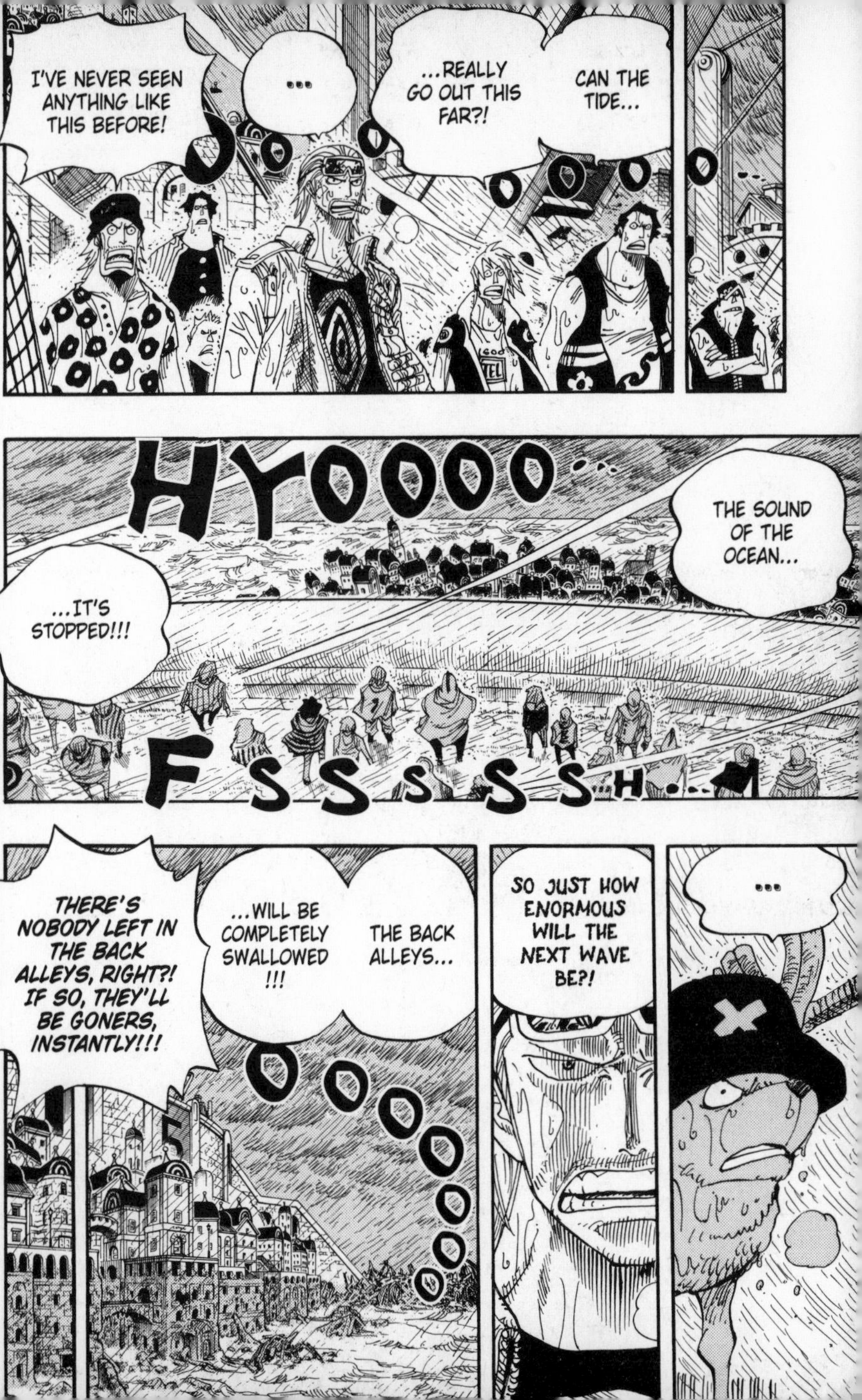
CAN THE TIDE...
...REALLY GO OUT THIS FAR?!
...
I'VE NEVER SEEN ANYTHING LIKE THIS BEFORE!
HYOOOO...
THE SOUND OF THE OCEAN...
...IT'S STOPPED!!!
FSSSSSH...
...
SO JUST HOW ENORMOUS WILL THE NEXT WAVE BE?!
THE BACK ALLEYS...
...WILL BE COMPLETELY SWALLOWED!!!
THERE'S NOBODY LEFT IN THE BACK ALLEYS, RIGHT?! IF SO, THEY'LL BE GONERS, INSTANTLY!!!

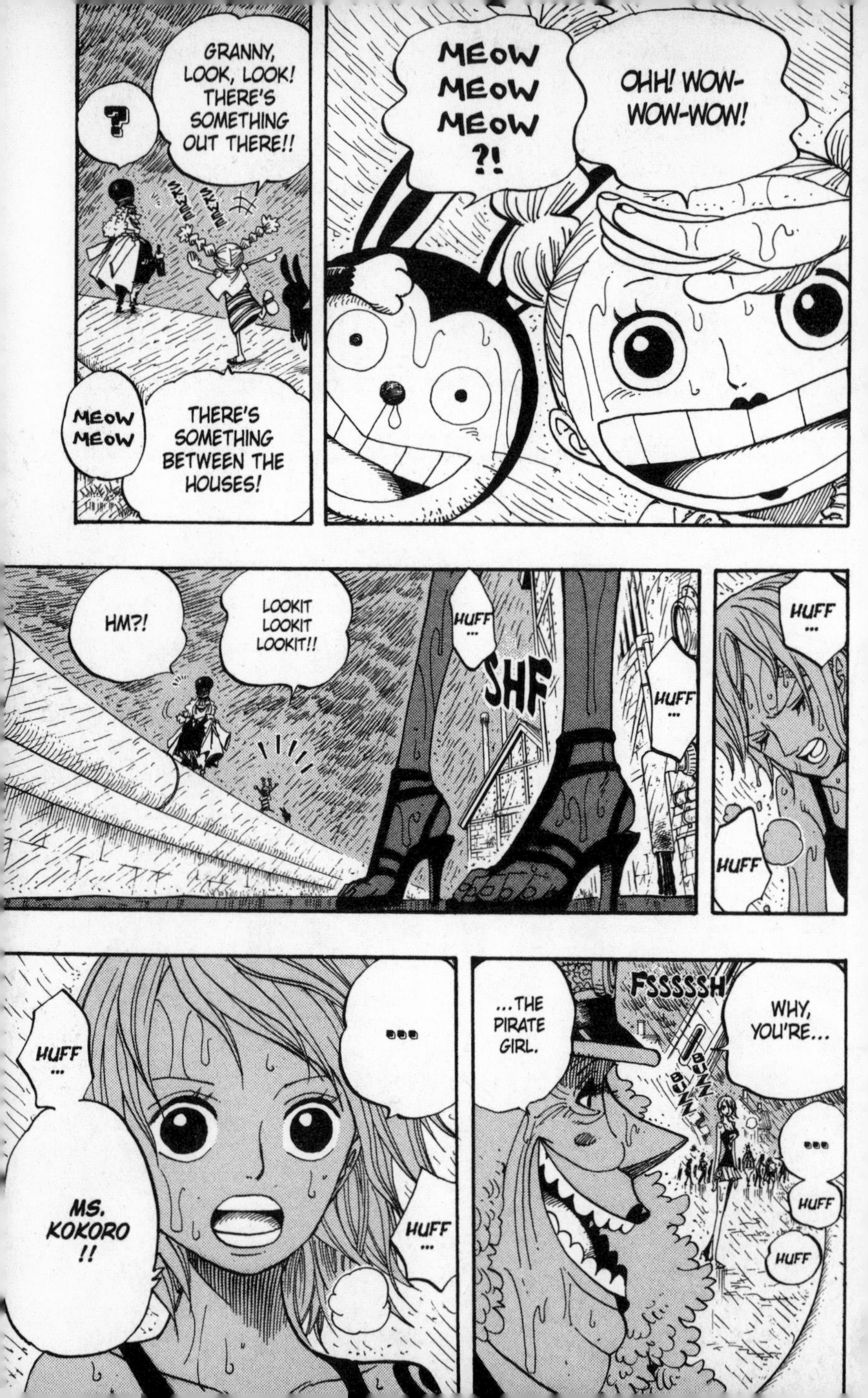
OHH! WOW-WOW-WOW!
MEOW MEOW MEOW ?!
GRANNY, LOOK, LOOK! THERE'S SOMETHING OUT THERE!!
?
THERE'S SOMETHING BETWEEN THE HOUSES!
MEOW MEOW
HUFF...
HUFF
HUFF...
SHF
HUFF...
LOOKIT LOOKIT LOOKIT!!
HM?!
WHY, YOU'RE...
FSSSSSH
...THE PIRATE GIRL.
BUZZ
BUZZ
...
HUFF
HUFF
...
HUFF...
MS. KOKORO!!
HUFF...

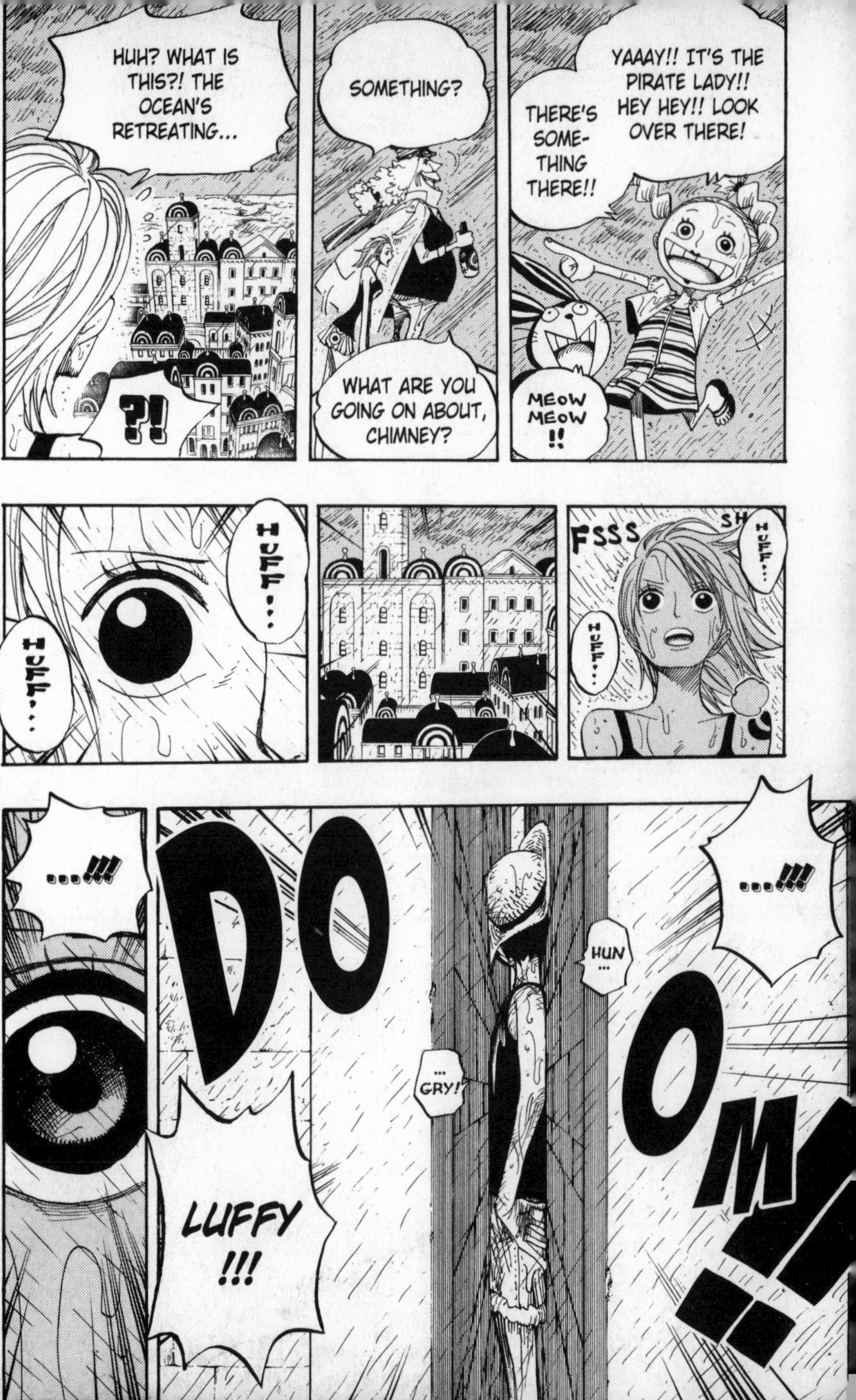
YAAAY!! IT'S THE PIRATE LADY!! HEY HEY!! LOOK OVER THERE!
THERE'S SOME-THING THERE!!
MEOW MEOW !!
SOMETHING?
WHAT ARE YOU GOING ON ABOUT, CHIMNEY?
HUH? WHAT IS THIS?! THE OCEAN'S RETREATING...
?!
FSSS
HUFF...
HUFF...
HUFF...
HUFF...
...!!!
HUN ...
... GRY!
DOOOM!!
...!!!
LUFFY !!!

Chapter 363:
AQUA LAGUNA

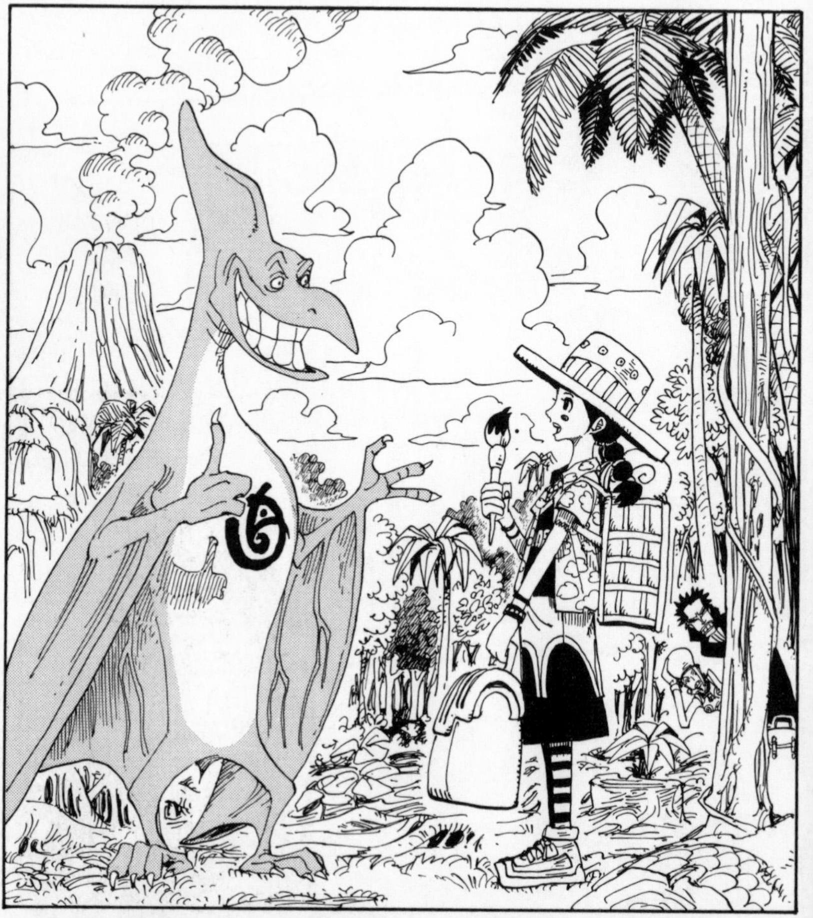

MS. GOLDEN WEEK'S BIG PLAN, A BAROQUE REUNION, VOL. 5:
"THE 'YELLOW-GREEN OF FRIENDSHIP' COLORS TRAP — GIVE US A RIDE."

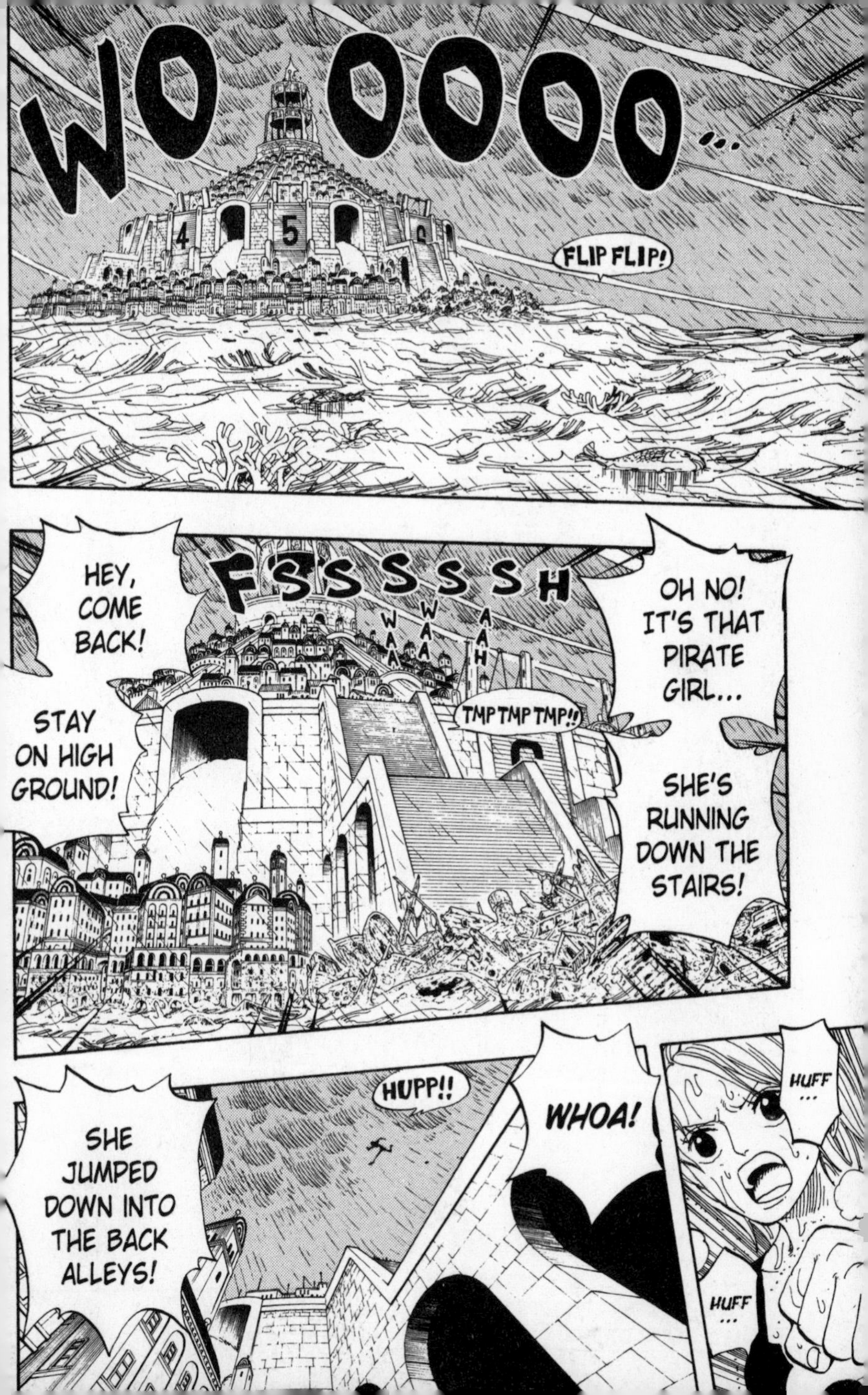
WO OOOO...
FLIP FLIP!
OH NO! IT'S THAT PIRATE GIRL...
SHE'S RUNNING DOWN THE STAIRS!
FSSSSSH
WAAA
WAAA
AAH
TMP TMP TMP!!
HEY, COME BACK!
STAY ON HIGH GROUND!
HUFF...
HUFF...
WHOA!
HUPP!!
SHE JUMPED DOWN INTO THE BACK ALLEYS!

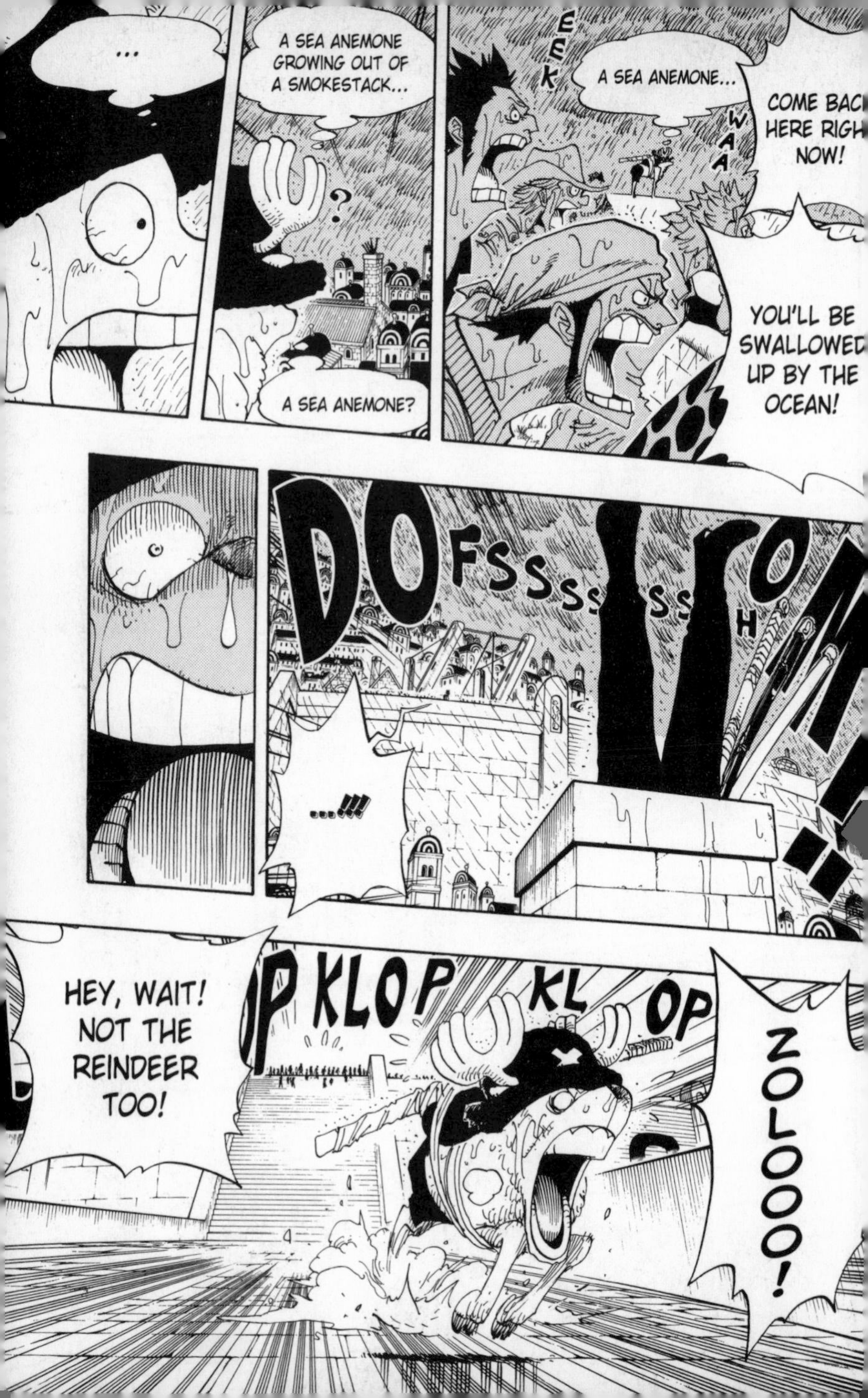

COME BAC HERE RIGH NOW!
YOU'LL BE SWALLOWED UP BY THE OCEAN!
EEK
A SEA ANEMONE...
WAA
A SEA ANEMONE GROWING OUT OF A SMOKESTACK...
?
A SEA ANEMONE?
...
DOFSSSSSSH
...!!!
ZOLOOO!
OP
KL
P KLOP
HEY, WAIT! NOT THE REINDEER TOO!

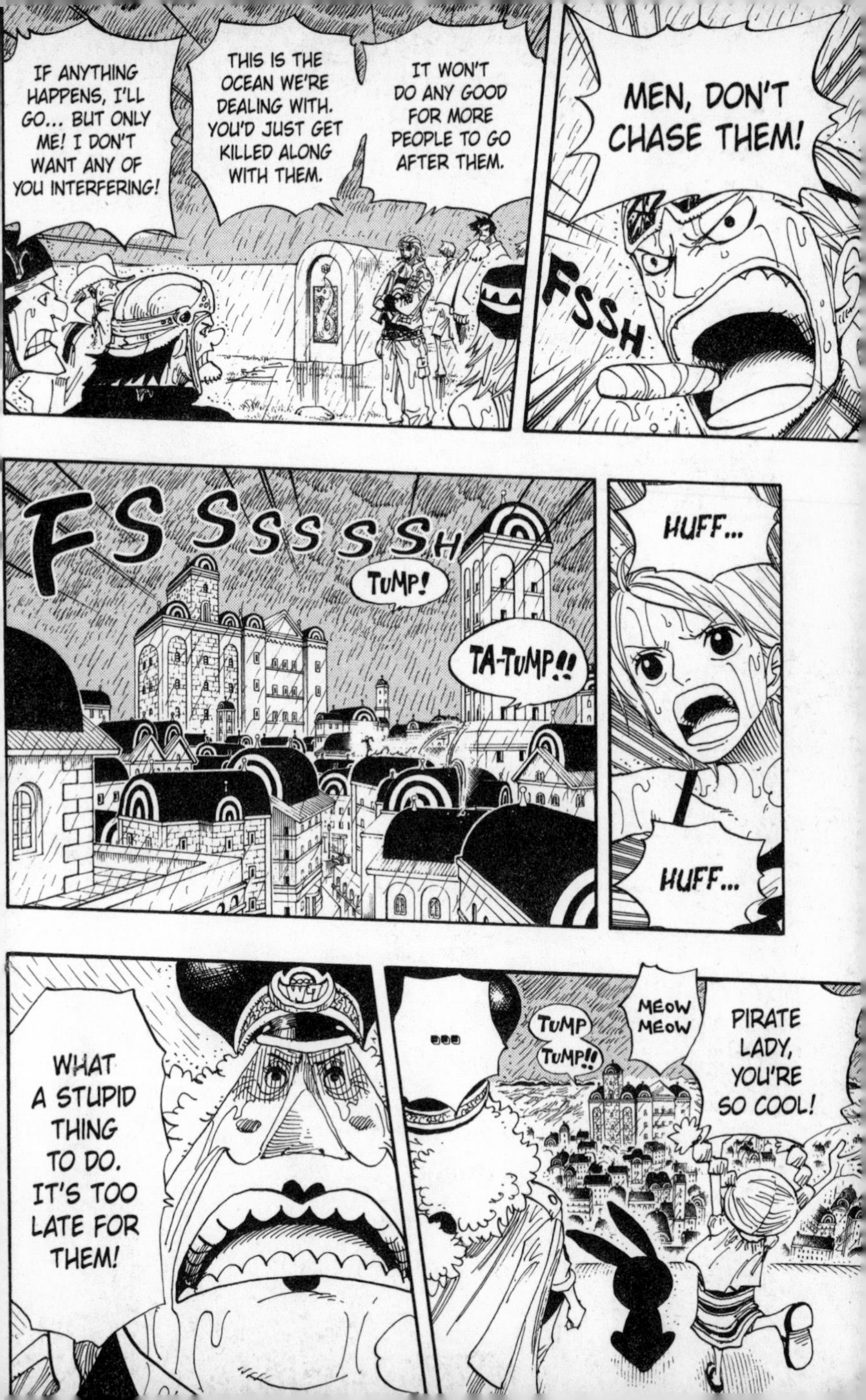
MEN, DON'T CHASE THEM!
FSSH
IT WON'T DO ANY GOOD FOR MORE PEOPLE TO GO AFTER THEM.
THIS IS THE OCEAN WE'RE DEALING WITH. YOU'D JUST GET KILLED ALONG WITH THEM.
IF ANYTHING HAPPENS, I'LL GO... BUT ONLY ME! I DON'T WANT ANY OF YOU INTERFERING!
HUFF...
HUFF...
FSSSSSSH
TUMP!
TA-TUMP!!
PIRATE LADY, YOU'RE SO COOL!
MEOW MEOW
TUMP TUMP!!
...
WHAT A STUPID THING TO DO. IT'S TOO LATE FOR THEM!

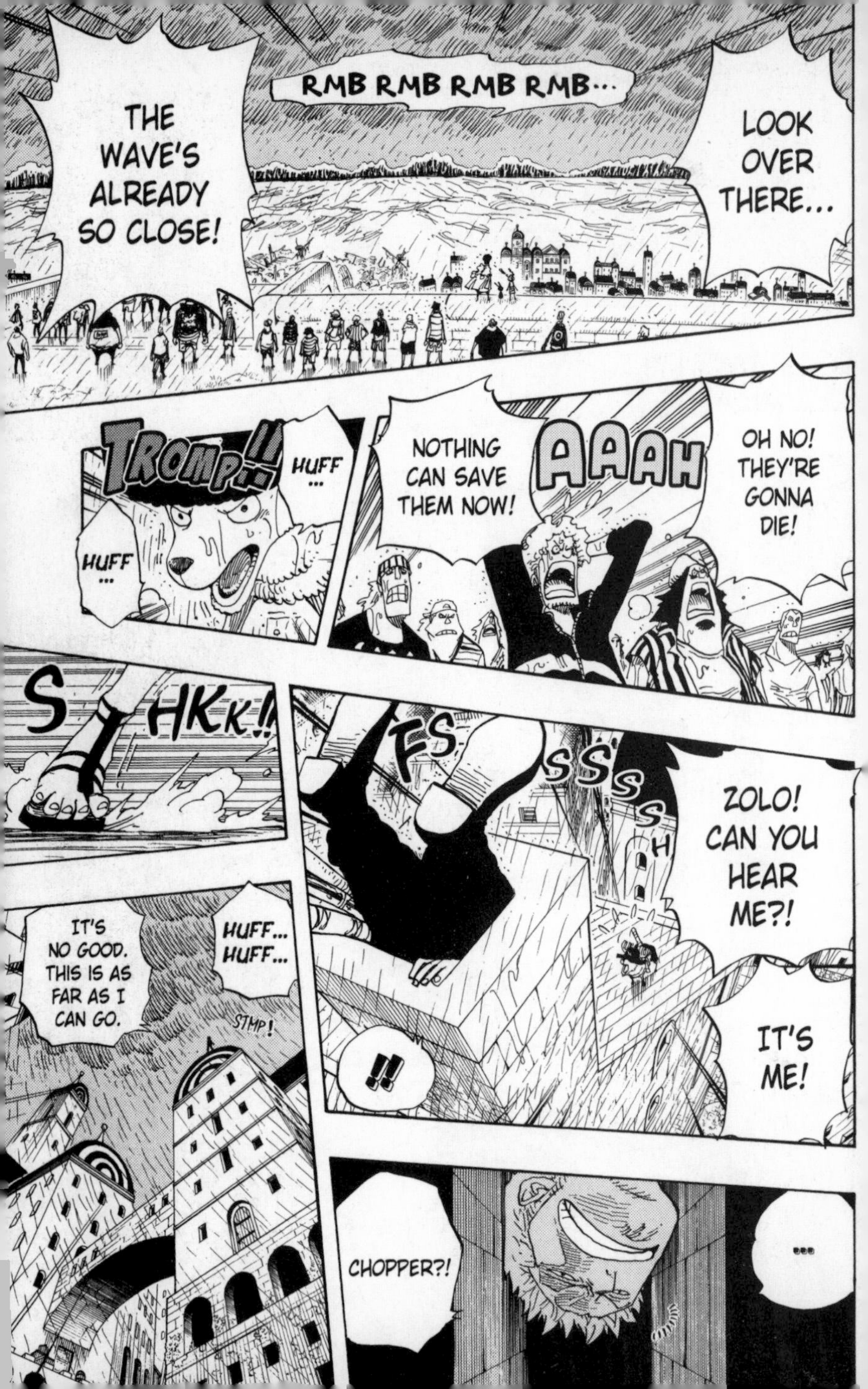

LOOK OVER THERE...
RMB RMB RMB RMB...
THE WAVE'S ALREADY SO CLOSE!
OH NO! THEY'RE GONNA DIE!
AAAH
NOTHING CAN SAVE THEM NOW!
HUFF ...
TROMP!!
HUFF ...
FS
SSSSSH
ZOLO! CAN YOU HEAR ME?!
IT'S ME!
!!
...
CHOPPER?!
SHKK!!
HUFF... HUFF...
IT'S NO GOOD. THIS IS AS FAR AS I CAN GO.
STMP!

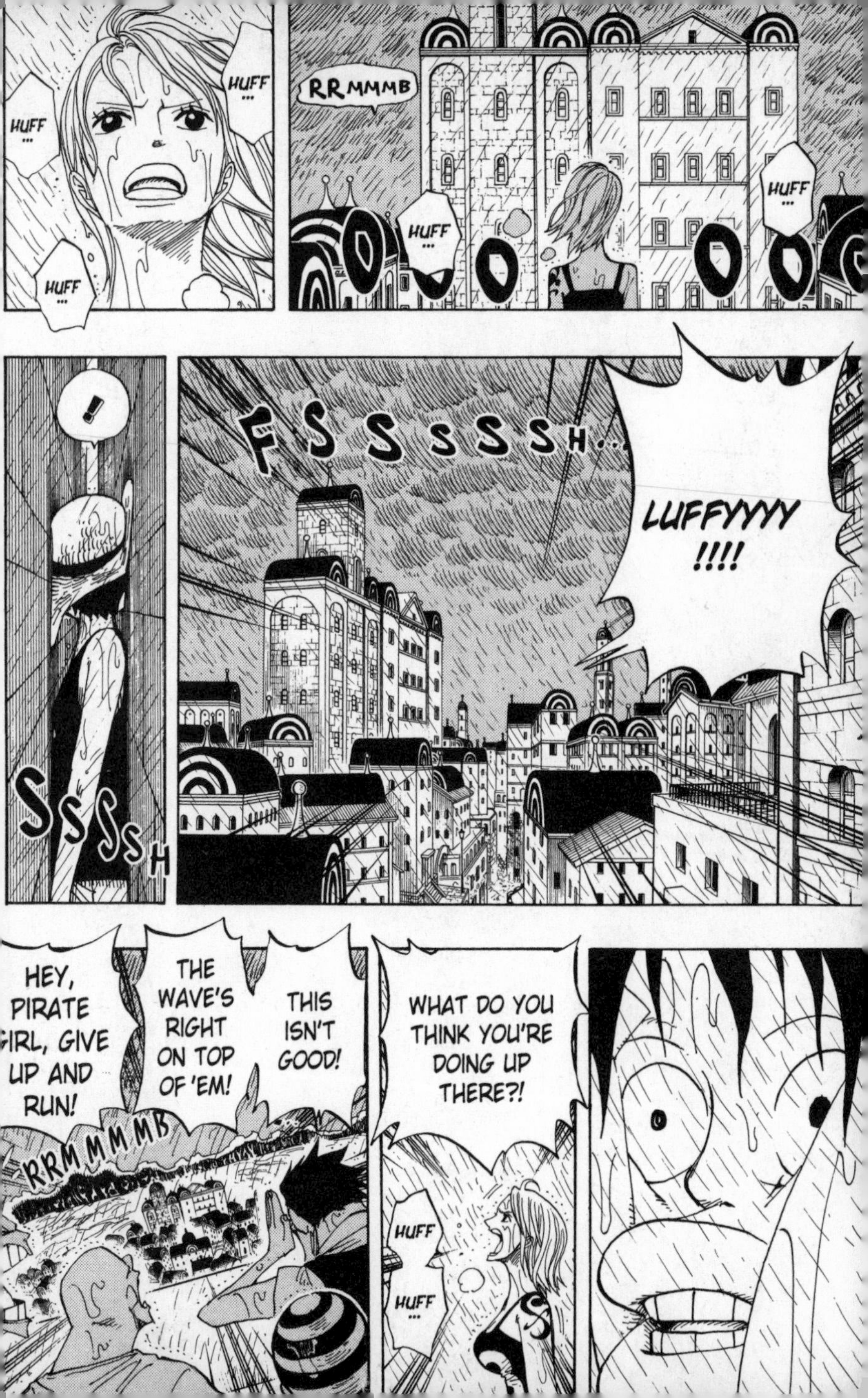
RRMMMB
HUFF...
HUFF...
HUFF...
HUFF...
HUFF...
LUFFYYYY!!!!
FSSSSSH...
!
SSSSH
WHAT DO YOU THINK YOU'RE DOING UP THERE?!
HUFF...
HUFF...
THIS ISN'T GOOD!
THE WAVE'S RIGHT ON TOP OF 'EM!
HEY, PIRATE IRL, GIVE UP AND RUN!
RRMMMMB

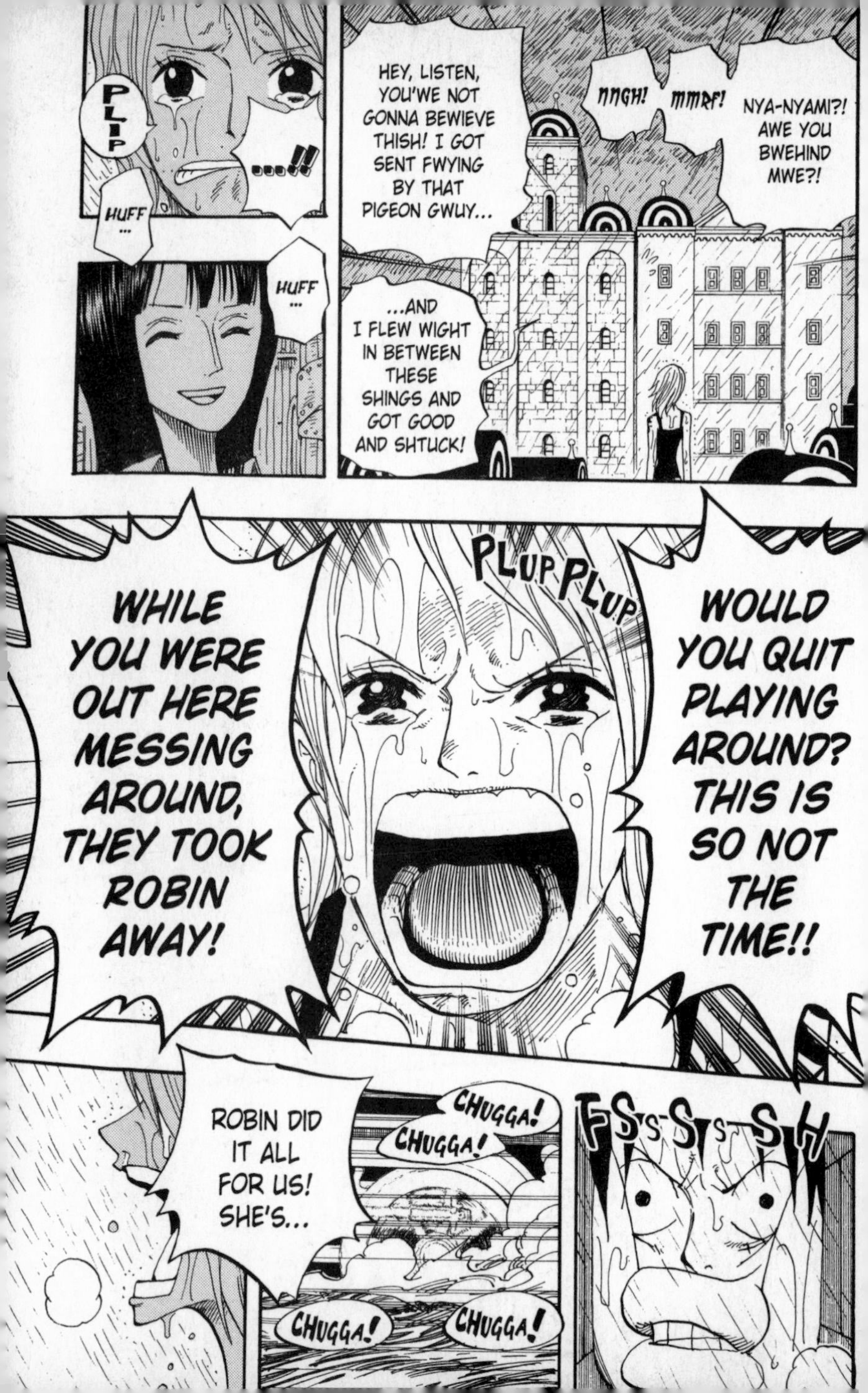
NYA-NYAMI?! AWE YOU BWEHIND MWE?!
MMRF!
NNGH!
HEY, LISTEN, YOU'WE NOT GONNA BEWIEVE THISH! I GOT SENT FWYING BY THAT PIGEON GWUY...
...AND I FLEW WIGHT IN BETWEEN THESE SHINGS AND GOT GOOD AND SHTUCK!
PLIP
...!!
HUFF ...
HUFF ...
WOULD YOU QUIT PLAYING AROUND? THIS IS SO NOT THE TIME!!
PLUP PLUP
WHILE YOU WERE OUT HERE MESSING AROUND, THEY TOOK ROBIN AWAY!
FSSSSSH
CHUGGA!
CHUGGA!
CHUGGA!
CHUGGA!
ROBIN DID IT ALL FOR US! SHE'S...

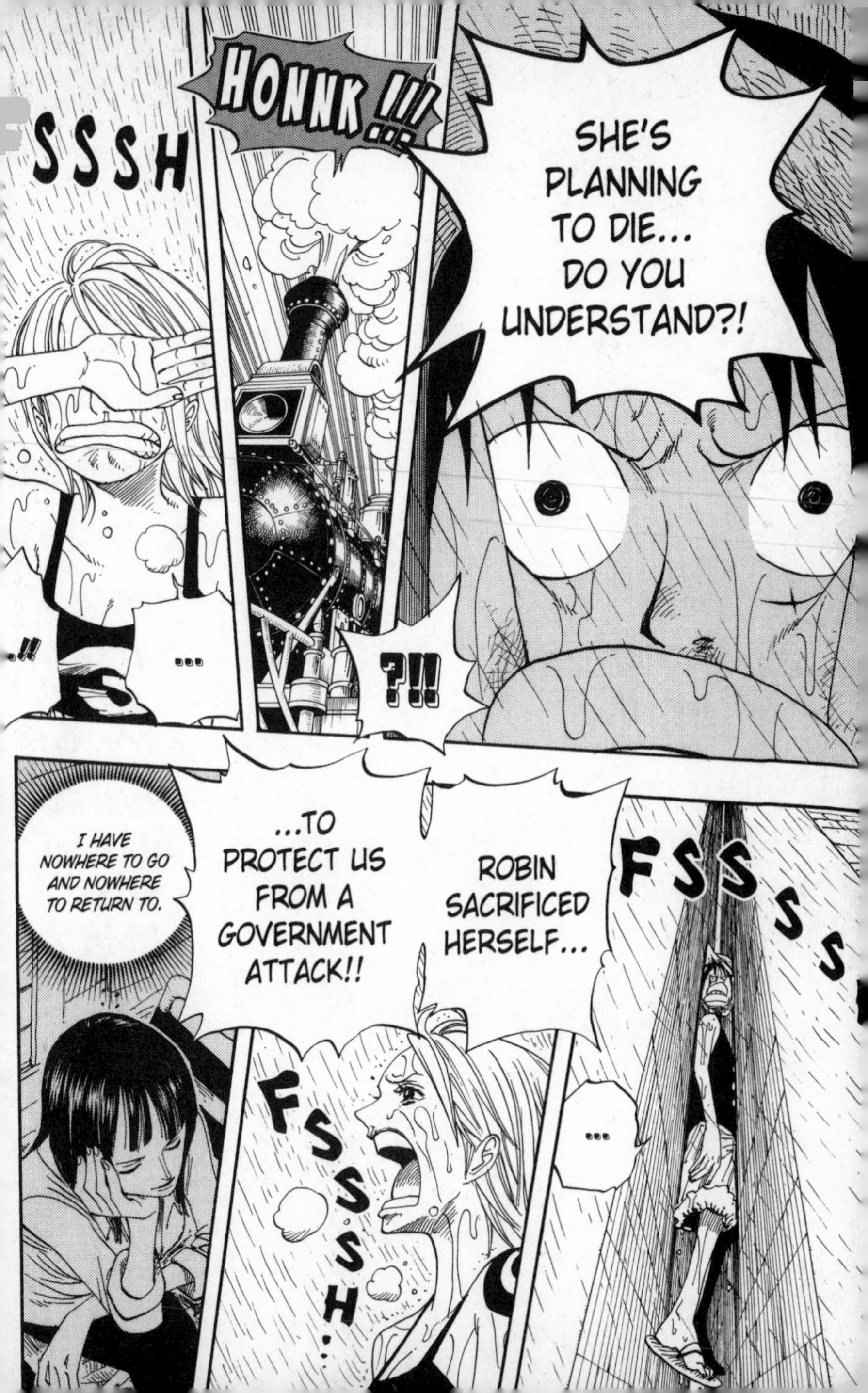
SHE'S PLANNING TO DIE... DO YOU UNDERSTAND?!
?!!
HONNK!!!
...
SSSH
..!!
FSSSSS
ROBIN SACRIFICED HERSELF...
...TO PROTECT US FROM A GOVERNMENT ATTACK!!
...
FSSSH
I HAVE NOWHERE TO GO AND NOWHERE TO RETURN TO.

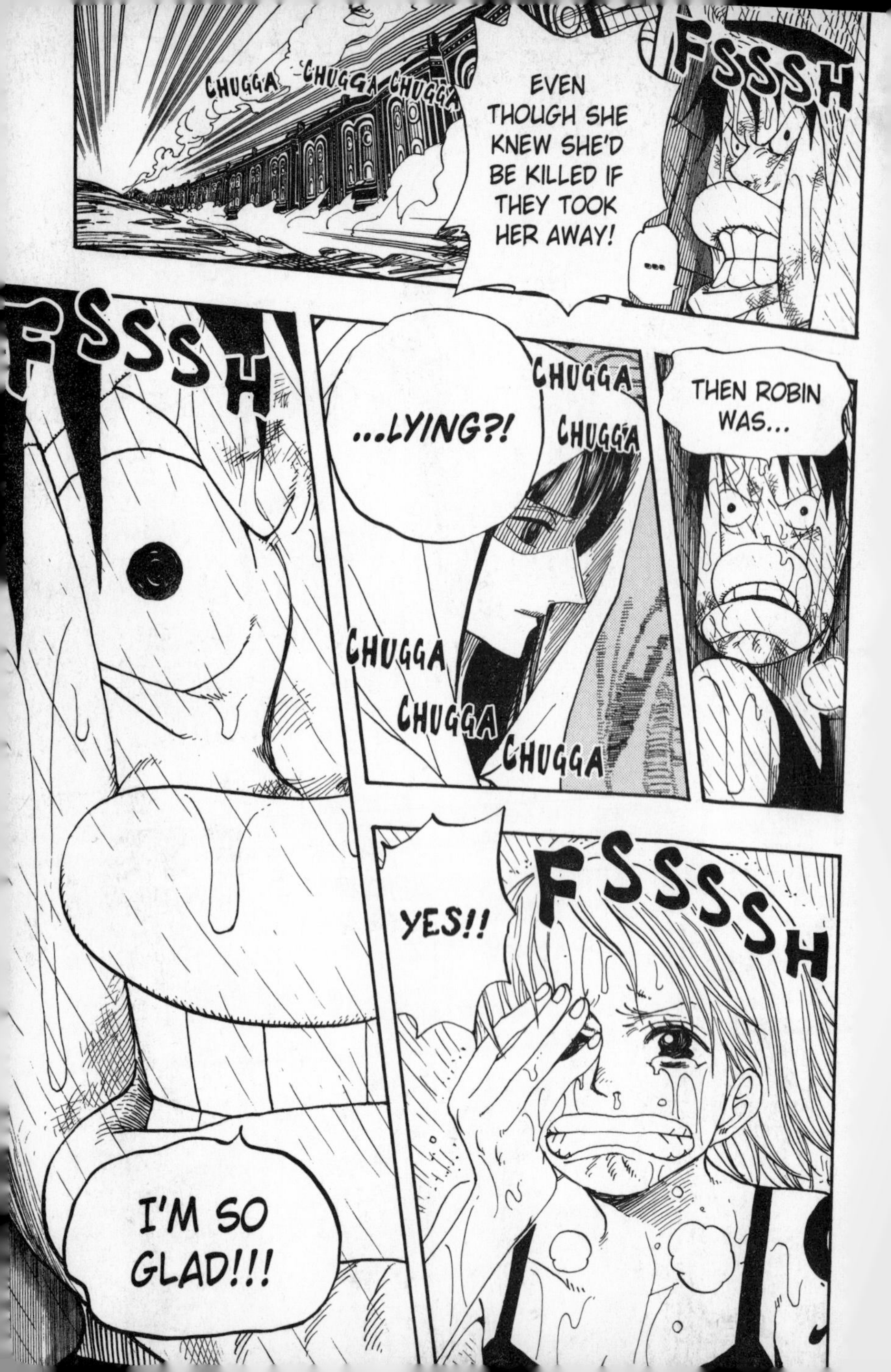
FSSSH
EVEN THOUGH SHE KNEW SHE'D BE KILLED IF THEY TOOK HER AWAY!
...
CHUGGA CHUGGA CHUGGA
THEN ROBIN WAS...
CHUGGA CHUGGA
...LYING?!
CHUGGA CHUGGA CHUGGA
FSSSSH
YES!!
FSSSH
I'M SO GLAD!!!

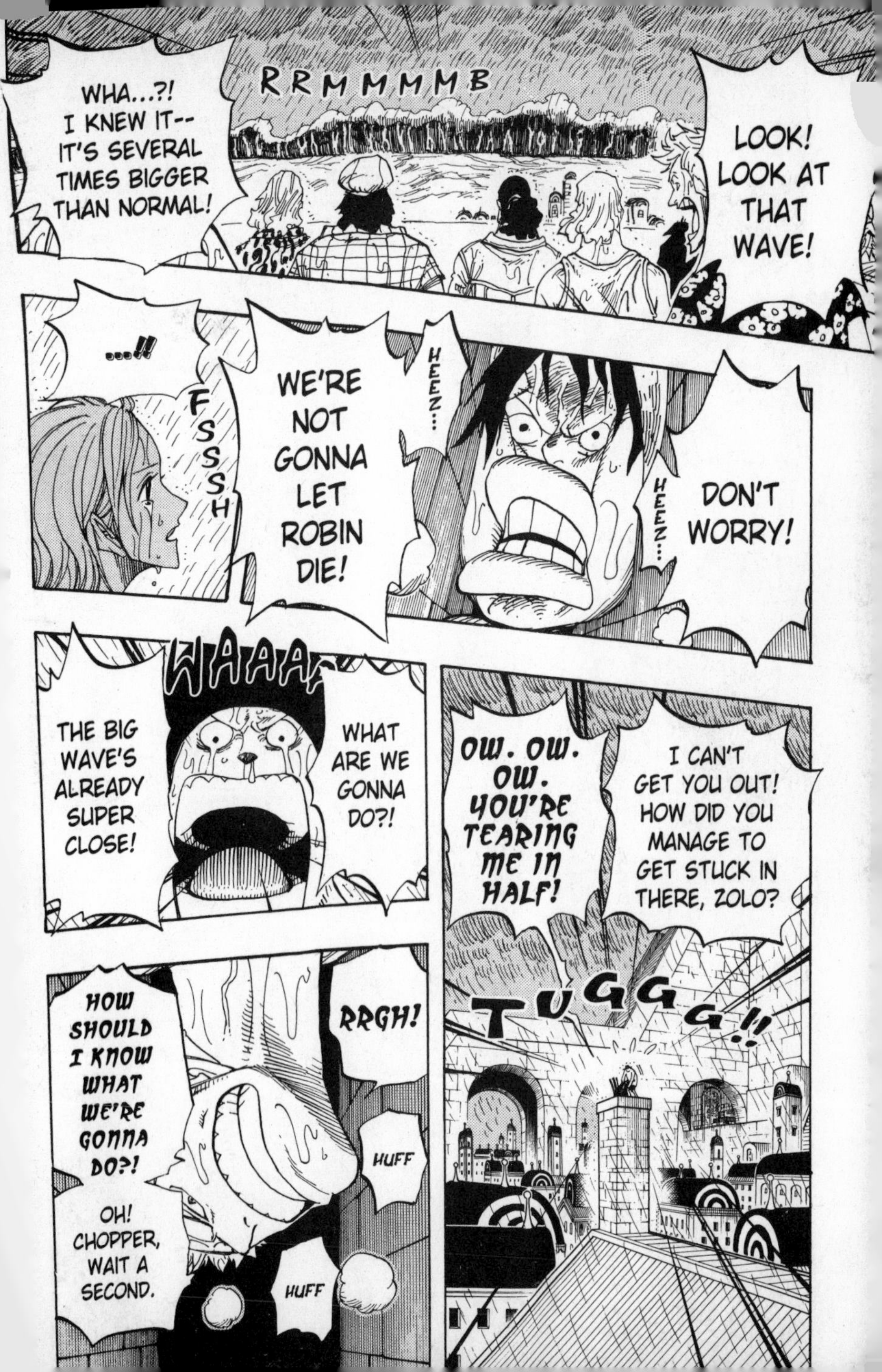
LOOK! LOOK AT THAT WAVE!
RRMMMMB
WHA...?! I KNEW IT-- IT'S SEVERAL TIMES BIGGER THAN NORMAL!
DON'T WORRY!
HEEZ...
HEEZ...
WE'RE NOT GONNA LET ROBIN DIE!
FSSSH
...!!
I CAN'T GET YOU OUT! HOW DID YOU MANAGE TO GET STUCK IN THERE, ZOLO?
OW. OW. OW. YOU'RE TEARING ME IN HALF!
TUGGG!!
WAAAA
WHAT ARE WE GONNA DO?!
THE BIG WAVE'S ALREADY SUPER CLOSE!
RRGH!
HOW SHOULD I KNOW WHAT WE'RE GONNA DO?!
HUFF
OH! CHOPPER, WAIT A SECOND.
HUFF

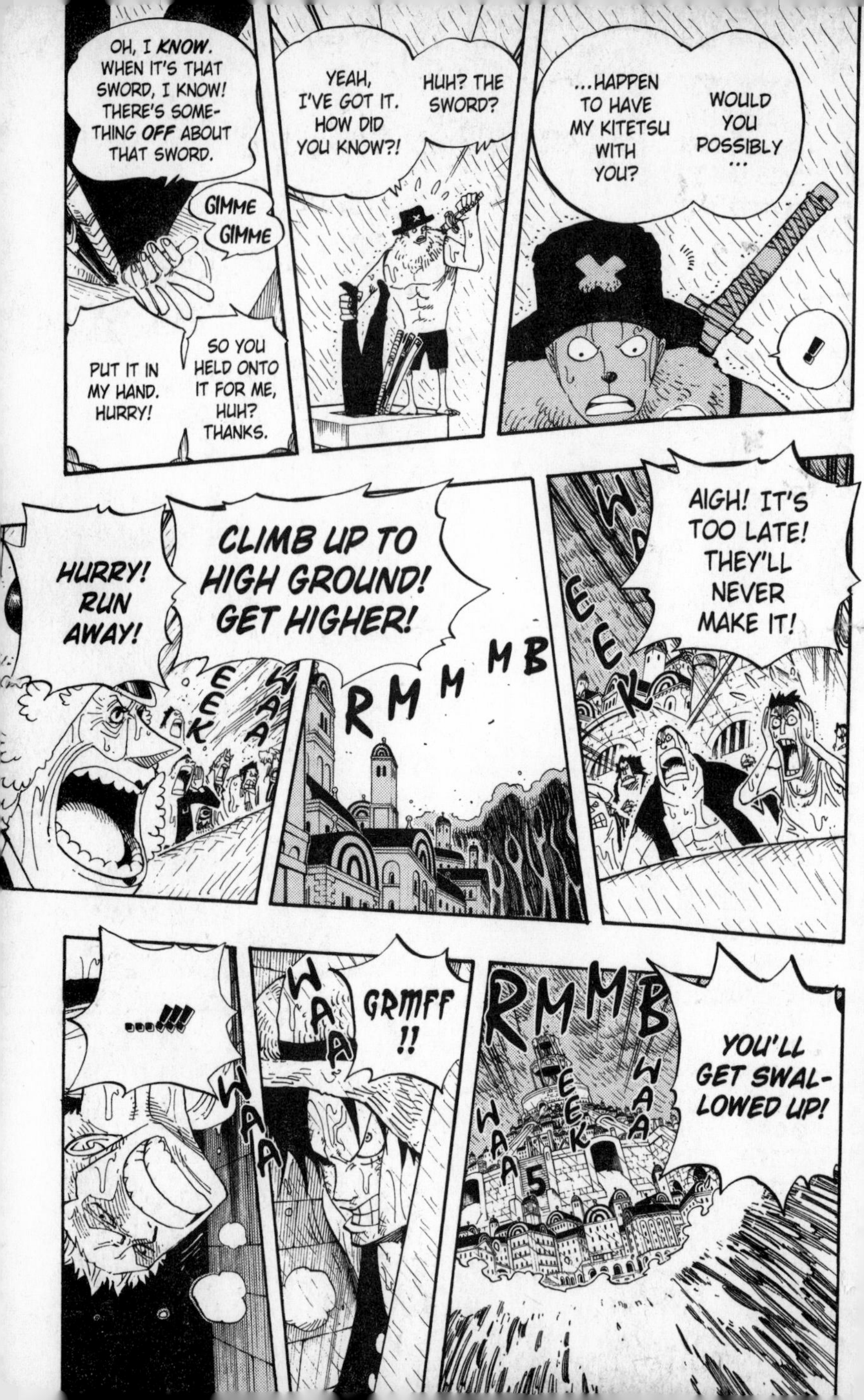
WOULD YOU POSSIBLY ...
...HAPPEN TO HAVE MY KITETSU WITH YOU?
!
HUH? THE SWORD?
YEAH, I'VE GOT IT. HOW DID YOU KNOW?!
OH, I KNOW. WHEN IT'S THAT SWORD, I KNOW! THERE'S SOMETHING OFF ABOUT THAT SWORD.
GIMME GIMME
SO YOU HELD ONTO IT FOR ME, HUH? THANKS.
PUT IT IN MY HAND. HURRY!
WAAA
EEEK
AIGH! IT'S TOO LATE! THEY'LL NEVER MAKE IT!
RMMMB
CLIMB UP TO HIGH GROUND! GET HIGHER!
WAAA
EEEK
HURRY! RUN AWAY!
RMMMB
WAAA
EEEK
WAAA
YOU'LL GET SWALLOWED UP!
WAAA
GRMFF !!
...!!!
WAAA

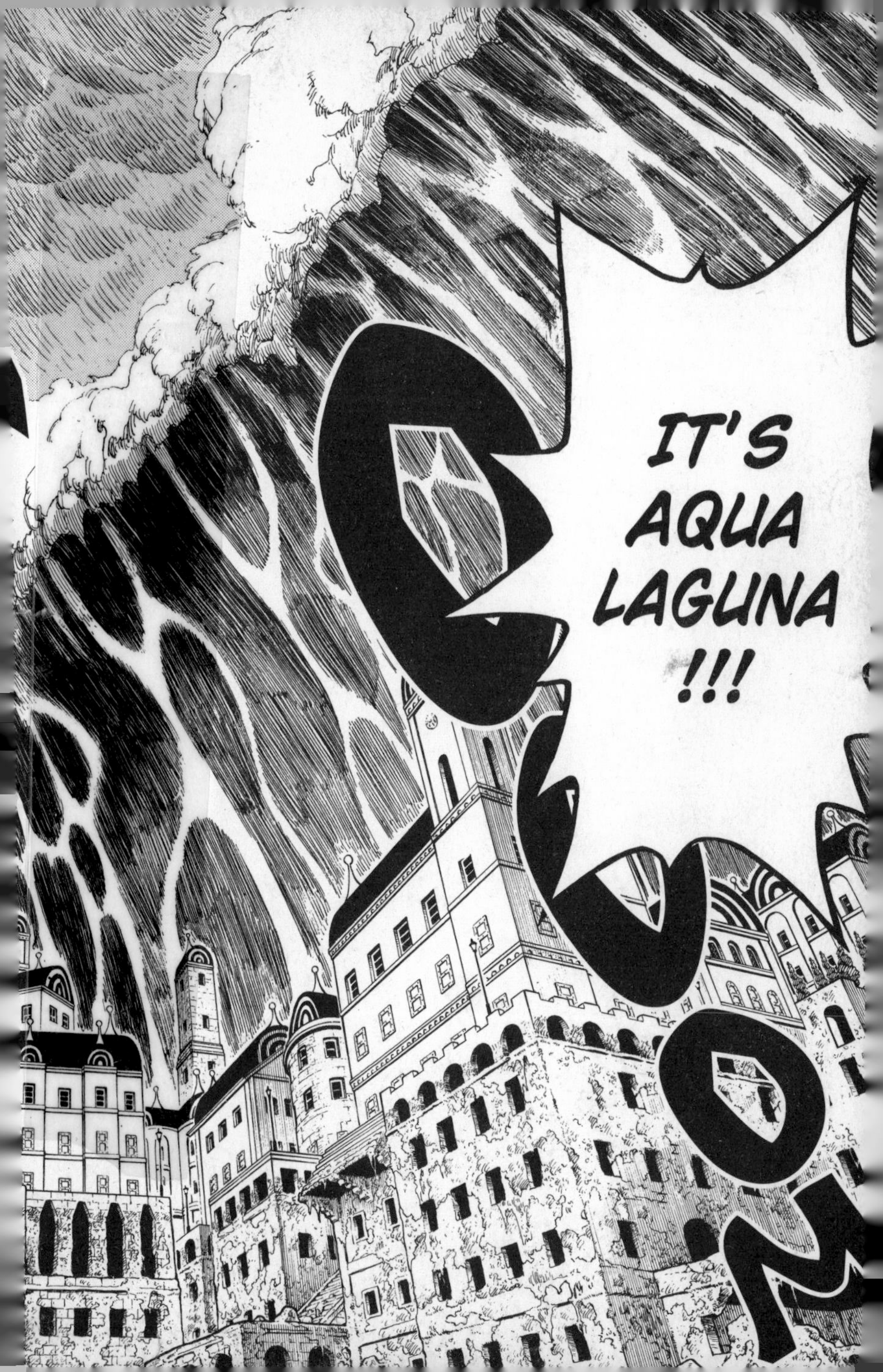
IT'S AQUA LAGUNA !!!

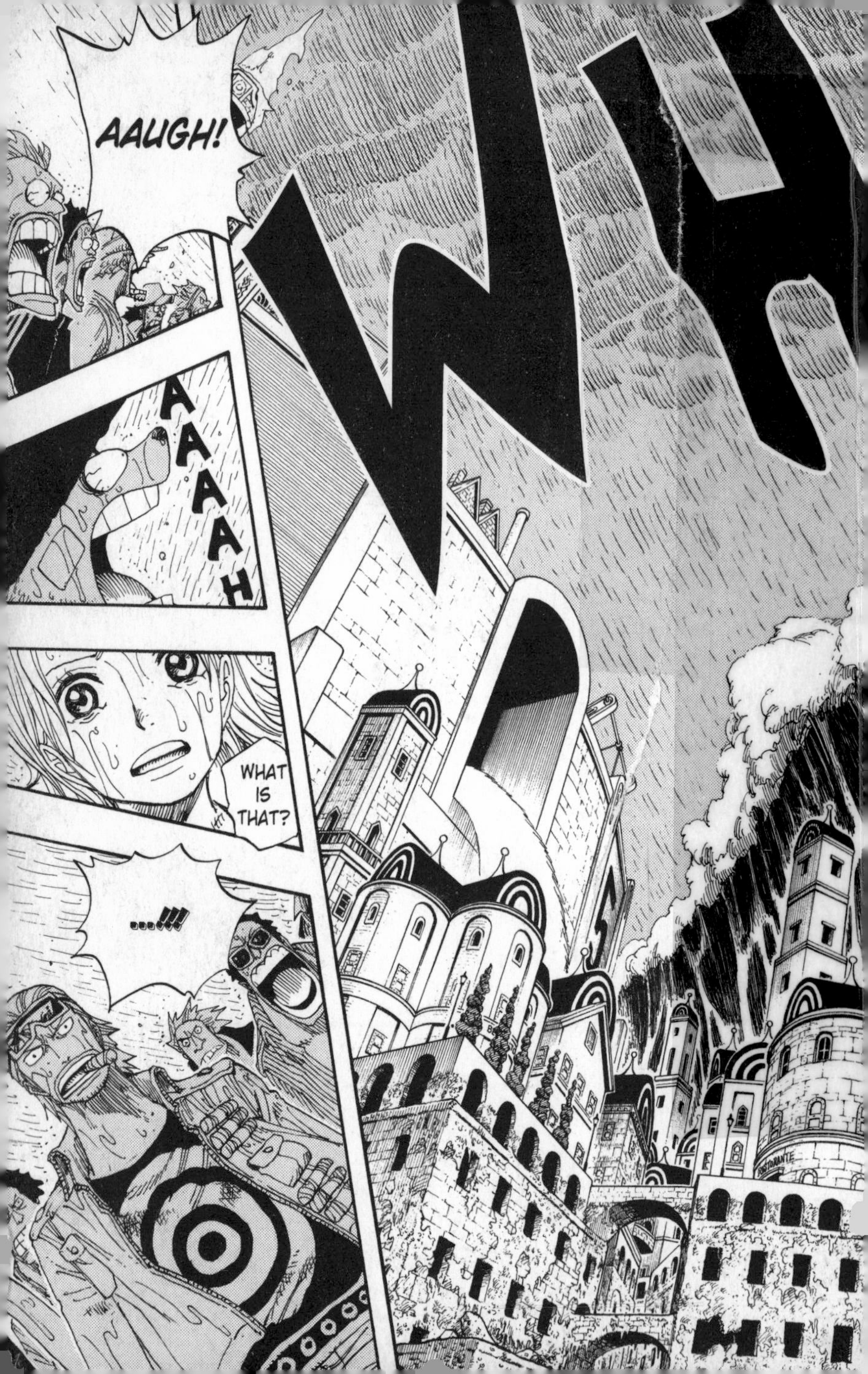
AAUGH!
AAAAH
WHAT IS THAT?
...!!!

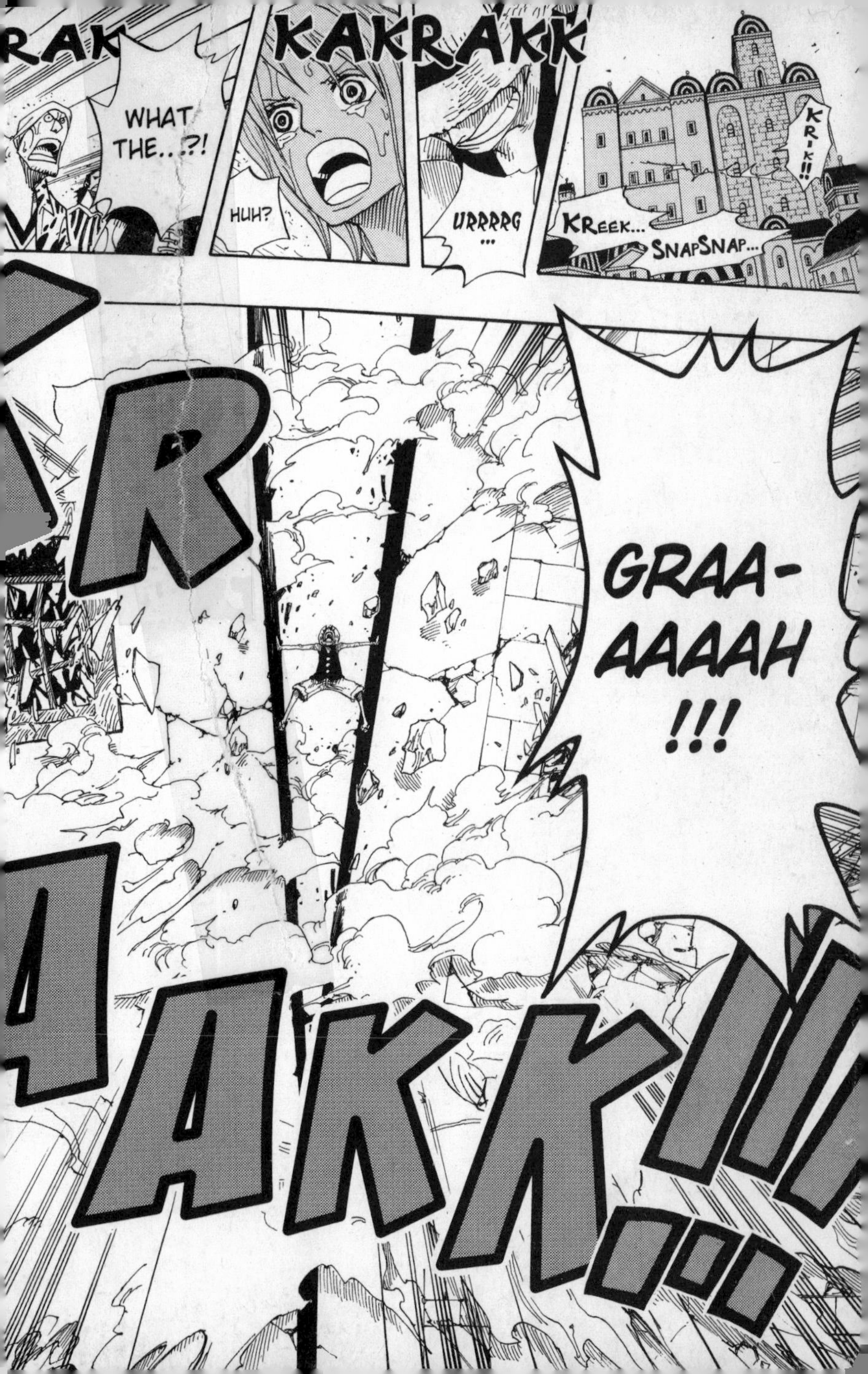
KRIK!!
KREEK...
SNAPSNAP...
URRRRG
...
KAKRAKK
HUH?
RAK
WHAT THE...?!
GRAA-
AAAAH
!!!
RAAKK...!!

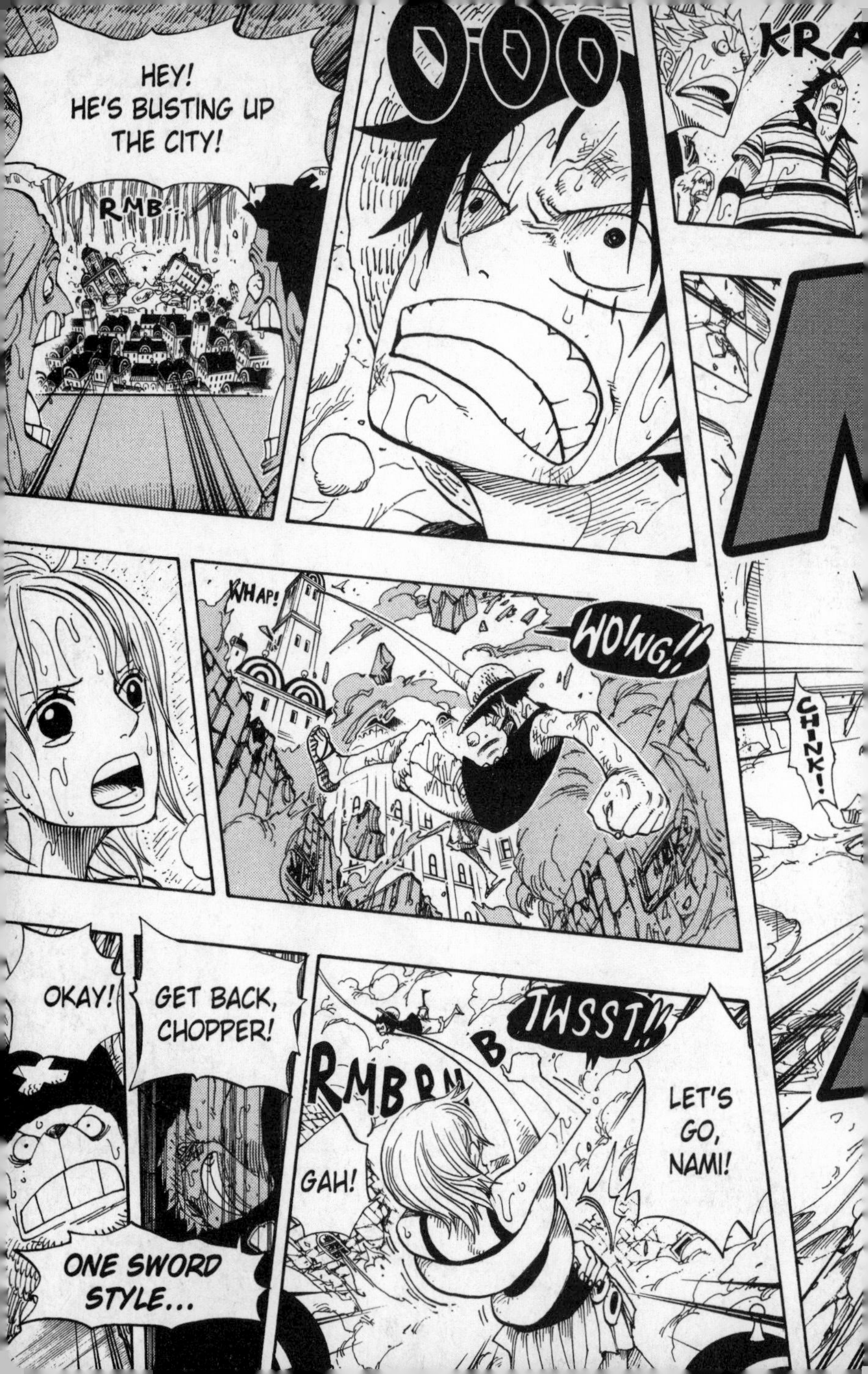
KRA
HEY! HE'S BUSTING UP THE CITY!
RMB...
CHINK!
WHAP!
WO!NG!!
LET'S GO, NAMI!
TWSST!!
B
RMBRN
GAH!
GET BACK, CHOPPER!
OKAY!
ONE SWORD STYLE...

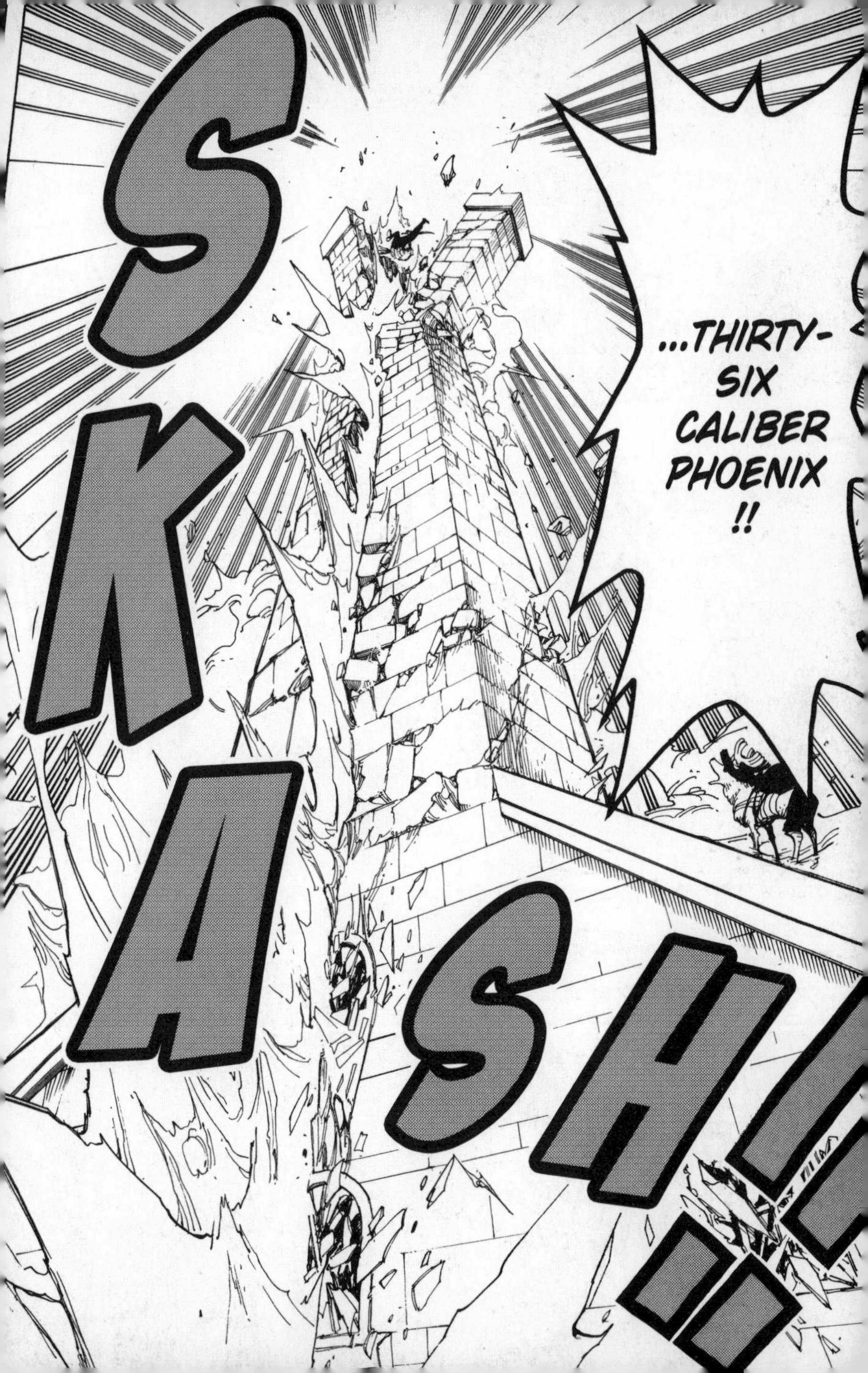
...THIRTY-SIX CALIBER PHOENIX !!
SKASH!!

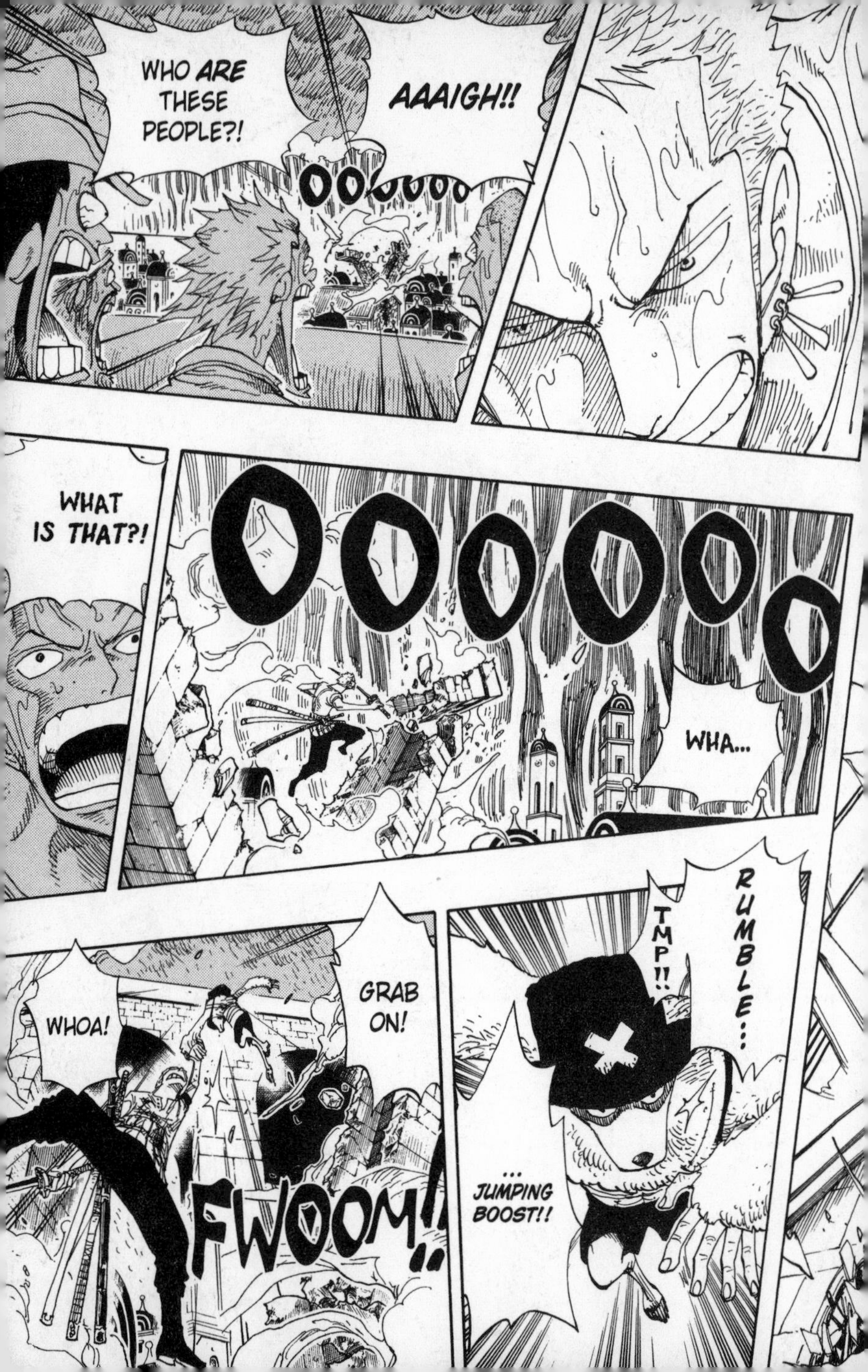
AAAIGH!!
WHO ARE THESE PEOPLE?!
OOOOOO
OOOOOO
WHA...
WHAT IS THAT?!
RUMBLE...
TMP!!
...JUMPING BOOST!!
GRAB ON!
WHOA!
FWOOM!!

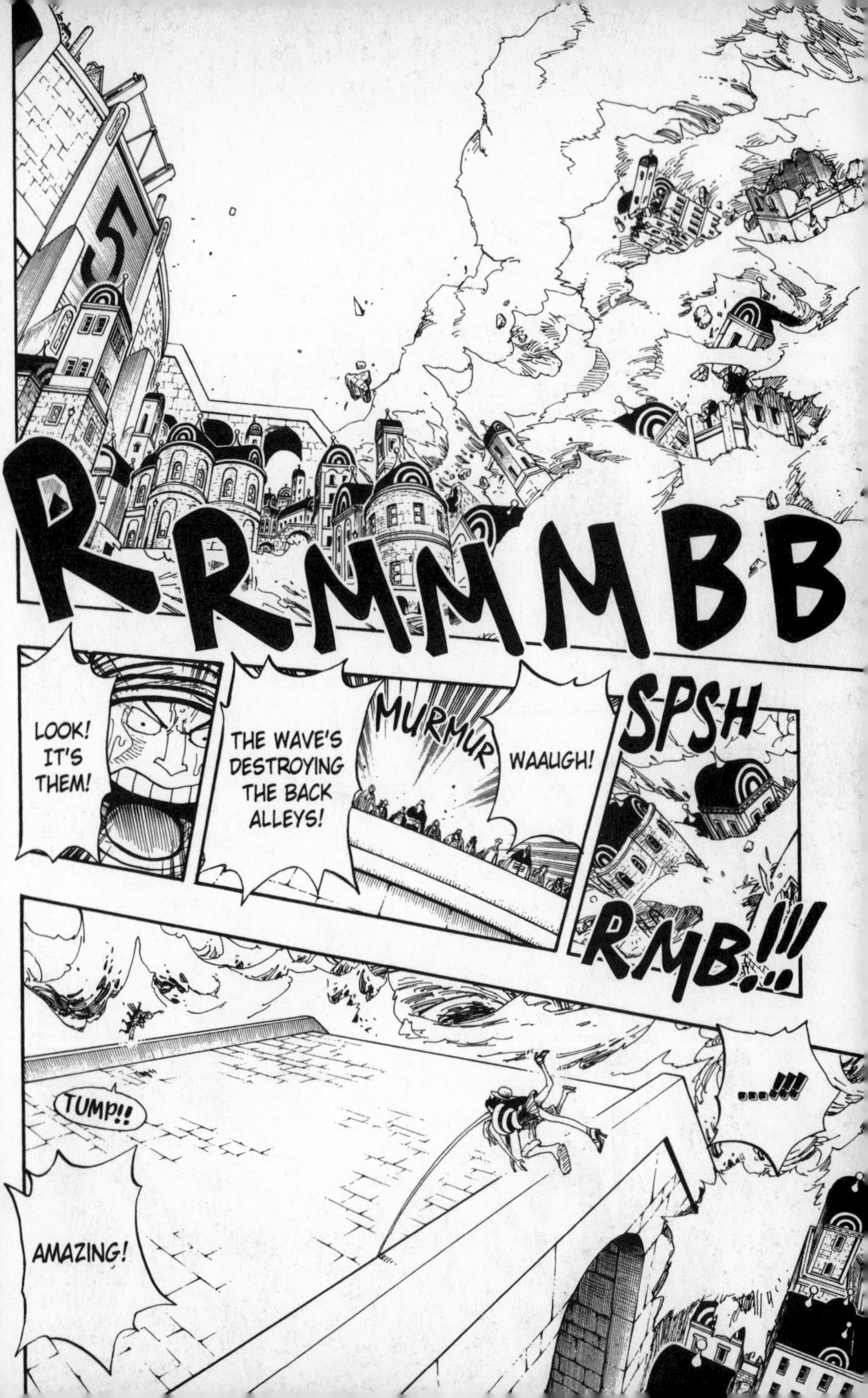
RRMMMBB
SPSH
RMB!!!
WAAUGH!
MURMUR
THE WAVE'S DESTROYING THE BACK ALLEYS!
LOOK! IT'S THEM!
...!!!
TUMP!!
AMAZING!

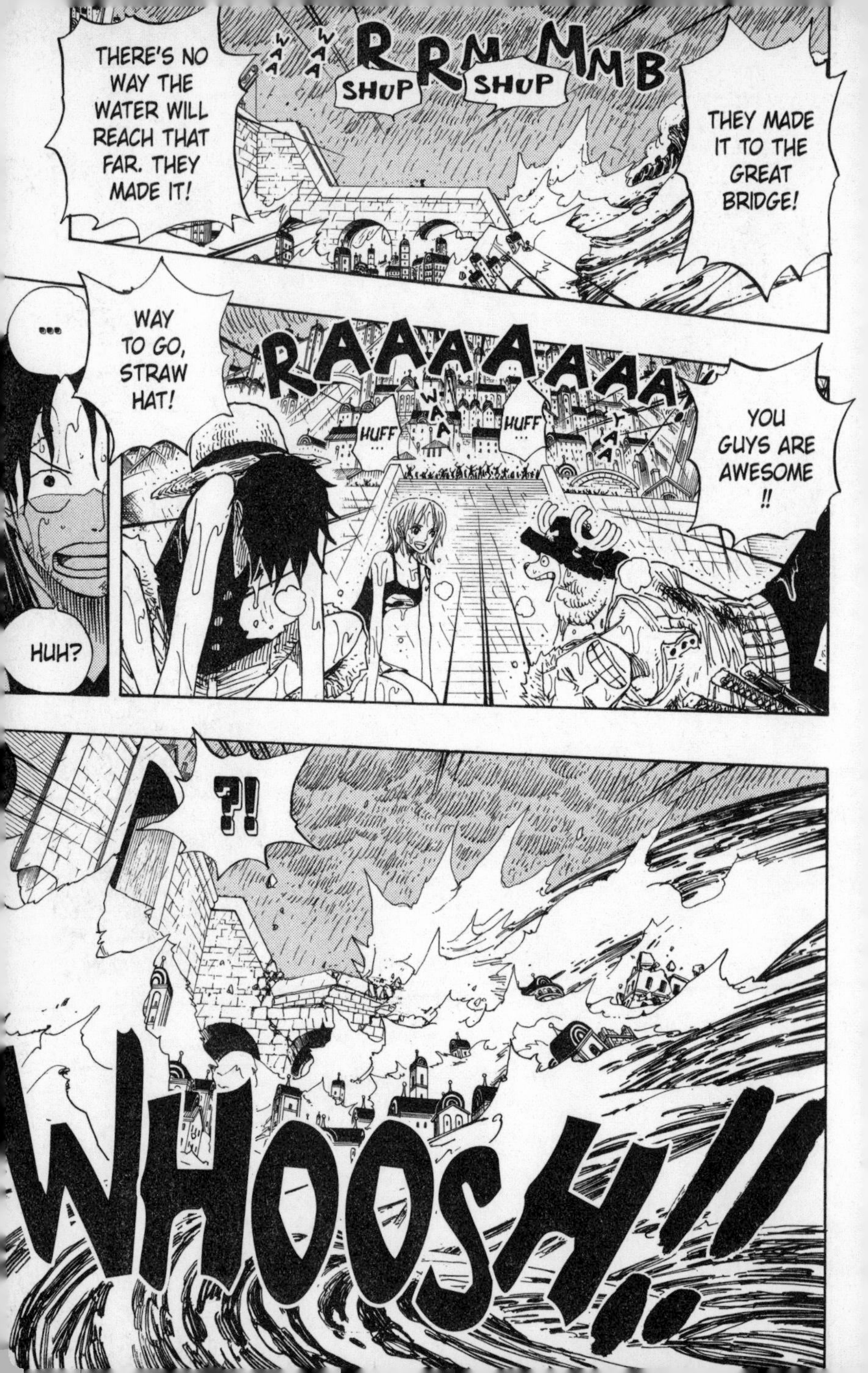
THEY MADE IT TO THE GREAT BRIDGE!
RRMMMB
SHUP SHUP
WAA
WAA
THERE'S NO WAY THE WATER WILL REACH THAT FAR. THEY MADE IT!
YOU GUYS ARE AWESOME !!
RAAAAAAA
YAAA
HUFF...
WAA
HUFF...
WAY TO GO, STRAW HAT!
...
HUH?
?!
WHOOSH!!

Chapter 364: KOKORO

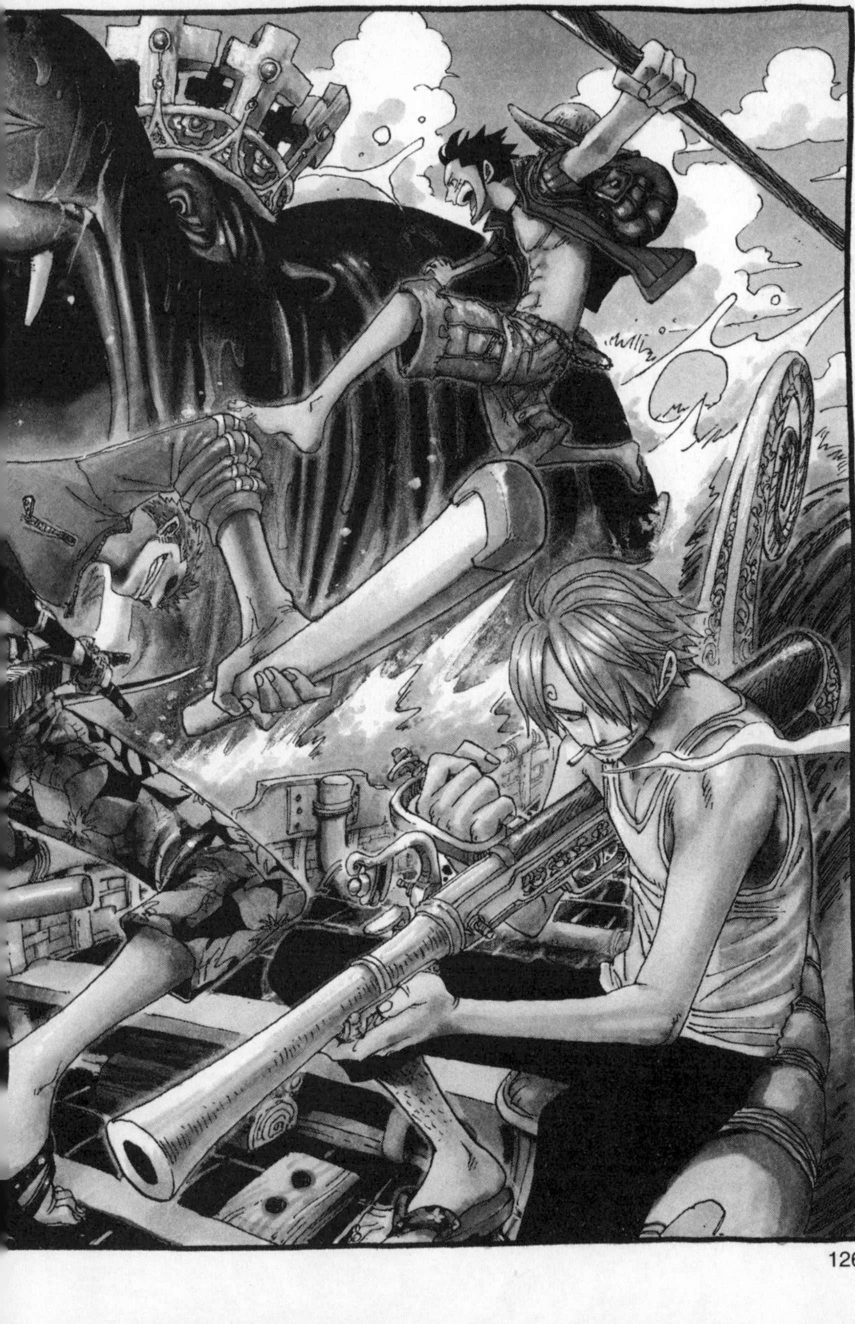

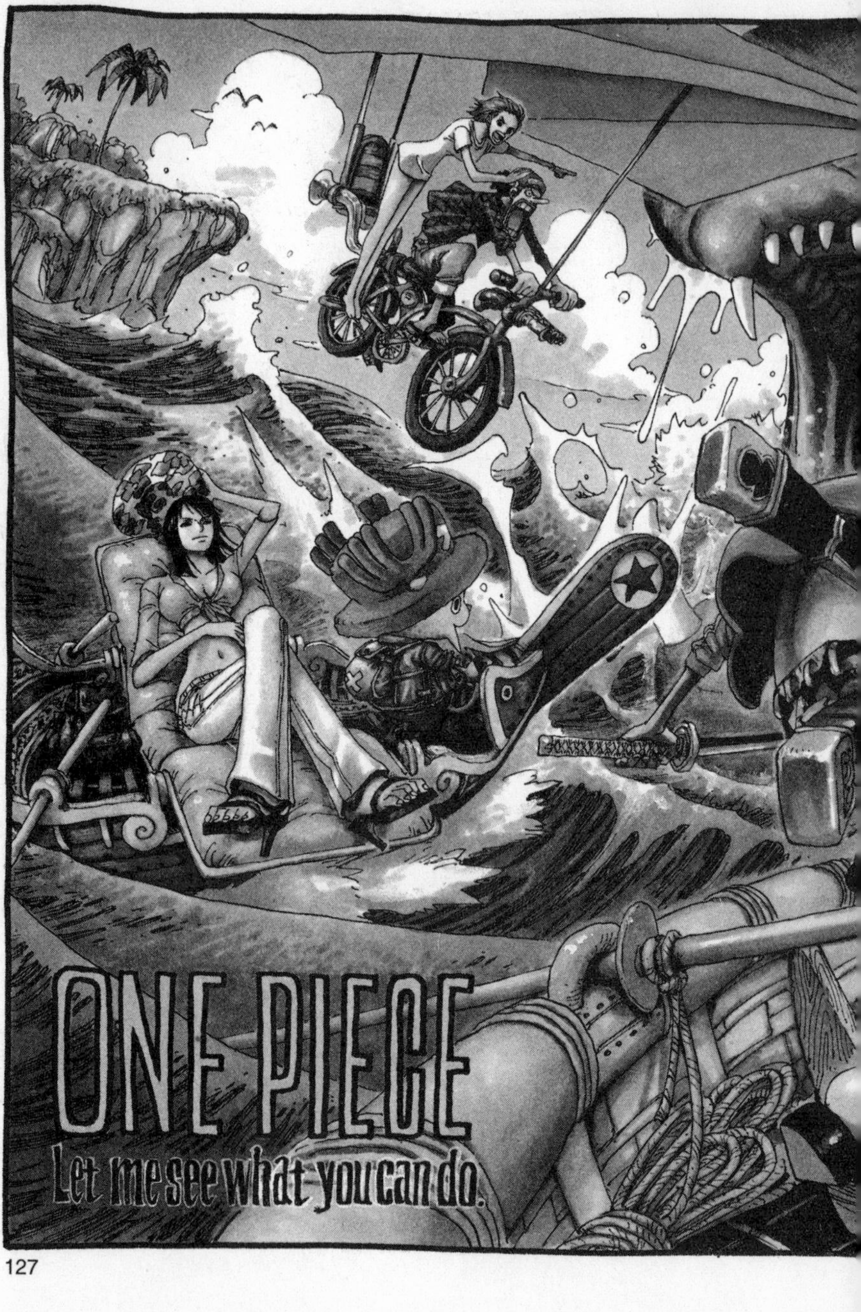
ONE PIECE
Let me see what you can do.

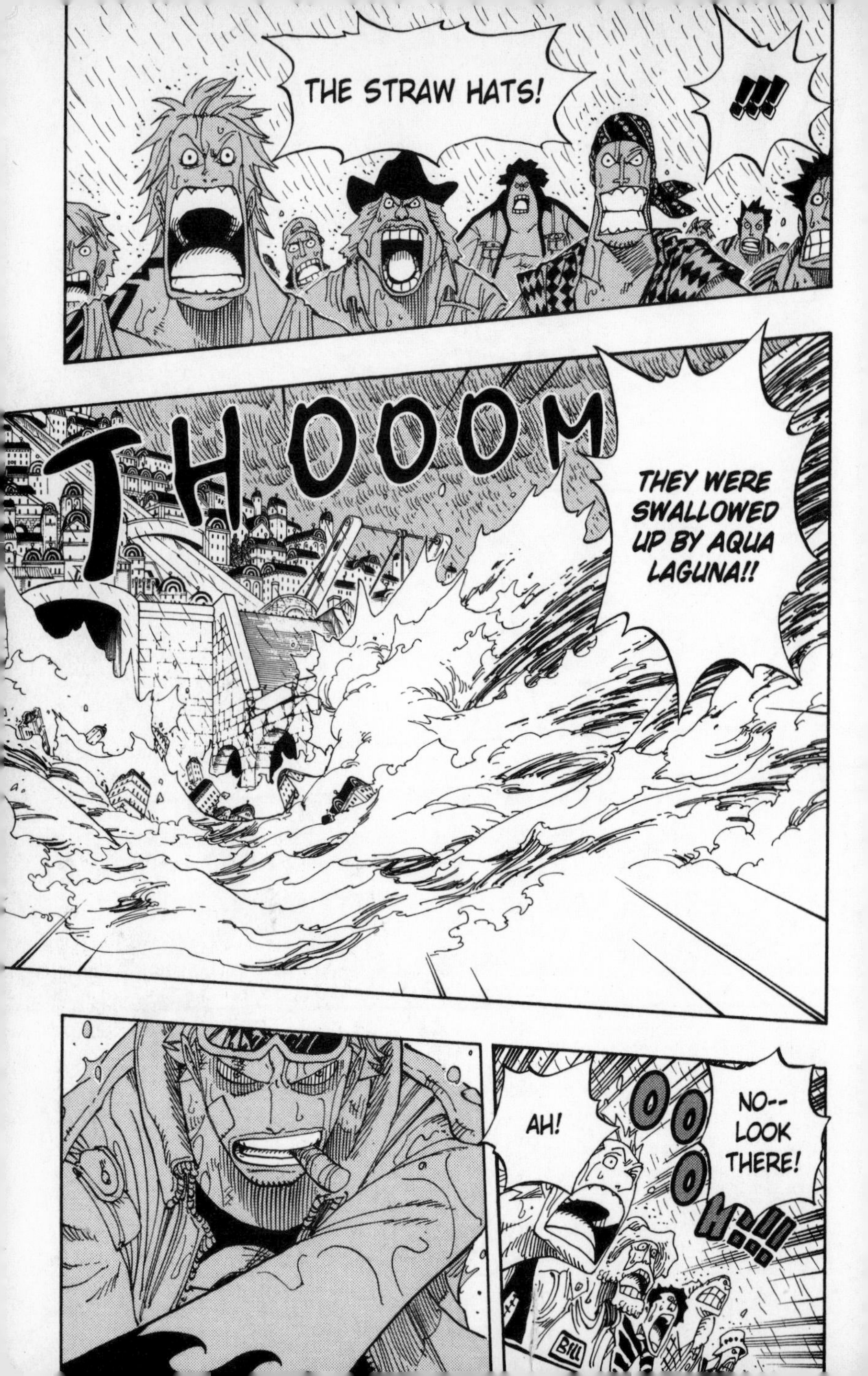
THE STRAW HATS!
!!!
THOOOM
THEY WERE SWALLOWED UP BY AQUA LAGUNA!!
NO-- LOOK THERE!
OOOOH!!!
AH!

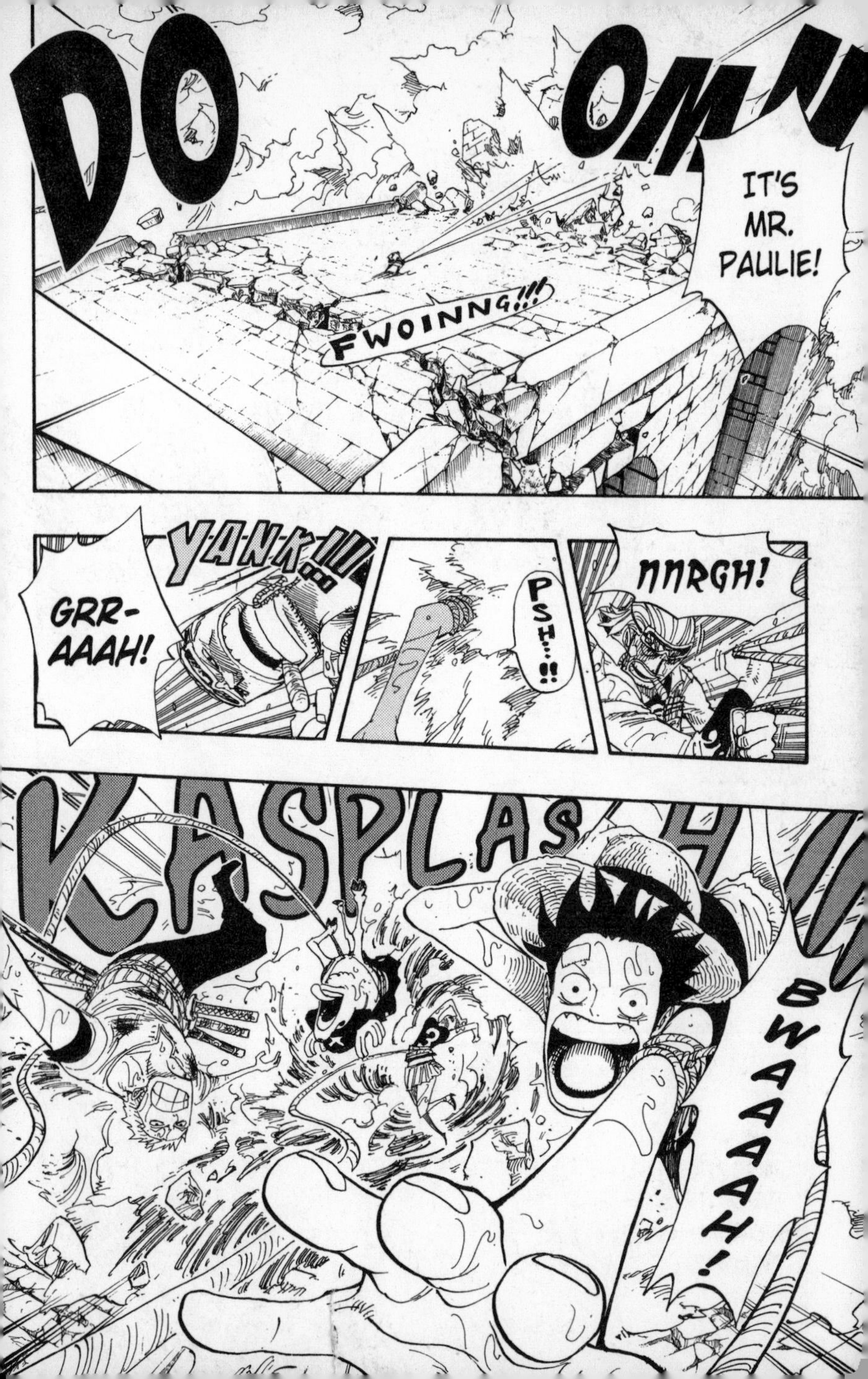
DOOM
IT'S MR. PAULIE!
FWOINNG!!!
NNRGH!
PSH...!!
YANK!!!
GRR-AAAH!
KASPLASH
BWAAAAAH!

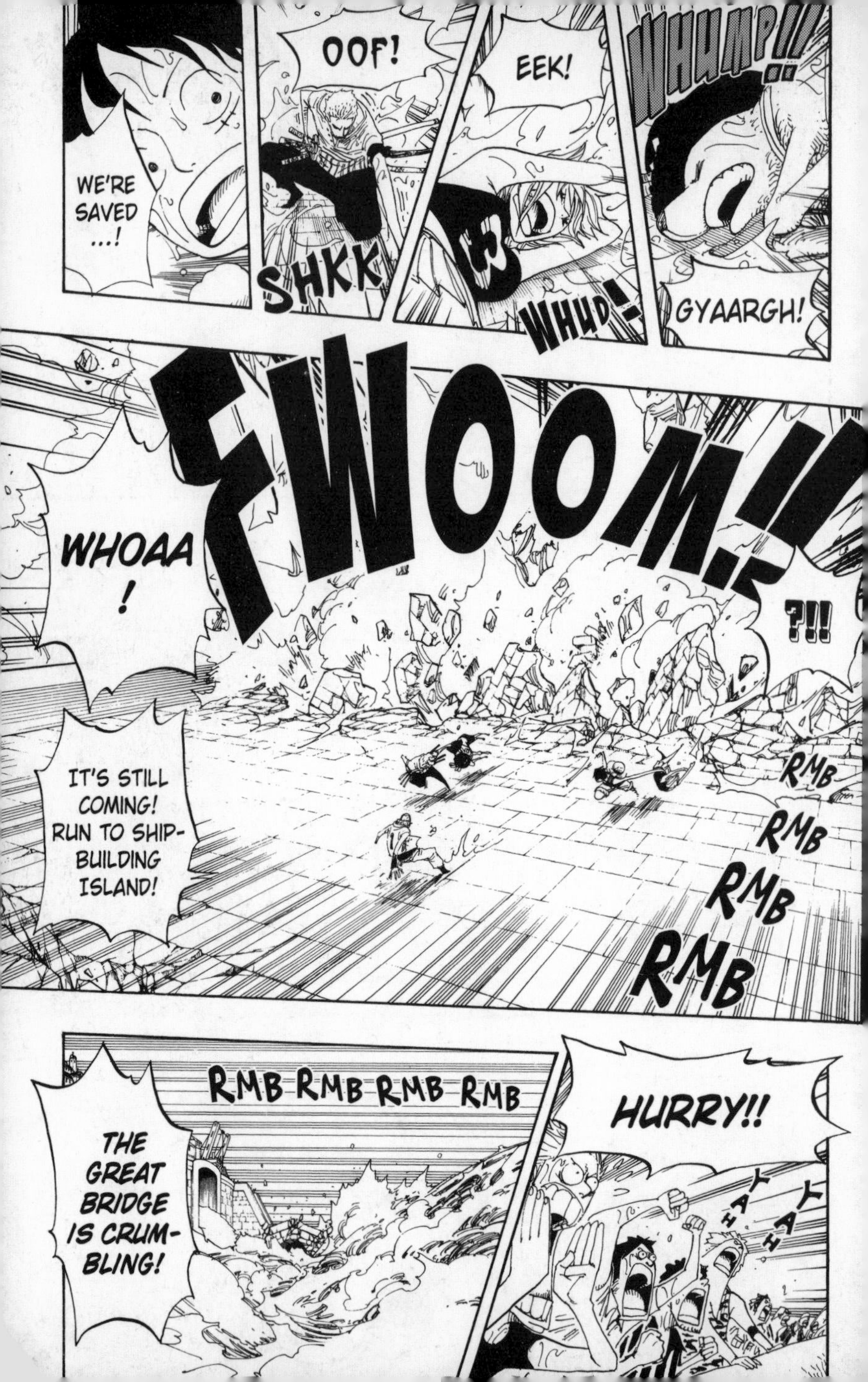
WHUMP!!
GYAARGH!
EEK!
WHUD!
OOF!
SHKK
WE'RE SAVED ...!
FWOOM!!
?!!
RMB
RMB
RMB
RMB
WHOAA!
IT'S STILL COMING! RUN TO SHIP-BUILDING ISLAND!
HURRY!!
YAH
YAH
RMB RMB RMB RMB
THE GREAT BRIDGE IS CRUM-BLING!

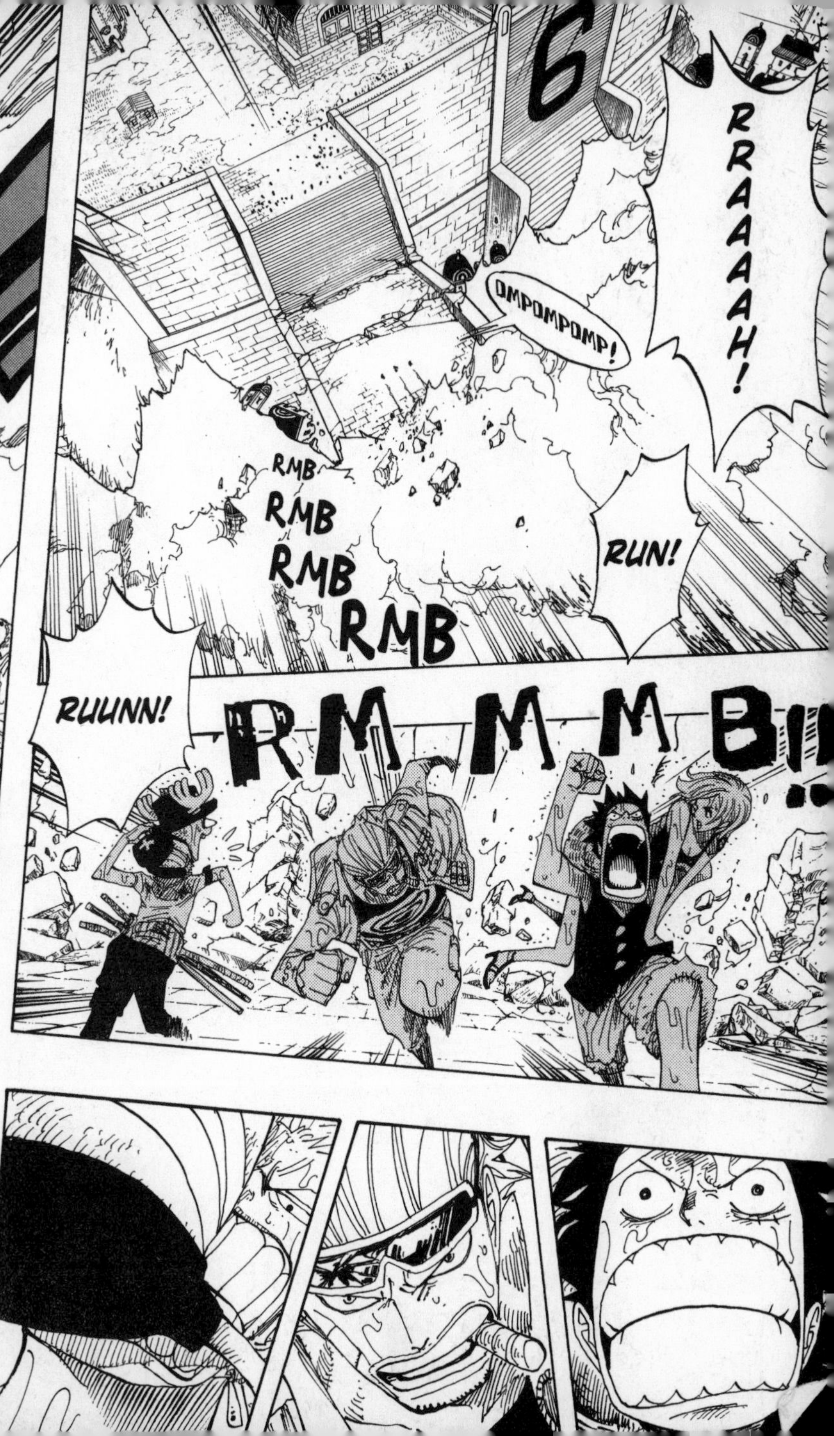
RRAAAAH!
6
OMPOMPOMP!
RMB
RMB
RMB
RMB
RUN!
RUUNN!
RMMMB!!

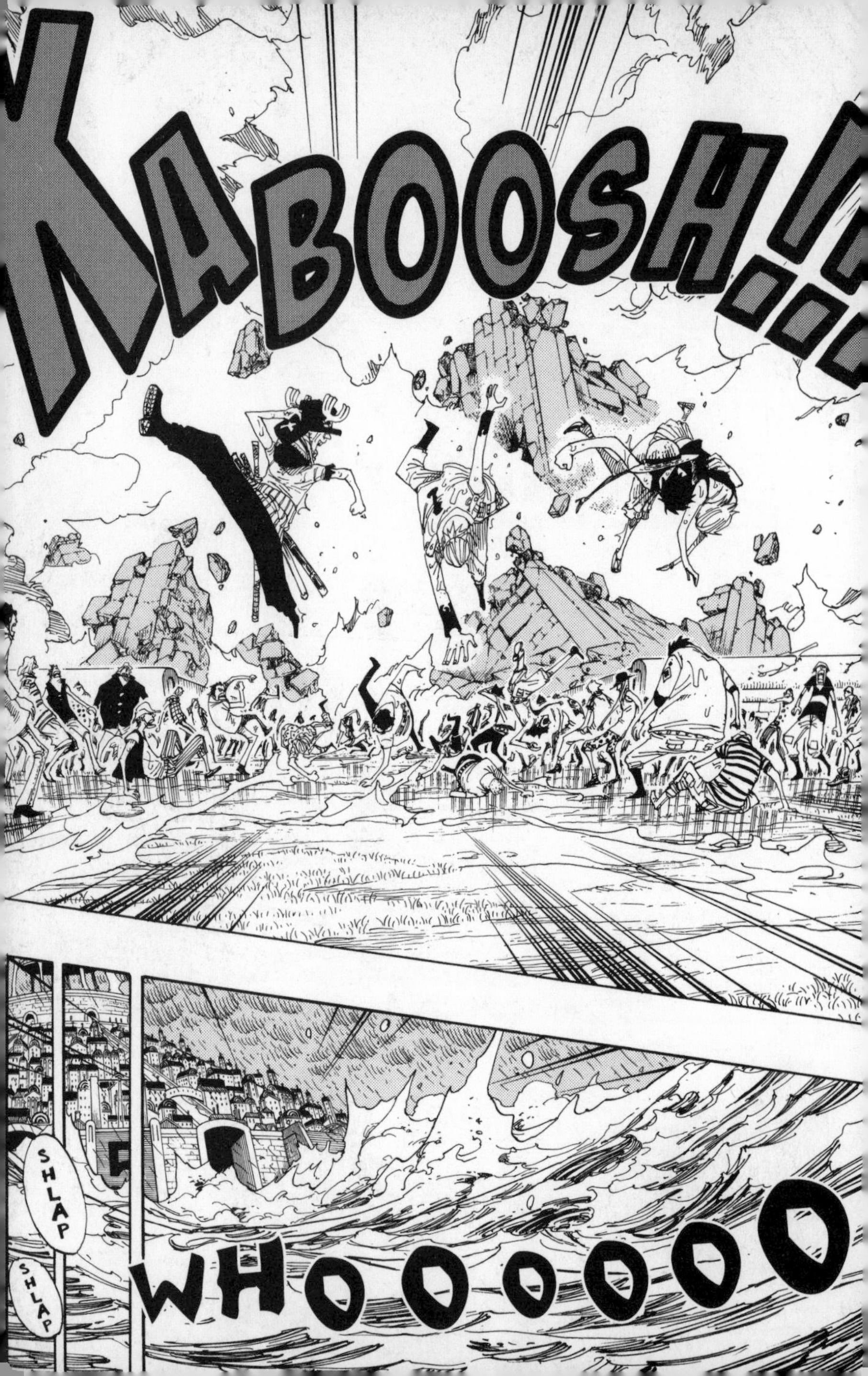
KABOOSH!!!
WHOOOOOOO
SHLAP
SHLAP

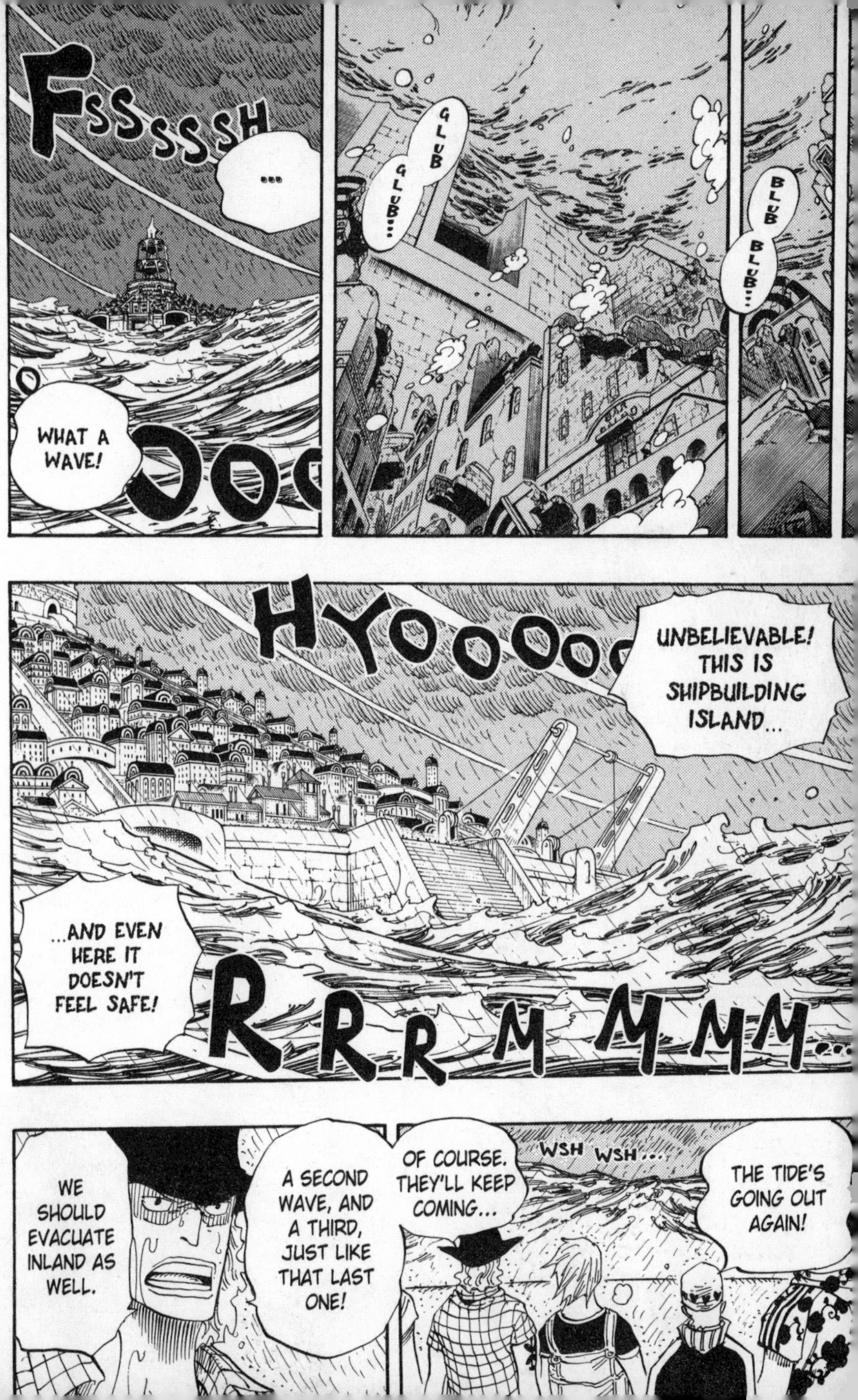
BLUB BLUB...
GLUB GLUB...
...
FSSSSSH
WHAT A WAVE!
DOOO
UNBELIEVABLE! THIS IS SHIPBUILDING ISLAND...
HYOOOO
...AND EVEN HERE IT DOESN'T FEEL SAFE!
RRRMMMM...
THE TIDE'S GOING OUT AGAIN!
WSH WSH...
OF COURSE. THEY'LL KEEP COMING...
A SECOND WAVE, AND A THIRD, JUST LIKE THAT LAST ONE!
WE SHOULD EVACUATE INLAND AS WELL.

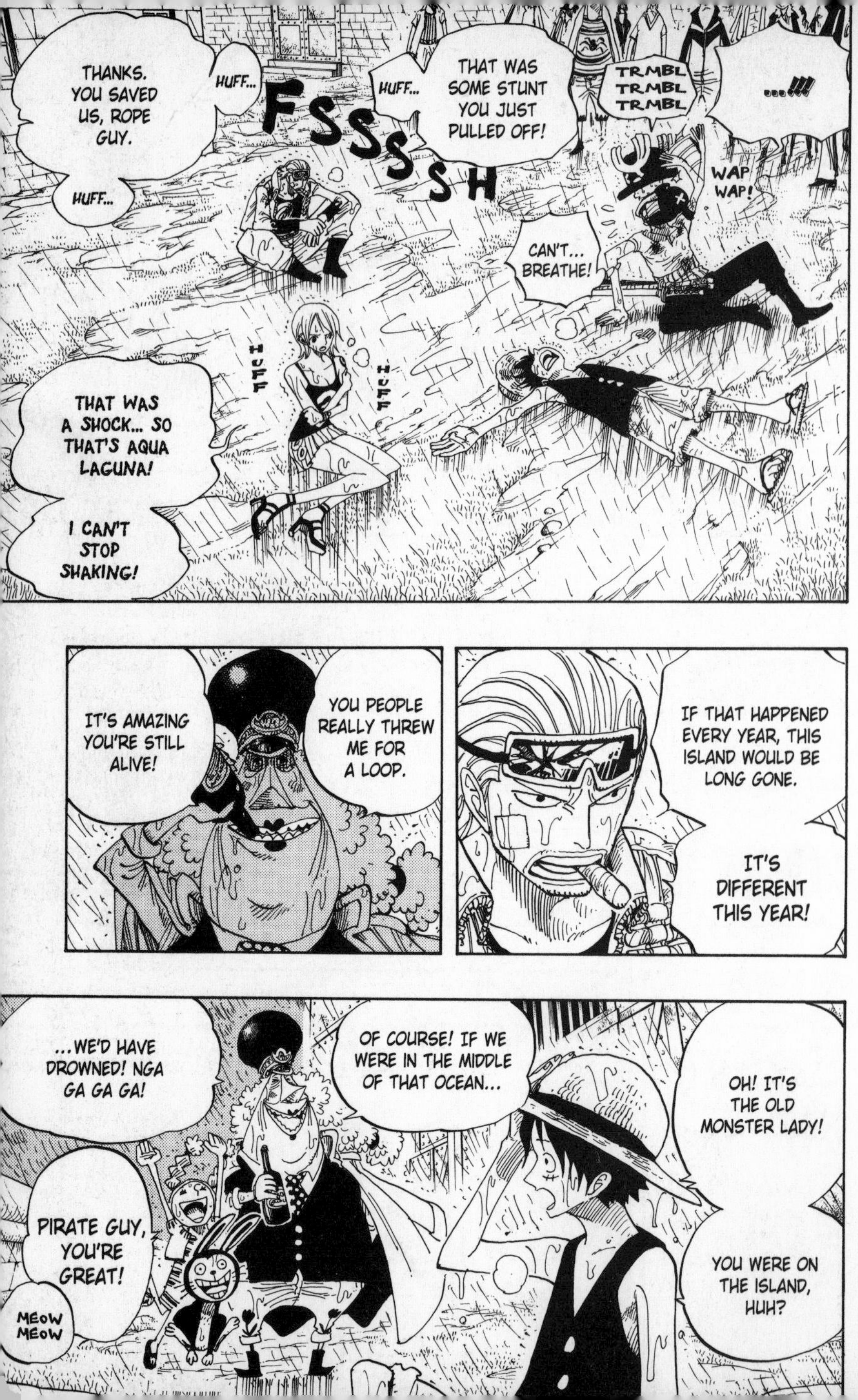
...!!!
TRMBL TRMBL TRMBL
WAP WAP!
THAT WAS SOME STUNT YOU JUST PULLED OFF!
HUFF...
FSSSSH
CAN'T... BREATHE!
HUFF...
THANKS. YOU SAVED US, ROPE GUY.
HUFF...
HUFF
HUFF
THAT WAS A SHOCK... SO THAT'S AQUA LAGUNA!
I CAN'T STOP SHAKING!
IF THAT HAPPENED EVERY YEAR, THIS ISLAND WOULD BE LONG GONE.
IT'S DIFFERENT THIS YEAR!
YOU PEOPLE REALLY THREW ME FOR A LOOP.
IT'S AMAZING YOU'RE STILL ALIVE!
OH! IT'S THE OLD MONSTER LADY!
YOU WERE ON THE ISLAND, HUH?
OF COURSE! IF WE WERE IN THE MIDDLE OF THAT OCEAN...
...WE'D HAVE DROWNED! NGA GA GA GA!
PIRATE GUY, YOU'RE GREAT!
MEOW MEOW

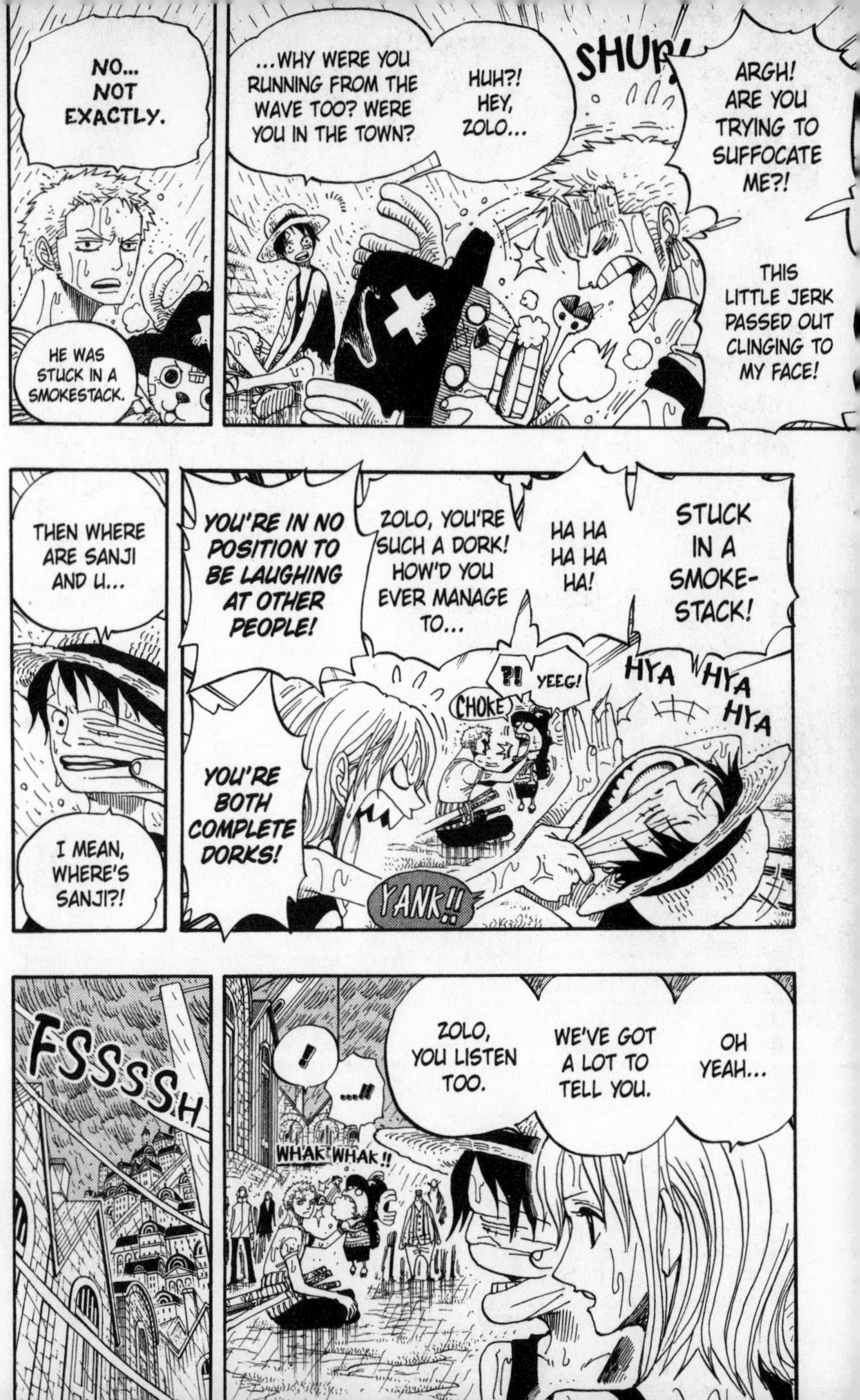
SHUP!
ARGH! ARE YOU TRYING TO SUFFOCATE ME?!
THIS LITTLE JERK PASSED OUT CLINGING TO MY FACE!
HUH?! HEY, ZOLO...
...WHY WERE YOU RUNNING FROM THE WAVE TOO? WERE YOU IN THE TOWN?
NO... NOT EXACTLY.
HE WAS STUCK IN A SMOKESTACK.
STUCK IN A SMOKE-STACK!
HA HA HA HA HA!
ZOLO, YOU'RE SUCH A DORK! HOW'D YOU EVER MANAGE TO...
YOU'RE IN NO POSITION TO BE LAUGHING AT OTHER PEOPLE!
HYA HYA HYA
YEEG!
?!
CHOKE
YOU'RE BOTH COMPLETE DORKS!
YANK!!
THEN WHERE ARE SANJI AND U...
I MEAN, WHERE'S SANJI?!
OH YEAH...
WE'VE GOT A LOT TO TELL YOU.
ZOLO, YOU LISTEN TOO.
!
...!!
WHAK WHAK!!
FSSSSH

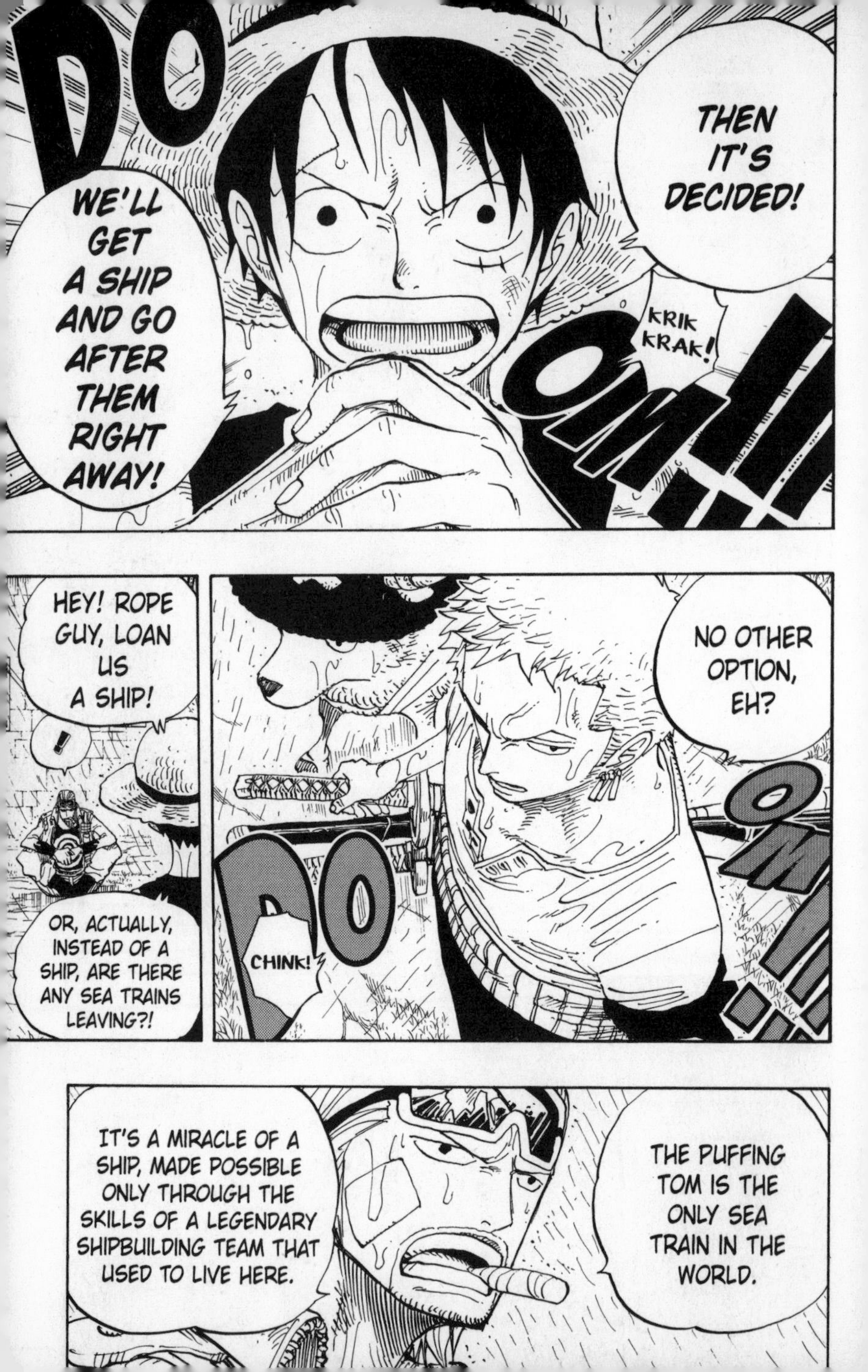

THEN IT'S DECIDED!
KRIK KRAK!
OM!!
DO
WE'LL GET A SHIP AND GO AFTER THEM RIGHT AWAY!
NO OTHER OPTION, EH?
OM!!
CHINK!
DO
HEY! ROPE GUY, LOAN US A SHIP!
!
OR, ACTUALLY, INSTEAD OF A SHIP, ARE THERE ANY SEA TRAINS LEAVING?!
THE PUFFING TOM IS THE ONLY SEA TRAIN IN THE WORLD.
IT'S A MIRACLE OF A SHIP, MADE POSSIBLE ONLY THROUGH THE SKILLS OF A LEGENDARY SHIPBUILDING TEAM THAT USED TO LIVE HERE.

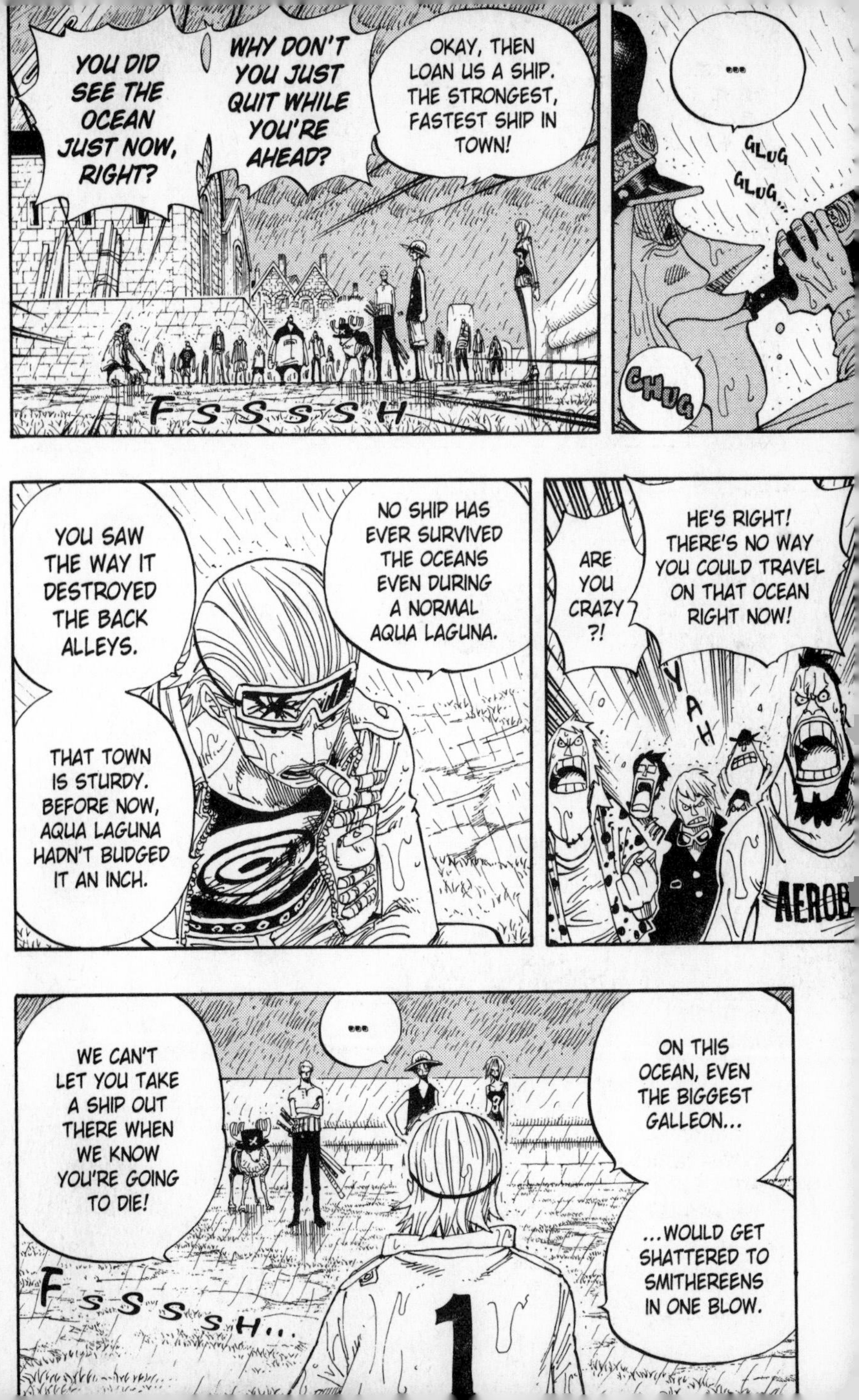
...
GLUG GLUG...
CHUG
OKAY, THEN LOAN US A SHIP. THE STRONGEST, FASTEST SHIP IN TOWN!
WHY DON'T YOU JUST QUIT WHILE YOU'RE AHEAD?
YOU DID SEE THE OCEAN JUST NOW, RIGHT?
FSSSSH
HE'S RIGHT! THERE'S NO WAY YOU COULD TRAVEL ON THAT OCEAN RIGHT NOW!
ARE YOU CRAZY?!
YAH
NO SHIP HAS EVER SURVIVED THE OCEANS EVEN DURING A NORMAL AQUA LAGUNA.
YOU SAW THE WAY IT DESTROYED THE BACK ALLEYS.
THAT TOWN IS STURDY. BEFORE NOW, AQUA LAGUNA HADN'T BUDGED IT AN INCH.
ON THIS OCEAN, EVEN THE BIGGEST GALLEON...
...WOULD GET SHATTERED TO SMITHEREENS IN ONE BLOW.
...
WE CAN'T LET YOU TAKE A SHIP OUT THERE WHEN WE KNOW YOU'RE GOING TO DIE!
FSSSSH...

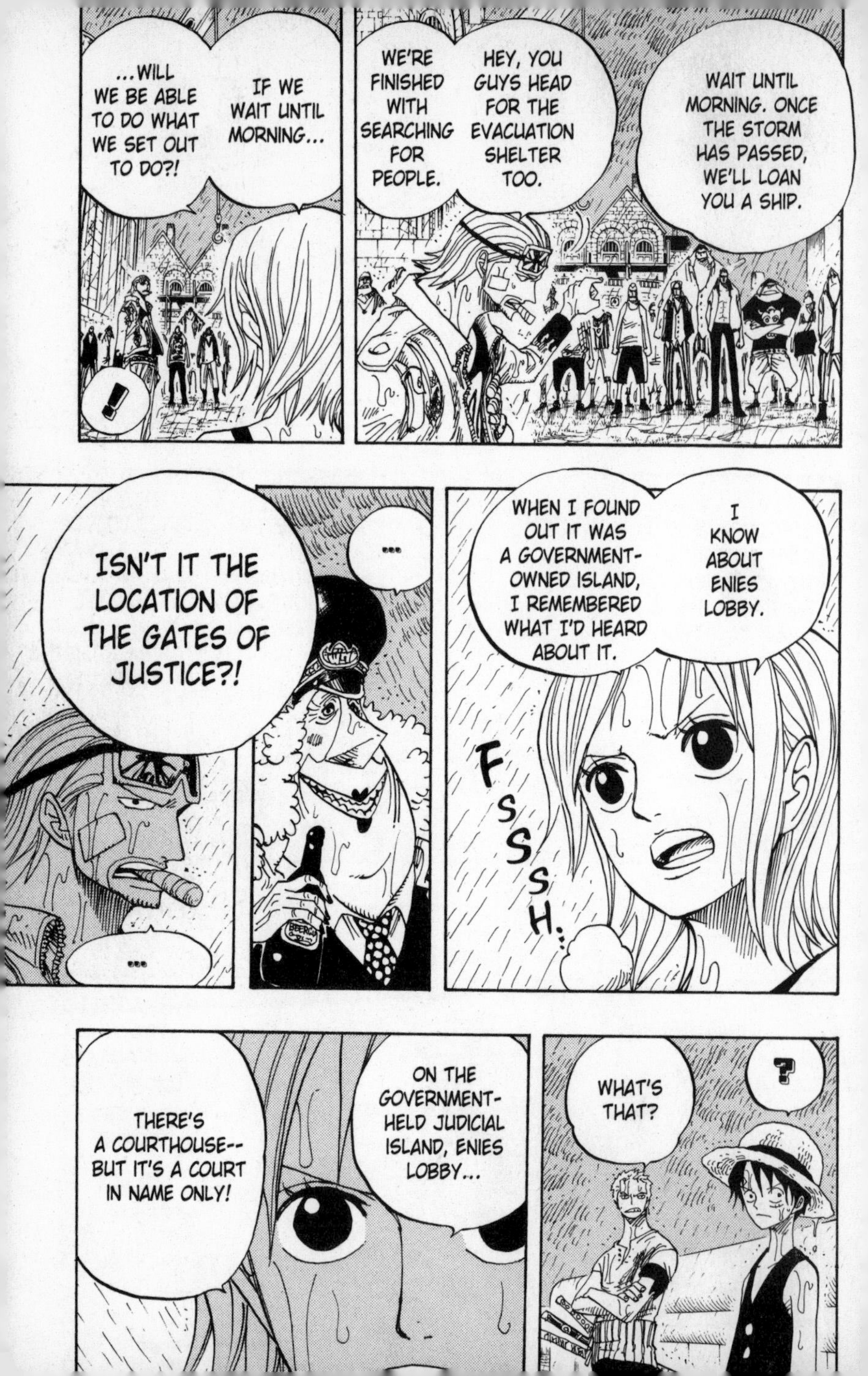
WAIT UNTIL MORNING. ONCE THE STORM HAS PASSED, WE'LL LOAN YOU A SHIP.
HEY, YOU GUYS HEAD FOR THE EVACUATION SHELTER TOO.
WE'RE FINISHED WITH SEARCHING FOR PEOPLE.
IF WE WAIT UNTIL MORNING...
...WILL WE BE ABLE TO DO WHAT WE SET OUT TO DO?!
!
I KNOW ABOUT ENIES LOBBY.
WHEN I FOUND OUT IT WAS A GOVERNMENT-OWNED ISLAND, I REMEMBERED WHAT I'D HEARD ABOUT IT.
FSSSH..
...
ISN'T IT THE LOCATION OF THE GATES OF JUSTICE?!
...
?
WHAT'S THAT?
ON THE GOVERNMENT-HELD JUDICIAL ISLAND, ENIES LOBBY...
THERE'S A COURTHOUSE-- BUT IT'S A COURT IN NAME ONLY!

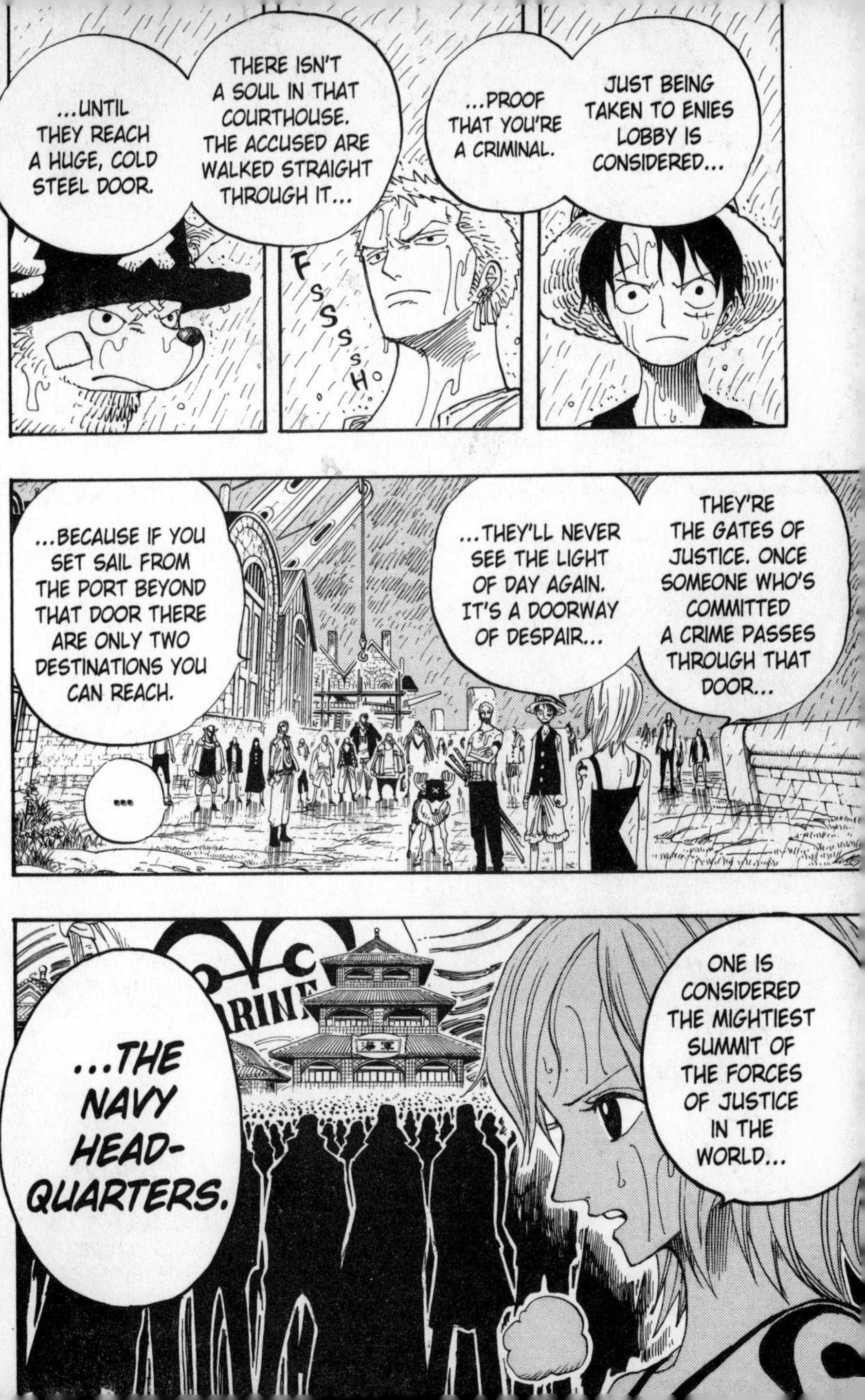
JUST BEING TAKEN TO ENIES LOBBY IS CONSIDERED...
...PROOF THAT YOU'RE A CRIMINAL.
THERE ISN'T A SOUL IN THAT COURTHOUSE. THE ACCUSED ARE WALKED STRAIGHT THROUGH IT...
FSSSSH
...UNTIL THEY REACH A HUGE, COLD STEEL DOOR.
THEY'RE THE GATES OF JUSTICE. ONCE SOMEONE WHO'S COMMITTED A CRIME PASSES THROUGH THAT DOOR...
...THEY'LL NEVER SEE THE LIGHT OF DAY AGAIN. IT'S A DOORWAY OF DESPAIR...
...BECAUSE IF YOU SET SAIL FROM THE PORT BEYOND THAT DOOR THERE ARE ONLY TWO DESTINATIONS YOU CAN REACH.
...
ONE IS CONSIDERED THE MIGHTIEST SUMMIT OF THE FORCES OF JUSTICE IN THE WORLD...
ARINE
...THE NAVY HEAD-QUARTERS.

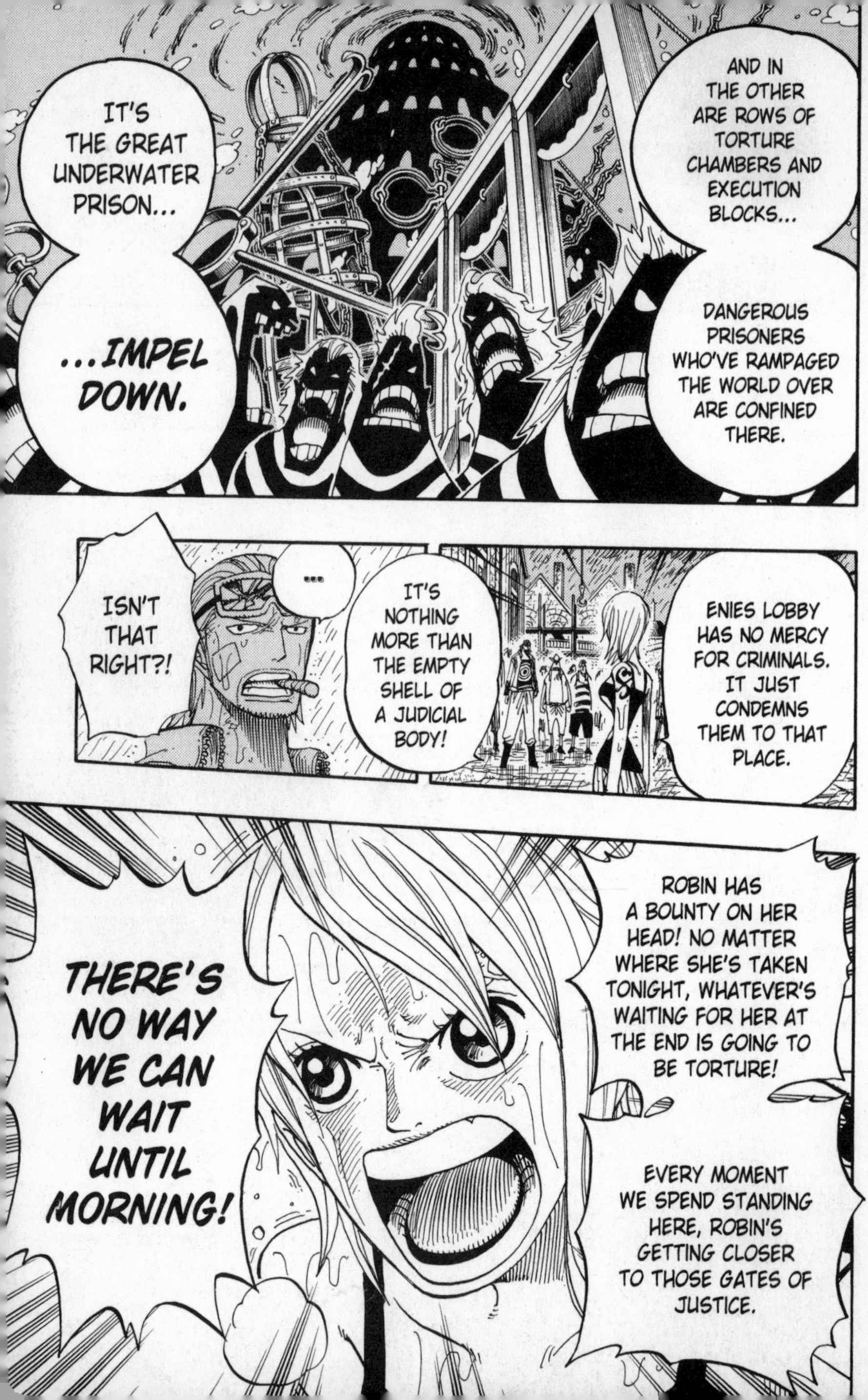
AND IN THE OTHER ARE ROWS OF TORTURE CHAMBERS AND EXECUTION BLOCKS...
DANGEROUS PRISONERS WHO'VE RAMPAGED THE WORLD OVER ARE CONFINED THERE.
IT'S THE GREAT UNDERWATER PRISON...
...IMPEL DOWN.
ENIES LOBBY HAS NO MERCY FOR CRIMINALS. IT JUST CONDEMNS THEM TO THAT PLACE.
IT'S NOTHING MORE THAN THE EMPTY SHELL OF A JUDICIAL BODY!
...
ISN'T THAT RIGHT?!
ROBIN HAS A BOUNTY ON HER HEAD! NO MATTER WHERE SHE'S TAKEN TONIGHT, WHATEVER'S WAITING FOR HER AT THE END IS GOING TO BE TORTURE!
EVERY MOMENT WE SPEND STANDING HERE, ROBIN'S GETTING CLOSER TO THOSE GATES OF JUSTICE.
THERE'S NO WAY WE CAN WAIT UNTIL MORNING!

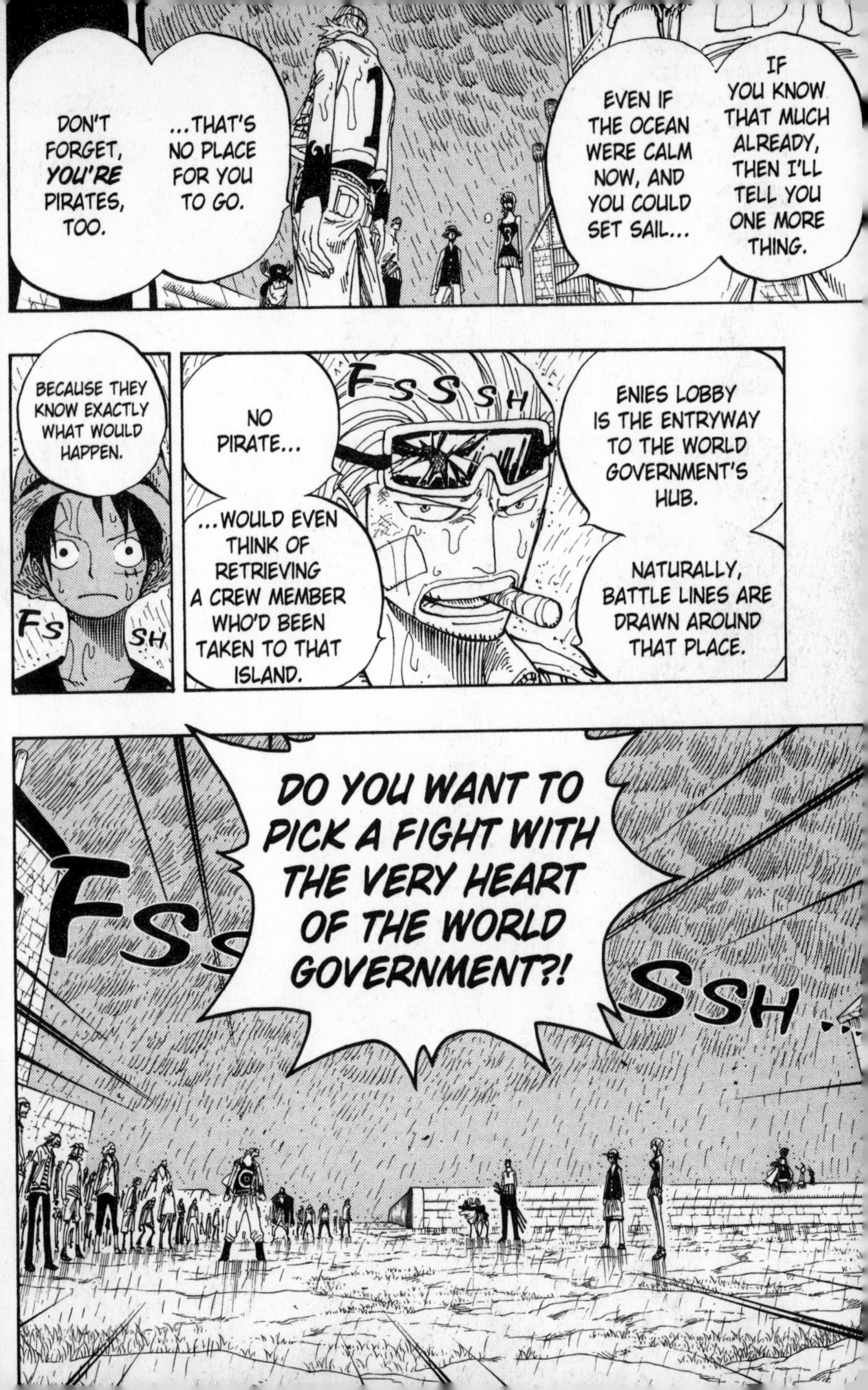
IF YOU KNOW THAT MUCH ALREADY, THEN I'LL TELL YOU ONE MORE THING.
EVEN IF THE OCEAN WERE CALM NOW, AND YOU COULD SET SAIL...
...THAT'S NO PLACE FOR YOU TO GO.
DON'T FORGET, *YOU'RE* PIRATES, TOO.
ENIES LOBBY IS THE ENTRYWAY TO THE WORLD GOVERNMENT'S HUB.
NATURALLY, BATTLE LINES ARE DRAWN AROUND THAT PLACE.
FSSSH
NO PIRATE...
...WOULD EVEN THINK OF RETRIEVING A CREW MEMBER WHO'D BEEN TAKEN TO THAT ISLAND.
BECAUSE THEY KNOW EXACTLY WHAT WOULD HAPPEN.
FS SH
DO YOU WANT TO PICK A FIGHT WITH THE VERY HEART OF THE WORLD GOVERNMENT?!
FSS SSH...

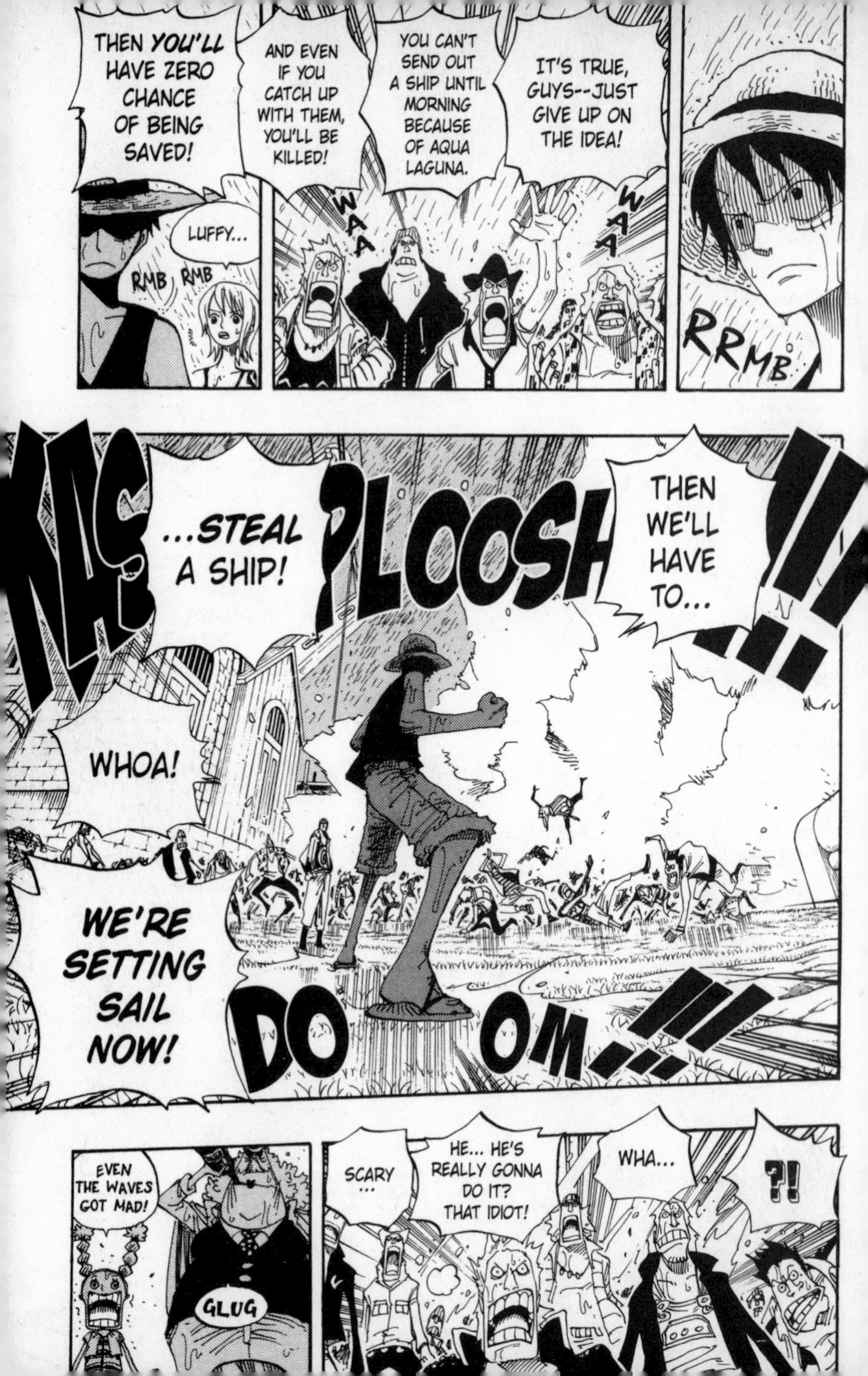
RRMB
IT'S TRUE, GUYS--JUST GIVE UP ON THE IDEA!
YOU CAN'T SEND OUT A SHIP UNTIL MORNING BECAUSE OF AQUA LAGUNA.
AND EVEN IF YOU CATCH UP WITH THEM, YOU'LL BE KILLED!
WAA
WAA
THEN YOU'LL HAVE ZERO CHANCE OF BEING SAVED!
LUFFY...
RMB RMB
THEN WE'LL HAVE TO...
PLOOSH
...STEAL A SHIP!
WHOA!
WE'RE SETTING SAIL NOW!
DO OM...!!!
?!
WHA...
HE... HE'S REALLY GONNA DO IT? THAT IDIOT!
SCARY...
EVEN THE WAVES GOT MAD!
GLUG

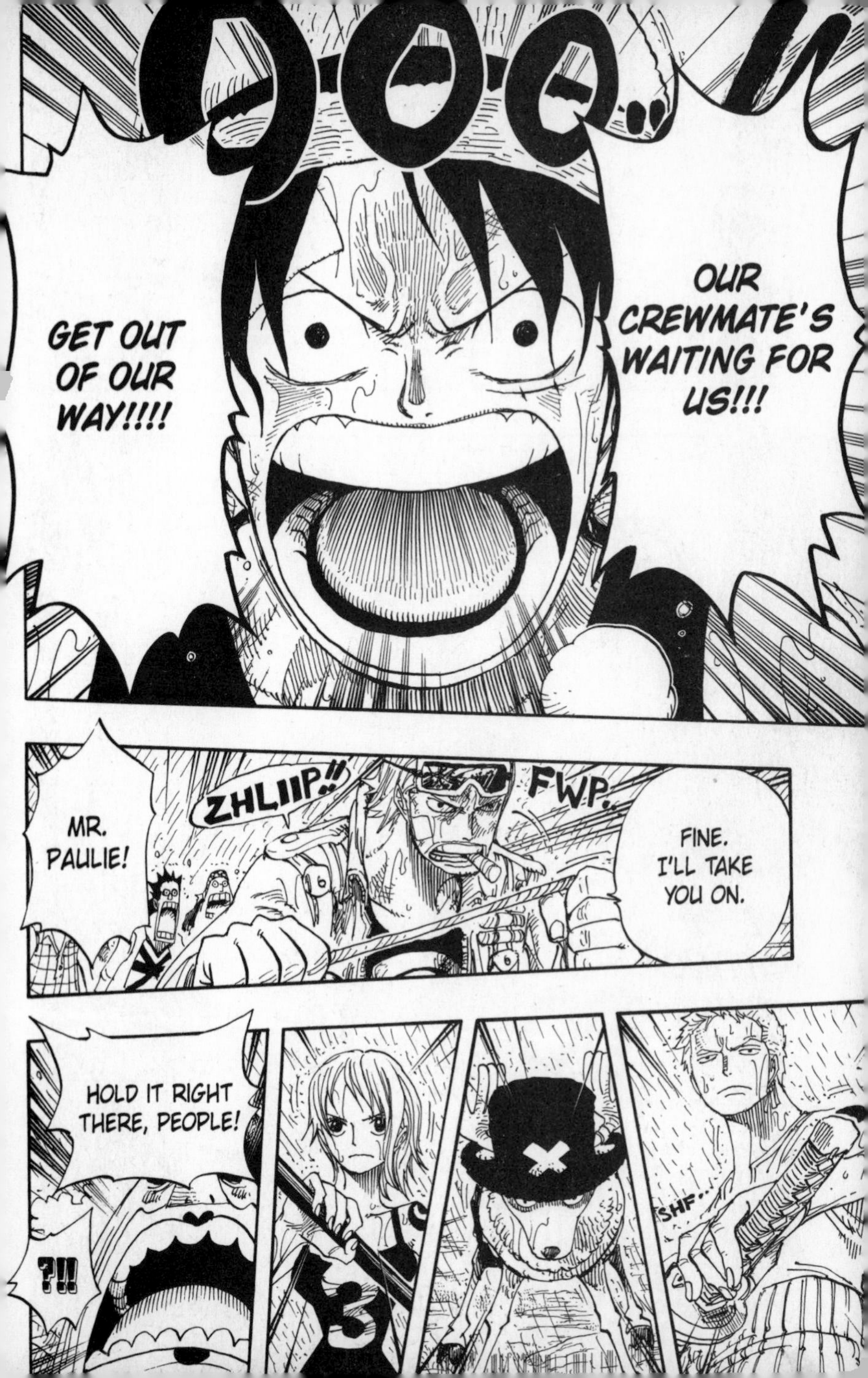
OUR CREWMATE'S WAITING FOR US!!!
GET OUT OF OUR WAY!!!!!
FINE. I'LL TAKE YOU ON.
FWP..
ZHLIIP!!
MR. PAULIE!
SHF...
HOLD IT RIGHT THERE, PEOPLE!
?!!

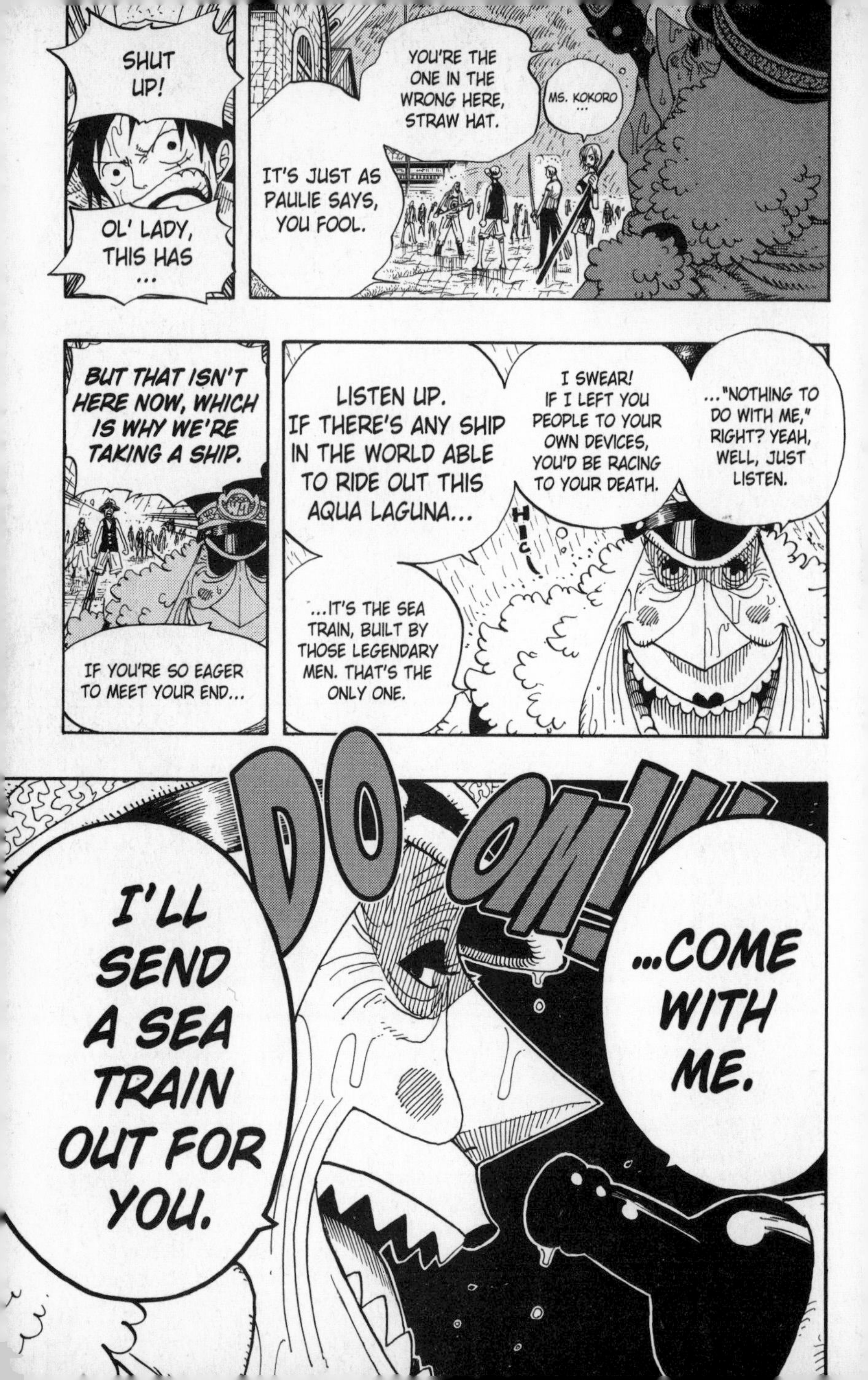
MS. KOKORO ...
YOU'RE THE ONE IN THE WRONG HERE, STRAW HAT.
IT'S JUST AS PAULIE SAYS, YOU FOOL.
SHUT UP!
OL' LADY, THIS HAS ...
..."NOTHING TO DO WITH ME," RIGHT? YEAH, WELL, JUST LISTEN.
I SWEAR! IF I LEFT YOU PEOPLE TO YOUR OWN DEVICES, YOU'D BE RACING TO YOUR DEATH.
HIC!
LISTEN UP. IF THERE'S ANY SHIP IN THE WORLD ABLE TO RIDE OUT THIS AQUA LAGUNA...
...IT'S THE SEA TRAIN, BUILT BY THOSE LEGENDARY MEN. THAT'S THE ONLY ONE.
BUT THAT ISN'T HERE NOW, WHICH IS WHY WE'RE TAKING A SHIP.
IF YOU'RE SO EAGER TO MEET YOUR END...
DOON!!
...COME WITH ME.
I'LL SEND A SEA TRAIN OUT FOR YOU.

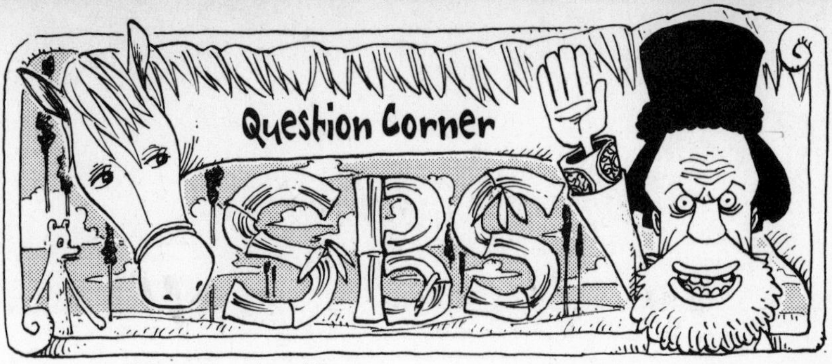

Question Corner
SBS

Reader: Would you pass the salt?

-- Yumi-chan

Oda: Oh, sure. Here you go.

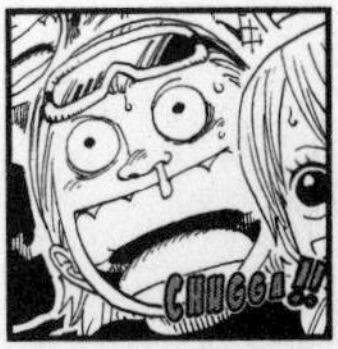

CHUGGA!!

Reader: Question for Odacchi! In Chapter 354: Sea Train, when the sea train sets sail, that snot-nosed guy on the lower left... Is that Paulie?! If you don't answer my question, I'll tie you up with rope! (Big ol' lie.)

--Meat-Meat-Meat-Meat-Meat

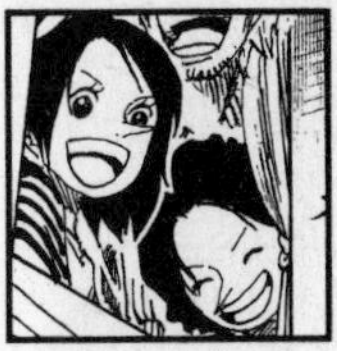

Reader: Oda Sensei! Oda Sensei! Those little girls who were riding on the sea train when it opened for service in vol. 37... Those were Mozu and Kiwi, weren't they? Ooh, ahh! They were so cute back then, and now! Now, they're so...! Daddy doesn't remember raising them to be like that! Oh, Daddy's sad. He's going to cry.

--Daddy (female)

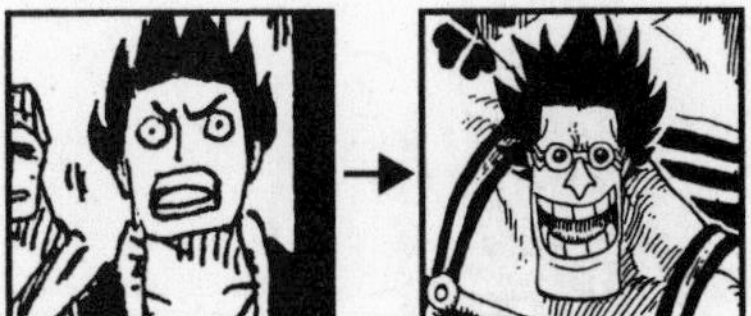

Oda: All right, lotsa letters came about these! Well, I assumed you guys would pick up on them; and that's why I drew 'em. They're both right. Paulie was really moved at the time; that emotion stayed with him, and now he's a great shipwright. And Kiwi and Mozu also wanted to become shipwrights, but they didn't pass Galley-La's test. Franky picked them up just as they were going delinquent, and the rest is history. And, on top of that, there was one more person ⬆ at that place with them: Zambai, the guy who holds the Franky Family together. He also intended to become a shipwright, then went delinquent. The Franky Family is comprised of a collection of Water Seven's failures and baddies. Franky is a benefactor to these people.

Chapter 365: ROCKETMAN!!

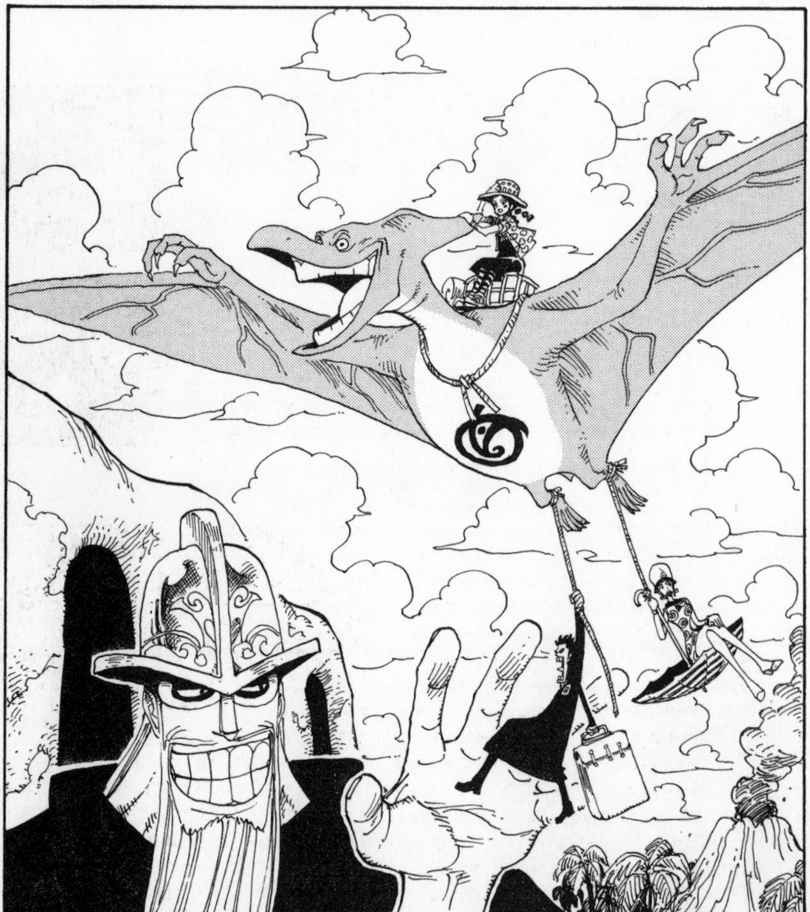

MS. GOLDEN WEEK'S BIG PLAN, A BAROQUE REUNION, VOL. 6: "GREAT ESCAPE FROM THE ISLAND OF GIANTS"

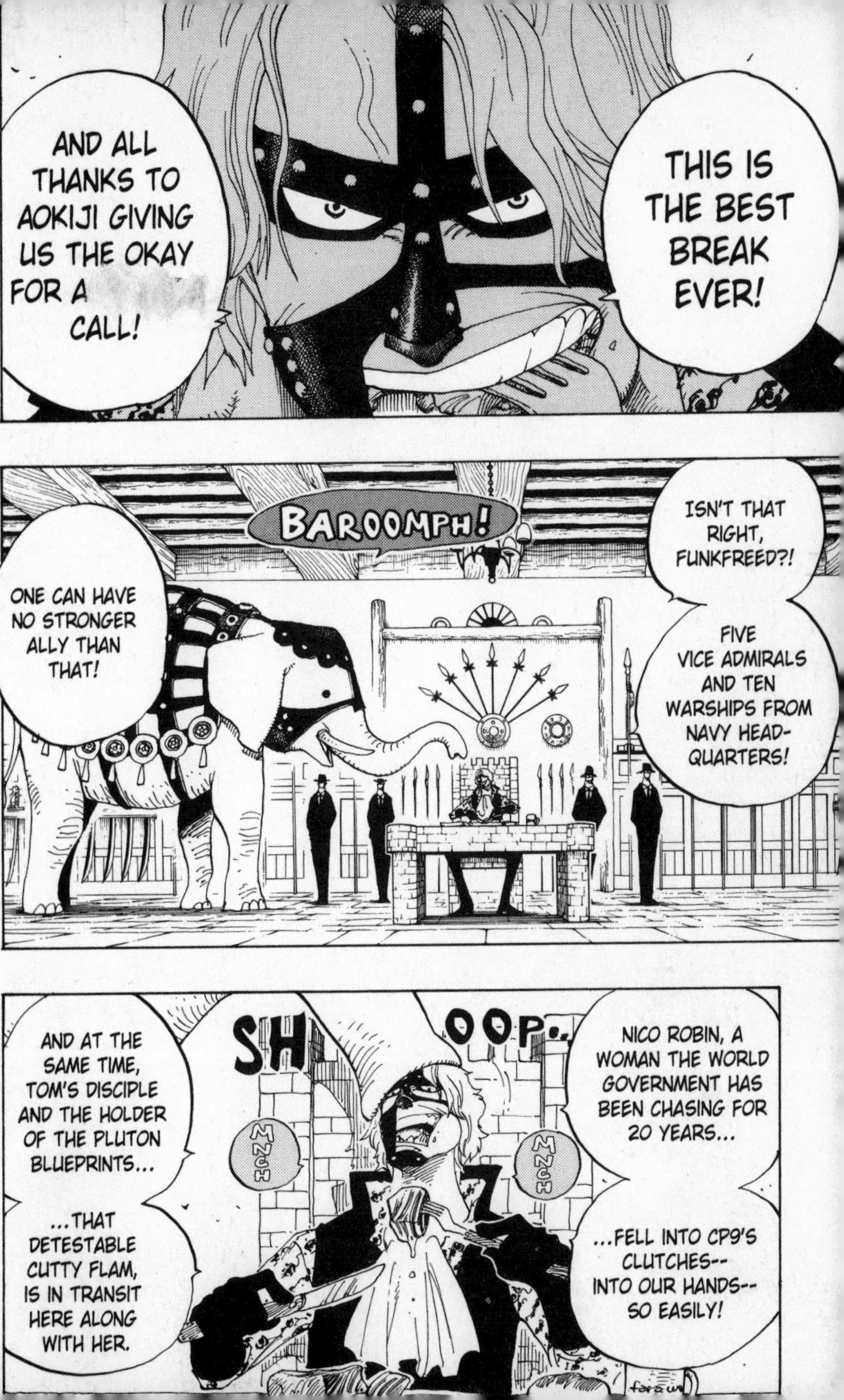
THIS IS THE BEST BREAK EVER!
AND ALL THANKS TO AOKIJI GIVING US THE OKAY FOR A CALL!
BAROOMPH!
ISN'T THAT RIGHT, FUNKFREED?!
FIVE VICE ADMIRALS AND TEN WARSHIPS FROM NAVY HEAD-QUARTERS!
ONE CAN HAVE NO STRONGER ALLY THAN THAT!
SHOOP..
NICO ROBIN, A WOMAN THE WORLD GOVERNMENT HAS BEEN CHASING FOR 20 YEARS...
...FELL INTO CP9'S CLUTCHES-- INTO OUR HANDS-- SO EASILY!
MNCH
MNCH
AND AT THE SAME TIME, TOM'S DISCIPLE AND THE HOLDER OF THE PLUTON BLUEPRINTS...
...THAT DETESTABLE CUTTY FLAM, IS IN TRANSIT HERE ALONG WITH HER.

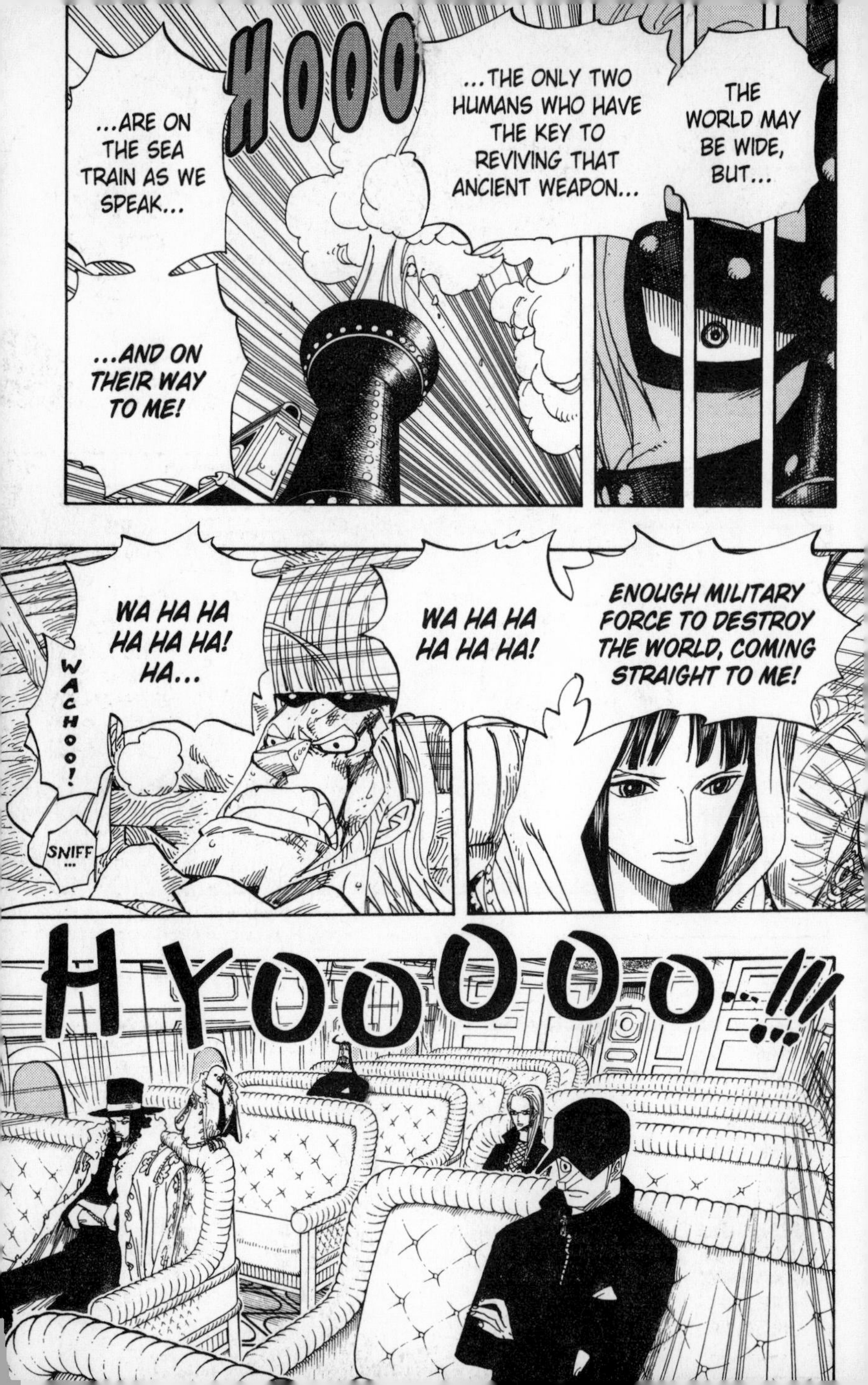
THE WORLD MAY BE WIDE, BUT...
...THE ONLY TWO HUMANS WHO HAVE THE KEY TO REVIVING THAT ANCIENT WEAPON...
HOOO
...ARE ON THE SEA TRAIN AS WE SPEAK...
...AND ON THEIR WAY TO ME!
ENOUGH MILITARY FORCE TO DESTROY THE WORLD, COMING STRAIGHT TO ME!
WA HA HA HA HA HA!
WA HA HA HA HA HA! HA...
WACHOO!
SNIFF...
HYOOOOO...!!

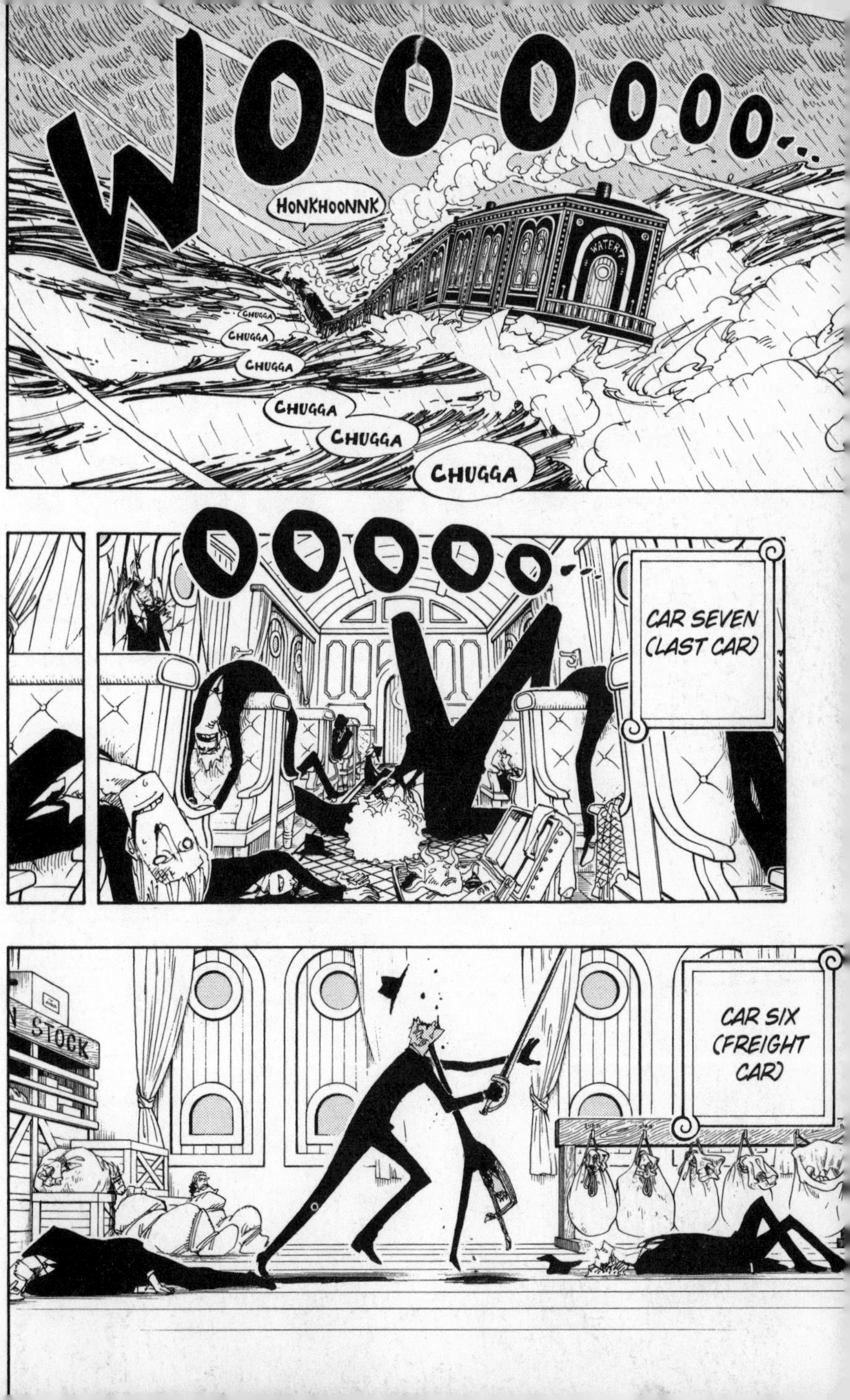
WOOOOOO...
HONKHOONNK
CHUGGA
CHUGGA
CHUGGA
CHUGGA
CHUGGA
CHUGGA
CAR SEVEN (LAST CAR)
OOOOO...
CAR SIX (FREIGHT CAR)
STOCK

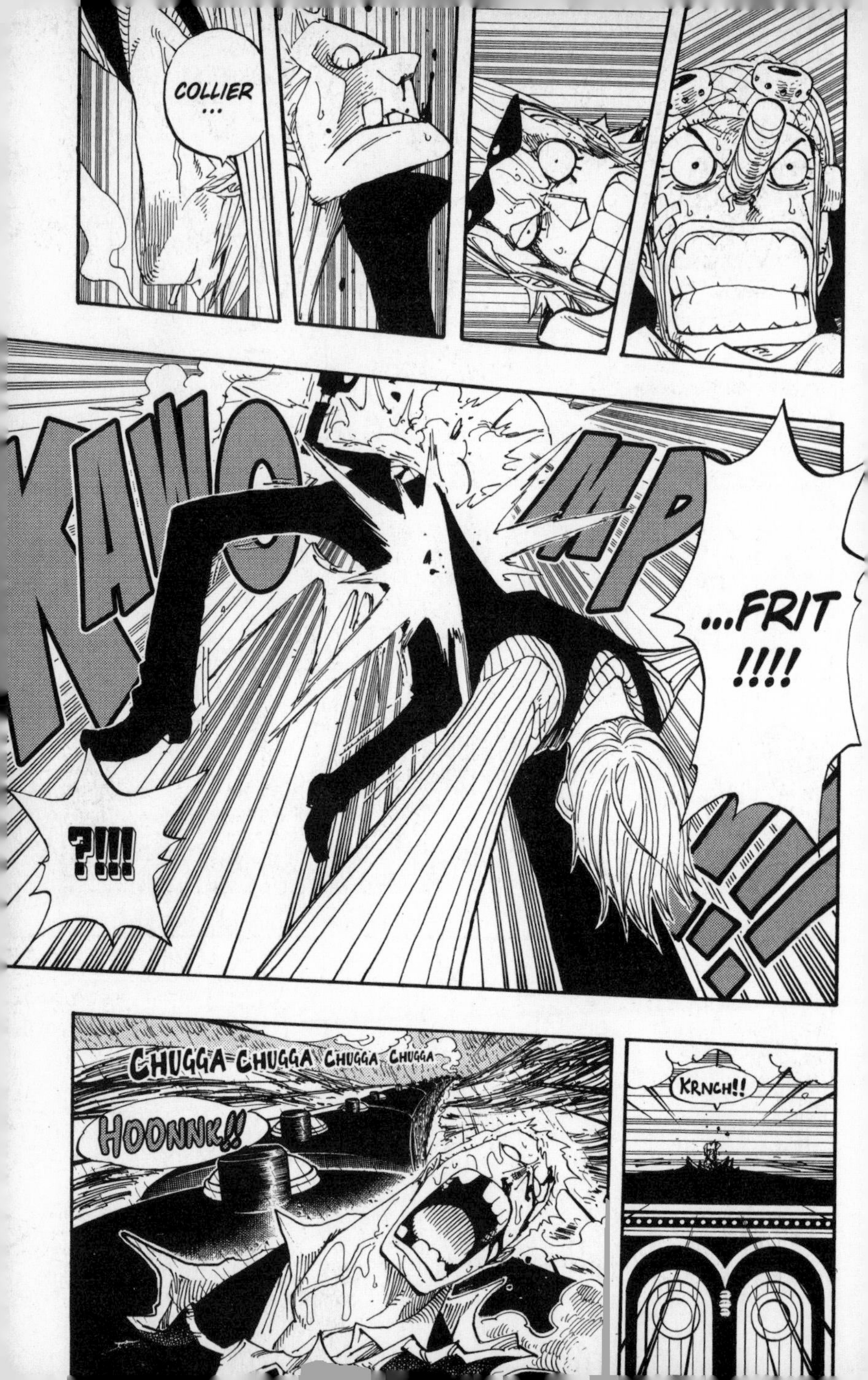
COLLIER ...
KAWOOMP
...FRIT !!!!
?!!!
KRNCH!!
CHUGGA CHUGGA CHUGGA CHUGGA
HOONNK!!

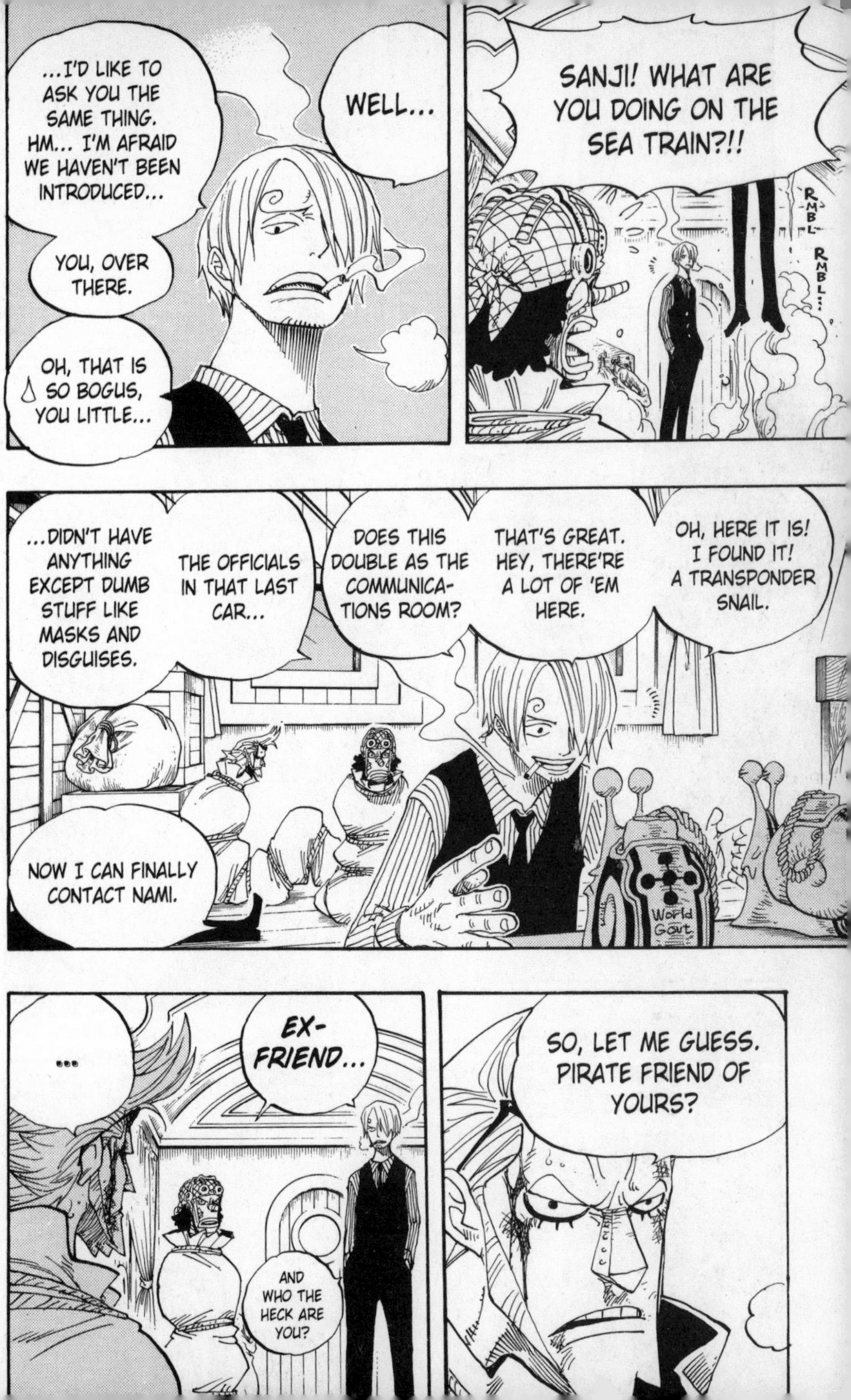
SANJI! WHAT ARE YOU DOING ON THE SEA TRAIN?!!
RMBL
RMBL...
WELL...
...I'D LIKE TO ASK YOU THE SAME THING. HM... I'M AFRAID WE HAVEN'T BEEN INTRODUCED...
YOU, OVER THERE.
OH, THAT IS SO BOGUS, YOU LITTLE...
OH, HERE IT IS! I FOUND IT! A TRANSPONDER SNAIL.
THAT'S GREAT. HEY, THERE'RE A LOT OF 'EM HERE.
DOES THIS DOUBLE AS THE COMMUNICATIONS ROOM?
THE OFFICIALS IN THAT LAST CAR...
...DIDN'T HAVE ANYTHING EXCEPT DUMB STUFF LIKE MASKS AND DISGUISES.
NOW I CAN FINALLY CONTACT NAMI.
World Govt.
SO, LET ME GUESS. PIRATE FRIEND OF YOURS?
EX-FRIEND...
...
AND WHO THE HECK ARE YOU?

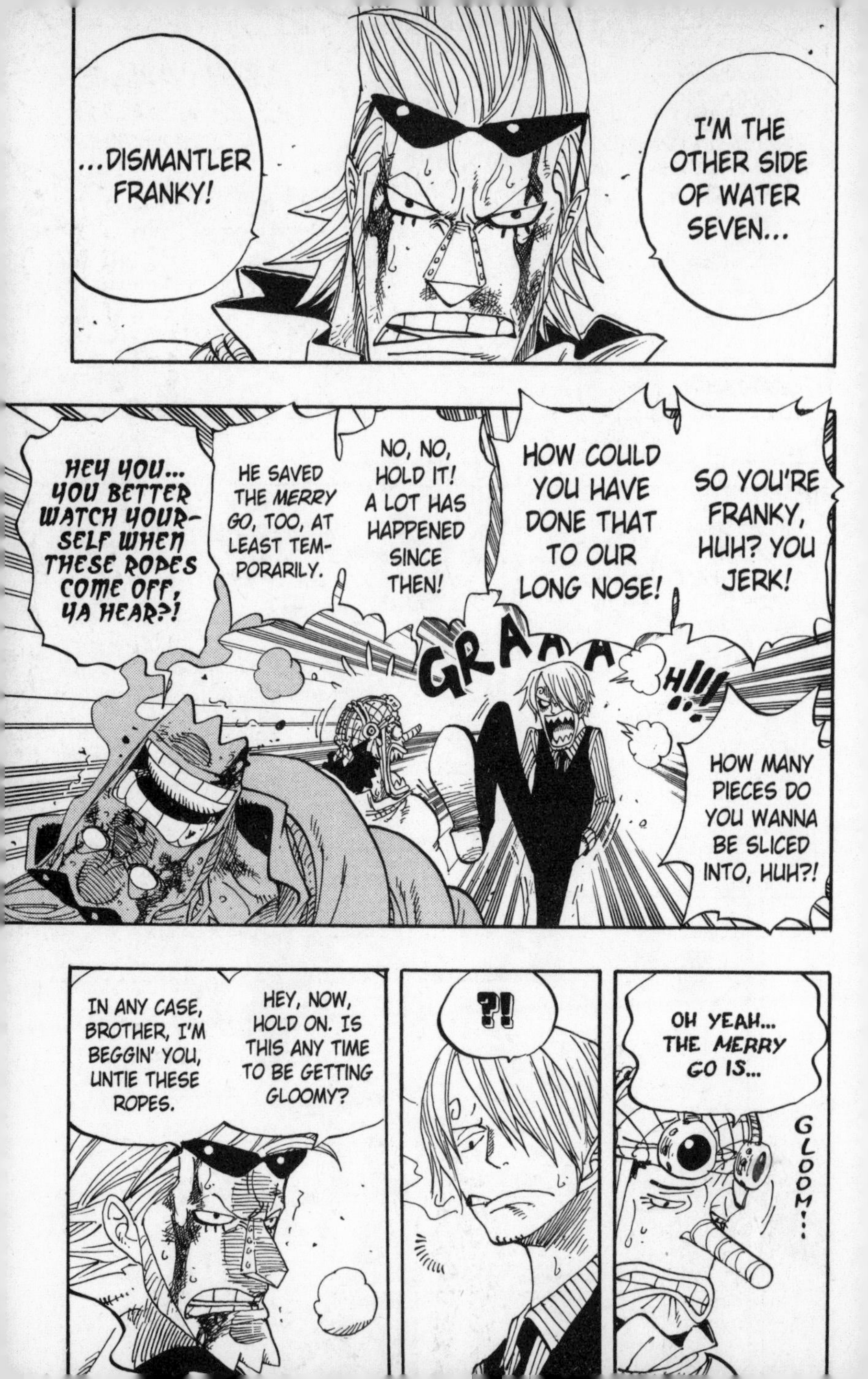
I'M THE OTHER SIDE OF WATER SEVEN...
...DISMANTLER FRANKY!
SO YOU'RE FRANKY, HUH? YOU JERK!
HOW COULD YOU HAVE DONE THAT TO OUR LONG NOSE!
GRAAAAH!!!
HOW MANY PIECES DO YOU WANNA BE SLICED INTO, HUH?!
NO, NO, HOLD IT! A LOT HAS HAPPENED SINCE THEN!
HE SAVED THE MERRY GO, TOO, AT LEAST TEMPORARILY.
HEY YOU... YOU BETTER WATCH YOURSELF WHEN THESE ROPES COME OFF, YA HEAR?!
OH YEAH... THE MERRY GO IS...
GLOOM...
?!
HEY, NOW, HOLD ON. IS THIS ANY TIME TO BE GETTING GLOOMY?
IN ANY CASE, BROTHER, I'M BEGGIN' YOU, UNTIE THESE ROPES.

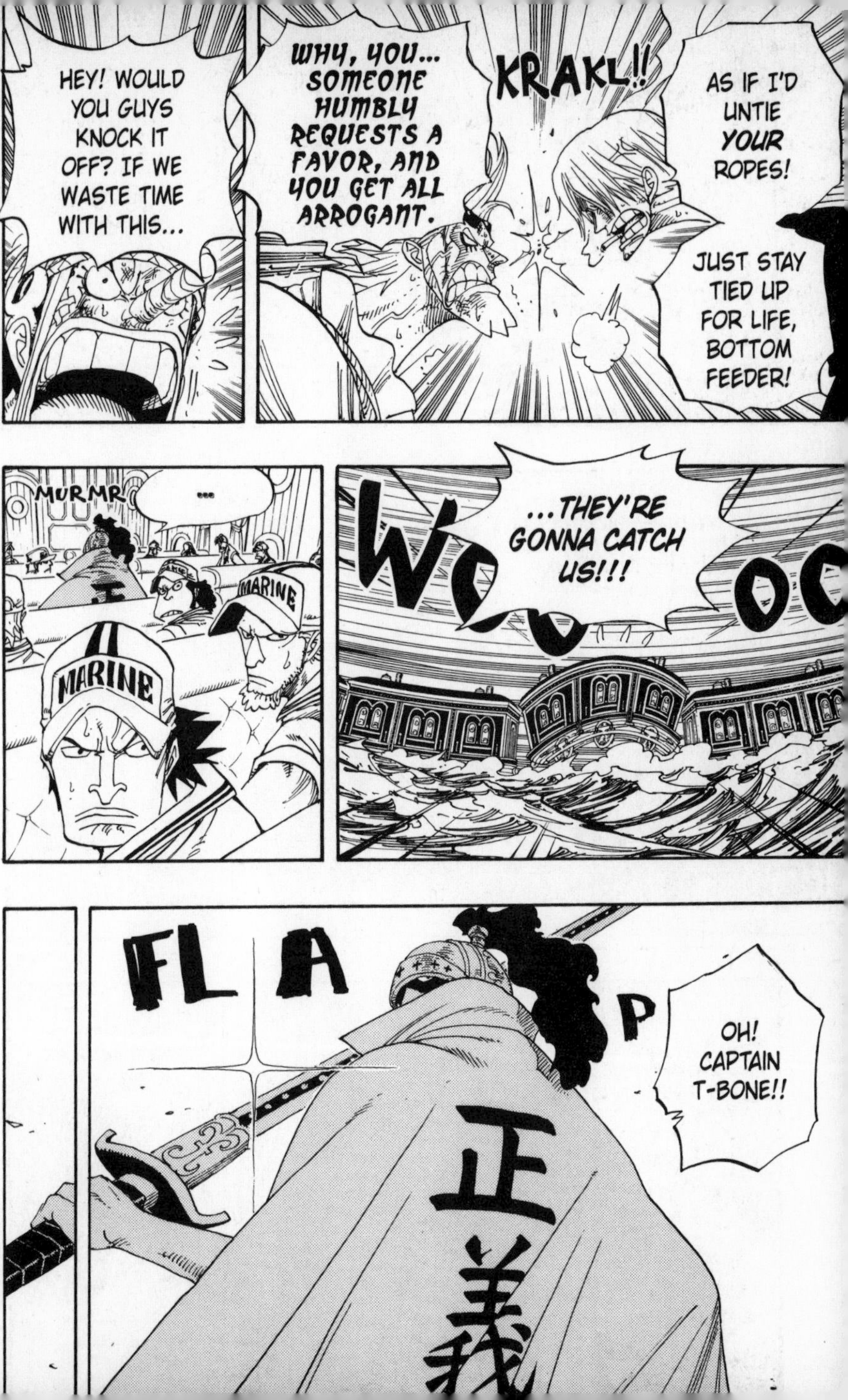
AS IF I'D UNTIE YOUR ROPES!
KRAKL!!
WHY, YOU... SOMEONE HUMBLY REQUESTS A FAVOR, AND YOU GET ALL ARROGANT.
JUST STAY TIED UP FOR LIFE, BOTTOM FEEDER!
HEY! WOULD YOU GUYS KNOCK IT OFF? IF WE WASTE TIME WITH THIS...
...THEY'RE GONNA CATCH US!!!
MURMR
...
MARINE
MARINE
FLAP
OH! CAPTAIN T-BONE!!
正
義

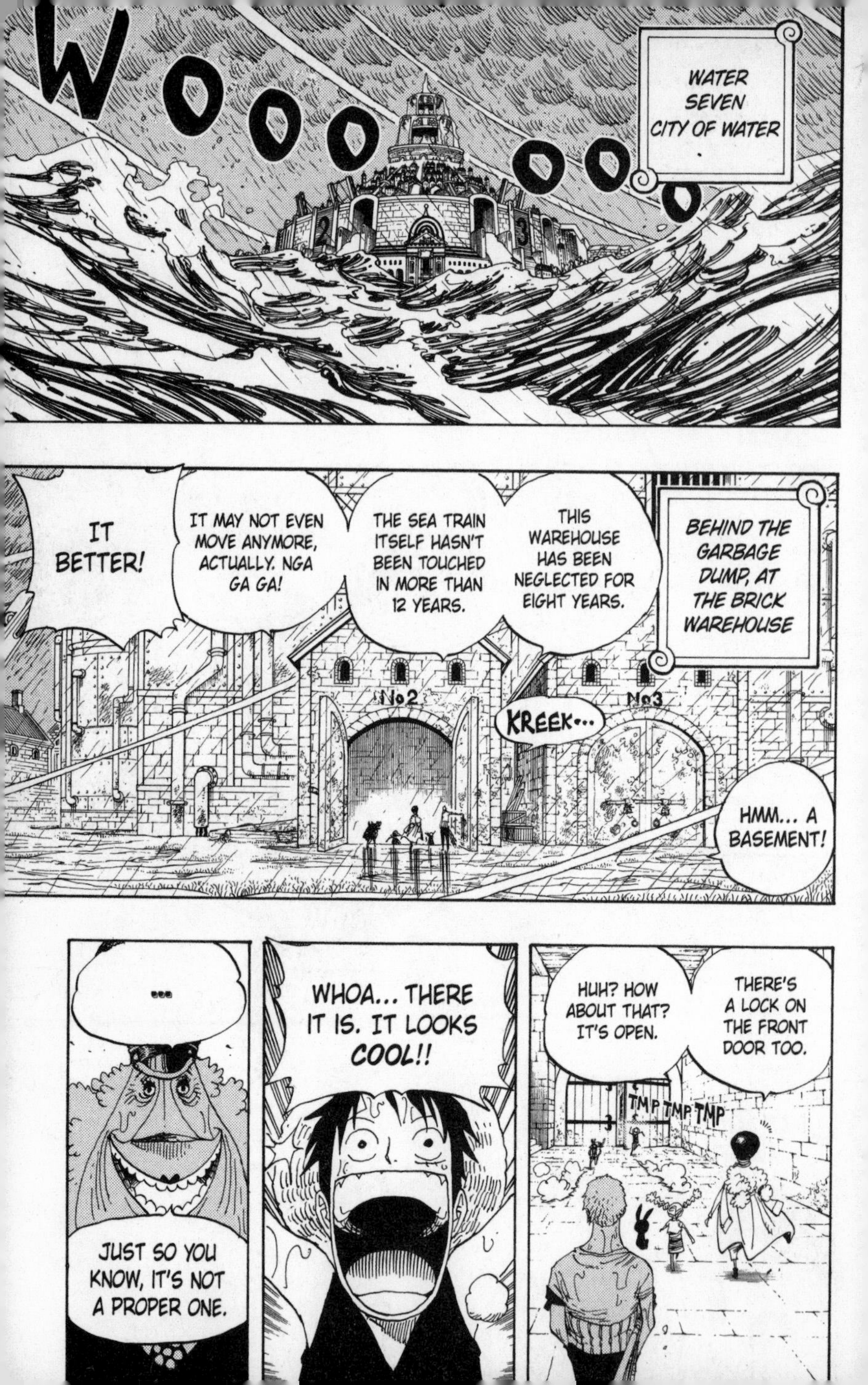
WATER SEVEN CITY OF WATER
WOOOOOOO
BEHIND THE GARBAGE DUMP, AT THE BRICK WAREHOUSE
THIS WAREHOUSE HAS BEEN NEGLECTED FOR EIGHT YEARS.
THE SEA TRAIN ITSELF HASN'T BEEN TOUCHED IN MORE THAN 12 YEARS.
IT MAY NOT EVEN MOVE ANYMORE, ACTUALLY. NGA GA GA!
IT BETTER!
No3
KREEK...
No2
HMM... A BASEMENT!
THERE'S A LOCK ON THE FRONT DOOR TOO.
HUH? HOW ABOUT THAT? IT'S OPEN.
TMP TMP TMP
WHOA... THERE IT IS. IT LOOKS COOL!!
...
JUST SO YOU KNOW, IT'S NOT A PROPER ONE.

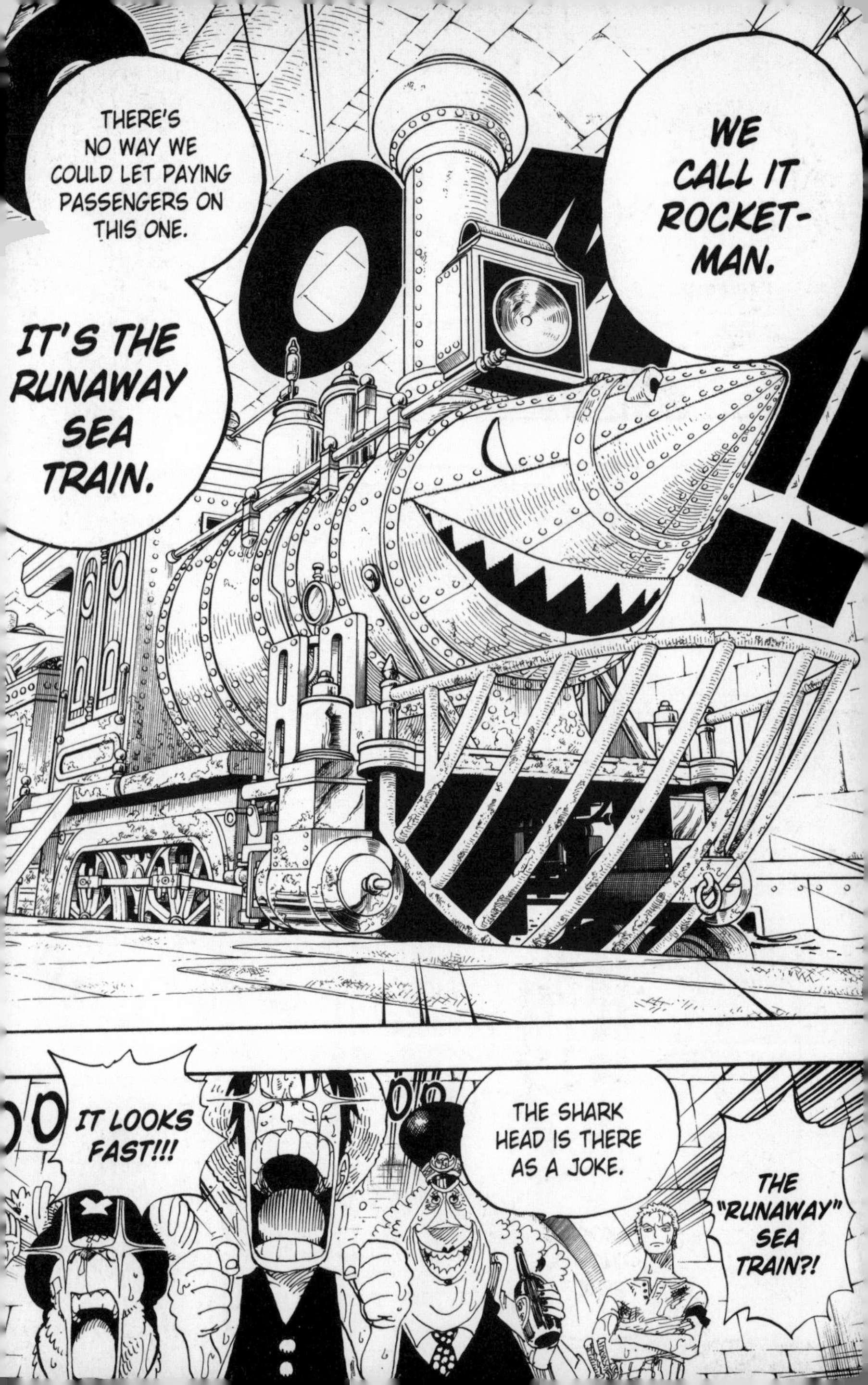
WE CALL IT ROCKET-MAN.
THERE'S NO WAY WE COULD LET PAYING PASSENGERS ON THIS ONE.
IT'S THE RUNAWAY SEA TRAIN.
THE "RUNAWAY" SEA TRAIN?!
THE SHARK HEAD IS THERE AS A JOKE.
IT LOOKS FAST!!!

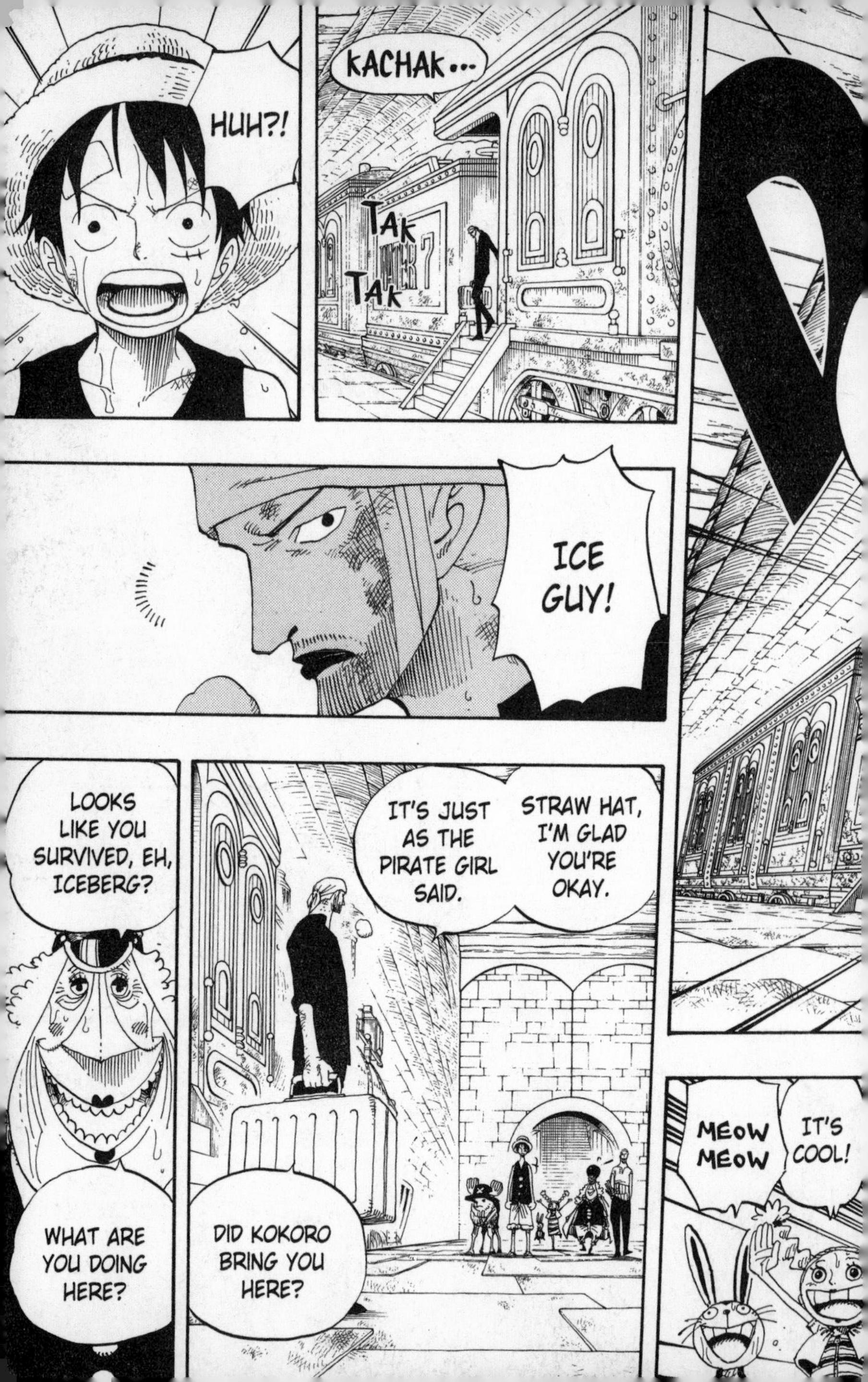
KACHAK...
TAK TAK
HUH?!
ICE GUY!
IT'S COOL!
MEOW MEOW
STRAW HAT, I'M GLAD YOU'RE OKAY.
IT'S JUST AS THE PIRATE GIRL SAID.
DID KOKORO BRING YOU HERE?
LOOKS LIKE YOU SURVIVED, EH, ICEBERG?
WHAT ARE YOU DOING HERE?

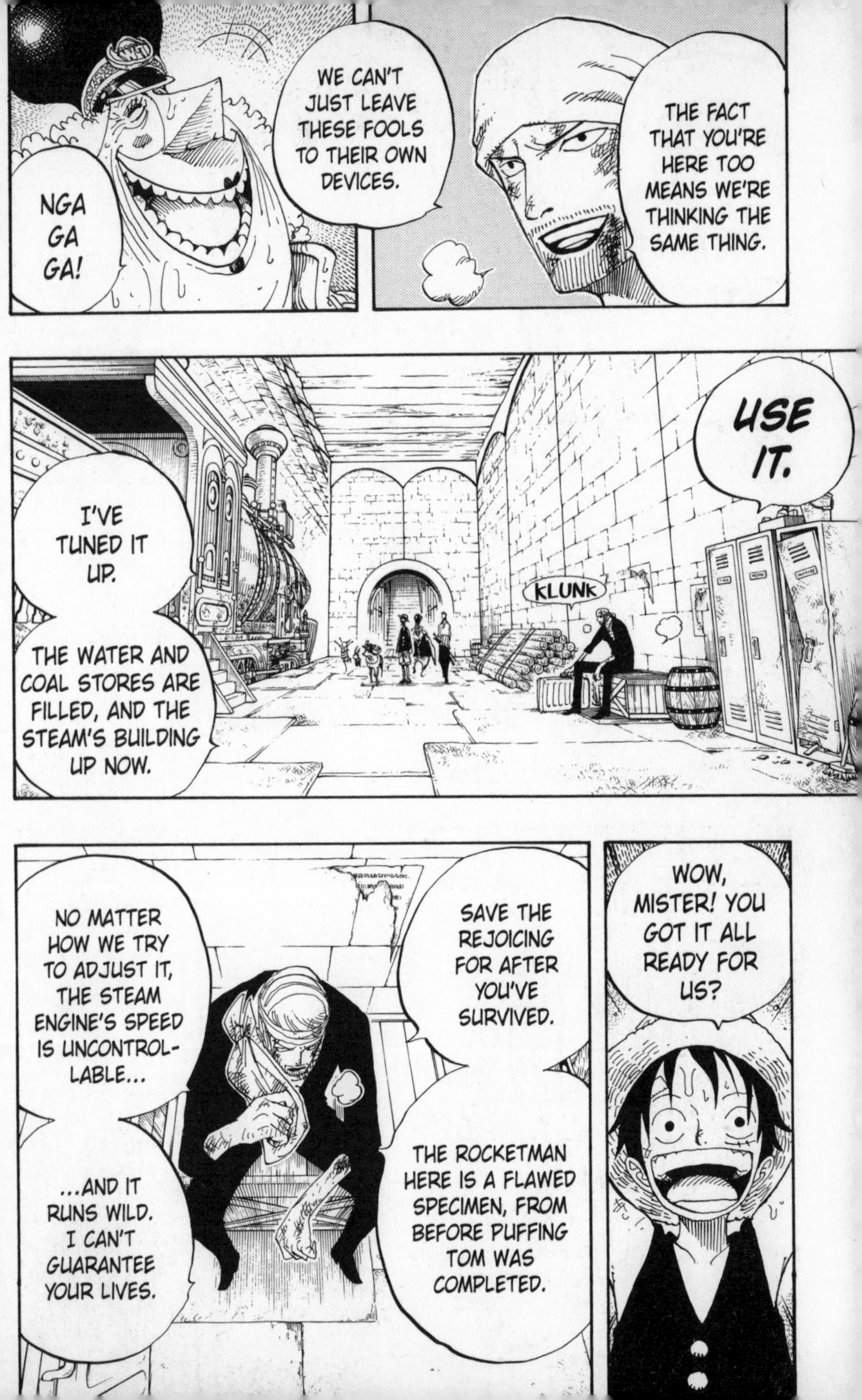
THE FACT THAT YOU'RE HERE TOO MEANS WE'RE THINKING THE SAME THING.
WE CAN'T JUST LEAVE THESE FOOLS TO THEIR OWN DEVICES.
NGA GA GA!
USE IT.
KLUNK
I'VE TUNED IT UP.
THE WATER AND COAL STORES ARE FILLED, AND THE STEAM'S BUILDING UP NOW.
WOW, MISTER! YOU GOT IT ALL READY FOR US?
SAVE THE REJOICING FOR AFTER YOU'VE SURVIVED.
NO MATTER HOW WE TRY TO ADJUST IT, THE STEAM ENGINE'S SPEED IS UNCONTROL-LABLE...
THE ROCKETMAN HERE IS A FLAWED SPECIMEN, FROM BEFORE PUFFING TOM WAS COMPLETED.
...AND IT RUNS WILD. I CAN'T GUARANTEE YOUR LIVES.

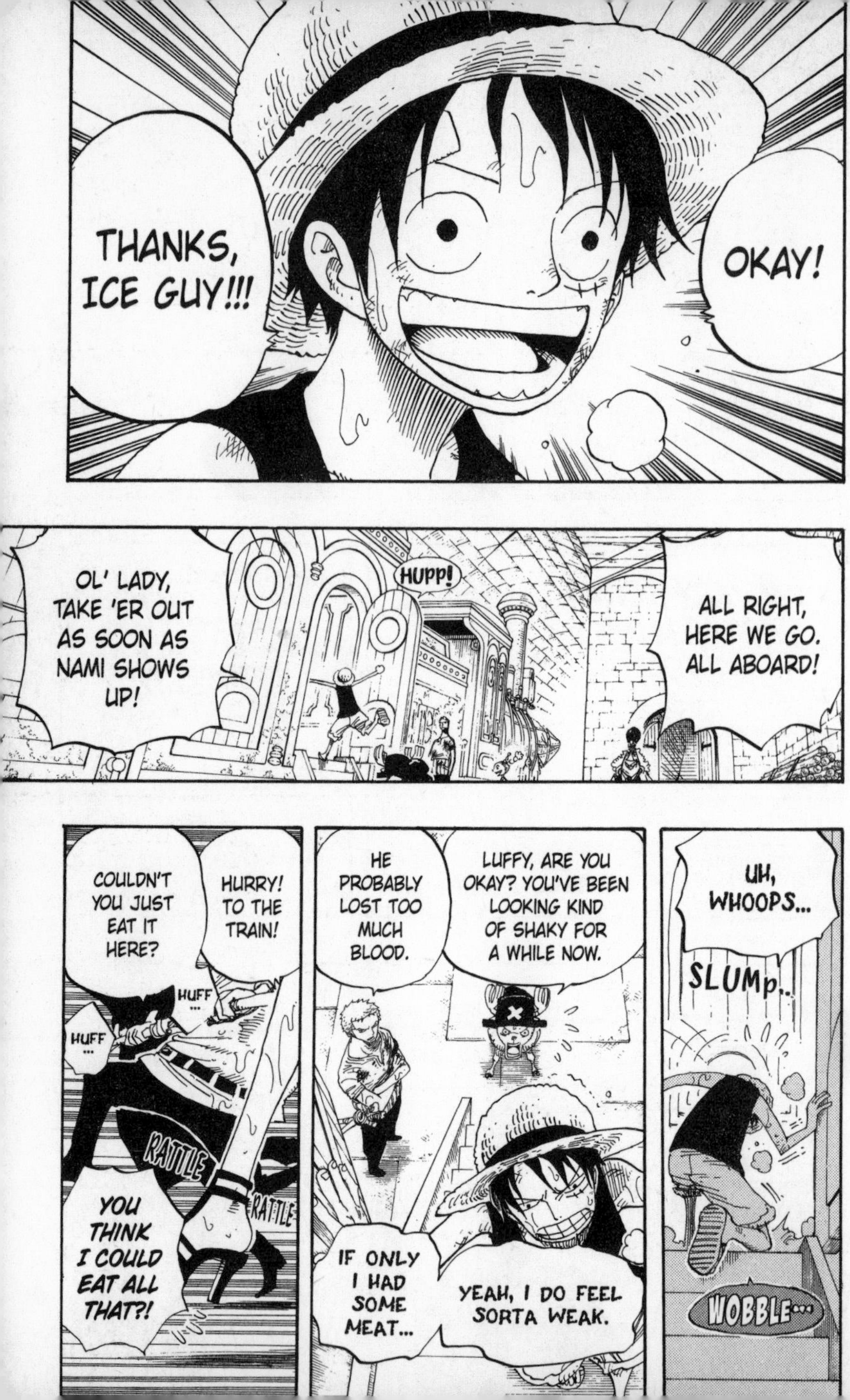

OKAY!
THANKS, ICE GUY!!!
ALL RIGHT, HERE WE GO. ALL ABOARD!
HUPP!
OL' LADY, TAKE 'ER OUT AS SOON AS NAMI SHOWS UP!
UH, WHOOPS...
SLUMp..
WOBBLE...
LUFFY, ARE YOU OKAY? YOU'VE BEEN LOOKING KIND OF SHAKY FOR A WHILE NOW.
HE PROBABLY LOST TOO MUCH BLOOD.
YEAH, I DO FEEL SORTA WEAK.
IF ONLY I HAD SOME MEAT...
HURRY! TO THE TRAIN!
COULDN'T YOU JUST EAT IT HERE?
HUFF...
HUFF...
RATTLE
RATTLE
YOU THINK I COULD EAT ALL THAT?!

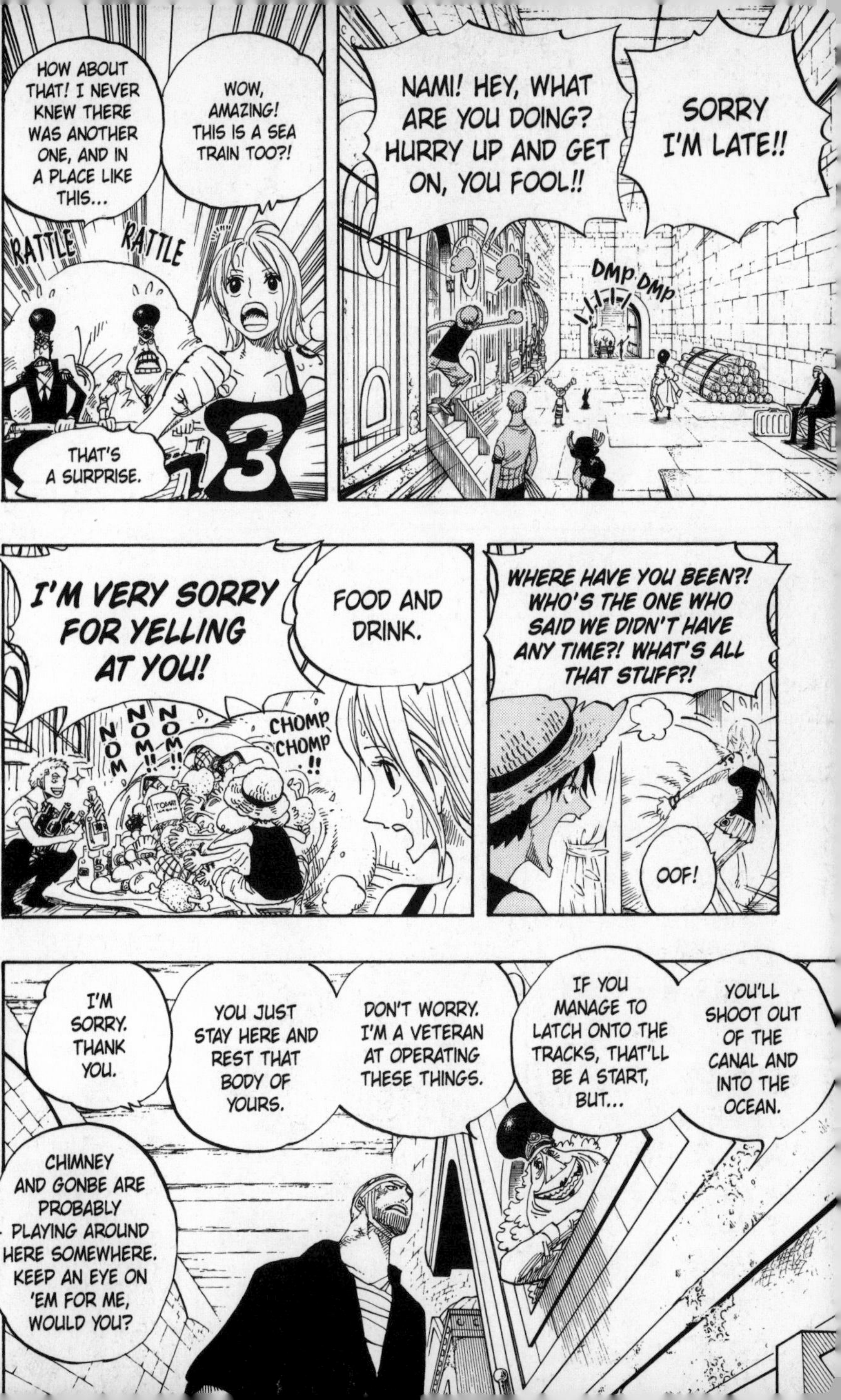
SORRY I'M LATE!!
NAMI! HEY, WHAT ARE YOU DOING? HURRY UP AND GET ON, YOU FOOL!!
DMP DMP
WOW, AMAZING! THIS IS A SEA TRAIN TOO?!
HOW ABOUT THAT! I NEVER KNEW THERE WAS ANOTHER ONE, AND IN A PLACE LIKE THIS...
RATTLE
RATTLE
THAT'S A SURPRISE.
WHERE HAVE YOU BEEN?! WHO'S THE ONE WHO SAID WE DIDN'T HAVE ANY TIME?! WHAT'S ALL THAT STUFF?!
OOF!
FOOD AND DRINK.
I'M VERY SORRY FOR YELLING AT YOU!
CHOMP CHOMP!!
NOM NOM!! NOM!!
YOU'LL SHOOT OUT OF THE CANAL AND INTO THE OCEAN.
IF YOU MANAGE TO LATCH ONTO THE TRACKS, THAT'LL BE A START, BUT...
DON'T WORRY. I'M A VETERAN AT OPERATING THESE THINGS.
YOU JUST STAY HERE AND REST THAT BODY OF YOURS.
I'M SORRY. THANK YOU.
CHIMNEY AND GONBE ARE PROBABLY PLAYING AROUND HERE SOMEWHERE. KEEP AN EYE ON 'EM FOR ME, WOULD YOU?

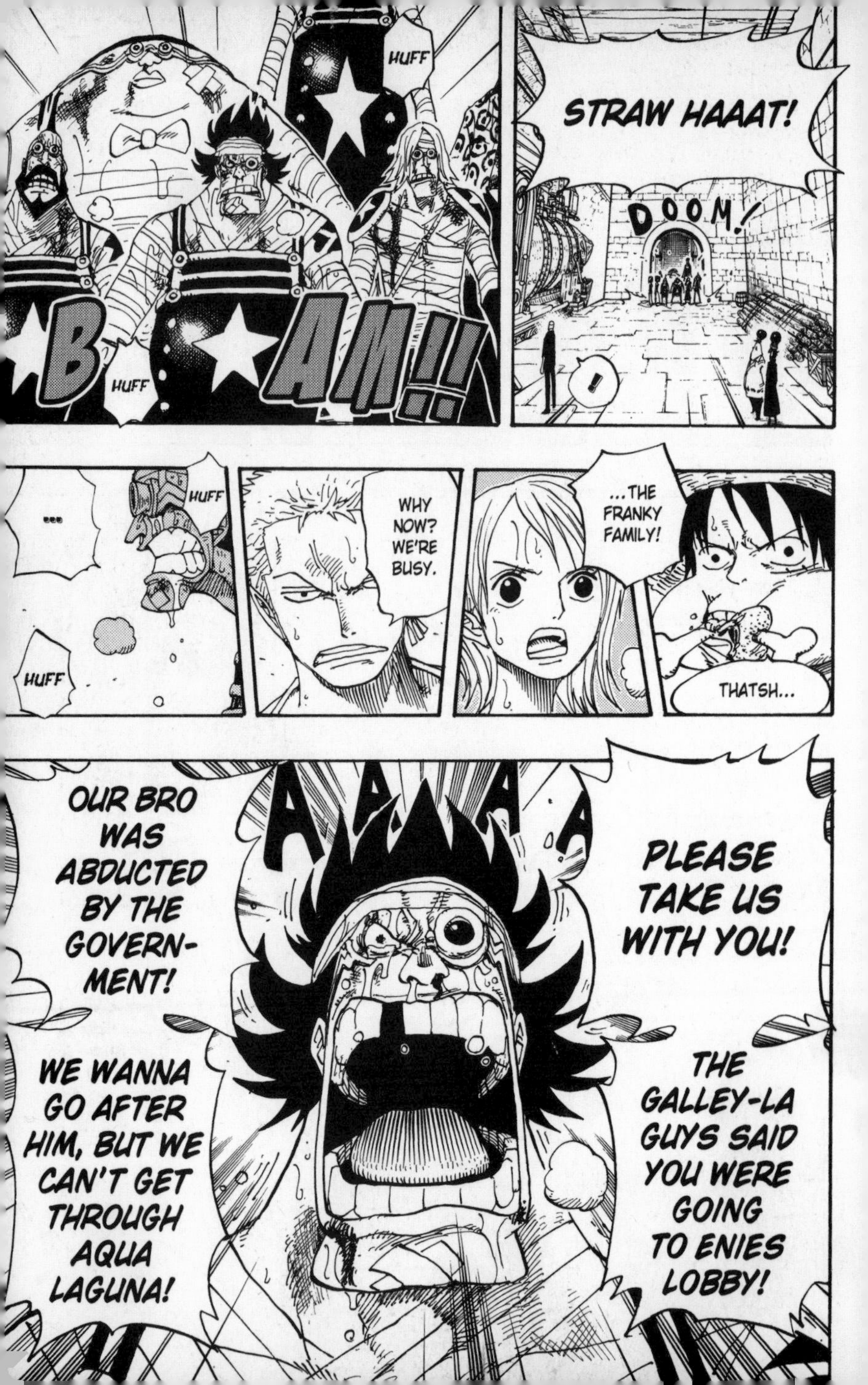
STRAW HAAAT!
DOOM!
!
HUFF
BAM!!
HUFF
THATSH...
...THE FRANKY FAMILY!
WHY NOW? WE'RE BUSY.
...
HUFF
HUFF
PLEASE TAKE US WITH YOU!
THE GALLEY-LA GUYS SAID YOU WERE GOING TO ENIES LOBBY!
OUR BRO WAS ABDUCTED BY THE GOVERN-MENT!
WE WANNA GO AFTER HIM, BUT WE CAN'T GET THROUGH AQUA LAGUNA!

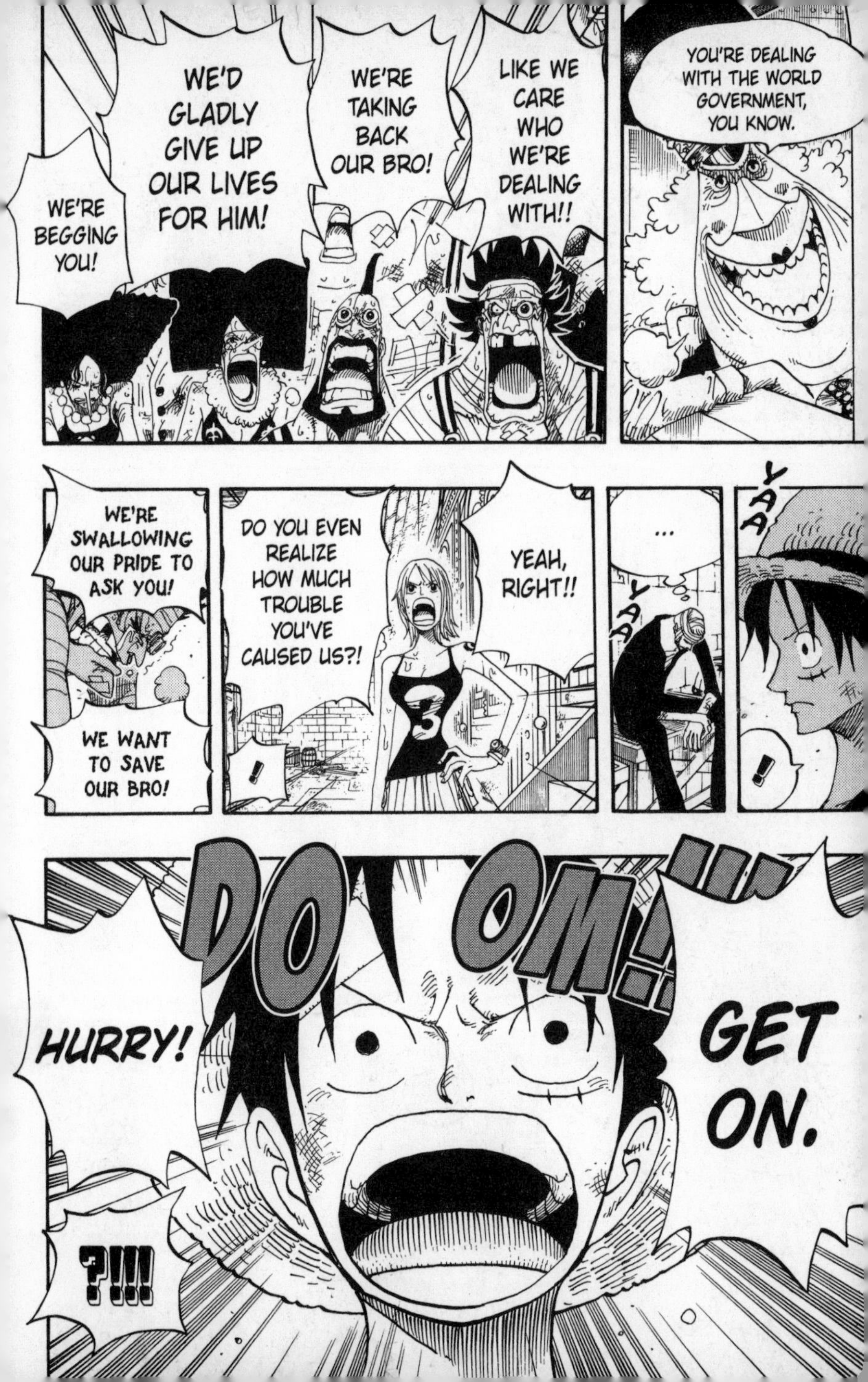
YOU'RE DEALING WITH THE WORLD GOVERNMENT, YOU KNOW.
LIKE WE CARE WHO WE'RE DEALING WITH!!
WE'RE TAKING BACK OUR BRO!
WE'D GLADLY GIVE UP OUR LIVES FOR HIM!
WE'RE BEGGING YOU!
YAA
!
...
YAA
YEAH, RIGHT!!
DO YOU EVEN REALIZE HOW MUCH TROUBLE YOU'VE CAUSED US?!
!
WE'RE SWALLOWING OUR PRIDE TO ASK YOU!
WE WANT TO SAVE OUR BRO!
DOOM!!
GET ON.
HURRY!
?!!!

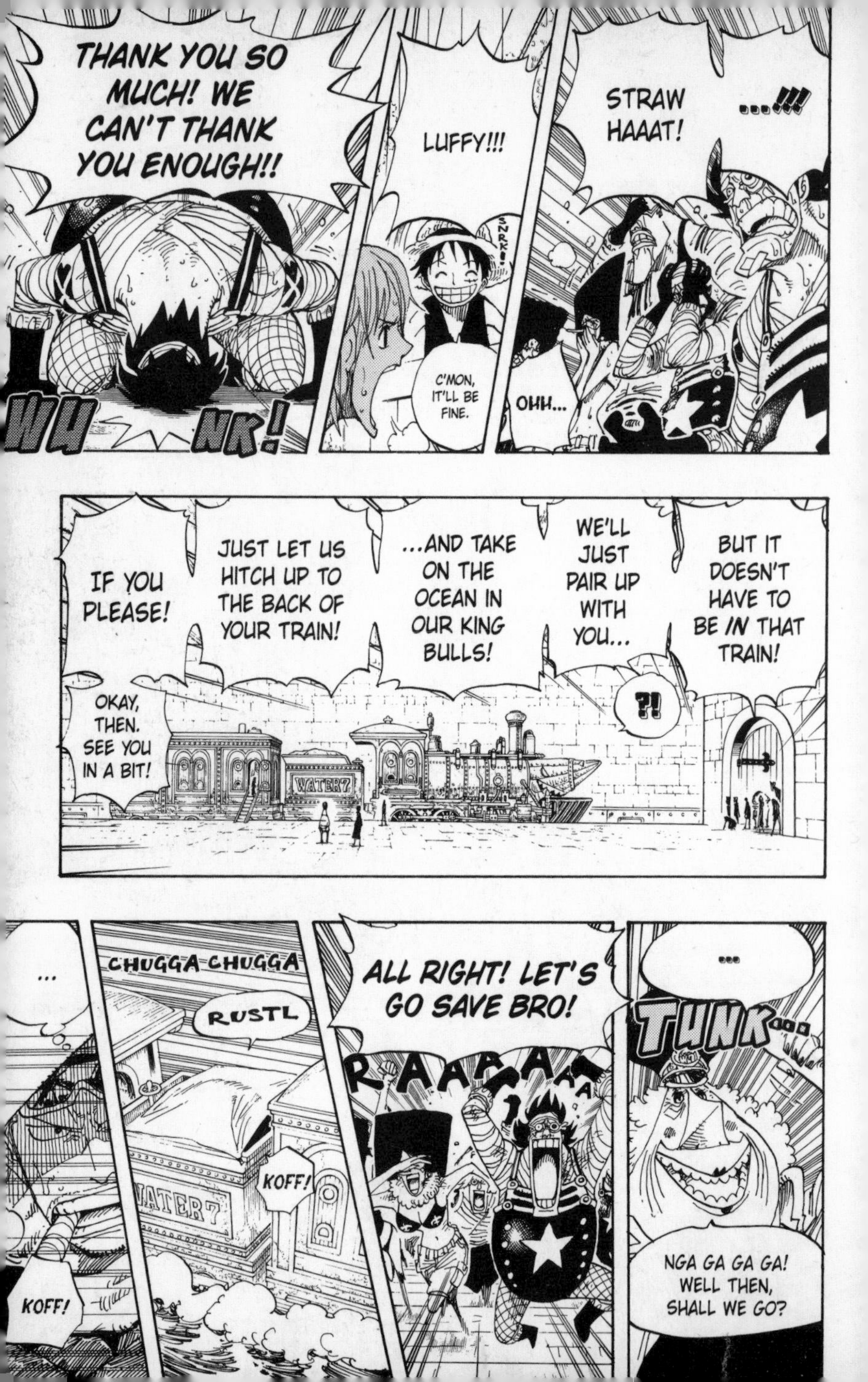
STRAW HAAAT!
...!!!
OHH...
LUFFY!!!
SNRK!
C'MON, IT'LL BE FINE.
THANK YOU SO MUCH! WE CAN'T THANK YOU ENOUGH!!
WHUNK!
BUT IT DOESN'T HAVE TO BE *IN* THAT TRAIN!
?!
WE'LL JUST PAIR UP WITH YOU...
...AND TAKE ON THE OCEAN IN OUR KING BULLS!
JUST LET US HITCH UP TO THE BACK OF YOUR TRAIN!
IF YOU PLEASE!
OKAY, THEN. SEE YOU IN A BIT!
WATER7
...
TUNK...
NGA GA GA GA! WELL THEN, SHALL WE GO?
ALL RIGHT! LET'S GO SAVE BRO!
RAAAAAA
KOFF!
CHUGGA CHUGGA
RUSTL
WATER7
KOFF!
...
KOFF!

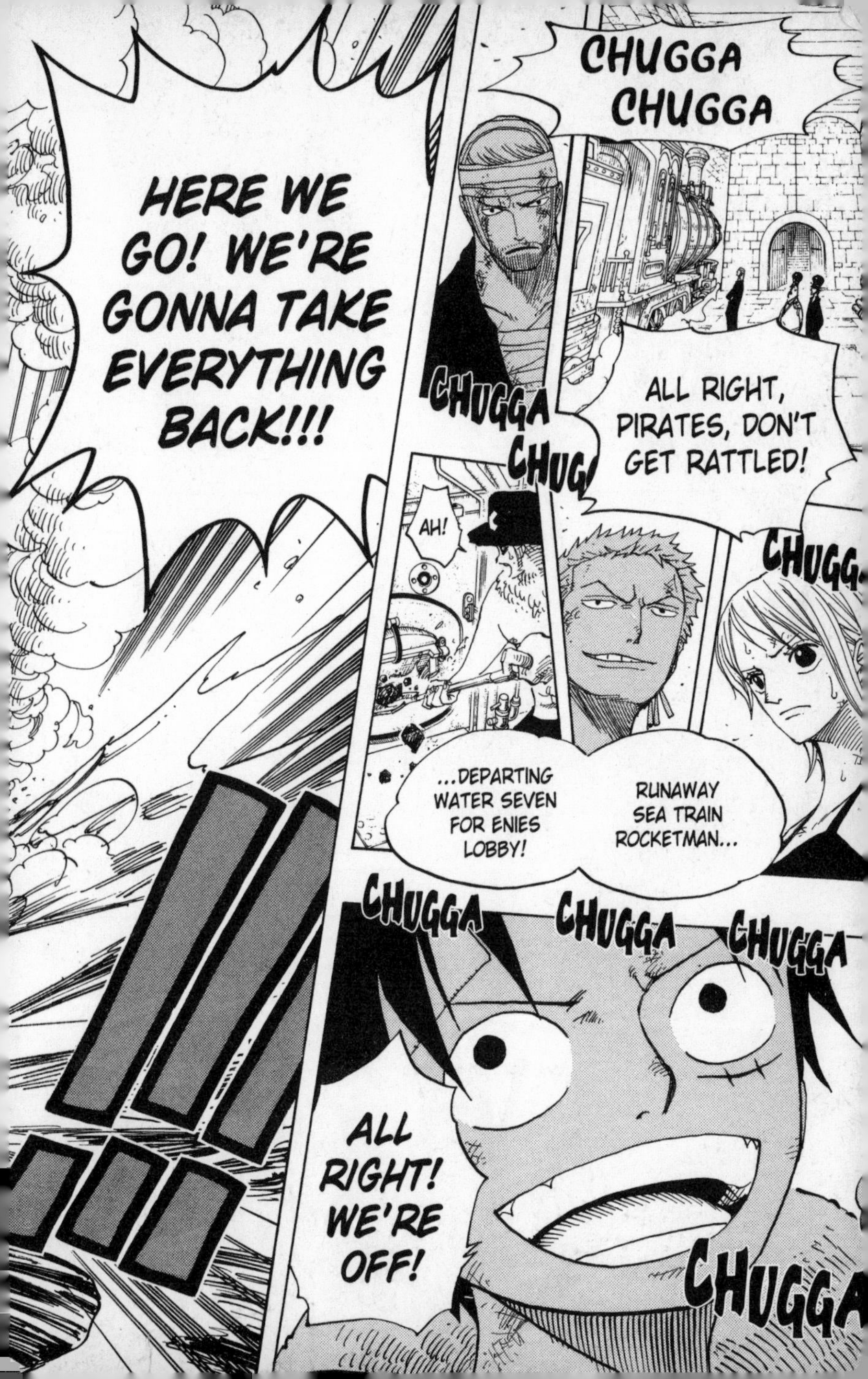
CHUGGA CHUGGA
ALL RIGHT, PIRATES, DON'T GET RATTLED!
CHUGGA CHUGGA
CHUGG-
AH!
RUNAWAY SEA TRAIN ROCKETMAN...
...DEPARTING WATER SEVEN FOR ENIES LOBBY!
CHUGGA
CHUGGA
CHUGGA
ALL RIGHT! WE'RE OFF!
CHUGGA
HERE WE GO! WE'RE GONNA TAKE EVERYTHING BACK!!!

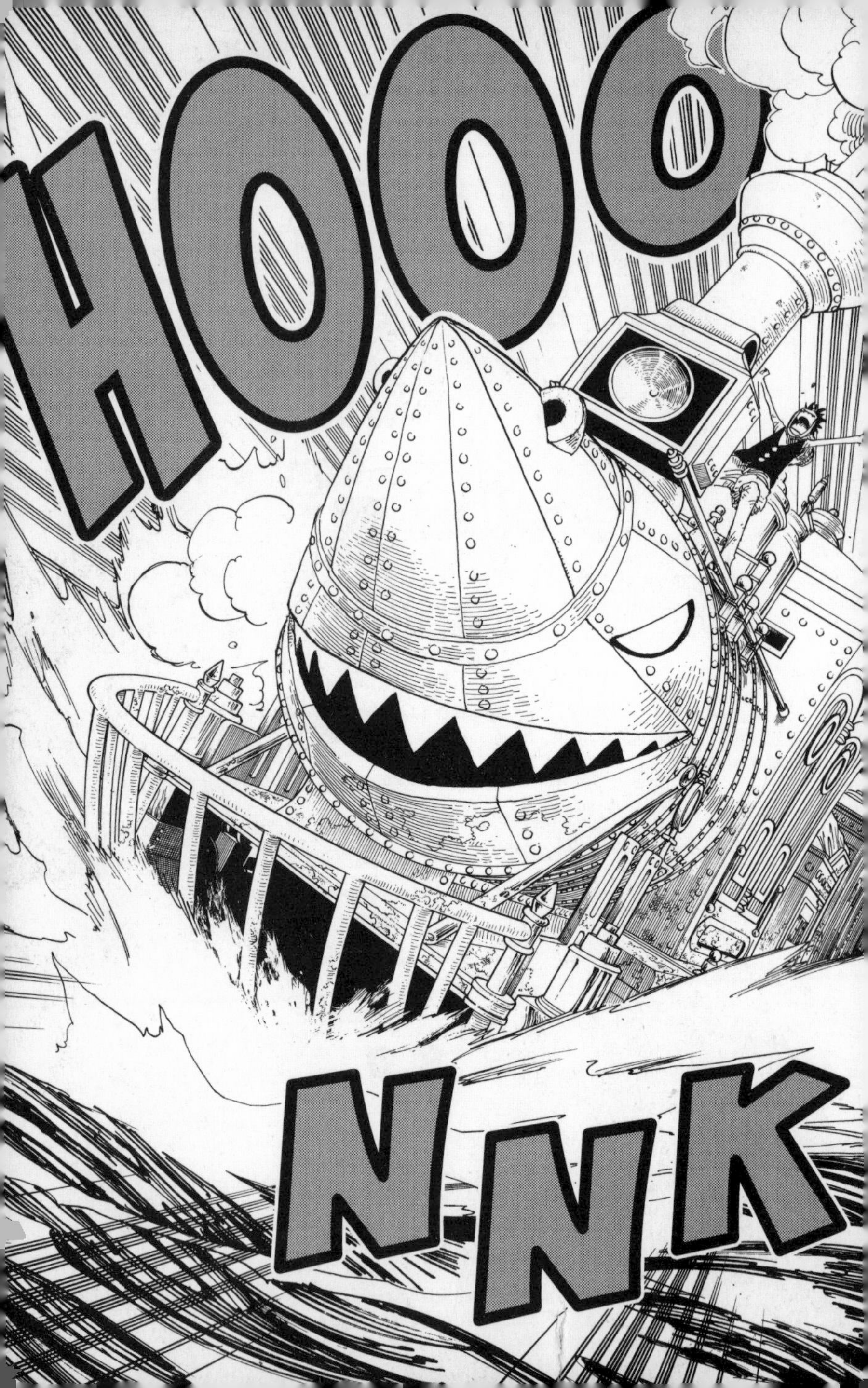
HOOO
NNK

Question Corner

Reader: I've got a request for you, Oda Sensei. ♥I'd like to see Eneru with his hat off, so draw him.

--Yuko-san

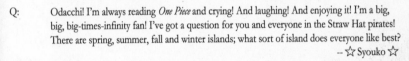

YA HA HA!

Oda: Okay, I drew him! ➡
W-Wow, that's a super curly perm!
He looks like an old lady! Uh-oh, I think
I might've gone too far this time. Run away!
(Running) Rumble-rumble KABOOOM! Gyaaaa!

Q: Odacchi! I'm always reading *One Piece* and crying! And laughing! And enjoying it! I'm a big, big, big-times-infinity fan! I've got a question for you and everyone in the Straw Hat pirates! There are spring, summer, fall and winter islands; what sort of island does everyone like best?

-- ☆ Syouko ☆

A: A question for everybody, huh? Okay, let's have them come out and answer!
Go on! You've got 16 stages to choose from, remember!
Summer Island (Summer, Spring, Fall, Winter), Spring Island (Summer, Spring, Fall, Winter), Fall Island (Summer, Spring, Fall, Winter), Winter Island (Summer, Spring, Fall, Winter).

Luffy: Let's see, I like... Well, I like summer, but snow makes me happy, so... Hmm...

Zolo: I like fall. Fall on Fall Island when it's easy to move around is good. I want to get stronger.

Nami: I like summer! Summer beaches on a Spring Island are really great.

Sanji: I like Robin on a Nami island ♡ *GIGGLE* ♡

Usopp: Are you an idiot? That's not even an answer! Parenthetically, I like... Hm. Summer on a Fall Island is perfect weather for weapons development! And you can fish at the same time.

Chopper: I can't handle heat. Spring on Winter Islands feels good, so I like that!

Robin: Fall on a Spring Island makes for perfect reading weather, so I think I like that. It seems as though you could really take it easy then

Luffy: Okay! I decided! I'm fine with anywhere, as long as there's meat!

Oda: Yes, yes. I don't know if that answered your question, but anyway, that's where we're ending the Question Corner for this volume--see you in the next one! Goodbye! Oh, and I like hot springs on a Summer Island in winter.

Chapter 366:
SORTIE!

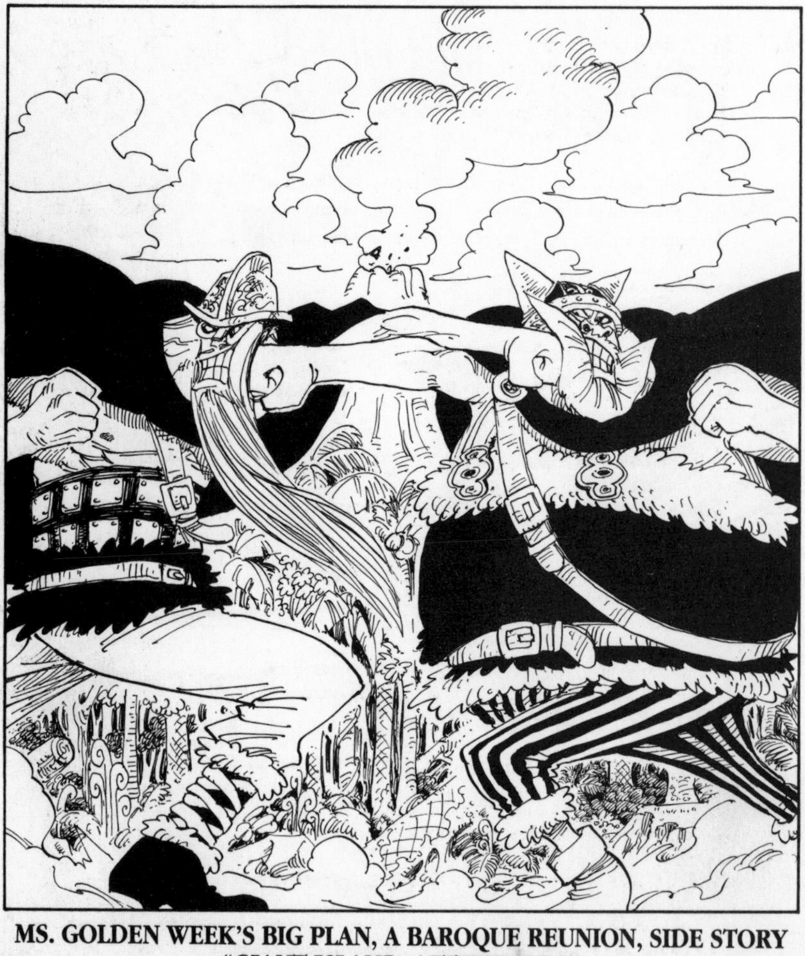

MS. GOLDEN WEEK'S BIG PLAN, A BAROQUE REUNION, SIDE STORY
"GIANT ISLAND, AFTERWARDS"

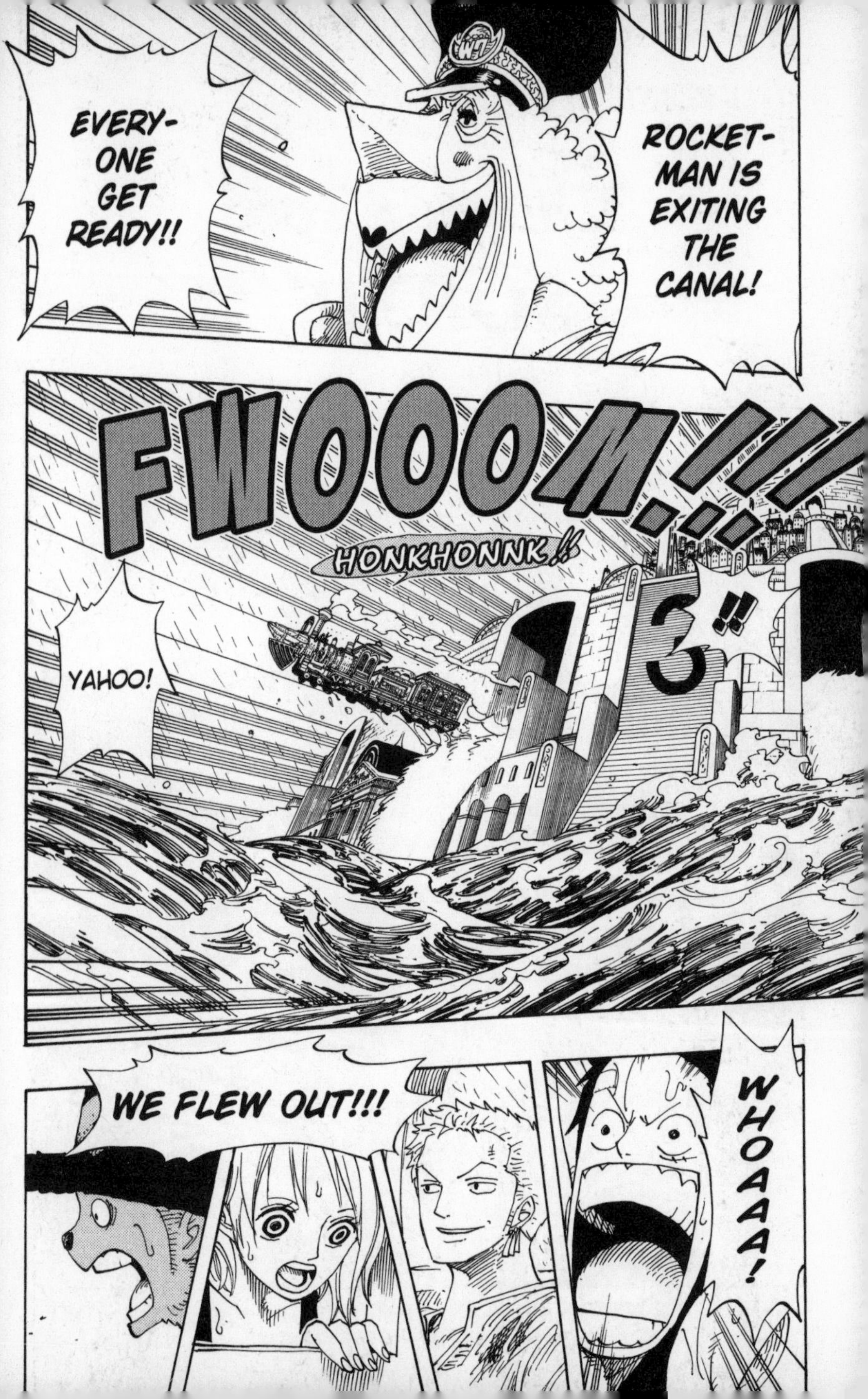
ROCKET-MAN IS EXITING THE CANAL!
EVERY-ONE GET READY!!
FWOOOM!!!!
HONKHONNK!!
3!!
YAHOO!
WHOAAAA!
WE FLEW OUT!!!

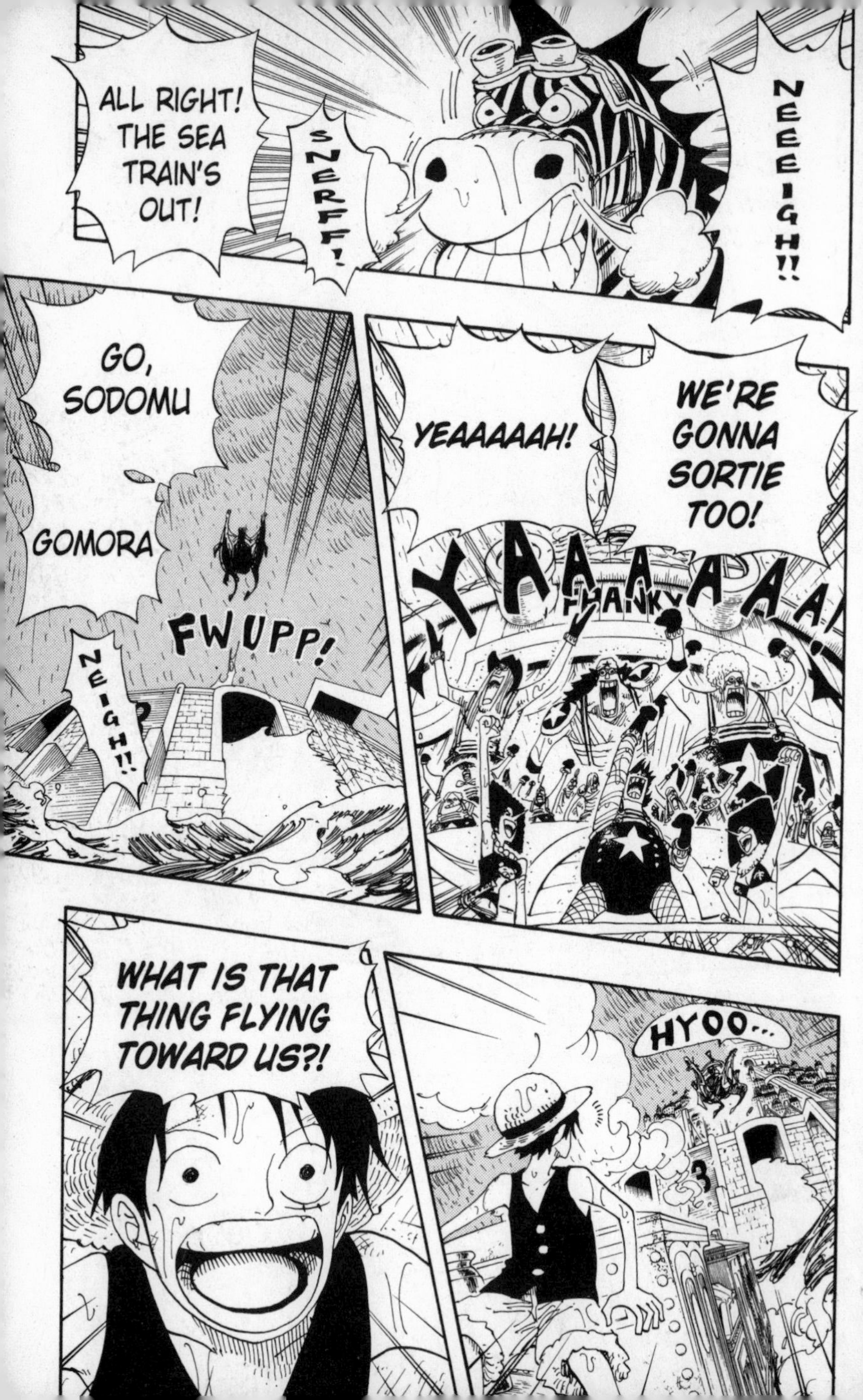
NEEEIGH!!
SNERFF!
ALL RIGHT! THE SEA TRAIN'S OUT!
WE'RE GONNA SORTIE TOO!
YEAAAAAH!
YAAAAAAA!
GO, SODOMU
GOMORA
FWUPP!
NEIGH!!
HYOO...
WHAT IS THAT THING FLYING TOWARD US?!

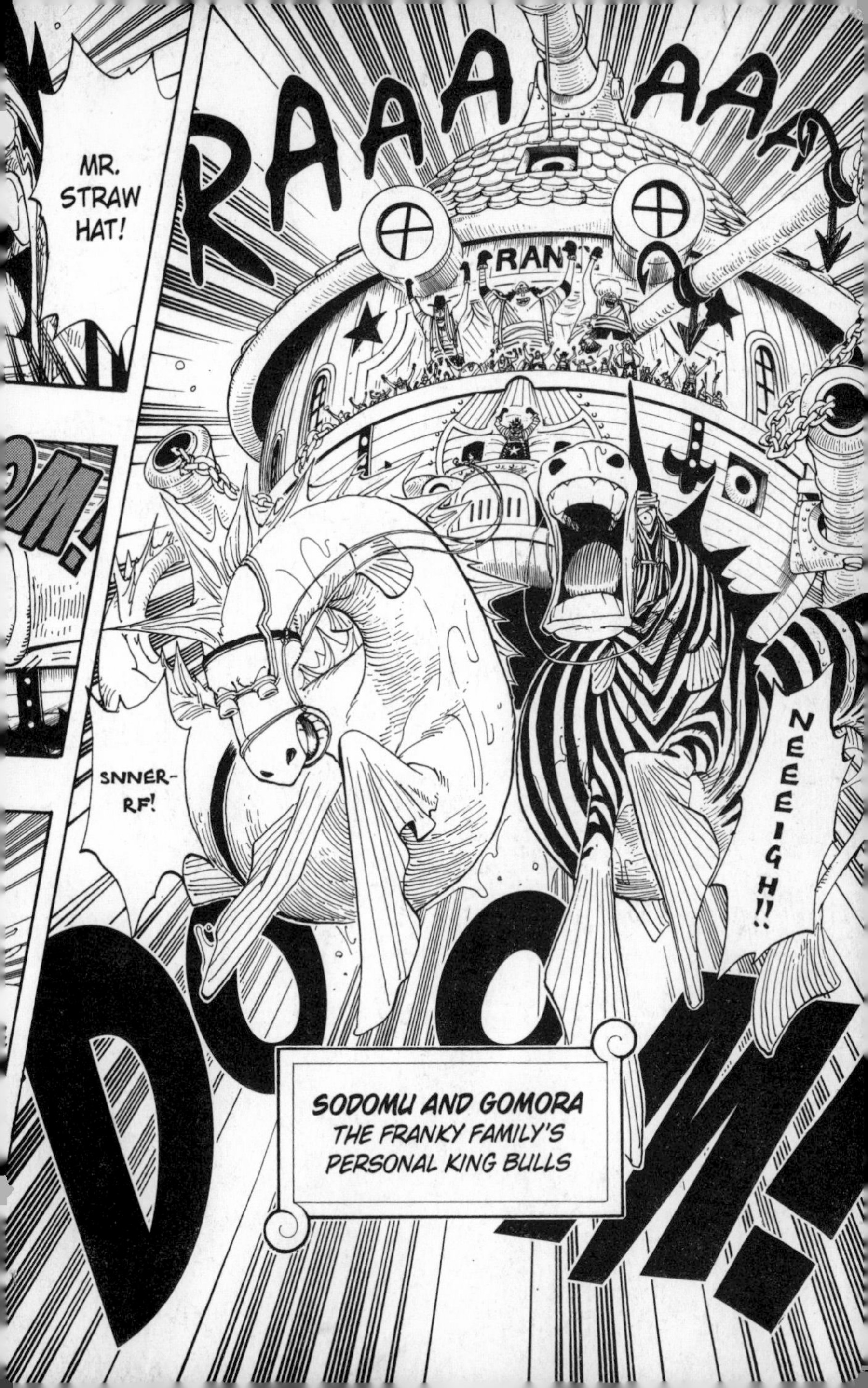
RAAAAAAA
NEEEIGH!!
DOOM!!
SODOMU AND GOMORA
THE FRANKY FAMILY'S
PERSONAL KING BULLS
MR. STRAW HAT!
SNNER-RF!

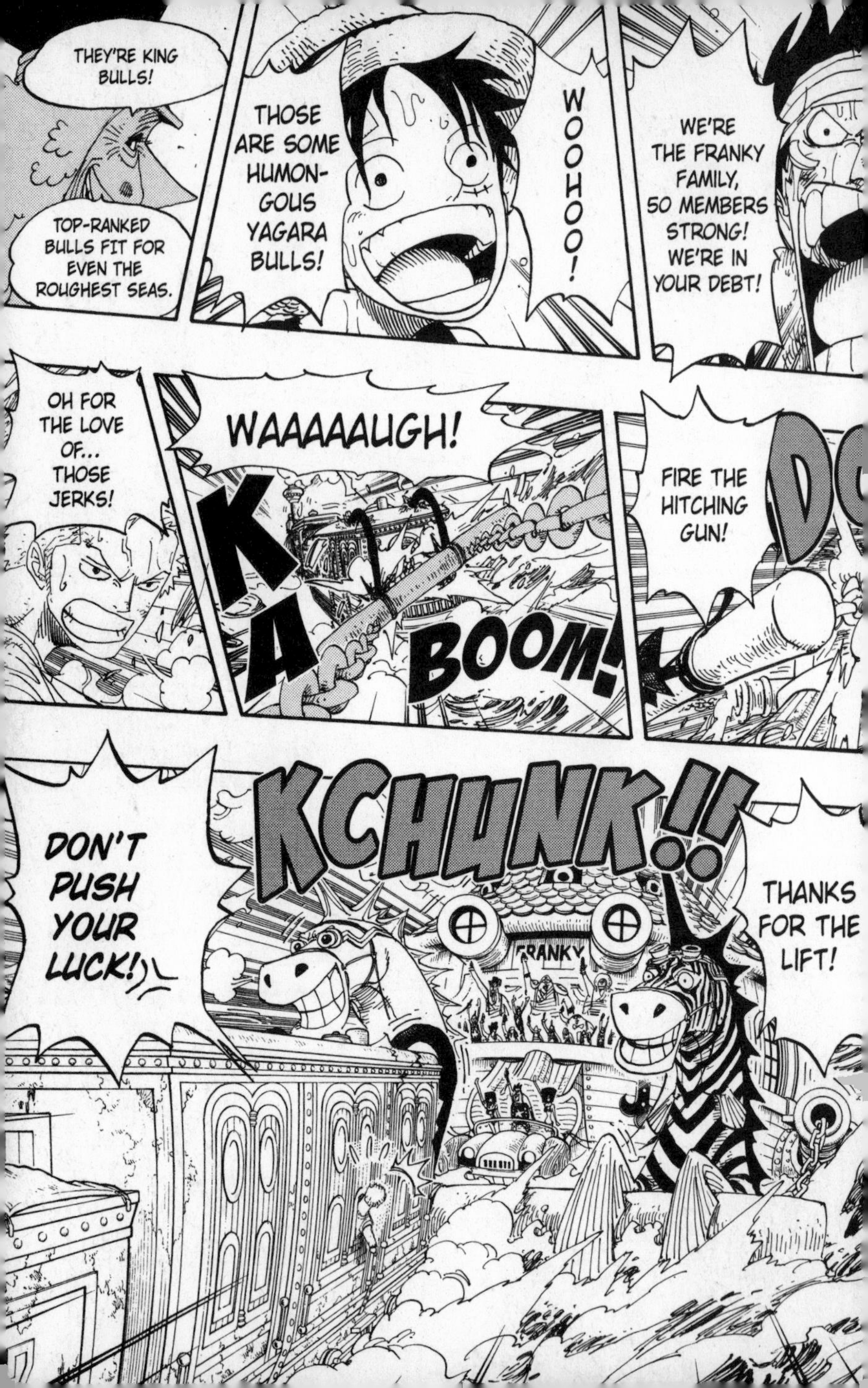
WE'RE THE FRANKY FAMILY, 50 MEMBERS STRONG! WE'RE IN YOUR DEBT!
WOOHOO!
THOSE ARE SOME HUMON-GOUS YAGARA BULLS!
THEY'RE KING BULLS!
TOP-RANKED BULLS FIT FOR EVEN THE ROUGHEST SEAS.
FIRE THE HITCHING GUN!
WAAAAAUGH!
KA
BOOM!
OH FOR THE LOVE OF... THOSE JERKS!
THANKS FOR THE LIFT!
KCHUNK!!
FRANKY
DON'T PUSH YOUR LUCK!

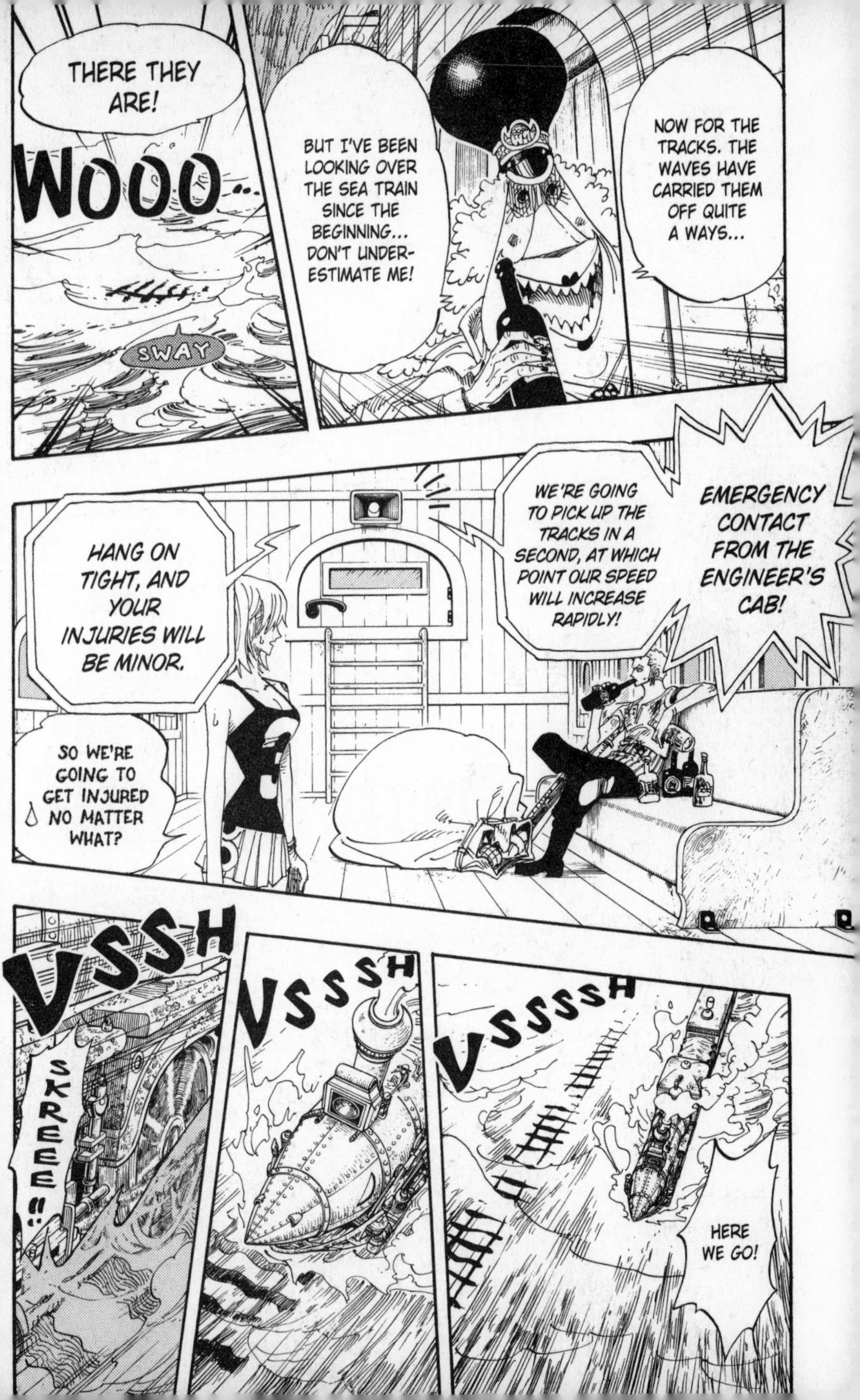
NOW FOR THE TRACKS. THE WAVES HAVE CARRIED THEM OFF QUITE A WAYS...
BUT I'VE BEEN LOOKING OVER THE SEA TRAIN SINCE THE BEGINNING... DON'T UNDER-ESTIMATE ME!
THERE THEY ARE!
WOOO...
SWAY
EMERGENCY CONTACT FROM THE ENGINEER'S CAB!
WE'RE GOING TO PICK UP THE TRACKS IN A SECOND, AT WHICH POINT OUR SPEED WILL INCREASE RAPIDLY!
HANG ON TIGHT, AND YOUR INJURIES WILL BE MINOR.
SO WE'RE GOING TO GET INJURED NO MATTER WHAT?
VSSSSH
HERE WE GO!
VSSSH
VSSH
SKREEE!!

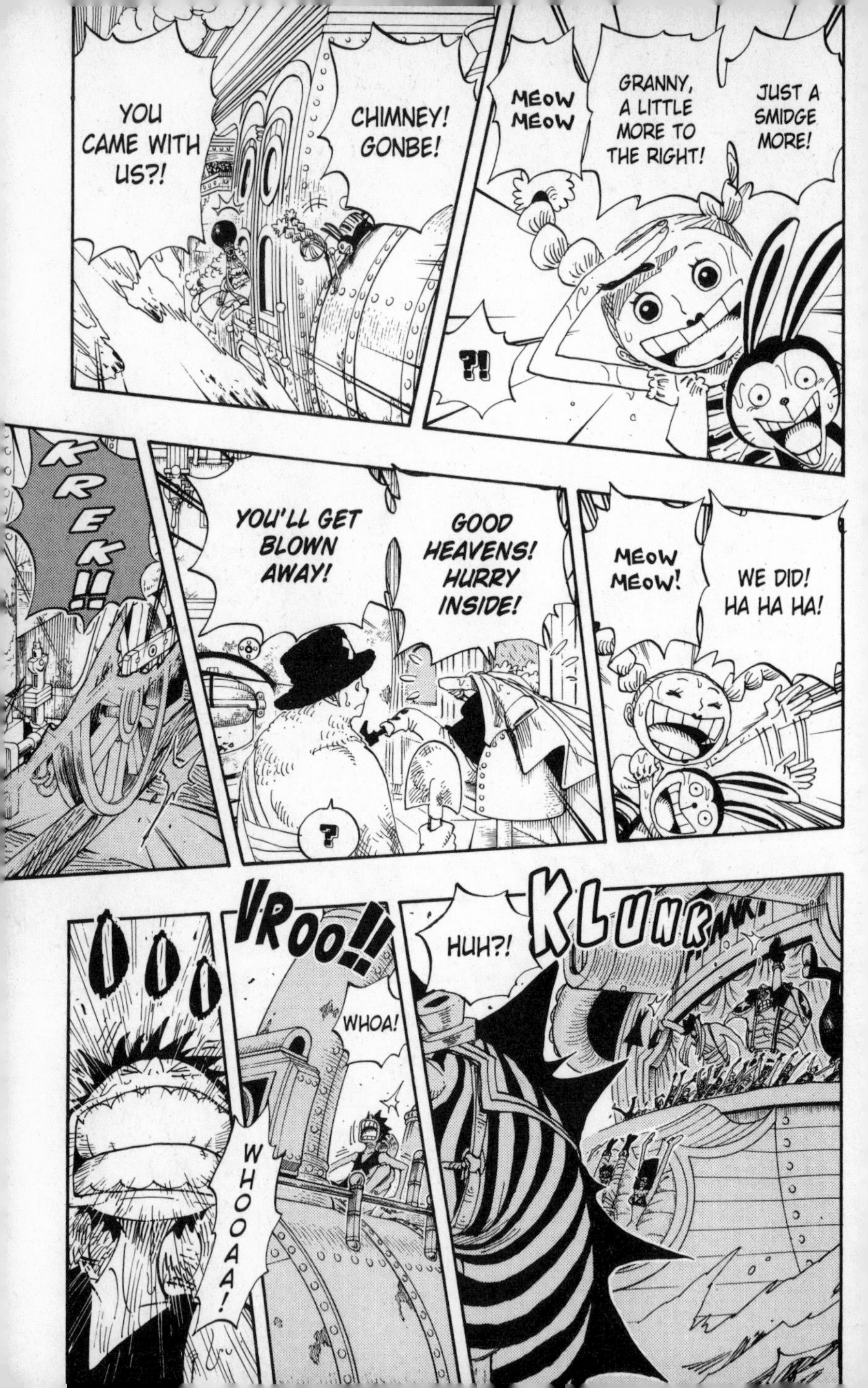
JUST A SMIDGE MORE!
GRANNY, A LITTLE MORE TO THE RIGHT!
MEOW MEOW
?!
CHIMNEY! GONBE!
YOU CAME WITH US?!
WE DID! HA HA HA!
MEOW MEOW!
GOOD HEAVENS! HURRY INSIDE!
YOU'LL GET BLOWN AWAY!
?
KREK!!
KLUNKANK
HUH?!
VROO!!
WHOA!
WHOOAA!

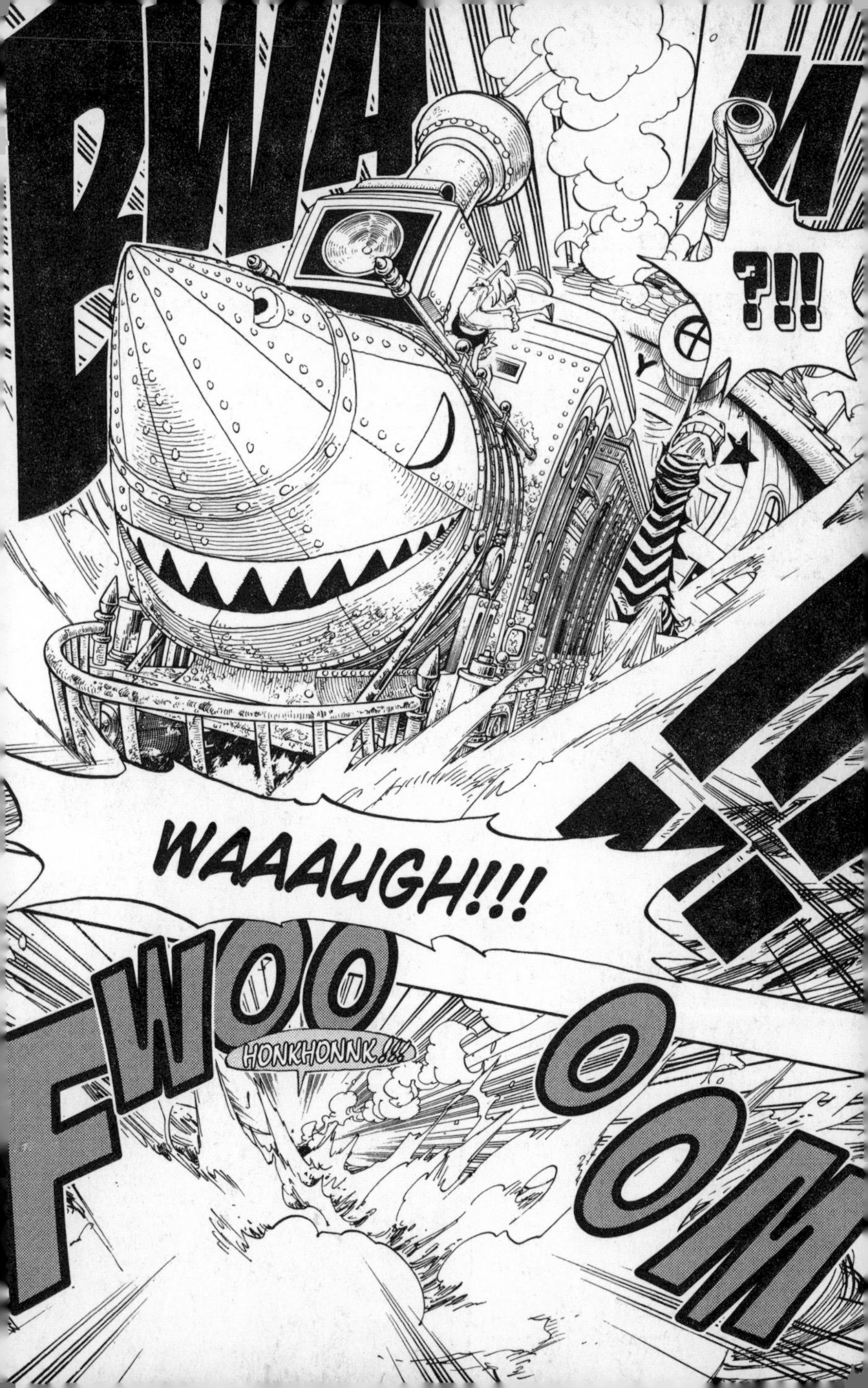
?!!
WAAAUGH!!!
HONKHONNK!!!

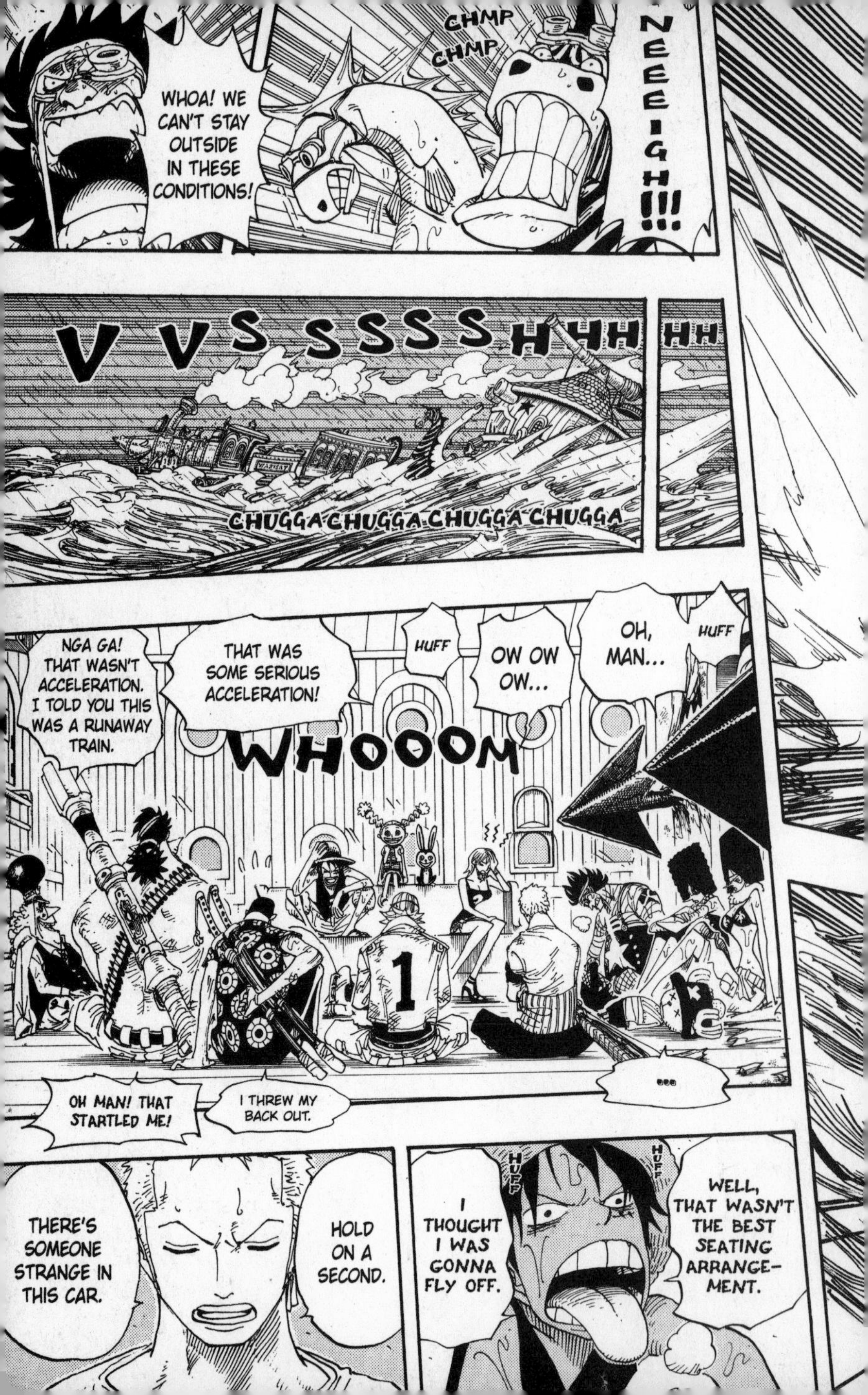
NEEEIGH!!!
CHMP CHMP
WHOA! WE CAN'T STAY OUTSIDE IN THESE CONDITIONS!
VVSSSSSHHH
HH
CHUGGA CHUGGA CHUGGA CHUGGA
OH, MAN...
HUFF
OW OW OW...
HUFF
THAT WAS SOME SERIOUS ACCELERATION!
NGA GA! THAT WASN'T ACCELERATION. I TOLD YOU THIS WAS A RUNAWAY TRAIN.
WHOOOM
...
I THREW MY BACK OUT.
OH MAN! THAT STARTLED ME!
WELL, THAT WASN'T THE BEST SEATING ARRANGEMENT.
HUFF
HUFF
I THOUGHT I WAS GONNA FLY OFF.
HOLD ON A SECOND.
THERE'S SOMEONE STRANGE IN THIS CAR.

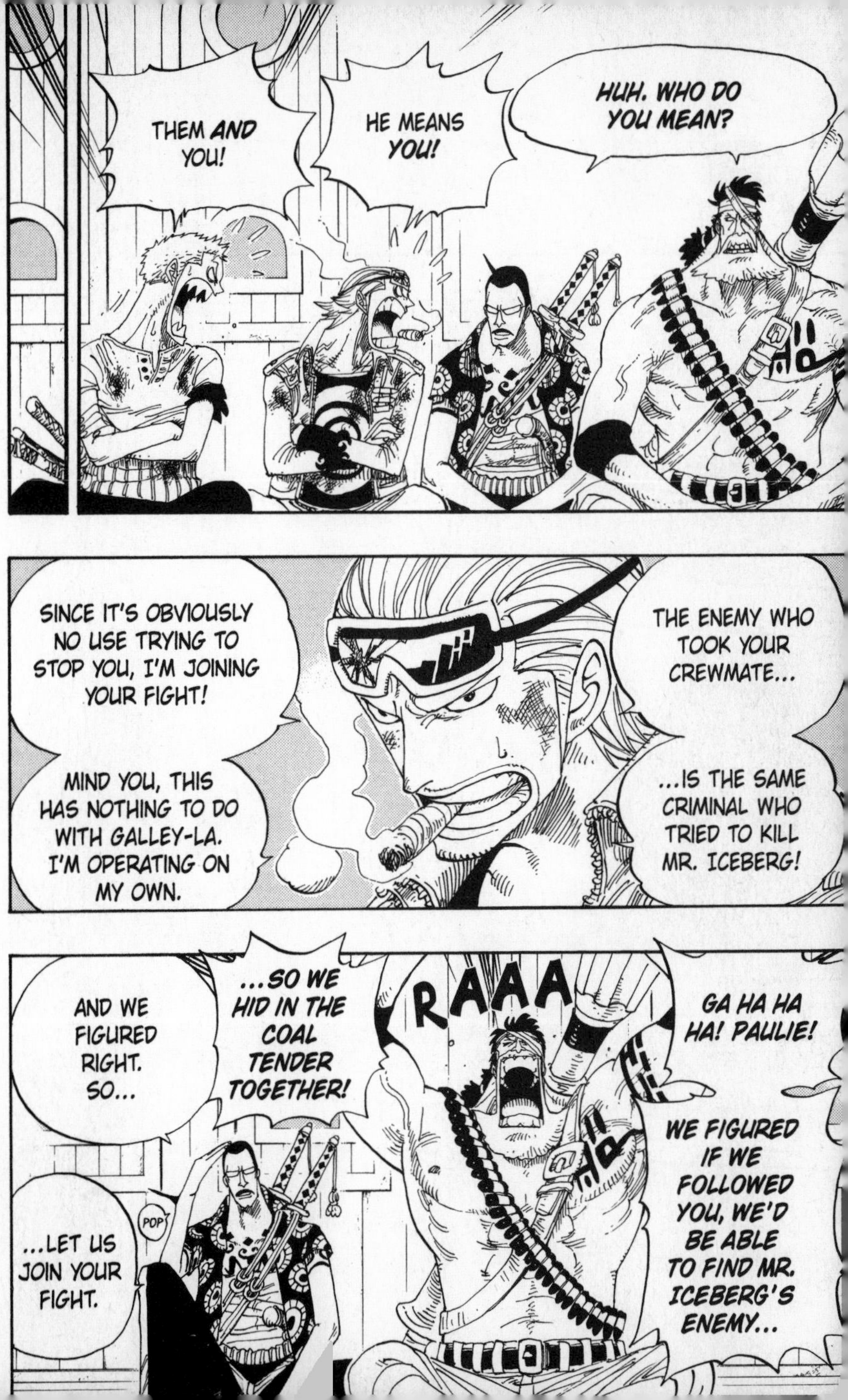
HUH. WHO DO YOU MEAN?
HE MEANS YOU!
THEM AND YOU!
THE ENEMY WHO TOOK YOUR CREWMATE...
...IS THE SAME CRIMINAL WHO TRIED TO KILL MR. ICEBERG!
SINCE IT'S OBVIOUSLY NO USE TRYING TO STOP YOU, I'M JOINING YOUR FIGHT!
MIND YOU, THIS HAS NOTHING TO DO WITH GALLEY-LA. I'M OPERATING ON MY OWN.
GA HA HA HA! PAULIE!
RAAA
WE FIGURED IF WE FOLLOWED YOU, WE'D BE ABLE TO FIND MR. ICEBERG'S ENEMY...
...SO WE HID IN THE COAL TENDER TOGETHER!
AND WE FIGURED RIGHT. SO...
POP
...LET US JOIN YOUR FIGHT.

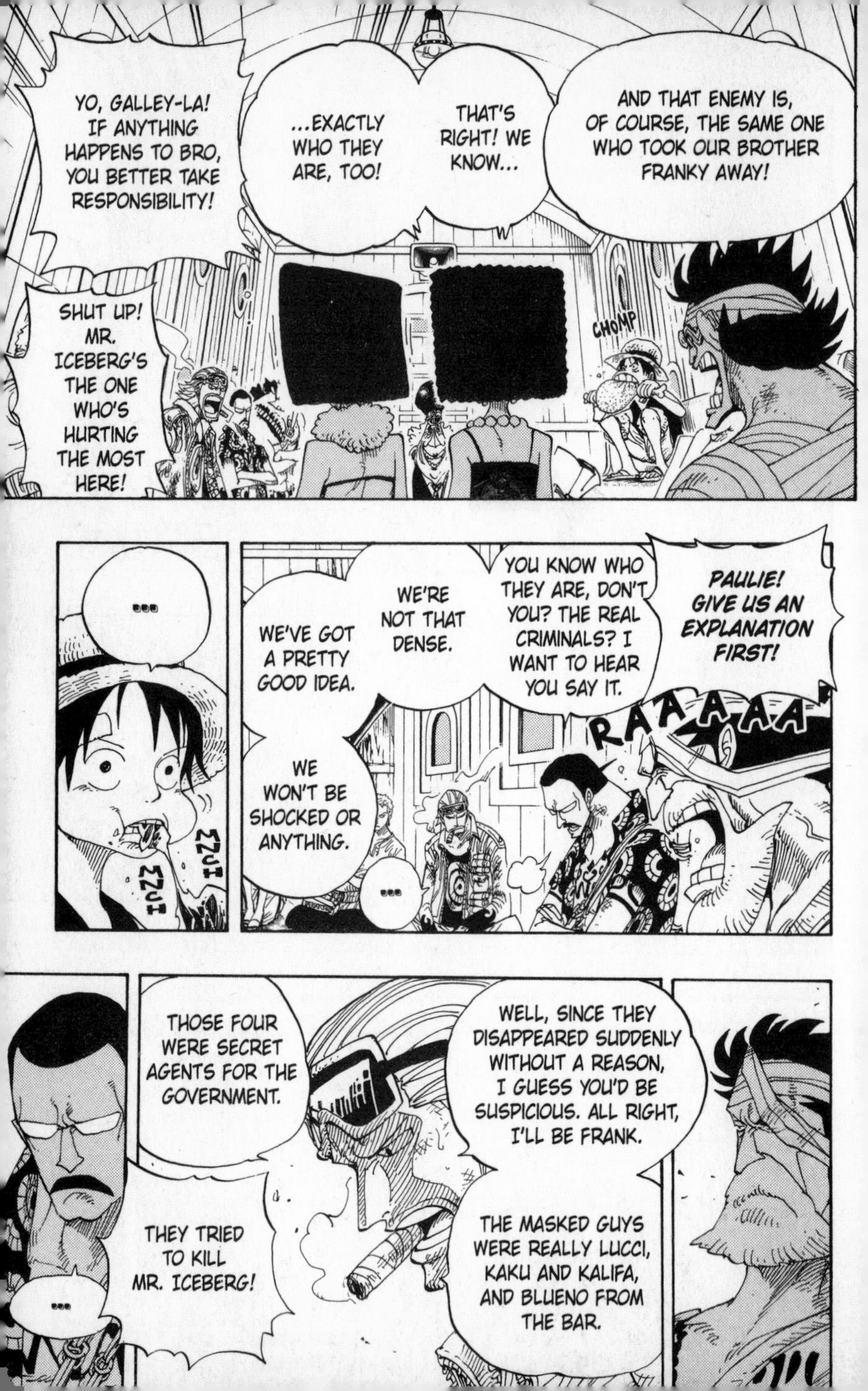
AND THAT ENEMY IS, OF COURSE, THE SAME ONE WHO TOOK OUR BROTHER FRANKY AWAY!
THAT'S RIGHT! WE KNOW...
...EXACTLY WHO THEY ARE, TOO!
YO, GALLEY-LA! IF ANYTHING HAPPENS TO BRO, YOU BETTER TAKE RESPONSIBILITY!
CHOMP
SHUT UP! MR. ICEBERG'S THE ONE WHO'S HURTING THE MOST HERE!
PAULIE! GIVE US AN EXPLANATION FIRST!
YOU KNOW WHO THEY ARE, DON'T YOU? THE REAL CRIMINALS? I WANT TO HEAR YOU SAY IT.
WE'RE NOT THAT DENSE.
WE'VE GOT A PRETTY GOOD IDEA.
RAAAAAA
WE WON'T BE SHOCKED OR ANYTHING.
...
...
MNCH
MNCH
WELL, SINCE THEY DISAPPEARED SUDDENLY WITHOUT A REASON, I GUESS YOU'D BE SUSPICIOUS. ALL RIGHT, I'LL BE FRANK.
THE MASKED GUYS WERE REALLY LUCCI, KAKU AND KALIFA, AND BLUENO FROM THE BAR.
THOSE FOUR WERE SECRET AGENTS FOR THE GOVERNMENT.
THEY TRIED TO KILL MR. ICEBERG!
...

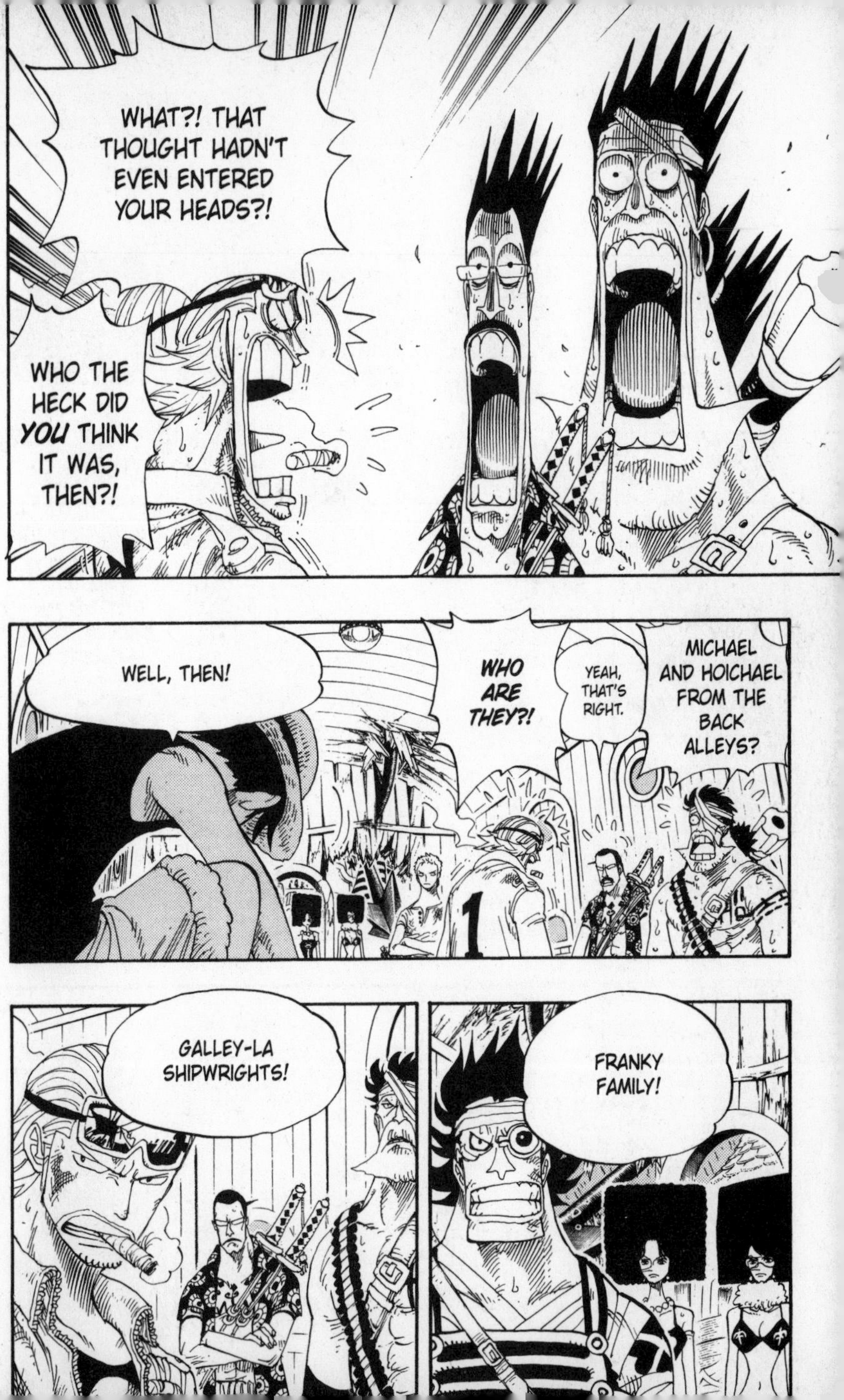
WHAT?! THAT THOUGHT HADN'T EVEN ENTERED YOUR HEADS?!
WHO THE HECK DID *YOU* THINK IT WAS, THEN?!
MICHAEL AND HOICHAEL FROM THE BACK ALLEYS?
YEAH, THAT'S RIGHT.
WHO ARE THEY?!
WELL, THEN!
FRANKY FAMILY!
GALLEY-LA SHIPWRIGHTS!

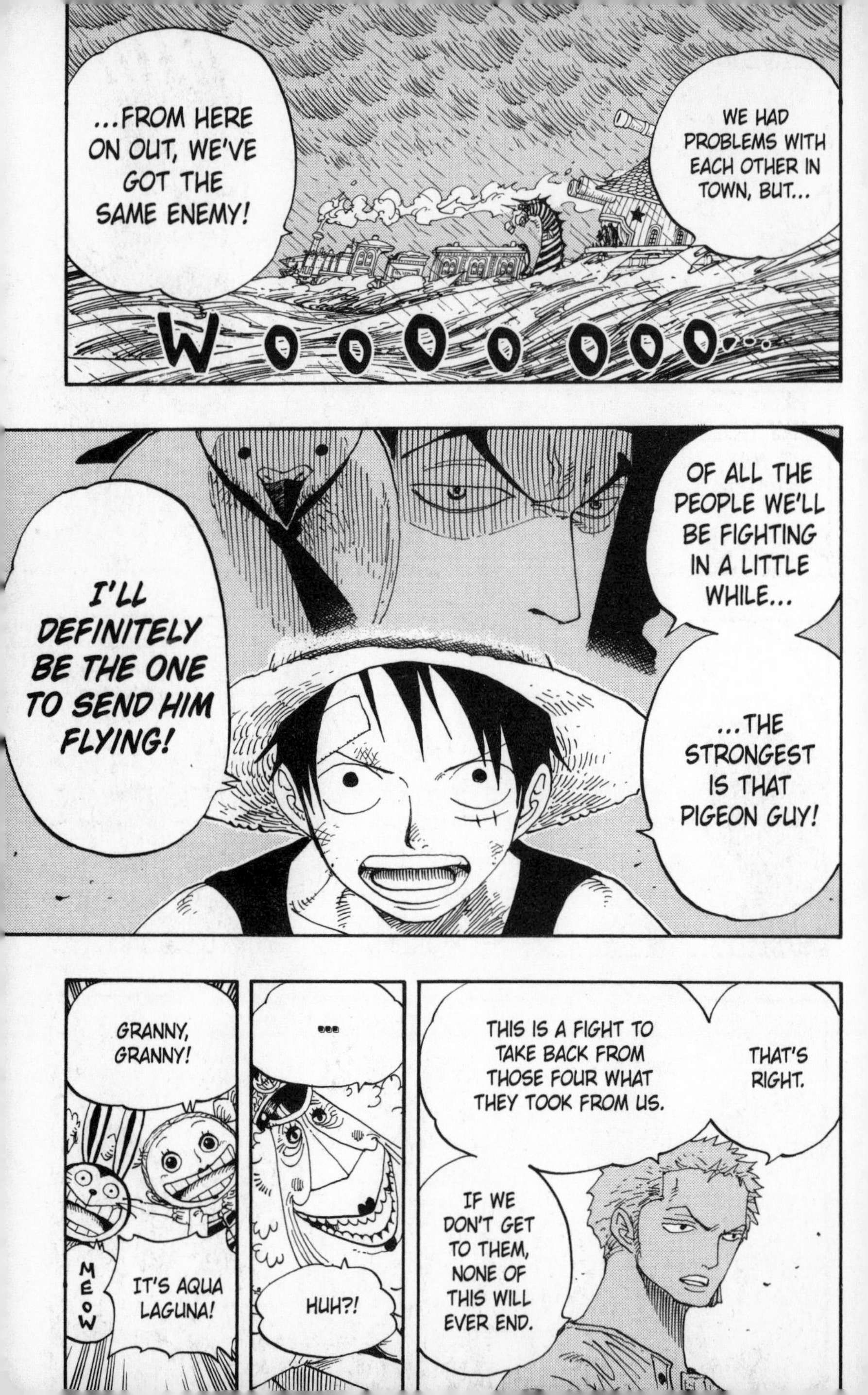
WE HAD PROBLEMS WITH EACH OTHER IN TOWN, BUT...
...FROM HERE ON OUT, WE'VE GOT THE SAME ENEMY!
WOOOOOOO...
OF ALL THE PEOPLE WE'LL BE FIGHTING IN A LITTLE WHILE...
...THE STRONGEST IS THAT PIGEON GUY!
I'LL DEFINITELY BE THE ONE TO SEND HIM FLYING!
THAT'S RIGHT.
THIS IS A FIGHT TO TAKE BACK FROM THOSE FOUR WHAT THEY TOOK FROM US.
IF WE DON'T GET TO THEM, NONE OF THIS WILL EVER END.
...
HUH?!
GRANNY, GRANNY!
IT'S AQUA LAGUNA!
MEOW

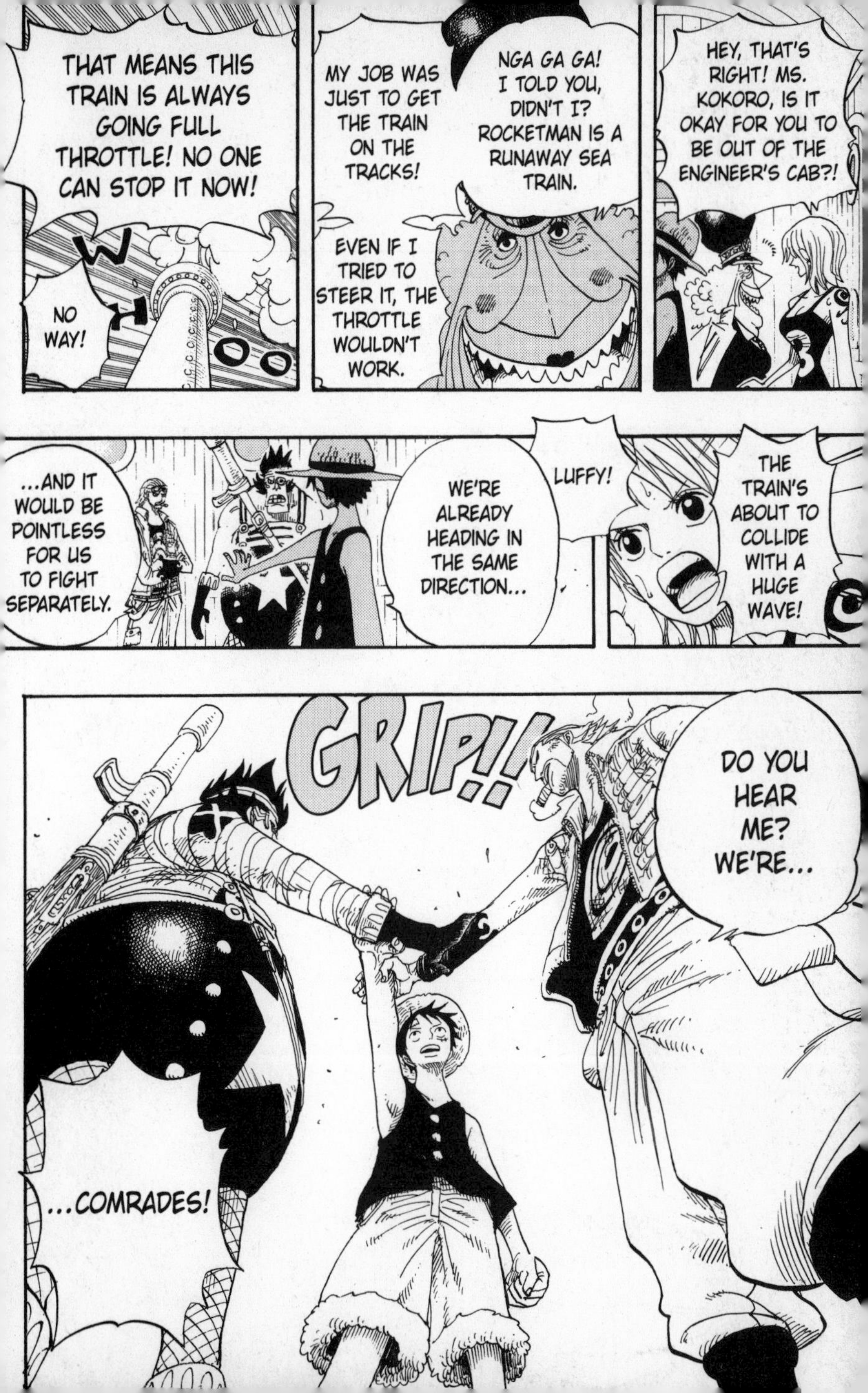
HEY, THAT'S RIGHT! MS. KOKORO, IS IT OKAY FOR YOU TO BE OUT OF THE ENGINEER'S CAB?!
NGA GA GA! I TOLD YOU, DIDN'T I? ROCKETMAN IS A RUNAWAY SEA TRAIN.
MY JOB WAS JUST TO GET THE TRAIN ON THE TRACKS!
EVEN IF I TRIED TO STEER IT, THE THROTTLE WOULDN'T WORK.
THAT MEANS THIS TRAIN IS ALWAYS GOING FULL THROTTLE! NO ONE CAN STOP IT NOW!
NO WAY!
LUFFY!
THE TRAIN'S ABOUT TO COLLIDE WITH A HUGE WAVE!
WE'RE ALREADY HEADING IN THE SAME DIRECTION...
...AND IT WOULD BE POINTLESS FOR US TO FIGHT SEPARATELY.
DO YOU HEAR ME? WE'RE...
GRIP!!
...COMRADES!

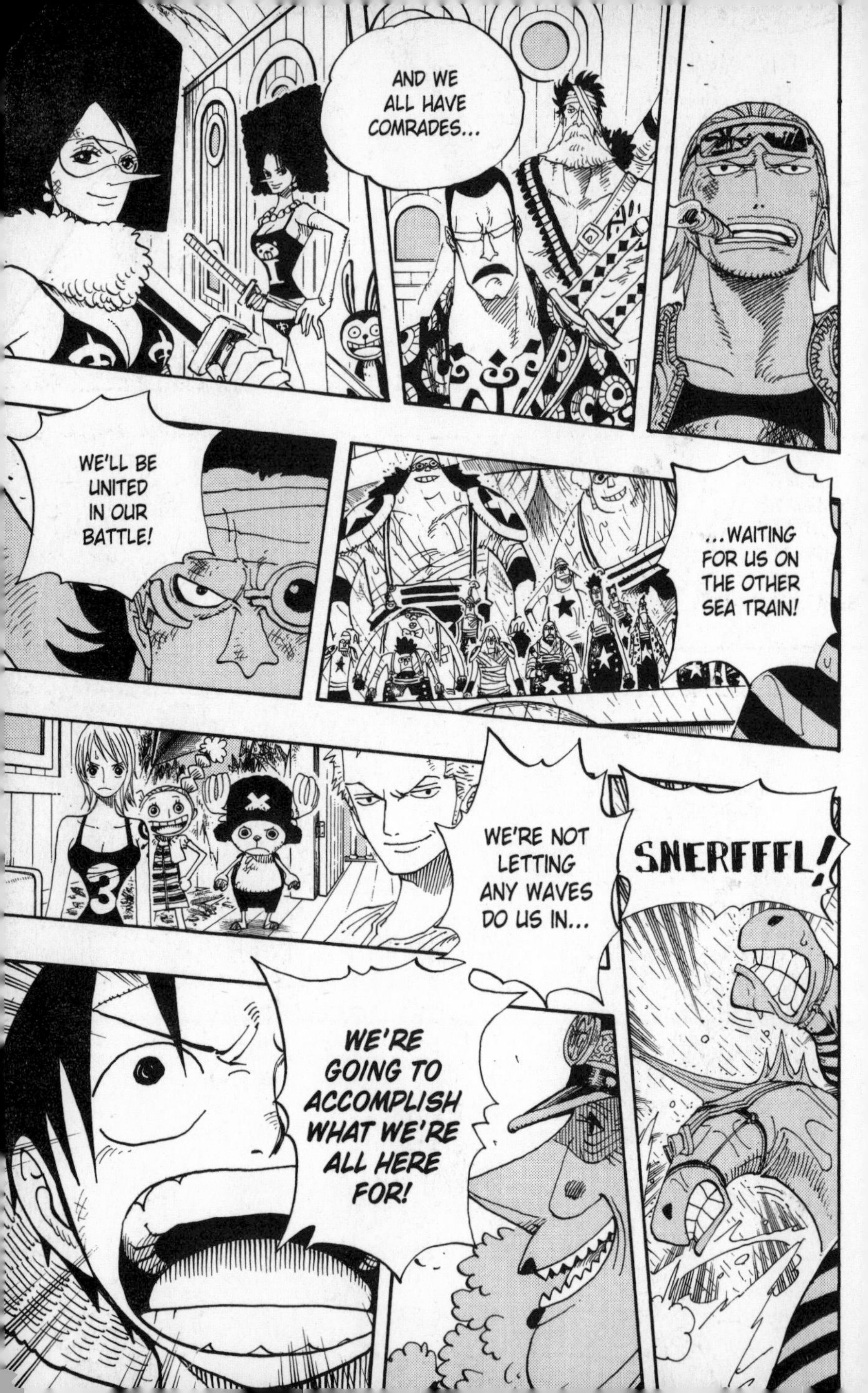
AND WE ALL HAVE COMRADES...
...WAITING FOR US ON THE OTHER SEA TRAIN!
WE'LL BE UNITED IN OUR BATTLE!
SNERFFFL!
WE'RE NOT LETTING ANY WAVES DO US IN...
WE'RE GOING TO ACCOMPLISH WHAT WE'RE ALL HERE FOR!

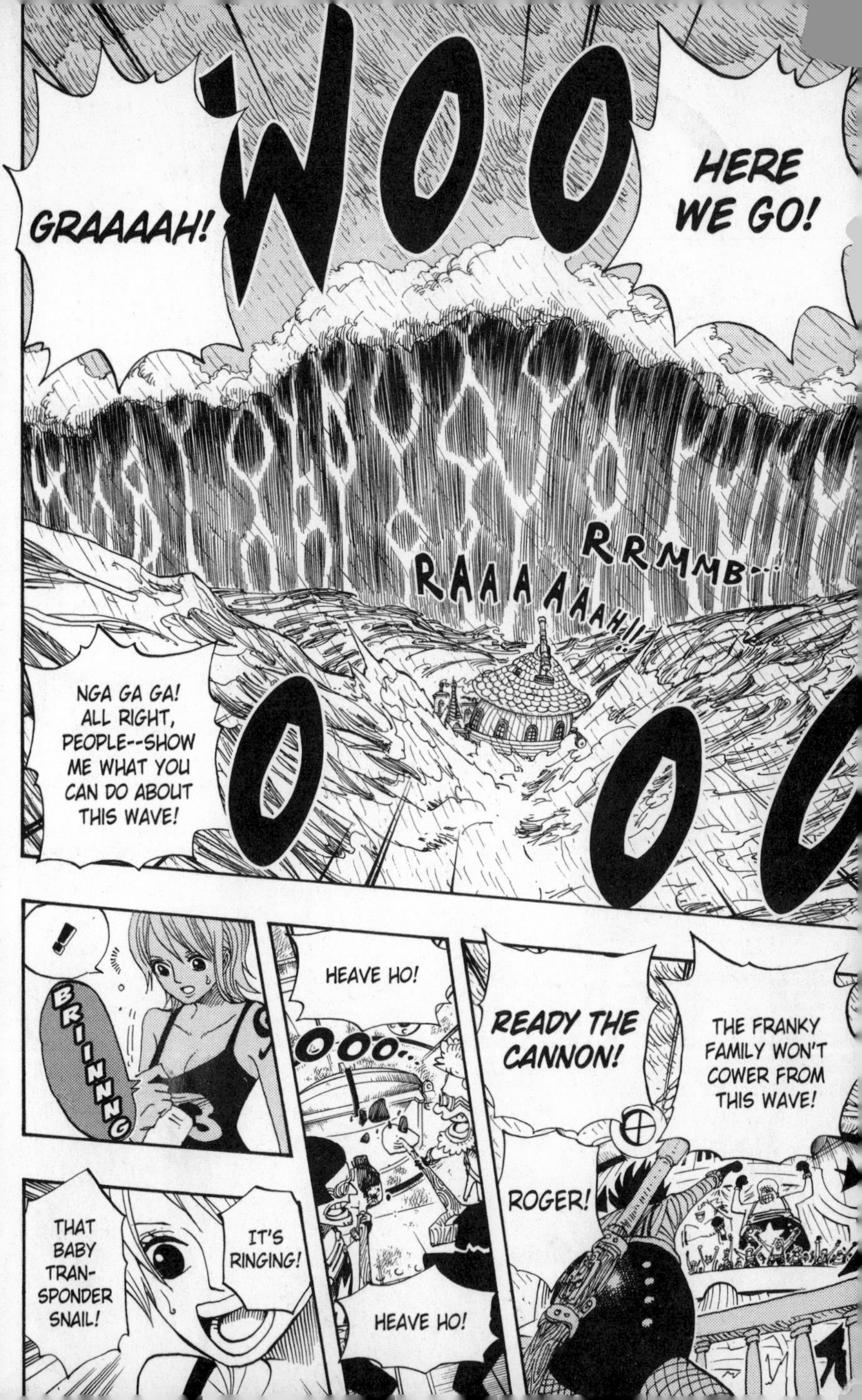
HERE WE GO!
WOO
GRAAAAH!
RRMMB...
RAAAAAAAH!!
OOO
NGA GA GA! ALL RIGHT, PEOPLE--SHOW ME WHAT YOU CAN DO ABOUT THIS WAVE!
THE FRANKY FAMILY WON'T COWER FROM THIS WAVE!
READY THE CANNON!
ROGER!
HEAVE HO!
OOOO...
HEAVE HO!
!
BRIINNG
IT'S RINGING!
THAT BABY TRANSPONDER SNAIL!

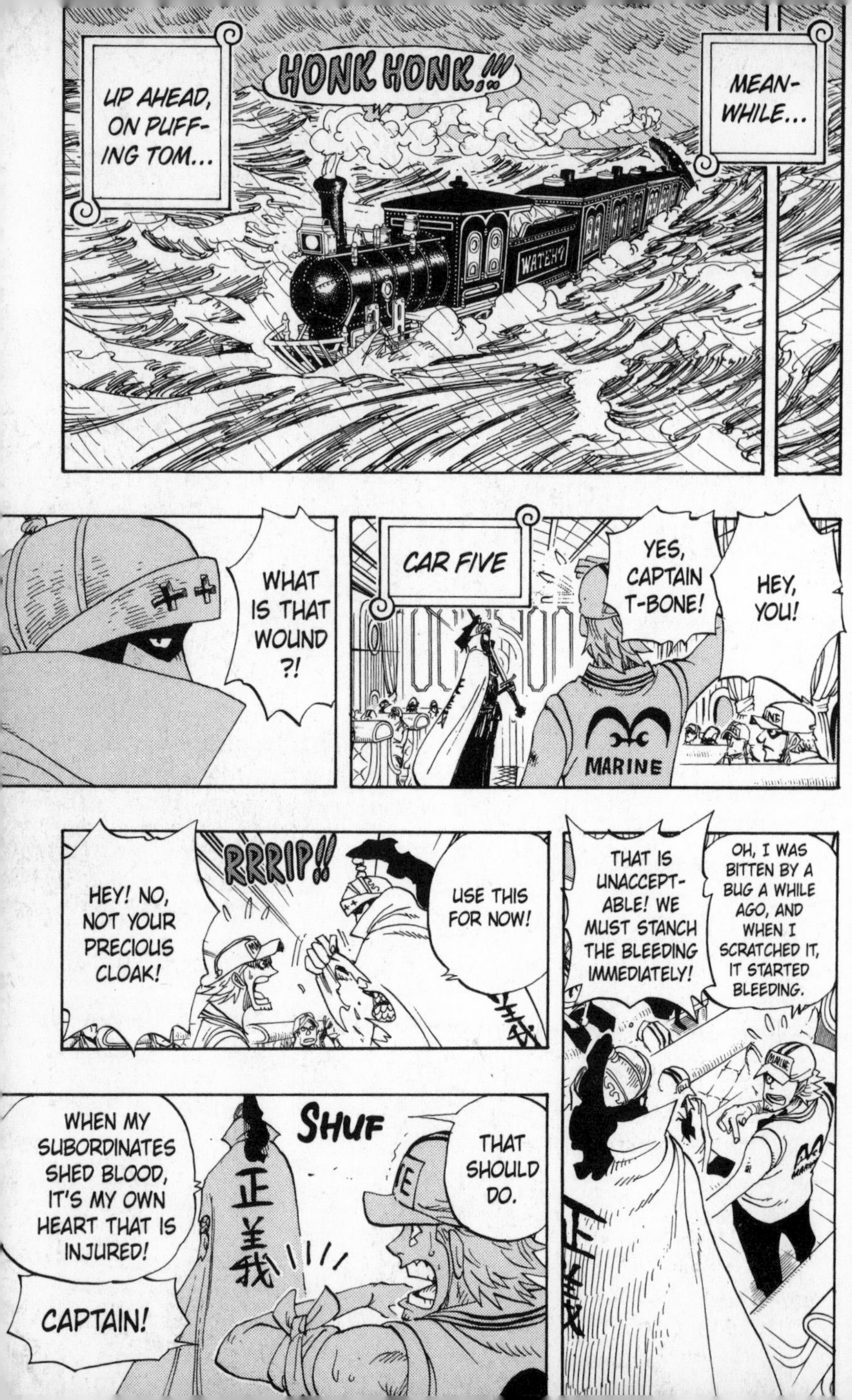
MEAN-WHILE...
UP AHEAD, ON PUFF-ING TOM...
HONK HONK!!!
HEY, YOU!
YES, CAPTAIN T-BONE!
CAR FIVE
MARINE
WHAT IS THAT WOUND?!
OH, I WAS BITTEN BY A BUG A WHILE AGO, AND WHEN I SCRATCHED IT, IT STARTED BLEEDING.
THAT IS UNACCEPT-ABLE! WE MUST STANCH THE BLEEDING IMMEDIATELY!
USE THIS FOR NOW!
RRRIP!!
HEY! NO, NOT YOUR PRECIOUS CLOAK!
THAT SHOULD DO.
SHUF
WHEN MY SUBORDINATES SHED BLOOD, IT'S MY OWN HEART THAT IS INJURED!
正義
CAPTAIN!

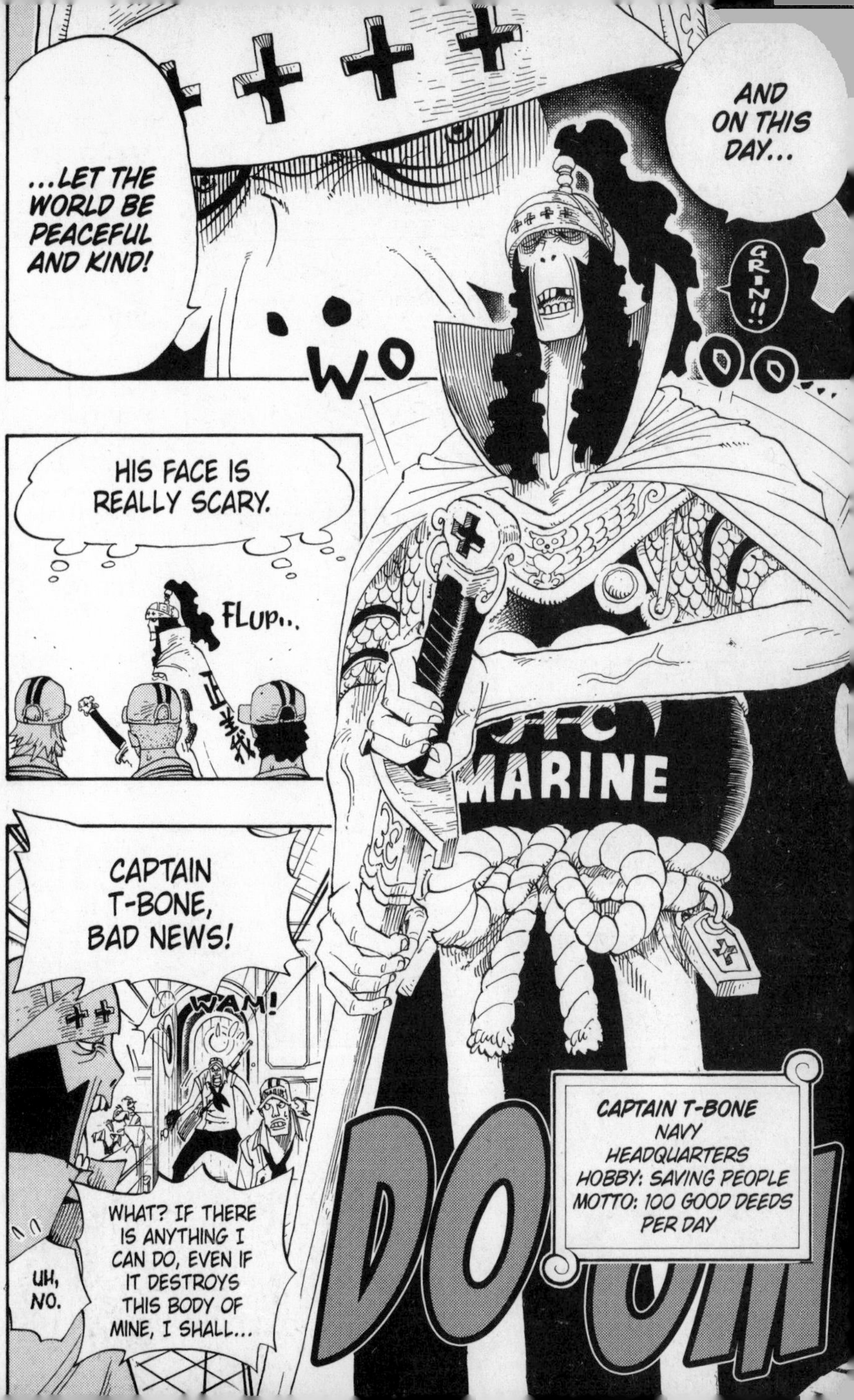
...LET THE WORLD BE PEACEFUL AND KIND!
AND ON THIS DAY...
GRIN!!
WO
OO...
MARINE
CAPTAIN T-BONE
NAVY HEADQUARTERS
HOBBY: SAVING PEOPLE
MOTTO: 100 GOOD DEEDS PER DAY
DO
HIS FACE IS REALLY SCARY.
FLUP...
CAPTAIN T-BONE, BAD NEWS!
WAM!
WHAT? IF THERE IS ANYTHING I CAN DO, EVEN IF IT DESTROYS THIS BODY OF MINE, I SHALL...
UH, NO.

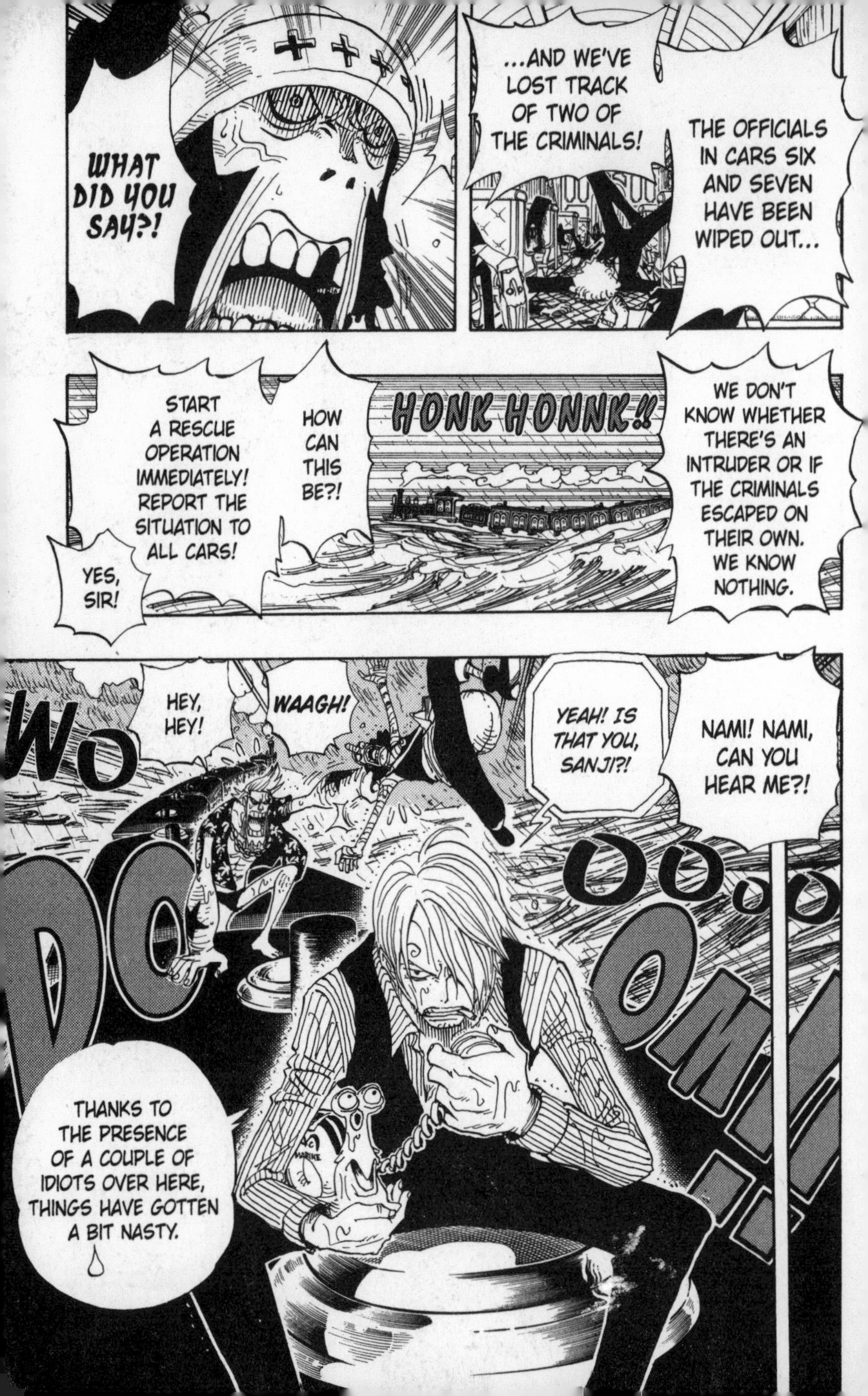
THE OFFICIALS IN CARS SIX AND SEVEN HAVE BEEN WIPED OUT...
...AND WE'VE LOST TRACK OF TWO OF THE CRIMINALS!
WHAT DID YOU SAY?!
WE DON'T KNOW WHETHER THERE'S AN INTRUDER OR IF THE CRIMINALS ESCAPED ON THEIR OWN. WE KNOW NOTHING.
HONK HONNK!!
HOW CAN THIS BE?!
START A RESCUE OPERATION IMMEDIATELY! REPORT THE SITUATION TO ALL CARS!
YES, SIR!
NAMI! NAMI, CAN YOU HEAR ME?!
YEAH! IS THAT YOU, SANJI?!
WAAGH!
HEY, HEY!
THANKS TO THE PRESENCE OF A COUPLE OF IDIOTS OVER HERE, THINGS HAVE GOTTEN A BIT NASTY.

Chapter 367:
SNIPER KING

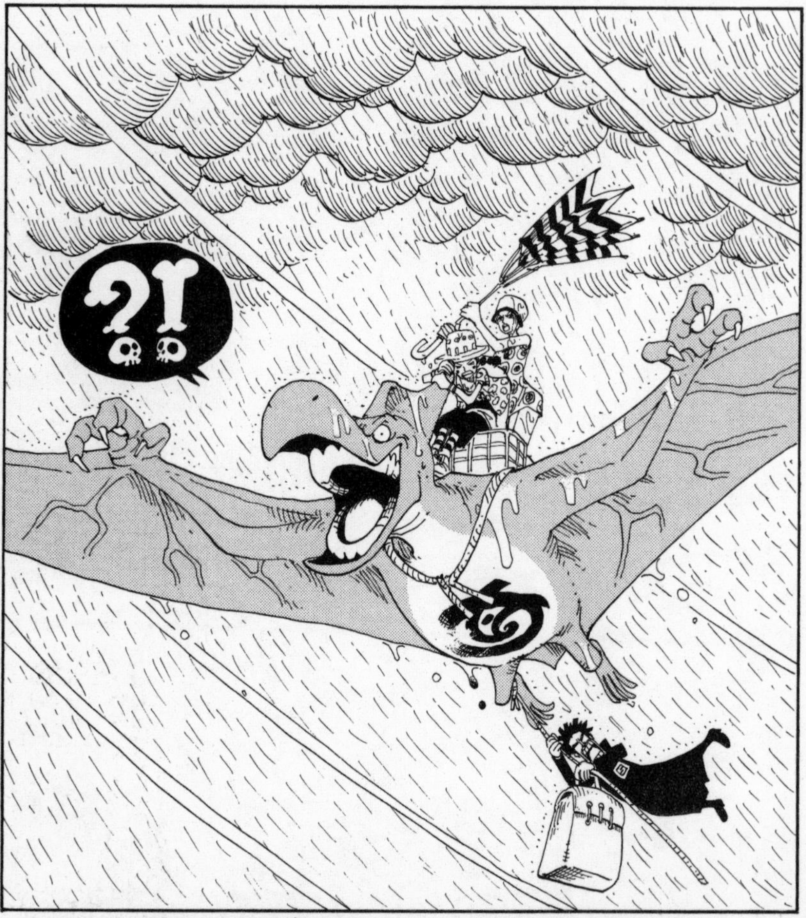
?!

MS. GOLDEN WEEK'S BIG PLAN, A BAROQUE REUNION,
VOL. 7: "INK WASHES OFF IN THE RAIN"

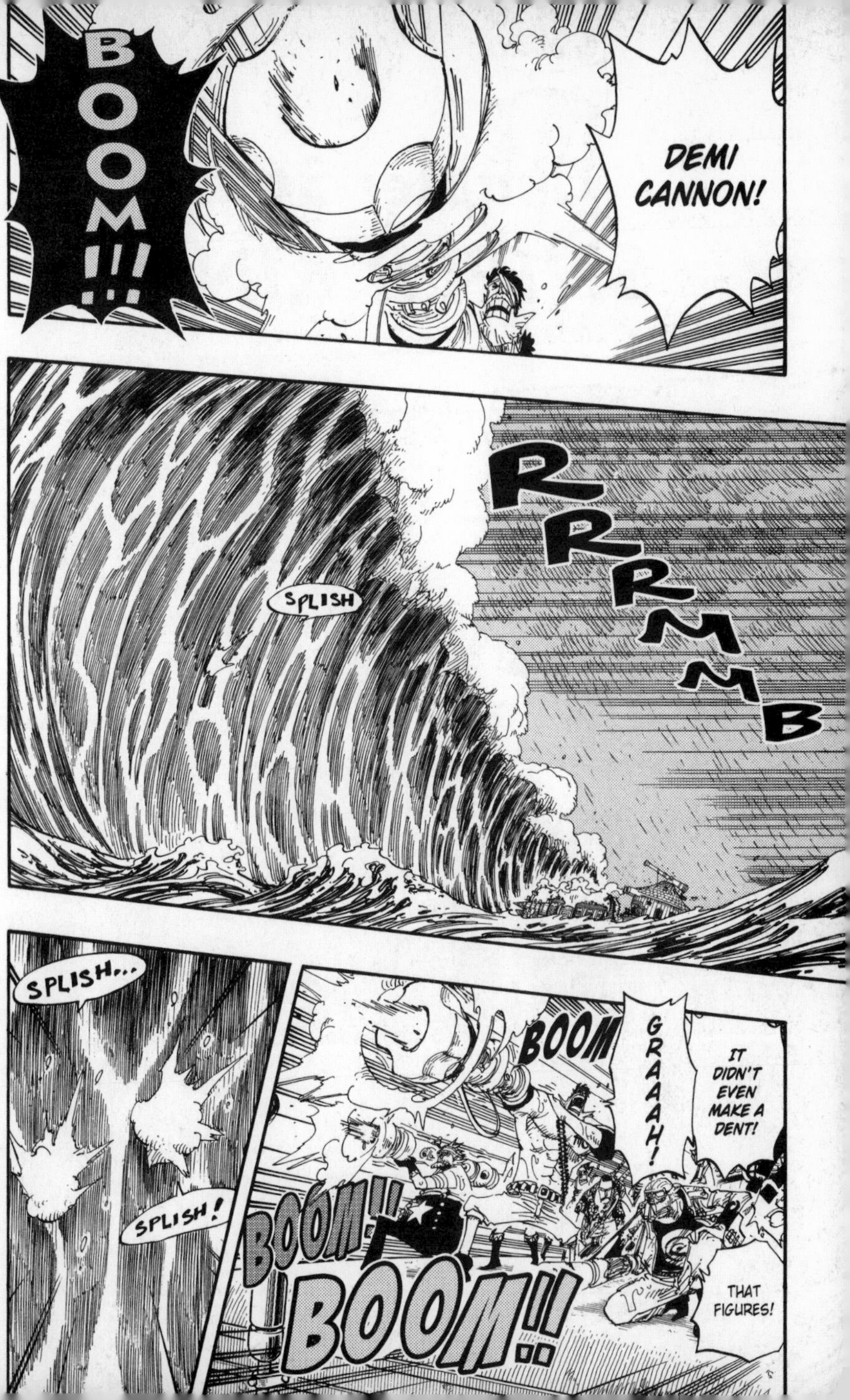
DEMI CANNON!
BOOM!!!
RRRRMMB
SPLISH
IT DIDN'T EVEN MAKE A DENT!
GRAAAH!
BOOM
THAT FIGURES!
BOOM!!
BOOM!!
SPLISH...
SPLISH!

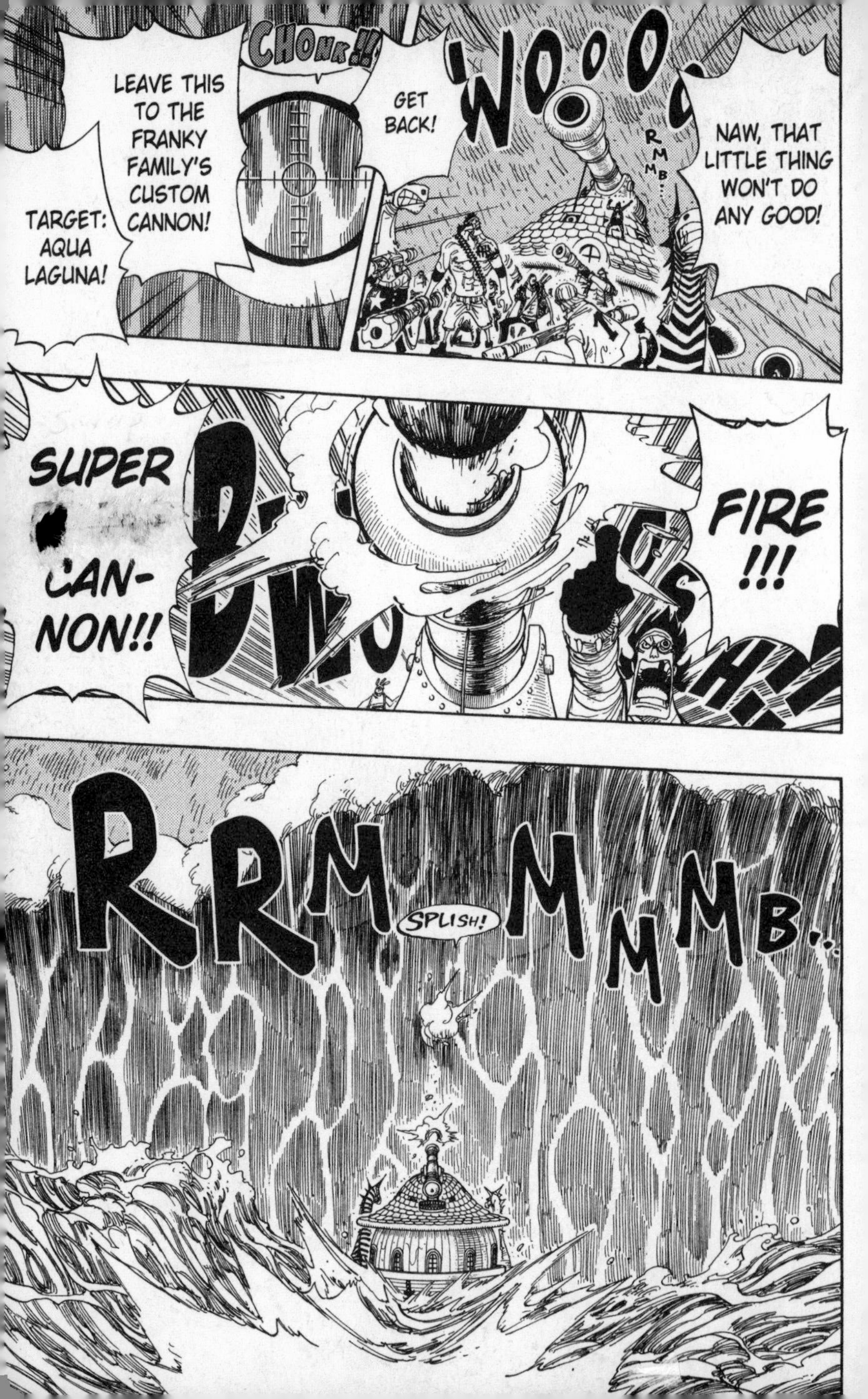
WOOOO
RMMB...
NAW, THAT LITTLE THING WON'T DO ANY GOOD!
GET BACK!
CHONK!!
LEAVE THIS TO THE FRANKY FAMILY'S CUSTOM CANNON!
TARGET: AQUA LAGUNA!
FIRE!!!
BWOOSH!!
SUPER
CAN-NON!!
RRRMMMMB...
SPLISH!

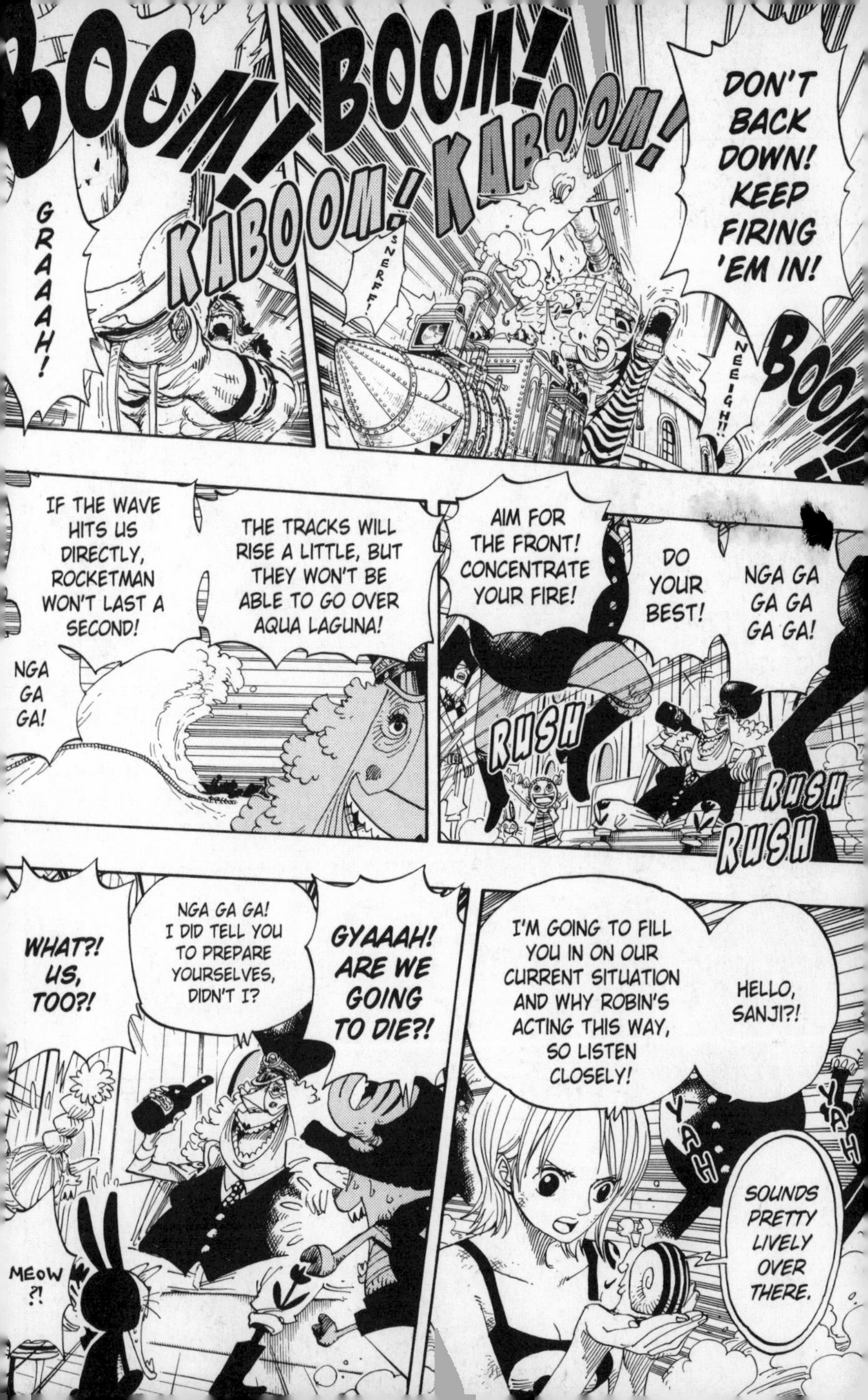
DON'T BACK DOWN! KEEP FIRING 'EM IN!
BOOM!
NEEIGH!!
KABOOM!
BOOM!
SNERFF!
KABOOM!
BOOM!
GRAAAAH!
NGA GA GA GA GA GA!
DO YOUR BEST!
AIM FOR THE FRONT! CONCENTRATE YOUR FIRE!
RUSH
RUSH
RUSH
THE TRACKS WILL RISE A LITTLE, BUT THEY WON'T BE ABLE TO GO OVER AQUA LAGUNA!
IF THE WAVE HITS US DIRECTLY, ROCKETMAN WON'T LAST A SECOND!
NGA GA GA!
HELLO, SANJI?!
I'M GOING TO FILL YOU IN ON OUR CURRENT SITUATION AND WHY ROBIN'S ACTING THIS WAY, SO LISTEN CLOSELY!
YAH
YAH
SOUNDS PRETTY LIVELY OVER THERE.
GYAAAH! ARE WE GOING TO DIE?!
NGA GA GA! I DID TELL YOU TO PREPARE YOURSELVES, DIDN'T I?
WHAT?! US, TOO?!
MEOW ?!

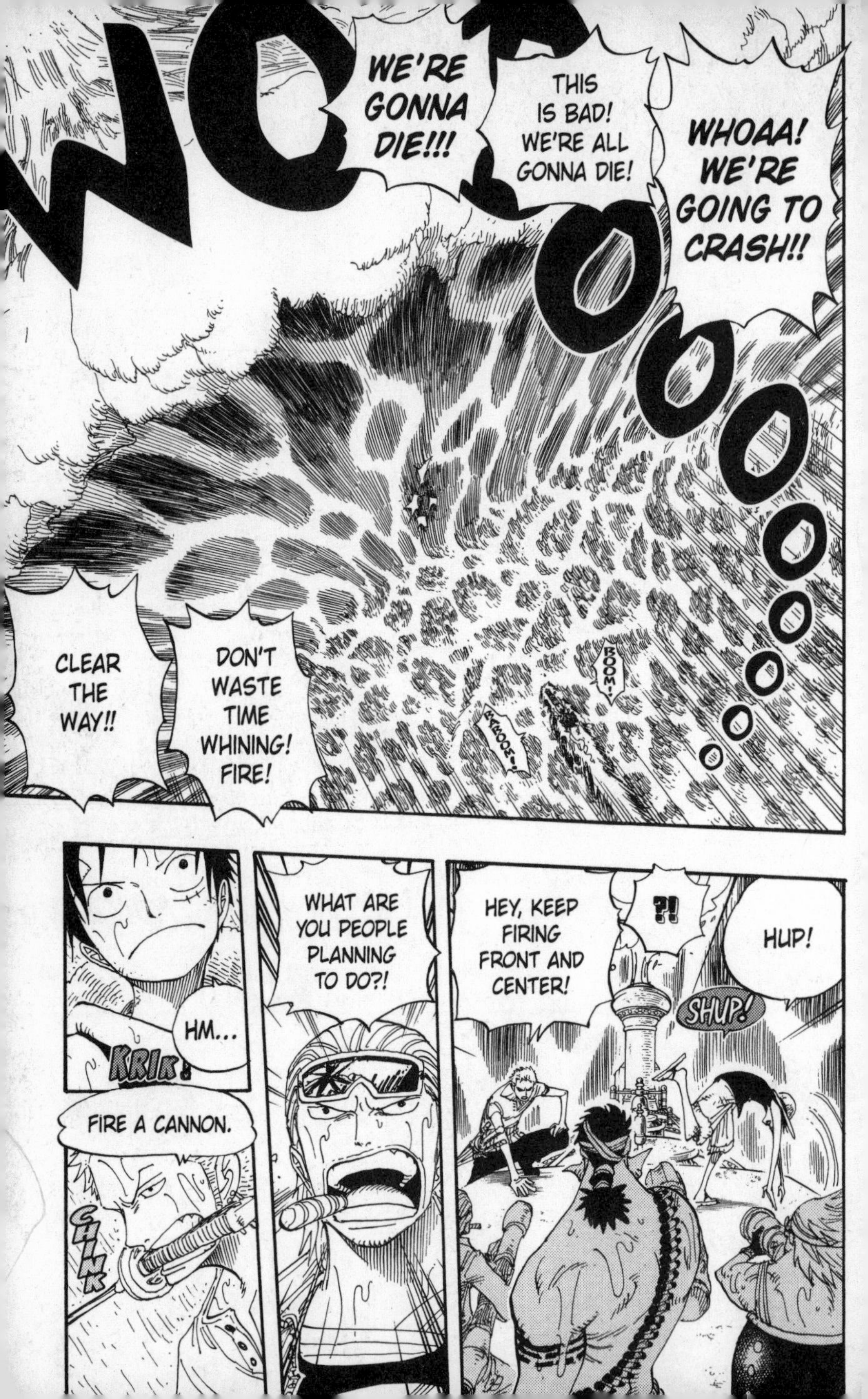
WHOAA! WE'RE GOING TO CRASH!!
THIS IS BAD! WE'RE ALL GONNA DIE!
WE'RE GONNA DIE!!!
BOOM!
KABOOM!
DON'T WASTE TIME WHINING! FIRE!
CLEAR THE WAY!!
HUP!
SHUP!
?!
HEY, KEEP FIRING FRONT AND CENTER!
WHAT ARE YOU PEOPLE PLANNING TO DO?!
HM...
KRIK
FIRE A CANNON.
CHINK

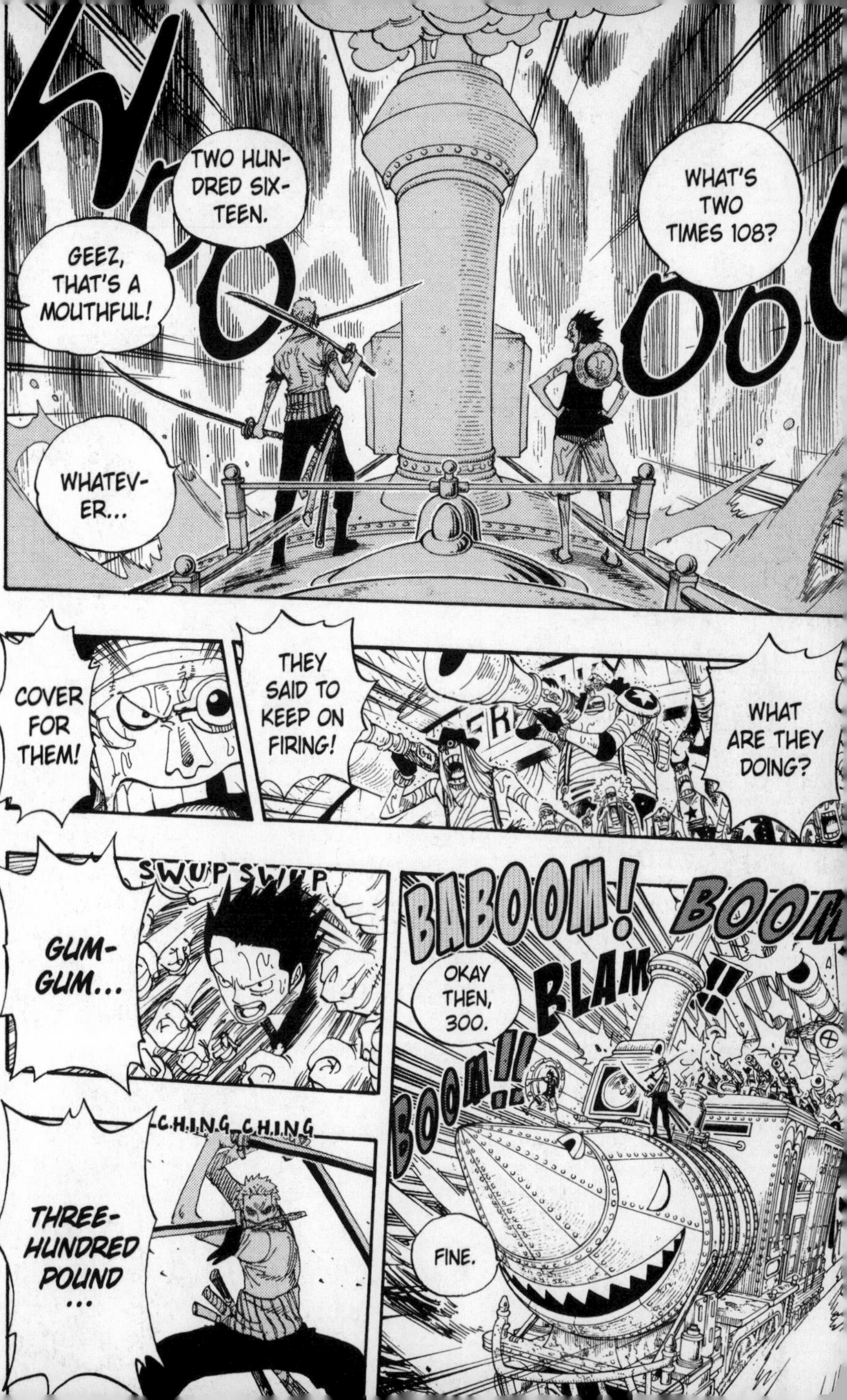
WHAT'S TWO TIMES 108?
TWO HUNDRED SIXTEEN.
GEEZ, THAT'S A MOUTHFUL!
WHATEVER...
WHAT ARE THEY DOING?
THEY SAID TO KEEP ON FIRING!
COVER FOR THEM!
BABOOM!
BOOM
BLAM!!
BOOM!!
OKAY THEN, 300.
FINE.
SWUP SWUP
GUM-GUM...
CHING CHING
THREE-HUNDRED POUND...

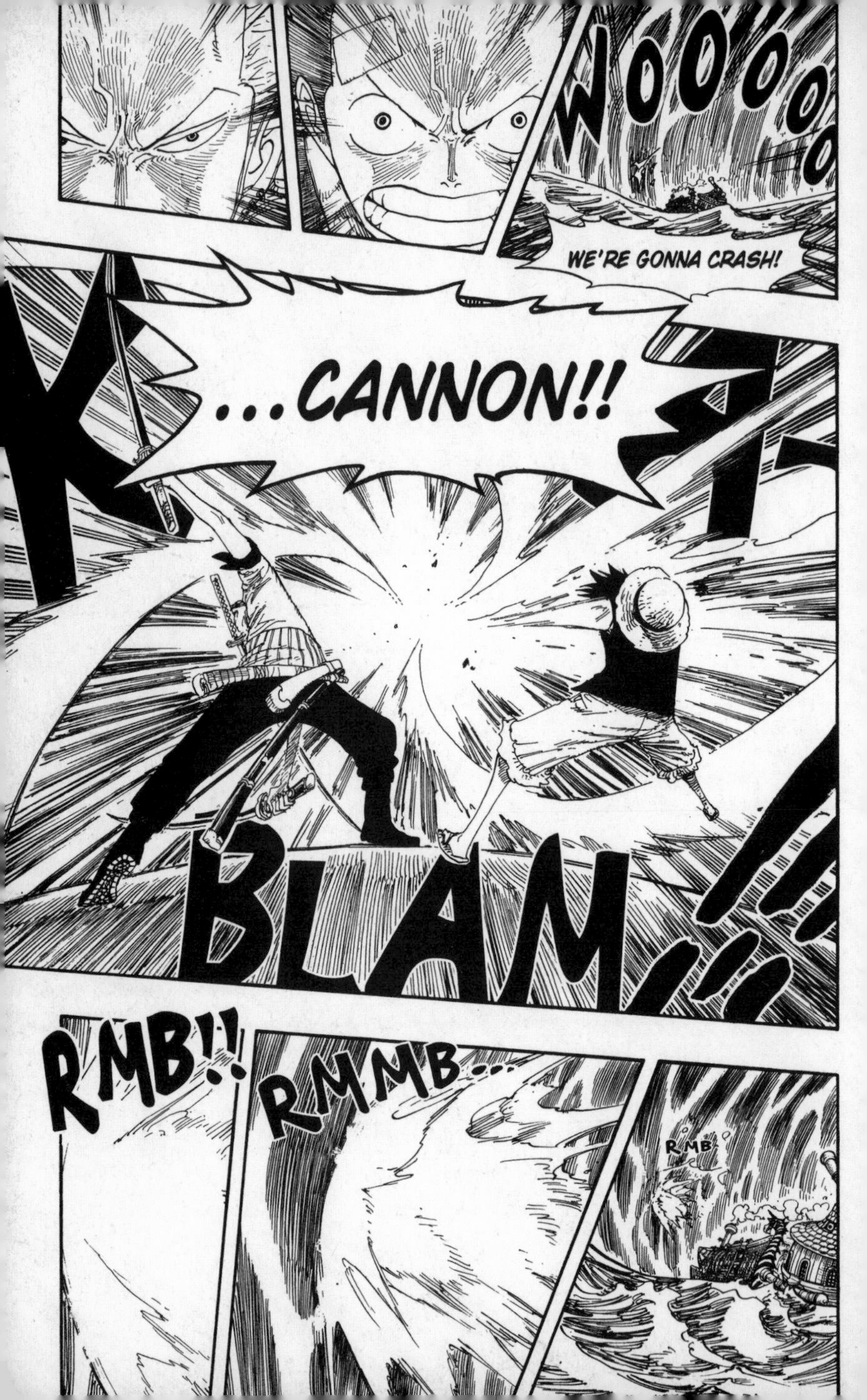
WOOOOO
WE'RE GONNA CRASH!
...CANNON!!
BLAM!!
RMB
RMMB...
RMB!!

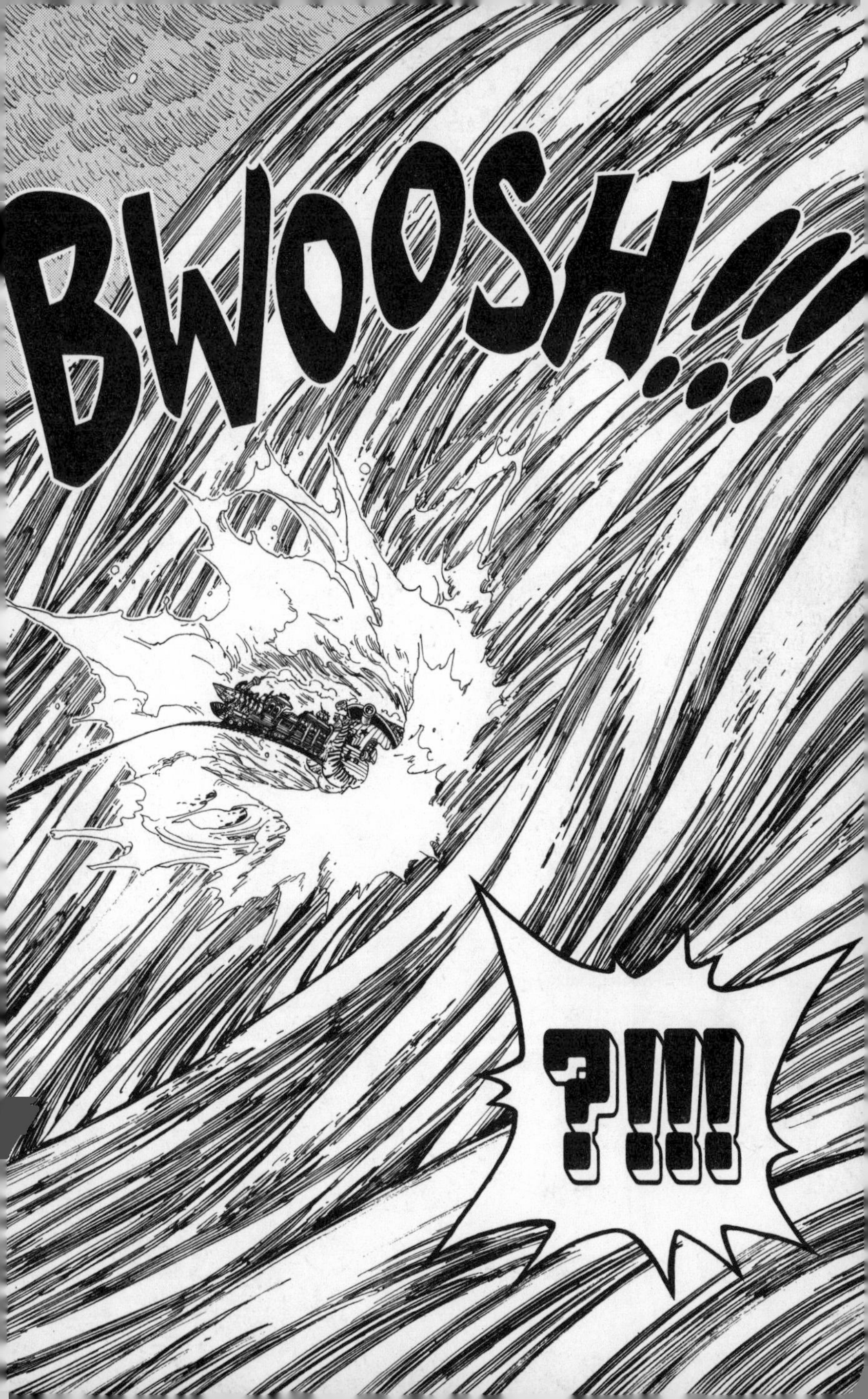
BWOOSH!!
?!!!

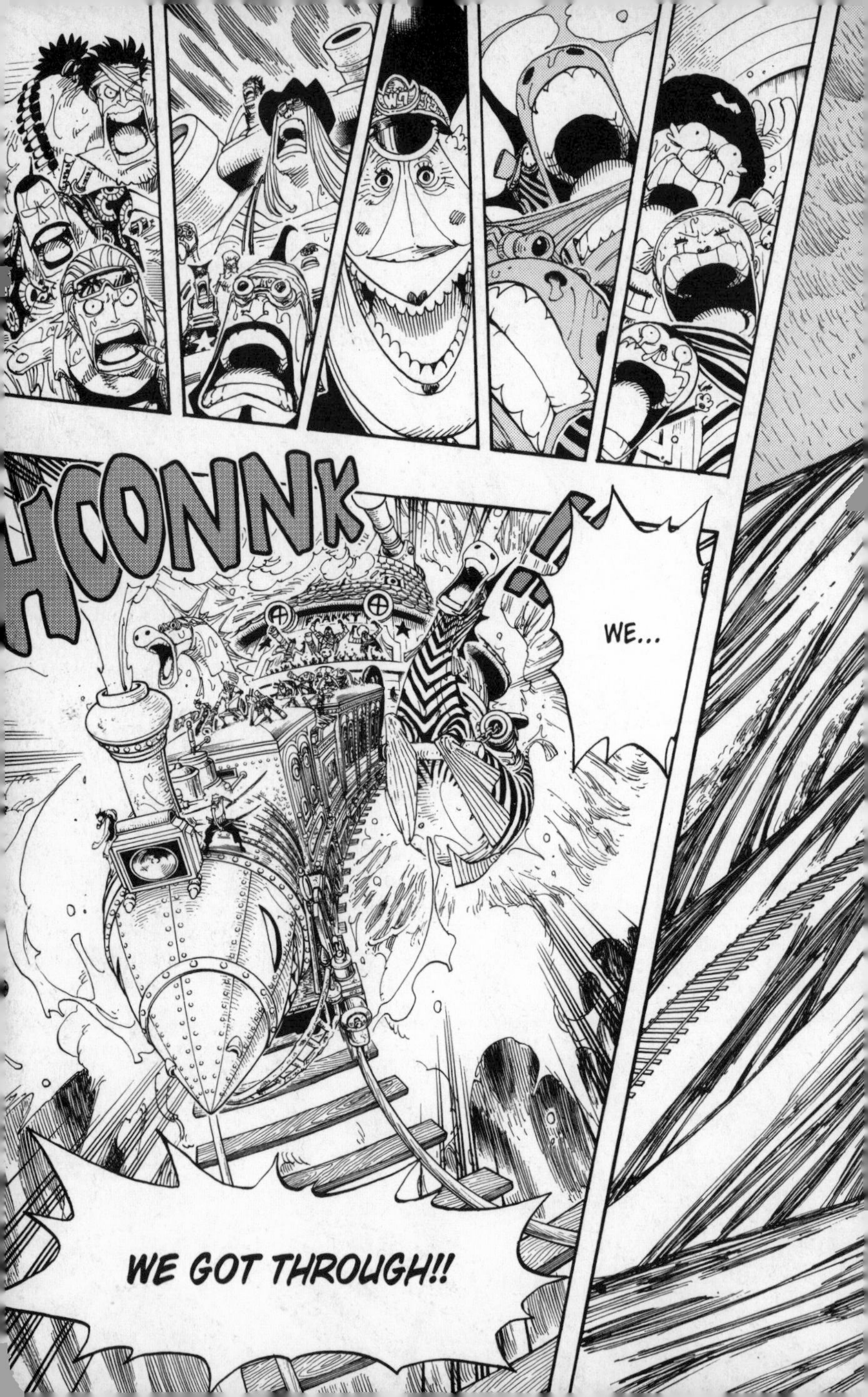
HCONNK
WE...
WE GOT THROUGH!!

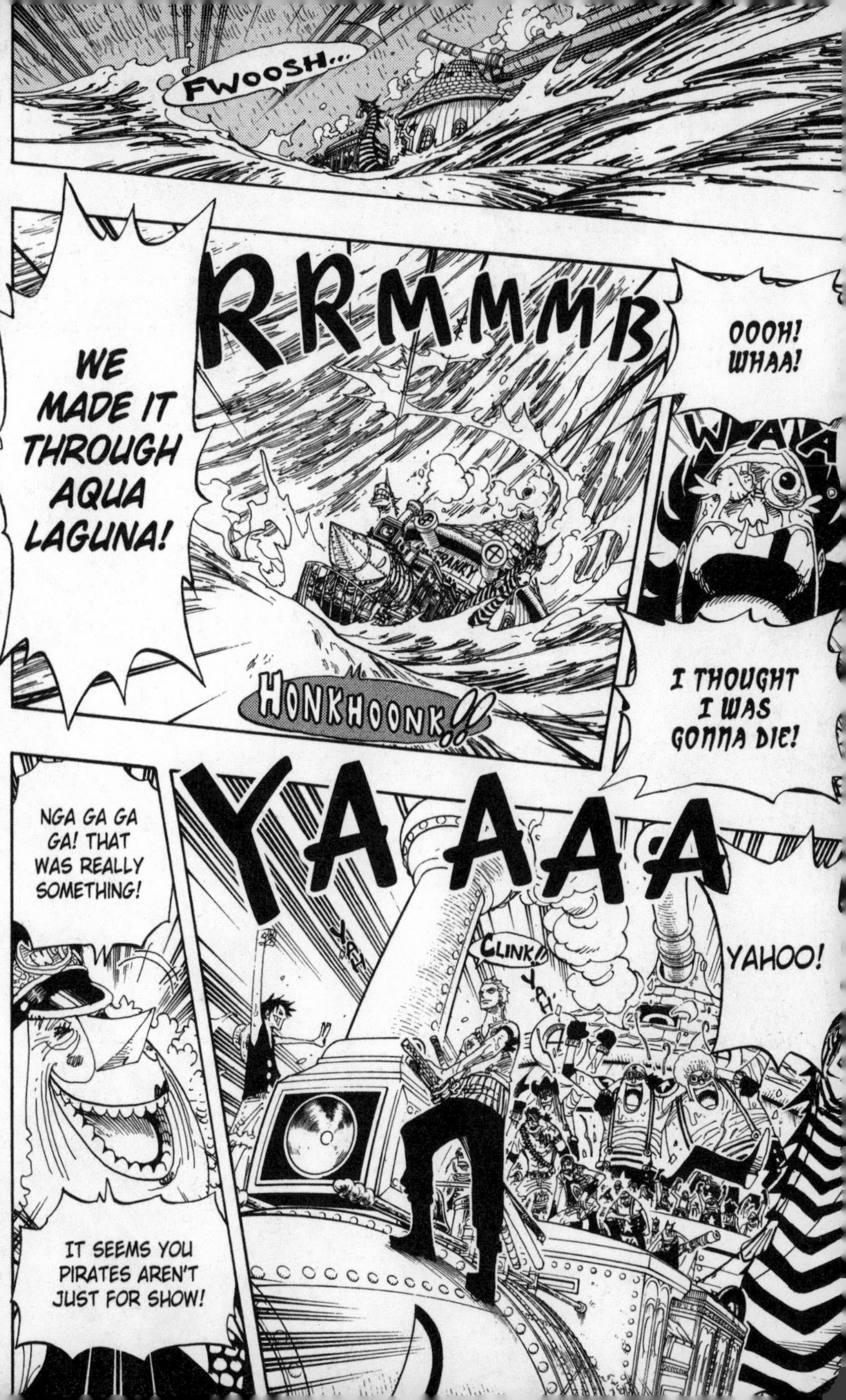
FWOOSH...
OOOH! WHAA!
WAAA
I THOUGHT I WAS GONNA DIE!
RRRMMMB
HONKHOONK!!
WE MADE IT THROUGH AQUA LAGUNA!
YAAAA
YAHOO!
CLINK!!
NGA GA GA GA! THAT WAS REALLY SOMETHING!
IT SEEMS YOU PIRATES AREN'T JUST FOR SHOW!

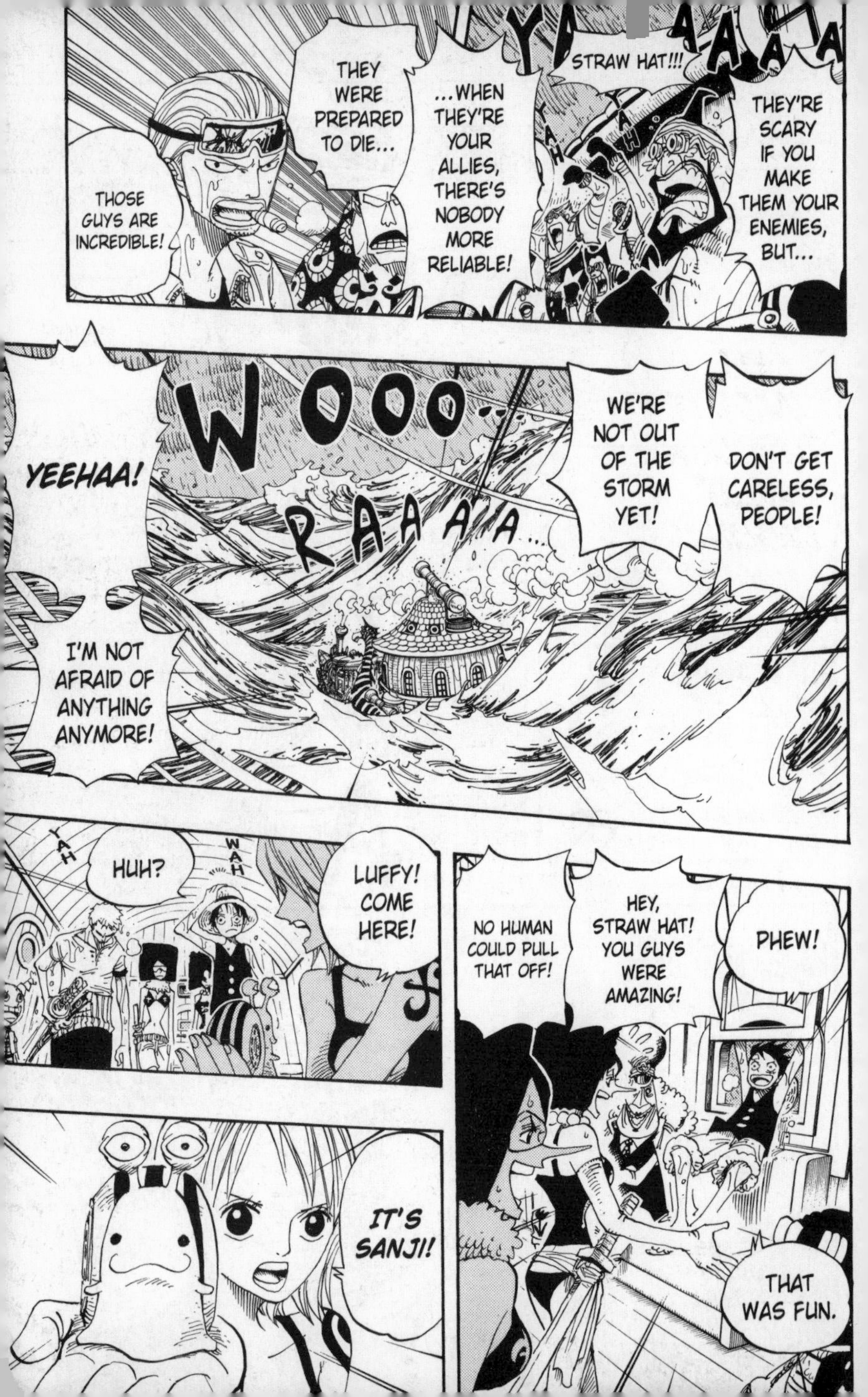
STRAW HAT!!!
THEY'RE SCARY IF YOU MAKE THEM YOUR ENEMIES, BUT...
...WHEN THEY'RE YOUR ALLIES, THERE'S NOBODY MORE RELIABLE!
THEY WERE PREPARED TO DIE...
THOSE GUYS ARE INCREDIBLE!
DON'T GET CARELESS, PEOPLE!
WE'RE NOT OUT OF THE STORM YET!
WOOO...
RAAAA...
YEEHAA!
I'M NOT AFRAID OF ANYTHING ANYMORE!
PHEW!
HEY, STRAW HAT! YOU GUYS WERE AMAZING!
NO HUMAN COULD PULL THAT OFF!
THAT WAS FUN.
LUFFY! COME HERE!
WAH
HUH?
YAH
IT'S SANJI!

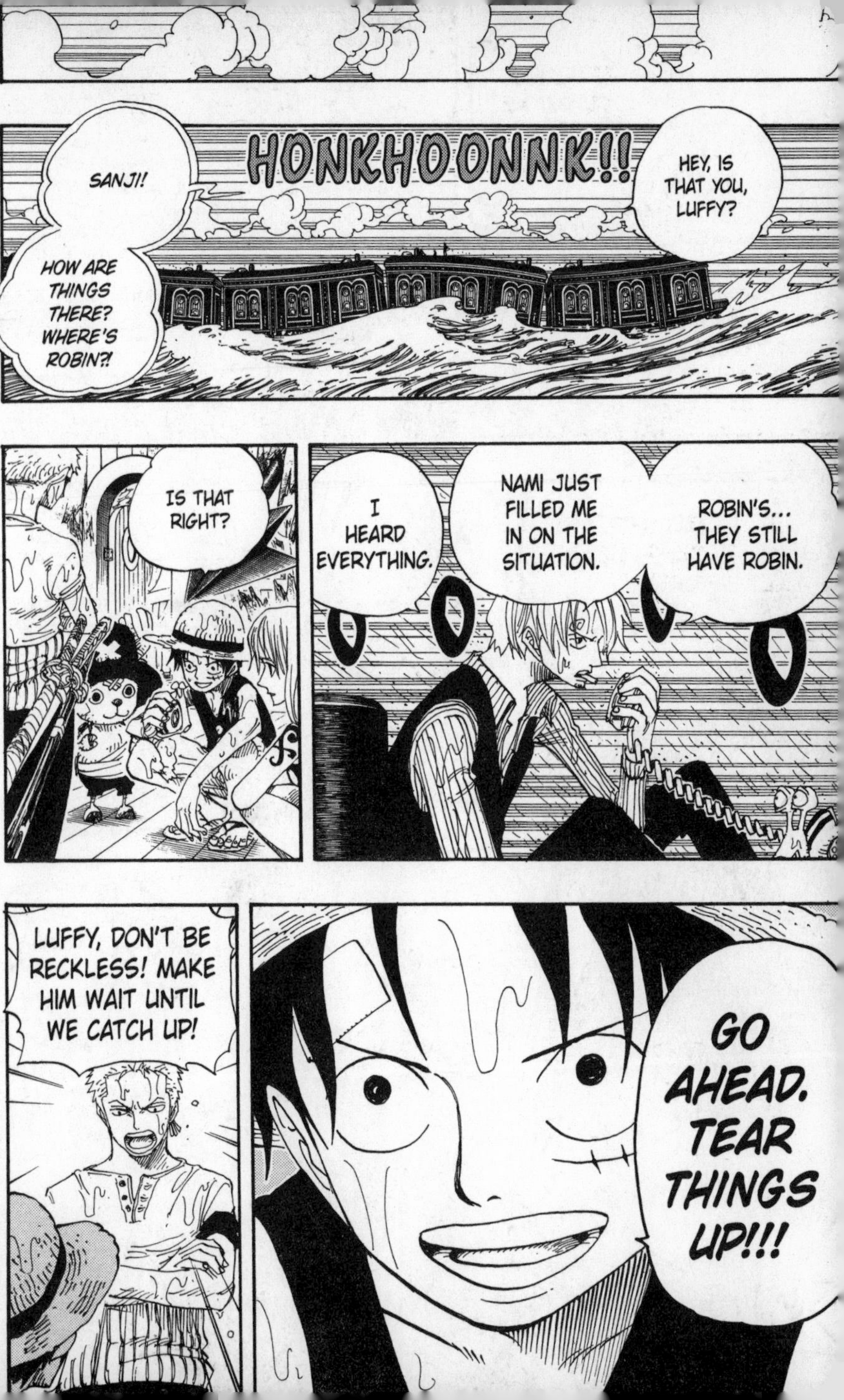
HEY, IS THAT YOU, LUFFY?
HONKHOONNK!!
SANJI!
HOW ARE THINGS THERE? WHERE'S ROBIN?!
ROBIN'S... THEY STILL HAVE ROBIN.
NAMI JUST FILLED ME IN ON THE SITUATION.
I HEARD EVERYTHING.
IS THAT RIGHT?
GO AHEAD. TEAR THINGS UP!!!
LUFFY, DON'T BE RECKLESS! MAKE HIM WAIT UNTIL WE CATCH UP!

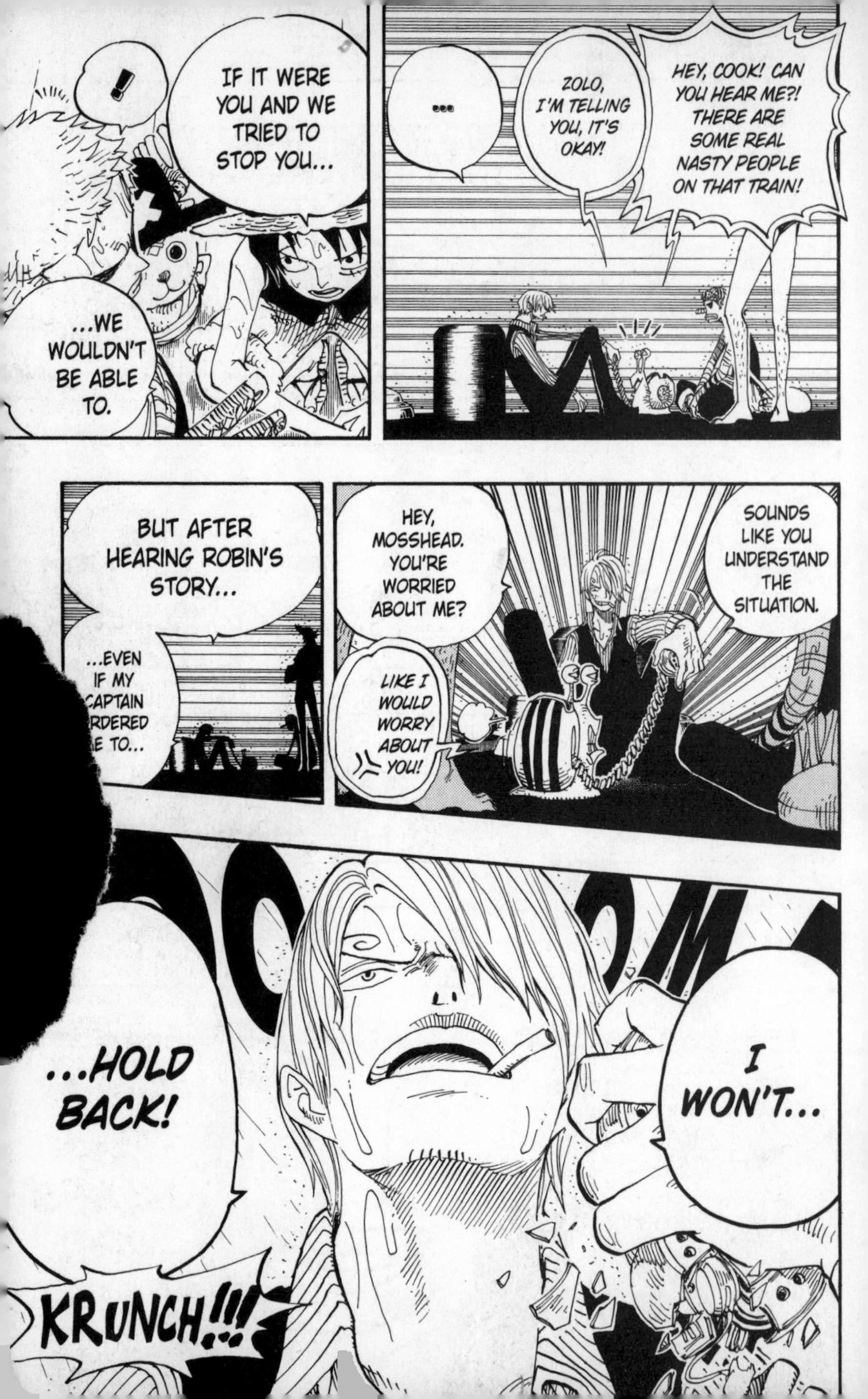
HEY, COOK! CAN YOU HEAR ME?! THERE ARE SOME REAL NASTY PEOPLE ON THAT TRAIN!
ZOLO, I'M TELLING YOU, IT'S OKAY!
...
!
IF IT WERE YOU AND WE TRIED TO STOP YOU...
...WE WOULDN'T BE ABLE TO.
SOUNDS LIKE YOU UNDERSTAND THE SITUATION.
HEY, MOSSHEAD. YOU'RE WORRIED ABOUT ME?
LIKE I WOULD WORRY ABOUT YOU!
BUT AFTER HEARING ROBIN'S STORY...
...EVEN IF MY CAPTAIN RDERED E TO...
I WON'T...
...HOLD BACK!
KRUNCH!!!

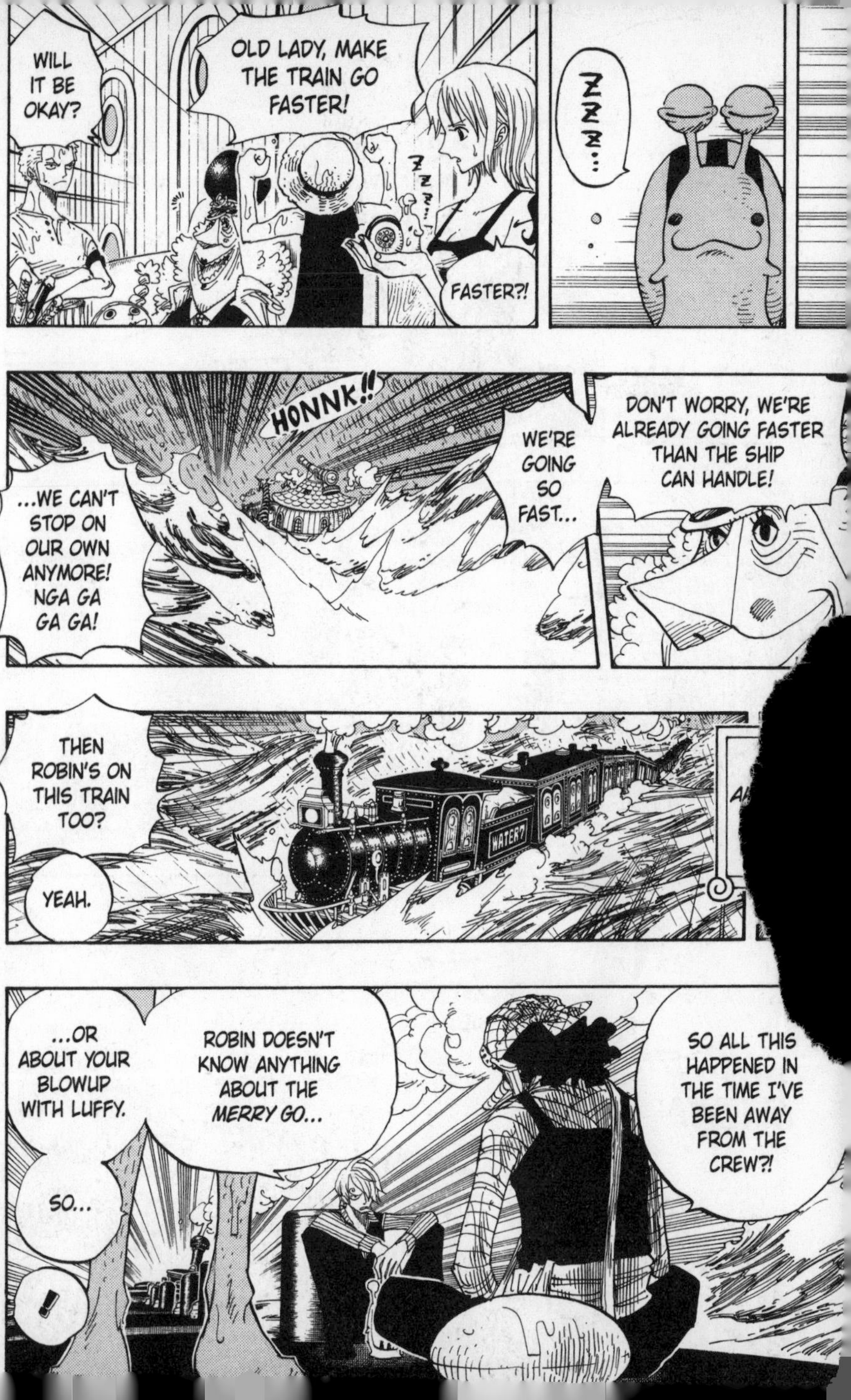
ZZZ...
OLD LADY, MAKE THE TRAIN GO FASTER!
WILL IT BE OKAY?
ZZZ...
FASTER?!
DON'T WORRY, WE'RE ALREADY GOING FASTER THAN THE SHIP CAN HANDLE!
WE'RE GOING SO FAST...
HONNK!!
...WE CAN'T STOP ON OUR OWN ANYMORE! NGA GA GA!
THEN ROBIN'S ON THIS TRAIN TOO?
WATER7
YEAH.
SO ALL THIS HAPPENED IN THE TIME I'VE BEEN AWAY FROM THE CREW?!
ROBIN DOESN'T KNOW ANYTHING ABOUT THE *MERRY GO*...
...OR ABOUT YOUR BLOWUP WITH LUFFY.
SO...
!

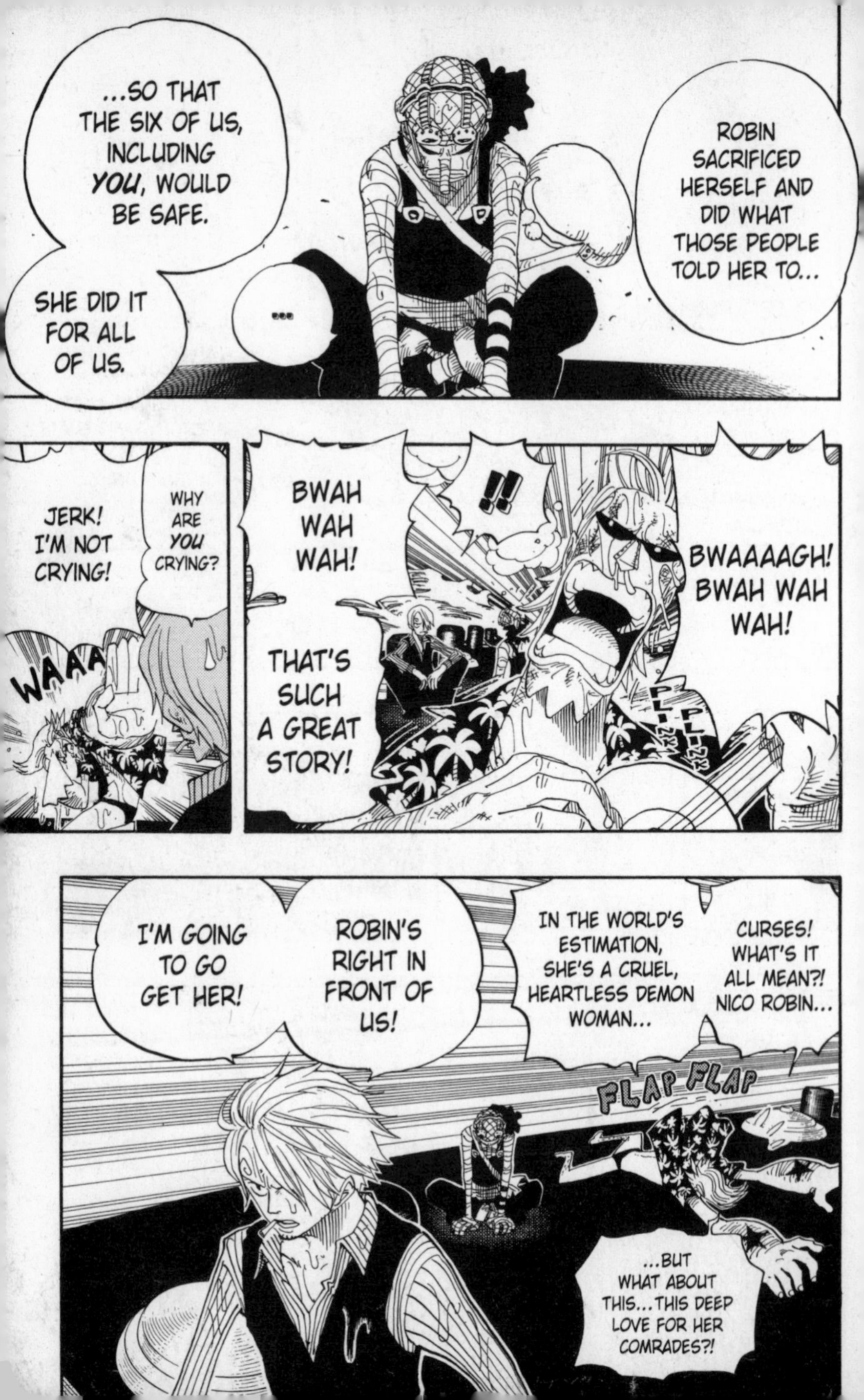
ROBIN SACRIFICED HERSELF AND DID WHAT THOSE PEOPLE TOLD HER TO...
...SO THAT THE SIX OF US, INCLUDING *YOU*, WOULD BE SAFE.
...
SHE DID IT FOR ALL OF US.
BWAAAAGH! BWAH WAH WAH!
!!
BWAH WAH WAH!
THAT'S SUCH A GREAT STORY!
PLINK
PLINK
WHY ARE *YOU* CRYING?
JERK! I'M NOT CRYING!
WAAA
CURSES! WHAT'S IT ALL MEAN?! NICO ROBIN...
IN THE WORLD'S ESTIMATION, SHE'S A CRUEL, HEARTLESS DEMON WOMAN...
ROBIN'S RIGHT IN FRONT OF US!
I'M GOING TO GO GET HER!
FLAP FLAP
...BUT WHAT ABOUT THIS...THIS DEEP LOVE FOR HER COMRADES?!

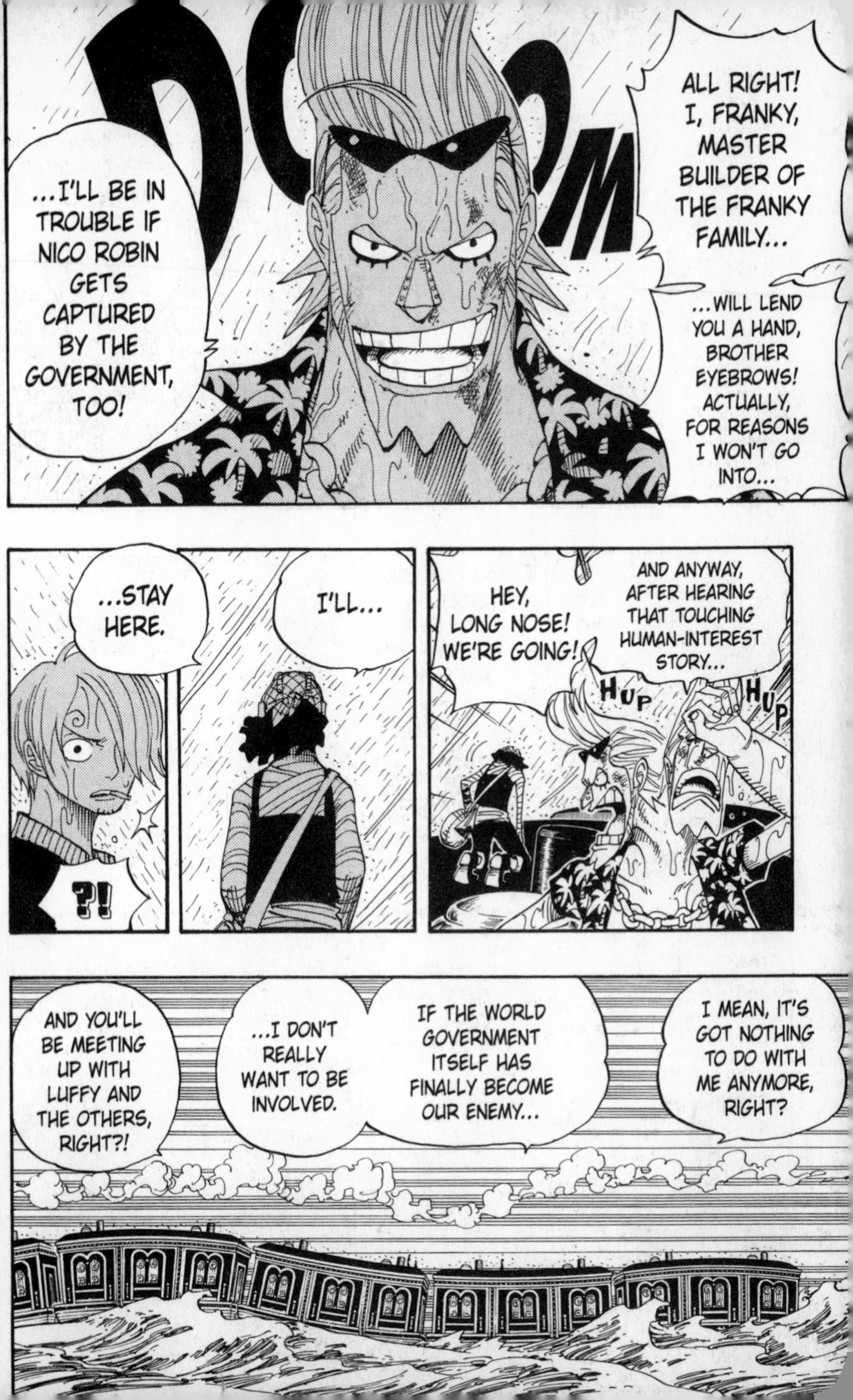
DOOM
ALL RIGHT! I, FRANKY, MASTER BUILDER OF THE FRANKY FAMILY...
...WILL LEND YOU A HAND, BROTHER EYEBROWS! ACTUALLY, FOR REASONS I WON'T GO INTO...
...I'LL BE IN TROUBLE IF NICO ROBIN GETS CAPTURED BY THE GOVERNMENT, TOO!
AND ANYWAY, AFTER HEARING THAT TOUCHING HUMAN-INTEREST STORY...
HEY, LONG NOSE! WE'RE GOING!
HUP
HUP
I'LL...
...STAY HERE.
?!
I MEAN, IT'S GOT NOTHING TO DO WITH ME ANYMORE, RIGHT?
IF THE WORLD GOVERNMENT ITSELF HAS FINALLY BECOME OUR ENEMY...
...I DON'T REALLY WANT TO BE INVOLVED.
AND YOU'LL BE MEETING UP WITH LUFFY AND THE OTHERS, RIGHT?!

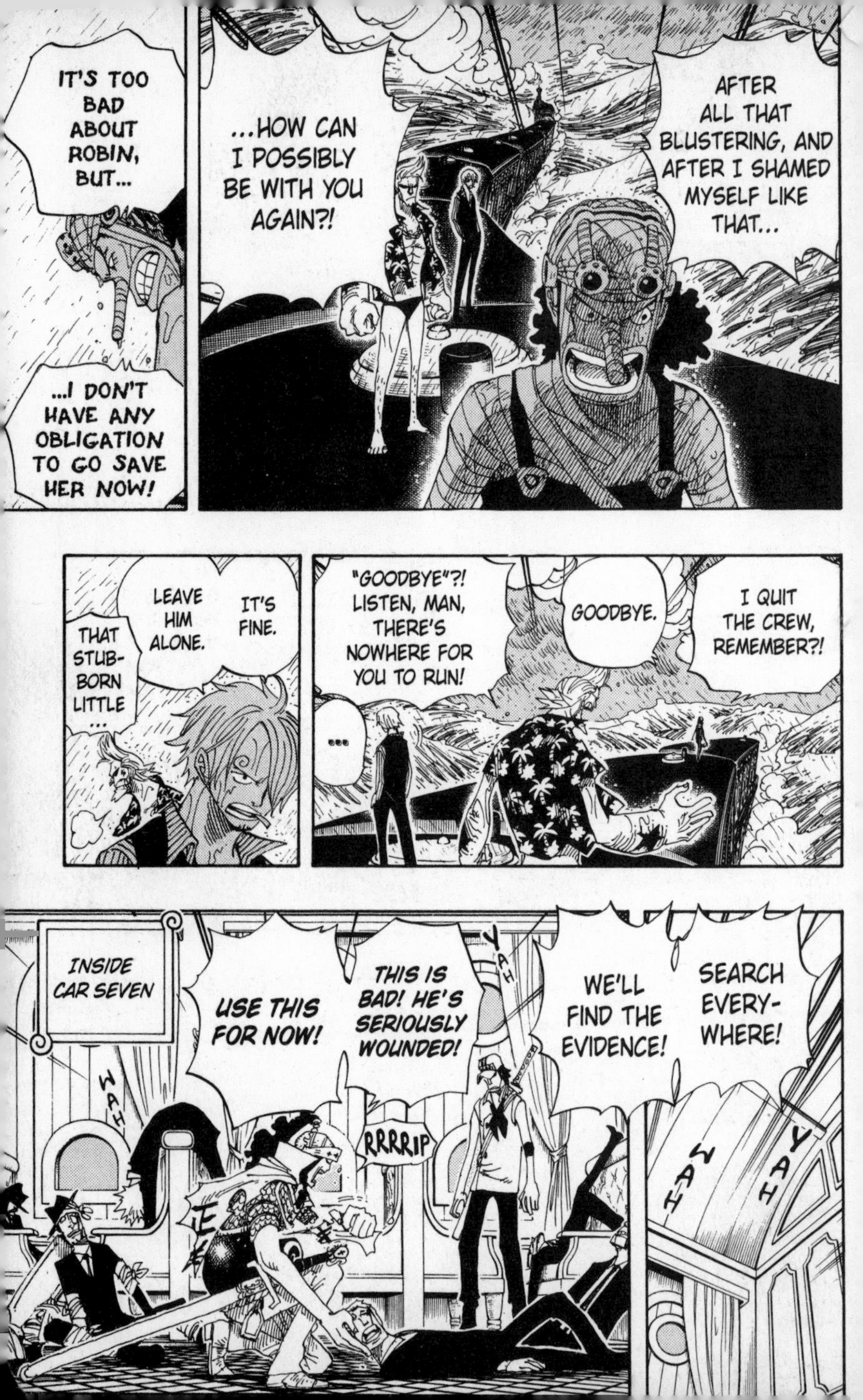
AFTER ALL THAT BLUSTERING, AND AFTER I SHAMED MYSELF LIKE THAT...
...HOW CAN I POSSIBLY BE WITH YOU AGAIN?!
IT'S TOO BAD ABOUT ROBIN, BUT...
...I DON'T HAVE ANY OBLIGATION TO GO SAVE HER NOW!
I QUIT THE CREW, REMEMBER?!
GOODBYE.
"GOODBYE"?! LISTEN, MAN, THERE'S NOWHERE FOR YOU TO RUN!
...
IT'S FINE.
LEAVE HIM ALONE.
THAT STUBBORN LITTLE ...
SEARCH EVERYWHERE!
YAH
WAH
WE'LL FIND THE EVIDENCE!
YAH
THIS IS BAD! HE'S SERIOUSLY WOUNDED!
RRRRIP
USE THIS FOR NOW!
INSIDE CAR SEVEN
WAH

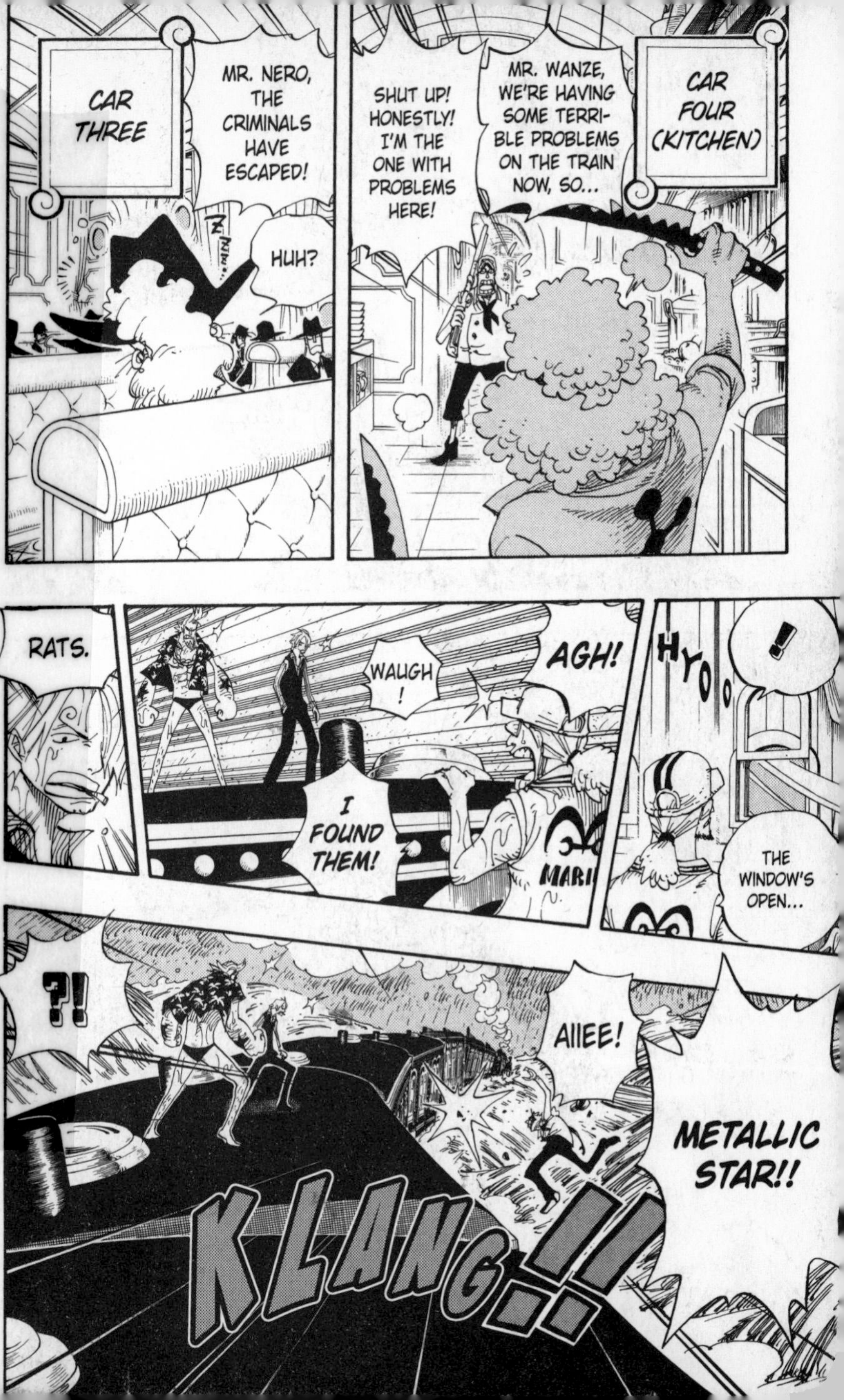
CAR FOUR (KITCHEN)
MR. WANZE, WE'RE HAVING SOME TERRIBLE PROBLEMS ON THE TRAIN NOW, SO...
SHUT UP! HONESTLY! I'M THE ONE WITH PROBLEMS HERE!
CAR THREE
MR. NERO, THE CRIMINALS HAVE ESCAPED!
HUH?
!
HYO
THE WINDOW'S OPEN...
AGH!
WAUGH!
I FOUND THEM!
MARI
RATS.
AIIEE!
?!
METALLIC STAR!!
KLANG..!!

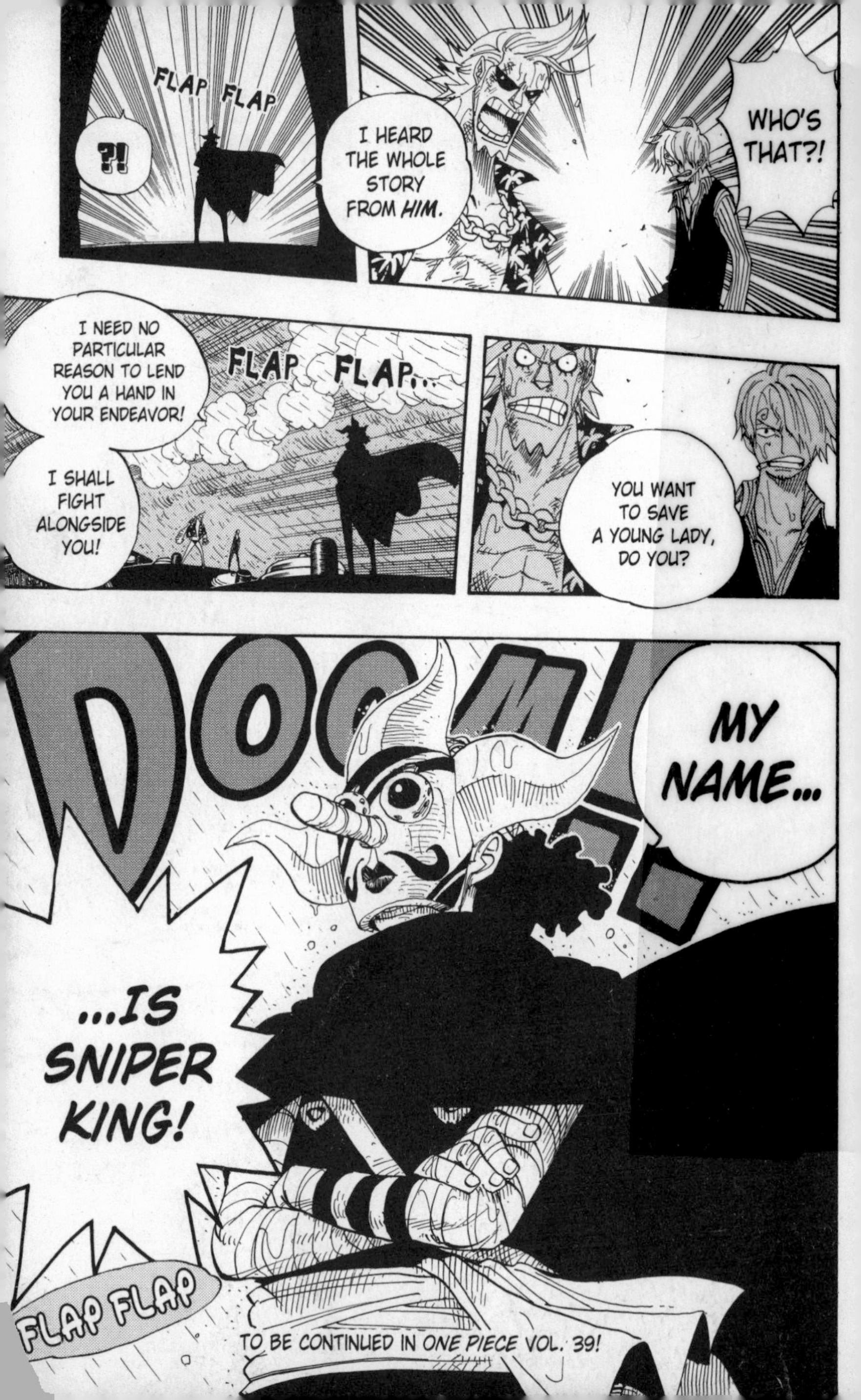
WHO'S THAT?!
I HEARD THE WHOLE STORY FROM *HIM*.
FLAP FLAP
?!
YOU WANT TO SAVE A YOUNG LADY, DO YOU?
FLAP FLAP...
I NEED NO PARTICULAR REASON TO LEND YOU A HAND IN YOUR ENDEAVOR!
I SHALL FIGHT ALONGSIDE YOU!
MY NAME...
...IS SNIPER KING!
FLAP FLAP
TO BE CONTINUED IN *ONE PIECE* VOL. 39!

COMING NEXT VOLUME:

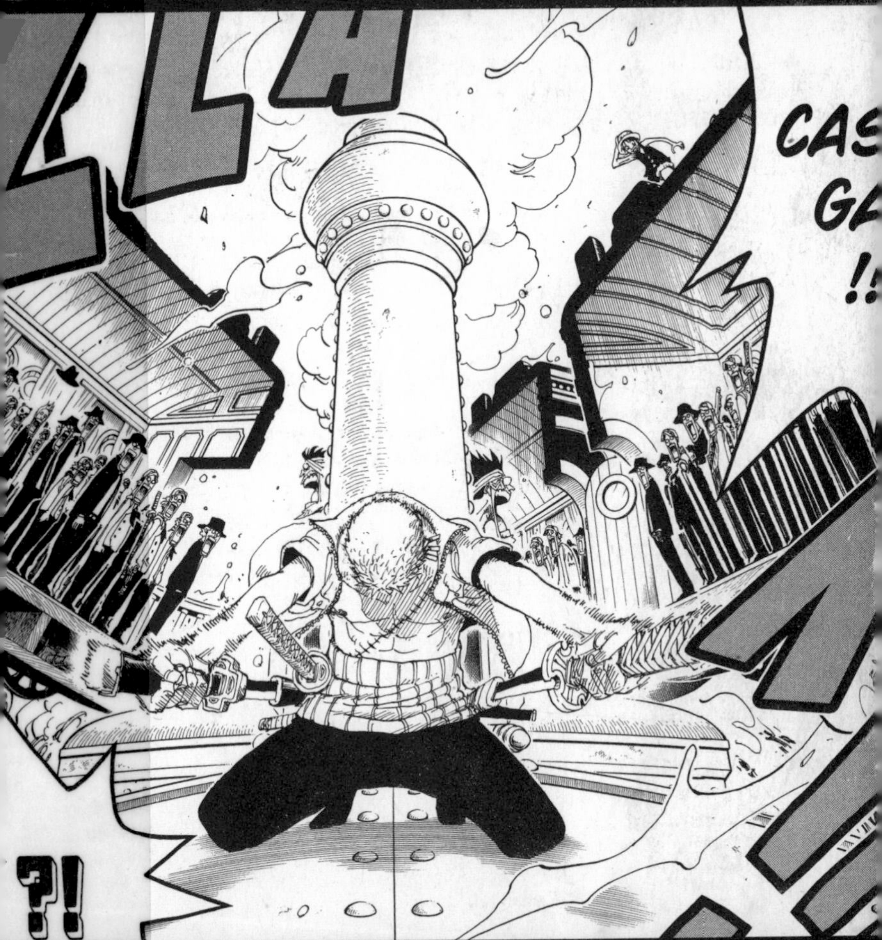
?!

Sanji, Usopp and Franky are on their own against the Navy as the rest of the Straw Hats hurry to catch up to the speeding Sea Train. But freeing Robin from the clutches of CP9 won't be an easy task with a train full of enemies. And even if they overcome all the fierce opponents to reach her, does she even want to be rescued?!

ON SALE APRIL 2010!